French Wine

The publisher gratefully acknowledges the generous support of the Ahmanson Foundation Humanities Endowment Fund of the University of California Press Foundation.

French Wine

A History

ROD PHILLIPS

University of California Press

University of California Press, one of the most distinguished university presses in the United States, enriches lives around the world by advancing scholarship in the humanities, social sciences, and natural sciences. Its activities are supported by the UC Press Foundation and by philanthropic contributions from individuals and institutions. For more information, visit www.ucpress.edu.

University of California Press
Oakland, California

© 2016 by Rod Phillips

Library of Congress Cataloging-in-Publication Data

Names: Phillips, Roderick, author.
Title: French wine : a history / Rod Phillips.
Description: Oakland, California : University of California Press, [2016] | "2016 | Includes bibliographical references and index.
Identifiers: LCCN 2016007020 (print) | LCCN 2016008371 (ebook) | ISBN 9780520285231 (cloth : alk. paper) | ISBN 9780520960770 (ebook)
Subjects: LCSH: Wine and wine making—France—History. | Wine and wine making—Social aspects—France—History. | Wine—Social aspects—France—History.
Classification: LCC TP553 .P48 2016 (print) | LCC TP553 (ebook) | DDC 338.4/766320944—dc23
LC record available at http://lccn.loc.gov/2016007020

Manufactured in the United States of America

25 24 23 22 21 20 19 18 17 16
10 9 8 7 6 5 4 3 2 1

In keeping with a commitment to support environmentally responsible and sustainable printing practices, UC Press has printed this book on Natures Natural, a fiber that contains 30% post-consumer waste and meets the minimum requirements of ANSI/NISO Z39.48–1992 (R 1997) (*Permanence of Paper*).

To Janet

Contents

Illustrations

A Note on Usage

REGIONS AND THEIR WINES

Throughout this book I capitalize the names of French wine regions and use lowercase for the wines from those regions. Thus "Burgundy" refers to the region and "burgundy" refers to a wine from Burgundy.

CLAIRET AND CLARET

Clairet, a light red wine commonly made in France, was given the name "claret" in English. I refer to it as *clairet* when I discuss it in a French context and as "claret" in the context of Great Britain.

Introduction

France occupies a special position in the world of wine. Until the late twen-tieth century there was a broad and robust consensus, among wine profes-sionals and everyday wine consumers alike, that France produced the best wines in the world. Even today, despite the improvements in wines from other European countries and the appearance of high-quality wines from regions of the United States, Canada, Chile, Argentina, South Africa, Australia, and New Zealand, there is a residual sense that France's best wines are the world's best. How else can we explain the perennial obsession with each vintage in Bordeaux and Burgundy, two of France's most impor-tant and prestigious wine regions, and the ever-increasing popularity of champagne in the face of less expensive but high-quality sparkling wines from other parts of the world?

Cynics may point to simple inertia among professionals and consumers as an explanation and suggest that as fine wines from other countries find more secure footings in world markets, the wines of France will be put into a more realistic comparative context. In the meantime, despite sustaining some loss of global market share in the face of the rising production of New World wines, French wines continue to attract and fascinate consumers at all levels in a way that wines from no other country do. Only one wine is a household name internationally, and it is French: champagne. Even though many consumers might not know that champagne is made only in the French region of that name, and even though many use *champagne* gener-ically to refer to any sparkling wine, it is a name known the world over and a metaphor for quality and style.

Although no other French region has entered the popular lexicon in such a way, Bordeaux and Burgundy are widely regarded as benchmarks for wine quality. Until recently, blends of certain grape varieties (especially cabernet sauvignon and merlot) were commonly referred to as "Bordeaux blends," and New World producers of pinot noir and chardonnay still often (too often) claim that they make their wines "in a Burgundian style." Until appellation names were effectively protected in the early 2000s, many New World red wines (no matter what grape varieties were used to make them) were labeled "burgundy" and "bordeaux," and many sparkling wines were labeled "champagne." These branding practices were not confined to French appellations—there were many New World "ports" and "sherries"—but French regional names were the most commonly used for nonfortified wines.

The three most prestigious wine regions of France—Bordeaux, Burgundy (whose wine authorities would prefer us to refer to it as "Bourgogne"), and Champagne—may be the standard-bearers of French wine, but they represent only a sixth of France's vineyard area and a smaller fraction of its wine production. Other regions—notably Alsace, southwest France, and the Loire and Rhône valleys—are notable for their distinctive wines, and most French wine produced today comes from Mediterranean France, especially from the broad Languedoc region that is the cradle of French viticulture. The sheer diversity of French wines—in terms of styles, grape varieties used, and vineyard practices—not only makes generalizations about the wines of France hazardous, if not impossible, but also complicates the idea of "French wine." Yet despite qualifications regarding region and locality, it is nonetheless true that "French wine," as a beverage and an idea, has dominated wine cultures throughout the world for the past two centuries, and in some cases much longer. Better-off English wine consumers, for example, have been transfixed by claret (red wine from Bordeaux) since the Middle Ages, despite periodic fluctuations in its availability and reputation and the evolution of its style.

It is surprising, then, that no book in the English language has yet attempted to survey the long-term history of wine in France. Several such histories have been published in French. Marcel Lachiver's *Vins, vignes et vignerons: Histoire du vignoble français*, published in 1988, is a magisterial work that covers many of the themes of this book. Roger Dion's *Histoire de la vigne et du vin en France: Des origines au XIXe siècle* (1959), more limited in the time span it covers, is equally authoritative, and Dion and Lachiver established the shape of the long-term history of French wine. Gilbert Garrier's *Histoire sociale et culturelle du vin* (1995) ranges more widely but is predominantly about French wine. Each of these books is more than seven hundred pages long and densely detailed, and none of them has been translated into English.

MAP O.I. Main French wine regions

In writing *French Wine* I have set out to provide a readable and relatively compact history of the twenty-five hundred years that separate the
present from the time when Etruscans, Greeks, and Romans first brought
wine to ancient France and planted the first vineyards there. I have traced
this long history at a number of levels: the expansion and contraction of
regional and national vineyard areas; long- and short-term changes in the
volumes of wine produced; the effects of long- and short-term climate
shifts on viticulture and wine production; the emergence of recognizable
wine regions and designated appellations; changing methods of viticulture
and wine making; the marketing of wine locally and regionally within
France and internationally; the reception of wine on domestic and foreign
markets; diverging levels of quality and the emergence of prestigious wine
regions and estates; the evolving definition of *terroir;* the regulation of
wine production and sale and the prevention of fraud; patterns of wine

consumption in France; and the relationship of wine to gender, class, health, religion, and identity in France.

Covering a long period and multiple themes in a relatively short book has posed problems of selection, especially with respect to wine regions. I have not been able to give full coverage to all regions, and some readers might wish for more attention to the less-known and less attention to the better-known appellations. My selection sometimes depends on the availability of sources, but it is also strategic, in that I have tried to identify the dominant themes in each period and to use the case studies that best illustrate them. This has meant giving particular attention to Languedoc-Roussillon, Bordeaux, and Burgundy in some chapters and to Champagne and the Rhône and Loire valleys in others. In some chapters, less-known regions as diverse as Béarn, Cahors, the Nantais, Lorraine, Jura, and Gaillac come into focus. If some regions and their wines are not mentioned at all, it is not because they are unimportant but generally because they proved to be less illustrative of the themes that I focus on. To have included all France's wine regions and appellations would have produced indigestible lists of names.

On the other hand, engaging with many themes has enabled me to highlight a number that contextualize the history of French wine. Although only a small proportion of French wine was exported until the twentieth century (exports currently stand at about 30 percent of production), I have given attention to the export trade because it laid the foundation for the reputation that French wine gained as the best in the world. Some foreign aficionados, such as John Locke and Thomas Jefferson, deepened their appreciation of French wine by touring French wine regions, but most discovered it when it was exported. Bordeaux and Champagne were by far the most important sources of wines for export until the 1900s, and exports were vital to their wine industries. Several chapters of this book explore the changing interrelationship between the export of French wines and their reputation on foreign markets.

I have also brought Algeria more clearly into the frame of French wine. For decades during the twentieth century, "Algerian wine" was shorthand for cheap wine of poor quality, but from the late nineteenth century it played a vital role in sustaining France's wine supply. Until its independence in 1962, Algeria was part of France, and its contributions to French wine (the robust wines of Algeria were blended with the then relatively anemic wines of southern France) have too often been overlooked or understated. Algerian wine came to the rescue when French wine production plummeted during the phylloxera crisis of the late 1800s, and throughout the first half of the twentieth century it played a vital role in ensuring that French workers and their cafés had a regular supply of inexpensive *vin ordinaire*. The scale of Algeria's contribution should not be understated: shipments of wine from Algeria to metropolitan France represented three times the combined wine exports of France, Italy, and Spain in the 1930s and easily exceeded them until the early 1960s.

I have also placed French wine in a broader, international context. This includes comparing the area devoted to viticulture in France to those in Spain and Italy and explaining why the French were not as interested as the Spanish, Dutch, and English in spreading viticulture and wine production to their colonies in the 1500s and 1600s. By contrast, there are points when developments in France were not unique but part of transnational trends, such as the rise of organic and biodynamic wine making in the 1970s. These contexts are important for understanding what was going on in France.

A core part of the story of French wine is the struggle against fraud, adulteration, and counterfeit. These might be straightforward issues today, when wine, consumer, public health, and commercial laws tightly regulate the making and selling of wine. But definitions of wine adulteration have changed, and in the relatively lawless past there was often little agreement at any given time as to what constituted adulteration or fraud. Chaptalization—adding sugar to grape juice before fermentation to increase potential alcohol—has been practiced in France for centuries and was recommended by a government-approved publication in the early 1800s. But later that century, producers who did not chaptalize denounced it as a form of adulteration. Today it is permitted in a number of French appellations.

As for counterfeiting, the most common form was labeling a wine made in one region or locality as if it had been made in a more prestigious one that would fetch a higher price for the wine. But until the early 1900s, such practices (known in Burgundy as *équivalence*) were permitted, as long as the wine in question tasted like wine from the region on the label. Similarly, in the 1920s, Bordeaux's producers were permitted to blend in some non-Bordeaux wine to make theirs taste the way customers expected wines from Bordeaux to taste. Objections to such practices and the commercial advantages they were thought to give were fundamental to the development of the *appellation d'origine contrôlée* (AOC) rules that have regulated viticulture and wine making in France since the 1930s.

Other themes that ground the history of French wine are the commercial rivalries that pitted one region or locality against another and the negative consequences of heavy wine consumption on individuals and on society more generally. These are at odds with a common genre of wine writing that is celebratory and uncritical. It too often uses the idea of "tradition" to portray the history of French wine as a seamless narrative that links the Middle Ages (or some undefined past period) to the present through generations of noble small-scale vignerons (wine producers who cultivate their own vines) and aristocratic proprietors.

In fact, there are more discontinuities than continuities in the history of French wine, and given what we know about the conditions in which wines were made in the not too distant past, modern wine marketers would be well advised not to claim that their wines were made by "traditional" methods. Some writers may glorify the past and find "golden ages," but I find it hard to be enthusiastic about wines made indiscriminately from ripe, unripe, overripe, and rotten grapes that were crushed and fermented together, left in vats for weeks or months, and then stored in unseasoned, dirty, infected barrels. These were the wines that the mass of French wine drinkers consumed for centuries, until the nineteenth century. They more than adequately satisfied the nutritional, sensory, and cultural needs of their consumers, but must we think of them, in hindsight, as "authentic," "real," or "natural"?

Many aspects of the history of French wine, as distinct from the celebration of an uncritically imagined past, have been studied by generations of historians, and the subject has been given new life by the recent emergence of the history of food and drink as a field of research. Writing this book, I have been able to draw on the work of hundreds of historians and scholars from other disciplines who have written on such diverse topics as drinking wine in Gaul, the development of the appellation system, the phylloxera crisis, the wine trade in early modern France, and the origins of chaptalization. The bibliography lists the works I found most useful —I consulted many more—and I wish to thank all these scholars for making this synthesis possible. Unless otherwise noted, the translations are mine.

A number of colleagues and friends helped me as I was writing. Peter McPhee, W. Scott Haine, George Gale, Patricia Prestwich, Max Nelson, Joe Bohling, and Philip Whalen all read one or two chapters and gave me invaluable advice. Adam Zietnek generously shared his research on alcohol in the French army during World War I. Noelle Plack, Kolleen Guy, and Thomas Brennan read the whole manuscript carefully and critically and made many astute suggestions. I own any errors and shortcomings that remain in the text, but it is in far better shape for the guidance of these friends and colleagues. I also thank Michelle Fairbrother for her careful work with the maps and diagrams. At University of California Press, Blake

Edgar commissioned the book, and Kate Marshall, Francisco Reinking, Bradley Depew, and Zuha Khan saw it through the editorial and production processes. They couldn't have been more helpful and supportive. Juliana Froggatt was an efficient and sensitive copy editor, with whom it was a pleasure to work.

This book is dedicated to my friend Janet Dorozynski, a wine professional who lives in Ottawa. We have known each other for many years, often dine together, occasionally judge wines together, and frequently challenge each other with blind tastings. It's been a pleasure to know Janet, and I look forward to many more years of friendship and getting wines wrong. Along the way, others have had to listen to me go on about French wine, often over a glass of it. They include my daughter, Zoë, her husband, Mark, my friend Cynthia Mar, and my colleague and friend Paul Nelles.

Finally, a personal note about French wine. Some nonhistorian readers might think this book is not celebratory enough and does not extol the pleasures of French wine and its role in promoting civility and sophistication. Such associations and images were carefully constructed centuries ago (along with the idea that French wine is intrinsically healthy), and they are present in this book as historical constructs to be examined and explained, but not as perspectives. This does not mean that I approach French wines as nothing more than expressions of a historical process, to be dissected and analyzed but not enjoyed. As a wine writer and judge as well as a professional historian, I regularly travel to wine regions in many parts of the world, but I have a special affection for France and its wines. When I started studying wine as a teenager in New Zealand in the 1960s, I soon developed a small cellar, and my most prized acquisitions were two bottles of 1953 Château La Tour Carnet (a Fourth Growth in the 1855 Bordeaux Classification). I bought them in 1965 for about the price of a hamburger per bottle because, as the retailer said, "they're old." The following year two friends and I drank them as BYO wines with roast chicken and french fries at an Auckland restaurant called Lutèce (the French name of the Roman town that was on the site of what is now Paris) a few days before I emigrated to Canada.

I grew up at a time when French wine was thought to be the best in the world and when New World wine was generally to be avoided. Over the past decades, of course, everything has changed, and excellent wines are now produced in hundreds of wine regions in scores of countries around the world. But even though I have a healthy skepticism about reputations that have long outlived their original justification, French wine has an enduring allure for me. I have lived in France and I visit French wine regions and wineries often, and I'm still impressed by what I find. If I had to choose wines from only one country to keep me going on a desert island (a desert island with good cellaring facilities), that country would be France. So it has been a pleasure to immerse myself in the history of French wine, and I hope this book is equally enjoyable to read.

1. From the Beginnings to 1000 CE

As the history of French wine was beginning, about twenty-five hundred years ago, both of the key elements were missing: there was no geographical or political entity called France, and no wine was made on the territory that was to become France. As far as we know, the Celtic populations living there did not produce wine from any of the varieties of grapes that grew wild in many parts of their land, although they might well have eaten them fresh. They did cultivate barley, wheat, and other cereals to ferment into beer, which they drank, along with water, as part of their daily diet. They also fermented honey (for mead) and perhaps other produce.

In cultural terms it was a far cry from the nineteenth century, when France had assumed a national identity and wine was not only integral to notions of French culture and civilization but held up as one of the important influences on the character of the French and the success of their nation. Two and a half thousand years before that, the arbiters of culture and civilization were Greece and Rome, and they looked upon beer-drinking peoples, such as the Celts of ancient France, as barbarians. Wine was part of the commercial and civilizing missions of the Greeks and Romans, who introduced it to their new colonies and later planted vineyards in them. When they and the Etruscans brought wine and viticulture to the Celts of ancient France, they began the history of French wine.

Although the Romans were largely responsible for planting vineyards throughout France, the first wines known to have reached ancient France came from Etruria in central Italy, the territory that is now Tuscany. The Etruscans were producing wine by 800 BCE as a result of contact with the Phoenicians from the eastern Mediterranean, and by 625 BCE they had begun to ship it to ports on the Mediterranean coast of ancient France.[1] One shipment from sometime in the period 525–475 BCE, which never reached

9

its destination, lies in the wreck of an Etruscan vessel that sank in sixty meters (two hundred feet) of water off Grand Ribaud Island, a kilometer (0.6 miles) from the French coast east of Toulon. In its hold were about a thousand amphoras, pottery vessels used for storing and shipping wine, olive oil, and dry goods such as grain. The wine in this ship—which would have been sailing westward along the coast of ancient France, perhaps to the port of Lattara, where Etruscan merchants had warehousing facilities— amounted to about forty thousand liters (eleven thousand gallons), the equivalent of some fifty thousand modern bottles of wine.[2]

Much of the evidence of the Etruscan wine trade to Mediterranean France takes the form of amphoras excavated intact or in pieces from sea- and riverbeds and from sites on land. They were two-handled vessels with a pointed end and commonly held about forty liters (eleven gallons, or about fifty-three modern bottles), although Roman amphoras were often smaller, holding about twenty-five liters (seven gallons, or thirty-three bottles). Each center of amphora production worked its own variations on the basic shape, and some added designs, making it possible to identify their origins. Some (like those in the ship wrecked off Grand Ribaud Island) were sealed with cork stoppers, while others were sealed with clay, wood, or textiles. Stacked in layers in the hulls of ships—transportation was far cheaper by water than by land—amphoras were the principal means of shipping wine until wooden barrels replaced them in the second century CE.

Unlike ancient barrels, only parts of which have only rarely survived two thousand years,[3] untold numbers of ancient amphoras have survived burial underground and in water, enabling archaeologists to identify their provenance and scientists to identify their contents from chemical residues on their interior walls. Many of those retrieved from southern France and its coastal waters show chemical and botanical residues that almost certainly derive from grapes. The amphoras might have held fresh grapes, wine, or vinegar, but there is a high probability that they contained wine, because chemical analysis also showed other characteristics common to ancient wines: tartaric acid, which is indicative of grapes; tree resin, used as a preservative or flavoring; and herbs (such as rosemary, basil, and thyme) used to enhance the aromas and flavors of wine.

The seventh-century BCE Etruscan wine trade to Mediterranean ancient France might have been robust, but it soon declined in the face of competition from Greeks. In about 600 BCE, Phocaean Greeks from Anatolia (in modern Turkey) established the settlement of Massalia (now Marseille), which became the region's main port. Given the centrality of wine to their culture and diet, it is not surprising that Greeks took it with them wherever they went. Settlers needed a supply of wine for daily consumption, festivities, and religious purposes, and a wine trade was quickly established between Greece and its settlements throughout the Mediterranean. As the indigenous Celtic inhabitants of ancient France—the wealthier strata, at least—began to emulate the newcomers and drink wine, the trade grew so as to supply the expanded market. One sunken ship excavated by marine archaeologists was carrying an astonishing ten thousand amphoras, which would have contained as much as four hundred thousand liters (one hundred thousand gallons) of wine, the equivalent of half a million standard modern bottles. It is estimated that Greek merchants shipped ten million liters (2.6 million gallons) of wine to ancient France each year through Massalia alone.[4] Much of it was then shipped to other towns in Massalia's trading network, including Celtic communities along the coast and up the Rhône and Saône Rivers.

The Greeks not only imported wine but began to plant vines. By about 525 BCE they were making their own amphoras in Massalia, a very good indicator that they were producing wine locally; there would have been no reason to produce amphoras if there was nothing to fill them with, and there are residues of grape seeds at a number of excavated sites in and near Massalia, including Nîmes.[5] This local wine production undercut the Etruscan wine trade to southern France, which went into decline but did not disappear entirely. It continued through Lattara, a coastal town south of what is now Montpellier and near the modern town of Lattes, where Vins de Pays d'Oc (the association of Languedoc wines) has its headquarters. In about 525 BCE, just as wine was beginning to be produced at Massalia, a complex of structures for warehousing and shipping goods both imported and for export was built at Lattara, which became the main port of entry for Etruscan wine. There must have been vineyards at Lattara too, as a limestone pressing platform was discovered there, along with piles of grape seeds. It dates from 425–400 BCE, about a century after the first evidence of wine being made in the region of Massalia.

On the basis of current knowledge we can conclude that wine was being produced on the Mediterranean coast of ancient France by about 500 BCE, two and a half millennia ago, and that Etruscans had imported it one or two centuries before that. These are the earliest known dates of wine-related activity in France, although it is quite possible that evidence will be found of even earlier wine trade and production there. Among the current unknowns is when the indigenous Celts, rather than Etruscan and Greek settlers, began to make wine, but at this point there is no evidence that they did so before the arrival of these newcomers.

If the Celts had made wine before the arrival of outsiders, they would have had to use indigenous wild vines that produced grapes that were generally too small, with too low a ratio of pulp to seeds and skin, to make pressing them very worthwhile. Wine must have been made on a commercial scale in ancient France only after exotic domesticated varieties (with larger berries and a higher pulp content) had been introduced or indigenous varieties had been selected and bred. The earliest evidence of domesticated grapes (but not of wine making) has been found at Port Ariane, very close to Lattes, and dates from the seventh to sixth centuries BCE, when the Etruscan wine trade began. Vines were sometimes transported long distances for replanting—in ships, they were planted in soil in the cool lower levels—and it seems likely that the first wine from French vineyards came from imported vines.

The vines planted at sites along the Mediterranean coast from about 500 BCE were the forerunners of the vineyards of the massive Languedoc-Roussillon wine region, which now accounts for a quarter of France's viticultural area. We do not know the extent of the earliest French vineyards or the volume of wine that they produced, but neither is likely to have been very substantial. Given the scale of imports from Etruria and from Greek vineyards in southern Italy, there was probably enough for some better-off groups within the indigenous Celtic populations to drink wine from time to time, especially on festive and other special occasions and perhaps for medical and therapeutic purposes. But the mass of the population must have continued to drink beer, water, and occasionally some mead. Even so, the Roman historian Justin ranked viticulture, along with urban life and constitutional government, as one of the benefits of civilization that the Greek settlers of Massalia had conferred on the indigenous inhabitants of the area.[6]

The wine cultures of the Greeks (and later the Romans) who settled in ancient France are important to understanding the impetus to develop viticulture and wine making there. Undoubtedly, these settlers consumed some of the wine imported into and produced in ancient France because it was a staple of the daily diet in their homelands. In Greece, vines were planted throughout the mainland and the islands of the Aegean Sea, and wine was consumed at all levels of society. Elite males drank wine in ritualized gatherings known as symposia, where it was diluted with water and the participants occupied themselves by talking, being entertained, playing wine-related games, and occasionally having sex.[7] Other classes in Greek society drank wine of varying quality, according to their rank and means.

Wine and the manner of drinking it were markers of social distinction in Greece, setting the upper classes off from the lower, and the Greek elites

used the same criteria to differentiate civilized people (thems
those who were uncivilized. The Greeks did not drink beer and w
ful not only of anyone who did but also of anyone who consum
improperly: by not diluting it with water or by drinking to the p
drunkenness. Scythians and Thracians were uncivilized by this count,
individuals such as Alexander the Great were despised as barbaric beca
they were heavy drinkers given to violence when they were drunk. In th
fifth century BCE, Greek writers added a further charge against beer: that
drinking it was "unmanly" and that it made men "effeminate."[8]

Wine was one of the benefits of civilization that the Greeks wanted to
confer on the beer-drinking Celts of ancient France, just as they had introduced it to southern Italy and later expanded wine production after coloniz-
ing Egypt in 300 BCE. In ancient France the Greek wine trade extended well
beyond the immediate coastal regions where the Greeks settled, and hundreds of thousands of amphoras lie buried on land and in riverbeds in
southern France. Concentrations can be found in such widely dispersed
locations as Toulouse in the southwest and Châlon-sur-Saône, in Burgundy,
in the east. There may well be hundreds of thousands of amphoras in the
bed of the Saône River alone, representing between five and ten million
liters (1.3 and 2.6 million gallons) of imported wine.

A particularly striking manifestation of the cultural impact of the Greek
wine trade is the treasure discovered in the subterranean burial chamber of
a Celtic princess of the Vix lineage near Châtillon-sur-Seine in Burgundy.
The Vix treasure includes not only jewelry, statues, and other luxury
objects but also a massive Greek krater, the receptacle used for mixing wine
and water at a symposium. Ornately decorated, more than a meter and a
half (five feet) in height, and holding more than a thousand liters (264 gallons), this krater—made of bronze rather than the usual ceramic—was
clearly more decorative than functional; many kraters held less than twenty
liters (five gallons) of wine and water. But together with other Greek wine
paraphernalia, such as pitchers and cups, that were also found in the tomb,
the Vix krater points to the high status of wine in the upper social echelons
of Celtic France under Greek influence.[9]

As important as the Etruscans and Greeks were in bringing viticulture
and wine drinking to ancient France, their activities pale in comparison with
those of the Romans, who began to incorporate France (which they called
Gallia, or Gaul) into their empire from the end of the second century BCE.
A Roman army crossed the Alps in 125 BCE and within a few years Rome
had control of the whole Mediterranean coastal area of Gaul as far as Spain.
A land route ran from the Alps to the Pyrenees, and the Romans created a

One

MAP 1.1. Ancient France

massive province that covered the territory now occupied by most of Languedoc-Roussillon and Provence. Called Narbonensis, it had its capital at Narbonne, which was colonized by Romans, and it stretched from the Toulouse region in the west to the Rhône valley in the east (see map 1.1).

At first the Romans imported their own wine into Gaul, principally from their main wine-producing region in Campania, and hundreds of thousands of Italian amphoras have been found around towns such as Autun, Roanne, and Châlon-sur-Saône, as well as in western France, at the mouth of the Loire and farther upstream as far as Angers. In southern France there are concentrations in the western districts of what was then Narbonensis, near Narbonne, Toulouse, Gaillac, and Rodez, and farther east, in the Nîmes region. Amphoras inscribed with the name of Porcius, a wine merchant of Pompeii, one of Campania's major wine-exporting centers, have been found near such towns as Toulouse, Agen, Bordeaux, and Saint-Foy-la-Grande, on the Dordogne River.[10] The distribution of amphoras gives us some idea of the geographical scope of the Romans' wine trade in Gaul by the first century CE. Toulouse itself became an important center for the Italian wine trade, and wine from Campania was shipped from there down the Garonne River to Bordeaux and to communities in southwest France. André Tchernia has estimated that between 150 and 25 BCE, some twelve million liters (three million gallons) of wine were shipped annually from Italy to Gaul. This was far more than the Roman settlers and army could consume, and indicates that there was a robust local market for it.[11] Not only that, but it is likely that some of the Campania wine that made its way to Bordeaux was forwarded to Roman Britain,[12] a forerunner of the massive Bordeaux wine trade with England that developed in the thirteenth century.

The wine trade from Italy was important, but the Roman colonization of southern Gaul also opened the way to viticulture. The Roman Senate had declared at the time when Narbonne was colonized that the "transalpine peoples" (the populations on the other side of the Alps from the perspective of Italy) should not be permitted to grow olives and vines, so as to protect the value of these products exported from Italy.[13] But Roman settlers were not prevented from doing so, and they soon planted vineyards (and olive trees) along the Mediterranean coast and in other areas of southern France. Within two centuries of arriving they began to extend viticulture wherever climate, soil, and other environmental conditions permitted. There was even a brief reversal of the wine trade between Italy and Gaul. When Mount Vesuvius erupted in 79 CE and buried Pompeii, the important wine trading town, it also destroyed many of the vineyards of Campania. To make up for shortages, some wine was imported from Gaul, as is shown by the presence of Gallic amphoras in Rome's port at Ostia and other towns of the region. This might have been the first significant export of French wine.

Roger Dion has suggested that two of the earliest Roman wine ventures in Gaul were vineyards at Gaillac, to the northeast of Toulouse, and near Vienne in the Rhône valley.[14] Gaillac was a center of amphora manufacture—a necessity for wine production at the time—and it was well situated for selling its wine: it is on the Tarn River, which runs into the Garonne River, giving easy access to markets in Toulouse and Bordeaux. In the first century BCE, Cicero wrote approvingly about the Toulouse wine trade, which most likely involved wine made in Gaillac.[15] The well-off inhabitants of Bordeaux drank wine from Gaillac before vines were planted in their own environs, and Gaillac and other regions of southwest France supplied the bulk of the wine for Bordeaux's wine trade well into the Middle Ages. As for the Rhône valley, the evidence of early Roman vineyards is less clear, but in the first century CE the historian Pliny the Elder reported vines near

Vienne, which the poet Martial wrote was well known for its wine. The nearby districts where vineyards are most likely to have been located were those known today as Côte-Rôtie and Hermitage, two of the Rhône valley's most prestigious appellations.

The promotion of viticulture and wine production by the Romans was largely driven by economic considerations, because wine was a profitable product. The Romans perceived the Celts as having a thirst for wine that was as keen as that of traders for profit. In the middle of the first century BCE, the Greek historian Diodorus commented, "The natural greed of many Italian merchants exploits the passion of the Gauls [Celts] for wine. On boats that follow the navigable rivers or on carts that roll across the plains, they transport their wine, which brings them unbelievable profits, going so far as to trade one amphora for one slave, so that the buyer gives up his servant to pay for drink."[16] It was not only slaves that Romans bought with wine; they used it as a medium of exchange for metals such as iron and copper and sometimes to buy entire mines.

Another driver of the trade and production of wine was the Romans' belief that consuming wine rather than beer would raise the cultural level of the Celts. It is not difficult to see in this the origins of later French claims that their wine was an important underpinning of their cultural superiority. Like the Greeks, the Romans were wine snobs who scorned beer for wine and judged other cultures partly by what they drank and how they drank it. At first, one historian argues, the Romans were caught between wanting to be part of "the civilized symposiastic world" and resisting "the libidinous associations of vinous excess"[17] so graphically catalogued by many Roman writers. To resolve the tension, Romans stressed the role of wine in making life possible and highlighted the excellence of wine from their peninsula. As they later extended their institutions throughout their empire, they transferred wine consumption to the elites of other societies.

As wine production in southern Gaul increased, it represented growing competition for wine producers on the Italian peninsula. By 70–80 CE, for example, a substantial wine trade between Roman Gaul and London had begun to cut into wine exports from Italy to England.[18] In 92 CE, Emperor Domitian ordered the grubbing up of half the vines in Gaul and Rome's other provinces outside Italy. Claiming that too much arable land was being turned to viticulture, he also forbade the planting of any more vines on the Italian peninsula itself. The purpose of the edict might have been to protect Rome from grain shortages, but it also protected Roman wine producers from too much competition from vineyards in Gaul and elsewhere. By the end of the first century CE, vineyards were being planted in some of the northern regions of Gaul, cooler areas where vines had not been expected to grow and where Italian wine producers had established solid and expanding markets. The production of wines in these regions—and not just mediocre wines, but ones that earned a good reputation—was a real threat, which Domitian's decree would have reduced, to the Italian wine trade.

An alternative explanation for the decree is that it reflected concern at the spread of vineyards into unsuitable areas—good for grain but not for vines—and the proliferation of poor-quality wine. Wine of this sort could not be traded, because it did not have the quality to support the added costs of transportation and still sell at a viable price in the destination market.[19] It was thus much more likely to be consumed locally. Seen from this perspective, Domitian's order was the first of many state interventions in French wine production, particularly from the Middle Ages to the present, that have aimed to shore up quality and ensure the stability of supply and demand. That said, it is not clear how effective the decree to rip up vines was. Poorly performing vines and vineyards in unsuitable locations might have been removed, but viticulture continued to advance throughout Gaul. This suggests that Domitian's order was widely ignored, and it was eventually repealed, in about 280.[20]

As we have seen, the Romans first intensively sponsored viticulture in Gaul in their province of Narbonensis, and it is unlikely to have extended beyond this Mediterranean-Rhône region until the first century CE. Several accounts from the late first century BCE suggest that no vines or olive trees were to be seen beyond the Cévennes Mountains, which mark the beginning of the Massif Central, and that forests and pastures dominated the landscape of northern Gaul. By the first century CE there are records of vineyards in these northern regions, but we do not know when vines were first planted there. The first known reports might date decades or even centuries after these vineyards were established; that is a reasonable inference when the initial reports refer to old vineyards.

Vines were first recorded in Bordeaux in the first century CE. The town of Bordeaux was a significant market in its own right, and its port allowed for exports farther afield. Transportation costs encouraged the planting of vineyards close to urban centers whenever it was practicable; Bordeaux and Paris were prime examples in France. The vineyards near Bordeaux steadily expanded, and in 380 the poet Ausonius, writing about his vineyard at Naujac to the northwest of the city, claimed that Bordeaux was already famous for its wine. It is not clear which areas near Bordeaux were first planted, but it is likely that the Romans favored the gravel soils just outside the city.[21]

Viticulture generally followed the routes of the Roman wine trade, often along rivers. In the early fourth century, vineyards were reported in Burgundy, but because the source notes that they were already old and neglected, the implication is that vines were growing there in the third century or perhaps earlier. Also in the fourth century, vines were being cultivated near Auxerre in the Yonne valley, and by the fifth century they had been planted in the Paris region. The poet and bishop Sidonius Apollinaris wrote in the fifth century of Limagne, in the valley of the Allier River, "The mountains form a belt of meadows at the top, with vineyards on the slopes, and farms in cultivated areas."[22]

Viticulture seems to have reached the Atlantic districts of the Loire valley somewhat later: it was only in the late 580s that Gregory of Tours reported vineyards and wine production in Nantes, near the mouth of the Loire River. It has been suggested that the late emergence of viticulture in the this region might have be due to opposition from the Roman authorities of Bordeaux, who wanted to protect their wines from competition.[23] On the other hand, wine presses dating from the first and second centuries have been identified near Saumur and Tours, farther inland along the Loire.[24] By 500, when the Roman domination of Gaul ended, wine production had been established in what are now France's best-known wine regions: Bordeaux, the Loire and Rhône valleys, Alsace, Champagne, and Burgundy. The Romans were also responsible for planting vineyards throughout much of western continental Europe, in England, and in central and eastern Europe as far east as Poland.

In the third century, two legal changes reshaped the pattern of viticulture in Gaul. The first was a 212 edict of Emperor Caracalla which enabled Celts to own vineyards. Only Roman citizens were permitted own them, but Caracalla's edict gave citizenship to almost all the free inhabitants (that is, nonslaves) of the Roman Empire. Even so, it is impossible to know how many Celts planted vineyards or purchased them from their Roman owners. The second legal change was Emperor Probus's repeal in about 280 of Domitian's decree ordering the pulling up of half the vines in the empire outside Italy and a ban on further planting. It is thought that, by giving Celts the freedom to plant vines and make wine, Probus was trying to get their support against the Germanic populations that eventually destroyed the Western Roman Empire.[25] Yet the practical effects of his policy were probably marginal, because, as the spread of viticulture shows, the original decree seems to have been widely ignored and largely unenforced. It did, nonetheless, clear the way in legal terms for the unrestricted extension of vineyards throughout Gaul.

The spread of viticulture beyond the warm Mediterranean coastal areas to the northern regions of France by the first centuries CE meant that grapes were growing in a wide range of climatic and soil conditions. This had implications for the selection of grape varieties: vines that had flourished in the warmer conditions of Greece, southern Italy, and Mediterranean France did not do well in cooler and wetter climates and either failed to produce grapes or produced grapes that did not ripen. Anyone planning to make wine had to identify at least one variety that would not only survive but also produce satisfactory yields and wine that met minimum acceptable quality levels. The Romans understood the technique of grafting vines and undoubtedly taught it to the Celts, and it is possible that the varieties eventually selected for cultivation in each region developed as hybrids of indigenous and introduced varieties. Alternatively, farmers might have planted their vineyards with a number of varieties and selected those that proved most suitable.

Of the myriad varieties that had the potential for wine production in Roman Gaul, two in particular stood out and were mentioned by a number of authors. Biturica, which was widely planted around Bordeaux, seems to have been an exotic variety that was imported (perhaps from the Basque country of northeast Spain) and was found to ripen in the wet and windy maritime climate there. Its origins are unclear, but it is an ancestor of the carmenet family, which includes the cabernet varieties—including cabernet sauvignon and cabernet franc, two of modern Bordeaux's key varieties for making red wine.[26]

The second was allobrogica, an indigenous variety grown widely in the northern Rhône in areas now occupied by appellations such as St. Joseph, Côte-Rôtie, and Hermitage. The Roman encyclopedist Celsus was already in the first decades of the first century CE praising wine made from allobrogica, which suggests that it must have been cultivated for quite some time before. Roman writers describe it as a late-ripening black grape suitable for cool climates, which could be harvested even after the first frost—an event that would have put an end to grapes in the Mediterranean regions. The most famous wine made from allobrogica was called *picatum* (pealike) for the flavor it gained from the resin coating of the amphoras that it was kept in, and several accounts of banquets mention it.[27] Allobrogica might be the variety known as mondeuse noire in Savoie, or it might have been a parent of mondeuse. Either way, because mondeuse is in the lineage of syrah,[28] the signature black grape of the northern Rhône valley today, allobrogica cultivated there for wine in Roman times contributed to the longer-term history of the Rhône valley wine region.

Other emerging wine regions drew on either imported or indigenous varieties. Wine producers at Gaillac, for example, could have used varieties such as fer servadou (known locally as braucol), from Spain's Basque region,[29] and the indigenous duras. (Both are used in Gaillac wines today.) But there is no reason to think that vineyards anywhere were planted with only one variety, as is common today. In the early modern period, when grape varieties were identified and studied more closely for their suitability to specific climate and soil conditions, it became clear that the common practice was to interplant several varieties in each vineyard. This meant that wines tended to be field blends: blends of varieties as they were planted in the vineyard, with the proportion of each mirroring its representation there. It was only much later, starting in the nineteenth century, that varieties were commonly separated in French vineyards, enabling the production of varietal wines (made from a single variety) and blends assembled in the winery rather than in the vineyard.

There is little information on the amount of wine produced or patterns of wine consumption in Gaul during the Roman period. Once wooden barrels were used for storing and shipping wine, much of the evidence of the wine trade began to rot away. (Metal hoops, which withstand erosion longer than wood, were not widely used until the eighteenth century.) A body of wine merchants in a particular locality would suggest that it had a vigorous wine trade, but the absence of evidence of such a group might mean either that a place had no merchants or that it did but they left no surviving records. Dion suggests that the presence of a large community of merchants in Lyon trading in imported wine during the second century CE probably meant there was no significant wine production in Burgundy, not far to the north, at that time. If there had been, the nearby wine would have priced the imported wine off the market, thereby eliminating the need for so many of these wine merchants.[30]

Not knowing how much wine was produced in Roman Gaul, we can only speculate about consumption patterns. We do not know if enough was made to enable the elites to drink wine on a regular, if not daily, basis, if people in the lower ranks of society ever drank wine, or if wine became integral to festivities. But we can be quite sure that beer remained the most widespread alcoholic beverage consumed in Gaul, and it is quite likely that Gaul resembled some earlier cultures that consumed both wine and beer. It is probable that in Gaul, as in ancient Egypt, everyone drank beer but the elites also drank wine. Alternatively, the elites might have consumed only wine, while the mass of the Celtic population drank both beer and wine. Undoubtedly there were regional variations, with wine consumption higher in wine-producing areas, where it would have been less expensive, and lower in areas to which wine had to be shipped.

To some extent we might be able to extrapolate Celtic wine-drinking patterns from the practices of the Romans themselves, because they were the sponsors of the emerging wine culture of Gaul. We must remember, however, that cultural practices are more often adapted than adopted wholesale from one culture by another—adapted, that is, to preexisting local social, economic, and other conditions. The critical difference between Gaul and Roman Italy in this respect was that Italians did not drink beer at all, whereas the Celts had plenty of beer and a limited supply of wine. It is likely, nevertheless, that in many respects the wine that the Celts drank was like the wine consumed by their Roman mentors: containing various additives, including salt water, honey, herbs, and spices.[31]

It is quite likely too that the Celts adopted some of the Roman beliefs about the medicinal properties and health benefits of wine. Like their Greek counterparts, Roman physicians believed that wine, consumed in moderate amounts, was generally good for the digestion. It is recommended for that purpose in the Bible, where Paul advises Timothy, "You should give up drinking only water and have a little wine for the sake of your digestion and the frequent bouts of illness that you have."[32] Alcohol is an effective medium for dissolving other substances, so wine was often used as the base of medicinal potions. Cato the Elder wrote that the flowers of certain plants (such as juniper and myrtle) soaked in wine were effective against such ailments as snakebite, constipation, gout, indigestion, and diarrhea.[33] It is not that beer was not thought to have medicinal properties: a number of Roman physicians believed it was generally beneficial, as well as therapeutic for such problems as coughs, intestinal worms, and (with mustard) arrow wounds.[34] In short, wine was added to the beer-based pharmacy available to the Celts.

There was a hierarchy of wines in Roman society. The better-off classes drank wine that had deep color, good body, and relatively high alcohol, the sort that could be diluted without becoming insipid. Grapes used for making higher-quality wine were often dried before pressing so as to intensify the flavors and raise the alcohol level of the wine. In contrast, poorer Romans drank wine called *lora*, which was pale, weak in flavor, and low in alcohol and was made by adding water to the sediment left over from making better wine. It is reasonable to think that such practices were adopted in Gaul, although we should note that "relatively high alcohol" probably meant about 10 to 12 percent by volume at this time, with most wine in the range of 7 to 8 percent, and lora having perhaps 2 or 3 percent.

As vineyards and wine production extended across Roman Gaul in the first five centuries CE, they were paralleled by Christianity. Although Christianity supplanted the pagan religions of the Celtic populations throughout France, it did so slowly and unevenly. Much like vines, Christianity took root in some areas before others and flourished more in some regions than others, and even as late as the Reformation, it had a tenuous hold on some of France's more isolated populations. Even so, Christianity was an important driver of viticulture and winemaking in much of the country, because of the role that Christian ideology, imagery, and ritual give to wine. A river of wine runs through the New Testament, where it is the most commonly cited beverage—beer is not mentioned, and water appears more often as a medium for spiritual cleansing than as a drink. The first miracle that Jesus performed was to turn water into wine, and wine represents the blood of Christ in the sacrament of Communion. A common medieval genre of painting, Christ in the winepress, depicts him bearing a cross and bleeding from the nail holes in his feet and hands and from his head, which the crown of thorns has punctured. His blood flows into the vat of grapes that he is treading, and the liquid that will be fermented into wine is an undifferentiated blend of grape juice and blood.

Many pre-Christian religions had wine deities (such as Dionysus in Greece and Bacchus in Rome), and wine plays an important and positive role in Jewish ritual and doctrine. In a negative example, God's threats to punish the Jews for disobedience often refer to making grapevines barren and depriving the Jews of wine. But although such religions made an explicit link between wine and a deity, none before Christianity had given wine such a central position. It has been suggested that Christ was often viewed as a wine god, and he certainly might have appeared that way to the Celts of Gaul, who, as beer drinkers before the arrival of the Etruscans, Greeks, and Romans, did not have a wine god. The simultaneous spread of Christianity and viticulture can only have strengthened this association.

Yet as Christianity spread and reinforced the growing wine culture of Roman Gaul, a threat arose in the form of the migrations of beer-drinking Germanic tribes that occupied western Europe between 300 and 500 and destroyed the Western Roman Empire. These migrations used to be called "barbarian invasions" because, in the minds of the Romans, the Germanic newcomers had no respect for Roman culture, including wine. Edward Gibbon, the eighteenth-century English historian and author of *The History of the Decline and Fall of the Roman Empire*, channeled Roman prejudices accurately. He described the ancient Germans as "immoderately addicted" to "strong beer, a liquor extracted with very little art from wheat or barley, and *corrupted* . . . into a certain semblance of wine" (italics in the original). The resulting concoction was "sufficient for the gross purposes of German debauchery." Yet Gibbon credited these crude Germans with an almost instinctive attraction to fine wine: "Those who tasted the rich wines of Italy, and afterwards Gaul, sighed for that one delicious species of intoxication." Here was one of the reasons for the barbarian invasions of western Europe, for, according to Gibbon, the Germans would rather obtain what they wanted—in this case, wine—by force than by honest work: "The intemperate thirst of strong liquors often urged the barbarians into the provinces on which art or nature had bestowed those much envied presents [wine]."[35]

These invasions seemed to herald an uncertain future for the survival of wine in Gaul because, according to Gibbon, the newcomers lusted after wine yet lacked the discipline and patience needed to produce it. Would the "barbarians" destroy the vineyards so painstakingly established by civilized Romans and patiently nurtured by them and by Celtic owners? Would they adopt a laissez-faire attitude toward them? Or would these Germanic tribes—contrary to expectations—promote the expansion of wine?

It is difficult to describe the impact of these invaders on wine production, largely because records on viticulture in this period are very patchy. If there were adverse effects, however, they are unlikely to have been the direct result of willful neglect or deliberate damage to vineyards. Ironically, if the most negative portrayal of Germanic wine drinking habits is accurate—that they could not get enough—we should expect the new arrivals to have wanted to stimulate rather than reduce wine production. Indeed, during the invasions by the Germanic tribes and the political turmoil that followed, viticulture in France seems to have not only flourished where it was already established but also spread. It was in the period of Germanic incursions that vineyards were consolidated and expanded in many regions, such as along the Seine, Yonne, and Loire Rivers.[36] Yet the kinds of evidence we would like to have to confirm the extent of wine production and trade are too often missing. The replacement of amphoras by wooden barrels by the end of the second century CE might have had advantages for shippers, but it has done a real disservice to historians.

The evidence, as sparse as it is, leads us to believe that there were continuities and even some regional growth in viticulture during the centuries when the various Germanic tribes vied for control of western Europe. For one thing, the newcomers seem to have supported wine production everywhere. Visigothic law codes, for example, set out severe punishments for anyone found guilty of damaging vineyards. The Visigoths who occupied the southwest of France for a century after the fall of Toulouse in 418 did not harm the vineyards of the Gallo-Roman villas of the region.[37] In Portugal, the Gothic king Ordono (who ruled from 850 until his death in 866) granted vineyards near Coimbra to a monastic order. Such examples suggest that the rulers who replaced the Romans took care to look after vineyards and that rather than the monasteries protecting wine production from the invaders, the latter might actually have expanded the church's holdings.

The Vikings, whose reputation for plundering is among the worst of those of the invading peoples, also seem to have had positive attitudes toward wine. In the northern Frankish river settlements, they developed permanent commercial interests that offset their better-known hit-and-run economic activities. In addition to consuming much of the produce themselves, they participated in the northern Frankish wine trade and controlled the river traffic to ports from which wine was shipped to England and other destinations.[38] In the Carolingian Empire, which dominated western Europe from the late eighth century, wine was the drink of the upper classes, and great men boasted of the quality of their wine. Powerful rulers in the German provinces tried to acquire land in the Paris basin and the Rhône valley, where vineyards flourished.[39]

There are some examples of vineyards being destroyed. The Franks are said to have destroyed vines after the battle of Vouillé, near Poitiers, in 507.[40] But the overriding weight of the evidence suggests that if there were negative effects on wine production following the collapse of the Roman Empire, they were not the result of deliberate policies of Europe's new rulers. Rather, they were the product of the shock waves felt throughout Europe as many smaller political units replaced the political and economic unity of the Roman Empire and as existing patterns of commerce were disrupted. Bordeaux, where Romans had introduced viticulture in the first century, is a striking example of the instability that some wine-producing regions experienced in this period. In the fifth century alone it was invaded successively by Goths, Vandals, Visigoths, and Franks. The Gascons arrived from Spain in the seventh century, and the Carolingian Franks took the area in the eighth.

The disruption of commercial links does not mean that the wine production of France was in crisis for the five hundred years after the collapse of the Roman Empire. It might have stagnated or even declined in regions particularly affected by armed or political conflict, but overall vineyards seem to have continued to flourish in most areas where they were established by the time the Roman Empire began to crumble. In some localities—such as Burgundy, where forests were cut down to make way for vineyards—the land area devoted to viticulture increased. In the ninth century, with the emergence of a stable political entity in the form of the Carolingian Empire, security and long-distance trade links were reestablished and the wine industry rebounded. A burst of population growth further stimulated the recovery of the wine trade from about 1000, the subject of the next chapter.

Perhaps the clearest evidence that viticulture prospered under the rulers who replaced the Romans was its expansion within the Christian church. Christianity, as we have seen, embraced wine, and by the Middle Ages it was common for cathedrals and other church entities to have their own vineyards. Religious houses, especially monasteries, are often credited with particular responsibility (perhaps too much) for advances in viticulture and wine making. In the sixth century, Saint Maurus founded the earliest important monastery in Gaul, on the south bank of the Loire River a few miles from Angers. Little is known about it, but tradition has it that chenin blanc, the signature white variety of many Loire valley appellations today, was first cultivated there.

We do know that Saint Maurus was a follower of Saint Benedict, whose rule for the monastic life was followed in many religious houses throughout Europe. Although some theologians thought that monks should never drink wine, each monk in a Benedictine monastery was permitted a daily ration of wine if he could not abstain from it entirely. This was a pragmatic concession to reality, for Benedict noted that "wine is no drink for monks; but, since nowadays monks cannot be persuaded of this, let us at least agree upon this, that we drink temperately and not to satiety." In practice this meant "we believe that a hermina [about a third of a liter or a third of a quart] of wine a day is sufficient for each. But those upon whom God bestows the gift of abstinence, they should know that they have a special reward." Because of the medicinal value attributed to it, a sick monk was to be allowed a greater wine ration at the discretion of the prior. Benedict added that when circumstances did not permit the full ration or, even worse, when no wine at all was available, the monks should not complain.[41]

Benedict's rule speaks to the popularity of wine in Italy, where the first Benedictine monasteries were established, and implies that it was more appropriately reserved for Communion than for everyday drinking by monks—although the Communion wine, having been blessed and become the blood of Christ, was not considered the same as the wine served with meals. Having reluctantly conceded that monks might drink wine daily, Benedict was careful to limit their intake. Like many others with responsibility for maintaining moral and social order, he was aware that overconsumption of wine could lead to disruptive and immoral behavior. The

Benedictine rule was among the first to set down precise guidelines for moderate and acceptable levels of wine consumption; similarly, modern public health guidelines take the form of recommended maximum servings of alcohol per day and per week. When monasteries were founded in Gaul, where beer was more commonly consumed than wine, the rule was modified so that if wine were unavailable, monks were permitted two herminas of "good beer"; this was twice the permitted amount of wine, doubtless in recognition that beer was lower in alcohol by volume and less intoxicating.

We should note that in France, which still had a predominantly beer-drinking culture, monasteries were centers of brewing as well as wine production. The original rule of Benedict was silent on beer, which was not consumed in Italy, but information on monks' diets in France shows that they drank both wine and beer and that the two were sometimes not differentiated. One analysis of diets in eighth- and ninth-century western European religious houses suggests that monks drank on average 1.55 liters (0.41 gallons) of ale or wine a day, while nuns consumed a little less, 1.38 liters (0.36 gallons). Laypeople at this time drank between 0.57 and 1.45 liters (0.15 and 0.38 gallons) of wine and between 0.57 and 2.3 liters (0.15 and 0.61 gallons) of ale daily.[42]

The caution with which Benedict approached wine drinking was in tension with the monastic calling to plant vineyards and make wine. There are scattered references to vines being cultivated at monasteries in Gaul between the sixth and ninth centuries, but we have little sense of the size of the vineyards or the scale of production. In the ninth century there is evidence of considerable production at some monasteries. In 814, the wealthy Benedictine abbey of Saint-Germain-des-Prés on the outskirts of Paris, owned twenty thousand hectares (fifty thousand acres) of cultivable land, three hundred to four hundred (741 to 988 acres) of which were planted with vines. These vineyards were not one single estate but were scattered among scores of small holdings throughout the countryside, none of them too far from the Seine or Marne River. Fewer than half were cultivated by the monks themselves, and most were leased to tenants who paid their rents and other tax obligations in wine. The annual yield of the vineyards directly farmed by the monks was about half a million liters (132,000 gallons) a year, and they received another hundred and forty thousand liters (37,000 gallons) from their tenants as taxes. About 20 percent of this might have been used in Communion and for normal consumption by the monks and their visitors, leaving the remainder for sale. Equally significant, the tenants who grew the vines retained at least six hundred thousand liters (160,000 gallons) for their own use or for sale, a volume that speaks loudly for considerable peasant consumption, the existence of a wine market or, most likely, both.[43]

Monasteries became important channels for extending viticulture throughout Gaul and the rest of Europe. Networks of religious houses, following the Benedictine and other rules, were established, and many of these monasteries planted vineyards so as to be self-sufficient in wine. No other abbey in Gaul produced as much wine as Saint-Germain-des-Prés, but many provided not only for their own needs—which included wine for Communion and for consumption by the monks and their visitors and their retinues—but also for sale on the local market. Monasteries thereby contributed to the broadening of secular wine consumption. But although wine had an important status in Christian imagery and ritual, it was not identified with Christianity in a banal sense, even though a number of Christian commentators had negative views of beer.[44] It has sometimes been thought that Celts who converted to Christianity gave up beer for wine as a sign of their rejection of paganism and embrace of the new, wine-centered religion, but Max Nelson writes that this was not so.[45] Converting indigenous elites from beer to wine might well have been more important to the Greeks and Romans as a sign of cultural maturity than to Christians as evidence of faith.

The Christian church, through its vineyard-owning bishops and monasteries, played a vital role in both the maintenance and the spread of viticulture during these times of turmoil, but it would be wrong to think that the church was alone in this.[46] The image of pious and diligent monks carefully protecting and nurturing their vines contrasts nicely with that of "barbarians" from the east looting cellars, emptying barrels of wine in drunken orgies, and lying about in intoxicated stupors. These stereotypes contribute to the notion that the period after the collapse of the Roman Empire could fittingly be called "the Dark Ages," but it is a gross distortion of the social, economic, and political character of Europe's new rulers.

Still, the church was intimately involved with wine. Taxes and tithes owed to it could be paid in wine, and it benefited from gifts of wine. In the sixth century, Gregory of Tours mentioned a pious widow who brought a measure of wine every day to her church. In the eleventh century, Robert, Earl of Leicester, gave the cathedral of Évreux, in Normandy, about eight hundred liters (two hundred gallons) of wine a year for the celebration of mass. This wine came from the earl's own vineyards. In the seventh century, the bishop of Cahors sent ten barrels of wine to his counterpart in Verdun.[47]

Various church entities produced their own wine, and in 816 the Council of Aachen decreed that every cathedral should have a college of canons, a group of nonmonastic clergy whose obligations would include planting and cultivating a vineyard. Individual bishops owned vineyards in their own right. In the sixth century, Felix, the bishop of Nantes, owned vineyards near that town, while in the tenth century the bishop of Tours planted a vineyard for the abbey of Saint Julien. Other bishops are reported to have been so devoted to viticulture, or perhaps to the consumption of its product, that they moved to locations more suitable for grape cultivation.[48] Gregory of Langres (later Saint Gregory) moved to Dijon, where he was close to the vineyards of Burgundy, and the bishop of Saint-Quentin moved his residence to Noyon on the Oise River, part of a region considered favorable for grape growing.[49]

The need to have wine for Communion might well have been an important motivation for cultivating vineyards, but little wine was necessary for this purpose. Early medieval Christians rarely took Communion, and church authorities often suggested that three times a year was an acceptable minimum. If every Christian who turned up to Communion took a sip of wine, the volume required would still have been negligible. Cathedrals, religious houses, bishops, and other church entities and clergy produced far more wine than was needed for this purpose, and the great bulk that the church and clergy produced was consumed in contexts that had little or nothing to do with religion. The many travelers who stopped and rested at monasteries expected to be fed and provided with wine, as did the occasional visitors (such as kings, princes, and bishops) who arrived with large and thirsty retinues, and the heads of religious houses often hosted banquets at which wine was served. Wine was needed too for daily consumption by monks and nuns. Bishops and the higher-ranking members of religious houses probably drank wine every day, and ordinary monks did so when their monastery had a vineyard. Where vineyards were less common and wine was more expensive, monks tended to drink beer on a daily basis and receive wine only on special occasions, such as feast days.

Although much attention has been paid to church (especially monastic) ownership of vineyards, many were owned by nobles and other wealthy secular proprietors who produced for their own consumption and for the market. Vineyards were as likely to be attached to the mansions and villas of these individuals as to cathedrals and monasteries. Wine was an obligatory offering to distinguished guests, and a banquet without wine became as unthinkable then as it often is now. A ninth-century monk, Héric, described cups studded with precious stones, from which members of a wealthy Gallo-Roman family in Auxerre drank wines of the highest quality, made from grapes grown in their own vineyards.[50]

The problem with describing and quantifying the vineyards that were not owned by the church is that many, perhaps most, of the records of land cultivated by secular proprietors have been lost. In contrast, the archives of monasteries have generally survived better, because religious orders have had long, continuous histories and because monks were not only highly literate but also valued and conserved the written word. If there are more records of church-owned than of secular-owned vineyards, we should not assume that they accurately or even broadly reflect actual ownership patterns. In fact, some of our knowledge of the extent of secular ownership comes from the bequest of vineyards to churches and monasteries in wills. In the sixth or seventh century, for example, Ementrud, a widowed Paris aristocrat, left property including vineyards on the banks of the Marne River to members of her entourage and to several Paris churches. She also bequeathed small vineyards to her slave, whom she emancipated. The widow's vineyards might have been quite substantial, as she divided them among eighteen individuals in addition to the churches.[51] Many vineyards such as these must have remained in secular hands, passing down from generation to generation but without leaving any records.

In some respects, monasteries and bishoprics had advantages that secular vine owners did not share. They enjoyed greater continuity of cultivation, because subdivision through inheritance did not threaten their properties. Laws relating to inheritance varied from place to place, but in many regions of France, landowners had to leave their property to more than one heir, forcing the division of land into smaller and decreasingly economical plots at each generation. Moreover, although monks are often thought of as unworldly and devoted to prayer for most of each day, they were in fact intensely involved in the material and natural world around them. They studied agricultural techniques, and it is likely that they adopted scientific methods of viticulture and experimented with grapes, as they did with other produce. They learned to clarify red wines with egg whites and white wines with isinglass (fish bladder), although it is not certain that they were innovators in these techniques.

Monks put the by-products of viticulture and wine making to myriad uses. Poor or spoiled wine was used as vinegar, and grapes not used for wine were eaten or turned into verjuice (the acidic juice of unripe grapes) for pickling ham and cheeses. Grape seeds were used as flavoring or as a source of oil for making soap. Finally, the leaves and excess wood of the vines were used as, respectively, autumn cattle feed and fuel.[52] But again, it is unlikely that these economical practices (now called "sustainable") were to be found exclusively on monastic vineyard properties.

The collapse of the western half of the Roman Empire threw much of Europe into instability, undoubtedly somewhat disrupting viticulture, wine production, and the wine trade. In the late eighth century, production and trade began to rebound, with the emergence of the stable political system of the Carolingian Empire, which extended over most of France and much of central Europe. Its first emperor, Charlemagne, encouraged wine production. He is said to have ordered the planting of the first vines in the Rhine district and to have given a part of the famous hill of Corton, in Burgundy, to the abbey of Saulieu. (This vineyard is now known as Corton-Charlemagne.) In the calendar he drew up to replace the Romans' Julian calendar, Charlemagne designated October as Windume-Manoth, the month of the wine harvest. Carolingian ordinances also regulated wine making to ensure proper levels of hygiene, and one went so far as to insist that grapes be pressed, not crushed by foot. This clearly had little impact on techniques of wine production, for treading grapes by foot continued for centuries afterward.

The Carolingian period was undoubtedly beneficial to one of France's wine regions in particular: Champagne. Many of its great abbeys were founded in the seventh century, including that of Saint-Pierre d'Hautvilliers, where Dom Pérignon was said to have invented sparkling wine a thousand years later. All of them planted vineyards (producing grapes for still, not sparkling, wines at the time), and within two centuries the vines of Champagne were extensive enough for distinctions to be made among districts. What undoubtedly gave Champagne's wines a boost was the coronation of Charlemagne's son Louis in the town of Reims in 816, when the highborn guests would have had ample opportunity to sample the local wines. As Reims became the traditional place for the coronation of French kings, the wines of Champagne gained an aura of royalty, an image intensified much later when *champagne* came to refer to the distinctive sparkling wine made in the region.

Intentionally or otherwise, the Carolingians adopted policies that promoted viticulture and wine production, but Charlemagne is reported to have been a moderate drinker; he rarely drank more than three cups of wine with dinner, and he prescribed harsh penalties for drunkenness. In the end, however, the recovery of wine production and trade was the result less of Charlemagne's specific policies concerning wine than of the political stability that settled on Europe after centuries of territorial conflict.

Perhaps the best argument for the persistence of viticulture and wine making in France and elsewhere in western Europe after the collapse of the Roman Empire is the evidence of continued and widespread wine consumption. Drinking alcohol (beer as well as wine) was integral to the middle and upper levels of European society—those who could afford to drink anything but water on a regular basis. The most important social affairs—electing leaders, determining matters of war and peace, and celebrating marriage—were handled during banquets and other occasions of communal drinking. Drinking was also a ritual that bonded men in particular together, and the consumption of large quantities of alcohol was seen as an act of manliness. In southern France, the bishop of Arles, who had strong views on heavy drinking, noted with dismay that drunks not only ridiculed those who did not drink to excess but also expressed doubts about their masculinity.

Bouts of heavy drinking were far from uncommon, and the historical record suggests that drunkenness was a cultural trait among better-off men. If the weight of documentary evidence is any guide, the Anglo-Saxon inhabitants of England were the worst offenders of all: there are more references to intoxication there than to drunkenness in the rest of Europe combined.[53] Yet there is no reason to think that people in France drank notably less. In the Merovingian period, which preceded the Carolingian, there are many records of public drunkenness that depict drinkers stumbling through the streets vomiting and, when they retained enough physical control and coordination, engaging in acts of violence.

As for the Carolingian period, one historian has described it as "an age obsessed with wine."[54] Bilingual Latin-Germanic conversation manuals generally began with the apparently vital phrase "Give me a drink," and public drinking houses were intrinsic to patterns of rural and urban sociability. For religious or more secular reasons, clerics appear to have been particularly devoted to wine. Whenever invasions of Normans threatened the Carolingian Empire, fleeing monks were said to have often tried to take their wine supplies with them. When in 845 the monks of the abbey of Saint-Germain-des-Prés returned after Normans attacked their community, they thanked God not only for their deliverance but also for the survival of their wine cellar, which meant that they would have enough wine to last until the following harvest.[55]

As the Christian church extended its sway over the populations of Europe, it not only promoted viticulture but also had to confront the reality that many of the faithful—lay and clergy alike—drank too deeply and too often. As a rich theme in the Bible and an element integral to church ritual, wine had to be approached positively, and questions of abuse and drunkenness were difficult to resolve. Although many church authorities condemned the excessive use of wine, there was a sense that alcoholic intoxication was a physical and emotional state related to spiritual ecstasy. A number of church fathers developed the notion of "sober intoxication" to describe a state of spiritual bliss achieved without the help of wine or beer, and this might have prompted the less godly to use wine as a shortcut.

For the most part, however, the church opposed heavy drinking and drunkenness, an issue discussed repeatedly not only by individual church leaders but also by church councils. It was seen as problematic from social, moral, and spiritual angles. The sixth-century Bishop Caesarius of Arles condemned drunkenness on three grounds: it led to violent and immoral behavior, it wasted money that could have gone to charity, and it was sacrilegious. The records of Caesarius's time vividly illustrate his complaints, for descriptions of violent, immoral, and impious behavior related to wine are legion. Eberulf, the treasurer of King Childebert II (570–95), "flung a priest on a bench, beat him with his fists and belaboured him with blows, to the point that he nearly breathed his last, simply because he had refused to give Eberulf wine when he was obviously drunk." There were complaints that people refused alms to the poor, telling them, "Go, go on, God will give to you," while they themselves consumed large quantities of expensive wine. As for sacrilege, drinkers toasted the angels and the saints with the same wine that rendered them drunk and immoral.

The clergy were no better in this respect than laypersons. Bishop Cautinus of Tours was reported to be "often so completely fuddled with wine that it would take four men to carry him from the table." The bishop of Soissons, for his part, was said to have been "out of his mind . . . for nearly four years, through drinking to excess," such that he had to be locked behind bars whenever there was a royal visit to the city.[56] Gregory of Tours complained that monks spent more of their time in taverns drinking than in their cells praying. In 847, the Council of Prelates decreed that any person in religious orders who habitually drank to the point of drunkenness should do forty days' penance—which in this case meant abstaining from fat, beer, and wine.

Drinking and drunkenness were also treated in penitentials, manuals for priests that listed the penances Christians should perform when they had committed sins. In general, the penalties imposed on clerics, who were expected to be able to exercise greater self-discipline, were more severe than those applied to laypeople, and high-ranking clergy were expected to perform greater penances than mere monks and parish priests. An early-eighth-century penitential attributed to the Venerable Bede sets out the penance for drinking to the point that it "changes the state of the mind and the tongue babbles and the eyes are wild and there is dizziness and distension of the stomach and pain follows." These symptoms sound like punishment enough, but further penance was demanded: the offender was to consume no meat or wine (surely easily given up for the first few days after such a bout of drinking) for three days if the offender was a layman, seven days if a priest, two weeks if a monk, three weeks if a deacon, four weeks if a presbyter, and five weeks if a bishop.[57]

The Burgundian penitential of 700–725 prescribes a penance of three forty-day periods of just bread and water for anyone who has vomited because of drunkenness or gluttony. Other penitentials set out more severe penances for when a communicant has vomited the Communion bread because of either eating or drinking too much. (Presumably this refers to wine consumed before, rather than during, Communion.) Another penitential, from Cambrai in northern France and dating from about 830, specifies, "One who is drunk then with wine or beer violates the contrary command of the Savior and his Apostles; but if he has a vow of holiness, he shall expiate his guilt for forty days on bread and water; a layman, indeed, shall do penance for seven days."[58] It is noteworthy that being restricted to water was considered a punishment. This strongly suggests that beer and wine had become part of the daily diet for many in France in this period.

The simple presence of drunkenness in these penitentials should not necessarily be understood as indicating that drunkenness was widespread in early medieval France. What is clear is that in many regions, particularly where it was produced or easily accessible, wine was an integral part of the diet and, even more so, of occasions of sociability and celebration, and drunkenness was viewed as a deplorable result in some cases. The church's attempts to deter excessive drinking represented an early phase of the long-term theme of trying to keep wine consumption in France at levels considered moderate.

The first fifteen hundred years of French wine, from the first plantings by Greeks in about 500 BCE to the spread of viticulture throughout France by 1000 CE, established some patterns and themes for the following centuries, which the next chapters will trace. The association of wine with Christianity and the role of the church in promoting viticulture remained important through to the French Revolution and beyond. The French medical profession fully embraced the association of wine with medicine and health until the twentieth century. The intervention of the central government in wine production, in the form of Domitian's decree, was only the first of many such examples in the history of French wine. These and other themes came into clearer focus in the Middle Ages, between the years 1000 and 1500.

2. The Middle Ages

1000–1500

From about the year 1000, climatic and social trends favored the expansion of viticulture and wine production in France. (In this chapter and the next, I refer to "France" even though the patchwork of predecessor duchies, counties, and other political entities was in the process of becoming a single state.) There was a short-lived but important climatic shift from the late 1000s to the mid-1300s that led to warmer winters and drier summers in many parts of Europe. It was not as dramatic as the changes in climate and temperature that have occurred since the 1900s, but it produced changes in vegetation and reduced the length of glaciers.[1] For our purposes, it was important for a moderation of growing conditions that enabled vines to grow successfully in more of France's northern regions and some areas with marginal viticulture to establish it more securely.

The population of France seems to have grown steadily during this period, although in the absence of reliable censuses we have to depend on estimates. They suggest that the number of inhabitants at least doubled in 250 years, rising from between six and ten million in 1100 to eighteen million in the mid-fourteenth century, before it declined dramatically as a result of the Black Death.[2] This growing population increased the demand for all kinds of goods and services, especially food and drink. As wine became part of the daily diet of more and more French men and women in the Middle Ages, the demand for it might well have more than doubled between 1000 and 1350.

To meet this demand, vines were planted in new regions and viticulture was intensified where it was already practiced. There were many disruptions and short-term setbacks—including poor harvests, wars, and plague—between 1000 and 1500. The vintages of 1314 to 1316, for example, were poor throughout France, and there were widespread complaints that the vineyards failed to achieve quantity and quality. Of 1315 it was frequently noted that the grapes "did not reach their proper maturity," and one chronicler wrote of the 1316 harvest, "there was no wine in the whole kingdom of France." That was an exaggeration, but grape harvests around Paris were as much as 80 percent lower than average that year.[3]

The Black Death that ravaged Europe from the middle to the end of the 1300s reduced the continent's population by as much as a third. It had a serious impact on agriculture, including viticulture, as the smaller population needed less food and drink and could mount only a reduced workforce. It is likely that the area under vines in France peaked in the 1300s and then declined until the 1500s, when the population began to increase significantly. In the intervening period, many vineyards were abandoned, and land was converted to other crops in districts where viticulture was marginal. In Normandy, where the climate was too cold and damp for grapes to ripen, apple orchards for cider production replaced many vineyards.

Yet overall this was a period of growth for French wine, and it saw the emergence of a wine industry. Although it might seem premature to refer to such a thing at this time, the institutions that underpinned an industry began to appear. Production was substantial, with hundreds of millions of liters of wine exported each year; export and domestic markets were developed, and regular trading routes and commercial protocols were defined; guilds began to regulate the production, sale, and trade of wine; and various levels of government began to tax and control various aspects of wine. It was produced by thousands of vignerons—individuals who cultivated vineyards and made wine—who worked on a small scale, as well as by larger church and secular proprietors, and it was increasingly made for dedicated markets inside and outside France.

Although vineyards had been planted in northern regions of France—areas such as the Loire valley, the Paris region, Alsace, and Champagne—they were still marginal and occupied very limited areas by 1000. Even when average temperatures rose, these remained cool-climate regions, and many vineyards depended on mesoclimates (the conditions of individual vineyard sites) to provide a long enough growing season for late-ripening varieties. Vineyards were often planted on the banks of rivers, especially broader rivers such as the Loire, Seine, and Yonne, which moderated winter temperatures and lengthened growing seasons by providing warmer conditions in spring and autumn. Proximity to rivers was also important because water was by far the least expensive way of transporting barrels of wine. As long as they were not too heavily loaded, flat-bottomed boats could navigate these rivers at many times of the year, and they provided an affordable way of getting wine from the vineyard to consumers, especially in the important Paris market. Water was such an important resource that there was a saying, "For a vine to be most prosperous, it must always be able to see water."[4]

Northern climates generally favored early-ripening grape varieties and produced wines that were relatively low in alcohol (8 to 10 percent seems to have been common) and high in acidity. Some of the regions that expanded in this period have since receded; viticulture in the Île-de-France, as the region around Paris was known, was often marginal, but its closeness to Paris sustained it for centuries. The cost of transportation was an important component in the final price of any commodity, and large volumes of quite mediocre but drinkable wine could be shipped the relatively short distance from these vineyards to Paris, where they could be sold at lower prices than wine that had to be transported over longer distances. Wine from more distant French regions was also shipped down the Seine River and through the port of Rouen in Normandy to England, trade facilitated because England and parts of Normandy were ruled by the same king until the early 1200s. In 1175, Henry II granted Rouen a monopoly on shipping wine to England, but this trade was quite small and paled against the Bordeaux trade that followed it.

Near the mouth of the Loire River, in the area near Nantes that the Muscadet appellations now occupy, vineyards were sparsely scattered until the thirteenth century. Before that, a few dozen could be found throughout the valleys to the north and south of the river and along its banks, and the only significant clusters were around and to the southwest of Nantes. Vines were planted on slopes as much as possible, to maximize exposure to the sun and to minimize the effects of frosts and flooding. Ships taking on salt from nearby Guérande began to load some of the wine produced around Nantes— it was called "wine for the sea"—and in the 1200s enough was being exported to England that the duke of Brittany imposed a tax on it. In the fourteenth and fifteenth centuries, vineyards expanded throughout the Loire valley as far as Sancerre, then well known for red wines probably made from pinot noir grapes. Nantes became a significant wine-exporting port, and by the 1550s some eighteen thousand barrels of wine were shipped from there each year.[5]

The grape varieties of many of the northern plantings of the earlier Middle Ages are often unknown to us, and the first recorded references to many recognizable grape varieties date from the fifteenth century and later: chenin blanc, then known as plant d'Anjou and now the main white grape of the appellations of the central Loire valley, was first mentioned in

1496, while melon de Bourgogne (the main grape variety of Muscadet) was first recorded by name in 1567.[6] Experience must have shown that white grape varieties often did better than dark-skinned varieties, that some withstood late spring and early autumn frosts better than others, and that varieties with thicker skins were more resistant to the rot and mildew that affected grapes in damp climates. After that, it was a matter of identifying varieties with high yields, so as to maximize the production of wine per unit of land.

In Burgundy, on the other hand, pinot noir was first mentioned earlier than many other varieties—in 1375, in relation to some wine from Burgundy that was being shipped from Paris to Brussels.[7] By this time the region was already becoming known for its wines made from pinot noir, even though it had been hard hit by plague and warfare in the early and mid-1300s, leading to neglect of vineyards, erosion of soil, and shortages of the skilled labor needed to cultivate the vines and make wine. It is possible that these conditions underlay the decision of a number of proprietors to increase their plantings of gamay, a variety known to have been used for wine in Burgundy as early as the 1360s. Although gamay (the signature variety of modern Beaujolais) made a wine that was widely considered inferior to that made from pinot noir, it delivered clear advantages: gamay was easier to cultivate than the notoriously sensitive pinot noir; gamay grapes ripened more quickly, so that they were at risk from autumn rains and other threats for a shorter time; and gamay vines had a much higher yield—two to four times that of pinot noir vines in the fourteenth century.

The decision to increase gamay stocks was understandable in the circumstances, but it was opposed by rival producers who clung to pinot noir and by Philip the Bold, the duke of Burgundy, who himself owned extensive pinot noir vineyards.[8] He declared in July 1395 that gamay was "a very bad" and "disloyal" variety that was repugnant to law and custom. Burgundy's wine trade was sagging under the impact of the Black Death, which reduced demand, but Philip attributed the decline to gamay-based wines, which he alleged were naturally bitter. According to the duke, merchants were adding hot water to this wine to sweeten it, but after the effect wore off, the wine reverted to type and became "quite foul." He ordered all gamay vines to be cut down within a month—that is, two months before the 1395 harvest, so at a point when they would have been laden with ripening grapes—and to be ripped out by the following Easter. Although Philip's tirade against gamay is well known, his defense of pinot noir is less so: in Burgundy, he said, it produced "the best and most precious wines in the Kingdom of France for nourishing and sustaining human beings."[9]

It is likely that many vignerons refused to pull out gamay (and destroy their livelihoods), because half a century later, in 1441, Philip the Bold's grandson Philip the Good renewed the attack. Gamay vines were "wicked vines" that made "bad and weak wines," he declared, in contrast to the "worthy and excellent wine" made from pinot noir.[10] Whatever the political reasons for these draconian orders and their observance by growers, the effect was to protect pinot noir as the signature red grape variety of Burgundy.

Between the thirteenth and fifteenth centuries, pinot noir scored another success as the wines of Beaune shot from obscurity to being regarded as some of the greatest of France. This was an exceptional case of quality overcoming the obstacles of geography, for although the region around Beaune was ideal for growing grapes, the town was not on any major waterway. To reach the profitable Paris market, wine from Beaune had to be moved by land to the Yonne River in the north before being shipped on barges to the capital, a route that added considerably to its end cost. Once they recognized the wine's quality, however, well-off Parisian consumers were willing to pay the price, even though a higher tax than those imposed on other French wines further inflated it: the Paris authorities applied to wines from Beaune a levy more than twice that imposed on wine from Auxerre and four times that on wine from around the city.

The popularity of Beaune wine among the rich, famous, and powerful enhanced its reputation. From the 1300s onward, it was ordered for the tables of successive French kings. In 1564, in the face of an impending visit by King Charles IX, the mayor of Dijon declined to present him with some of the reputable wine that was made close to the city, as we might expect a civic leader to do. Instead, he set up a special commission to go to Beaune to buy "the most exquisite wine that can be found to be presented to the king upon his arrival."[11]

There were also developments to the south of Beaune, in the Rhône valley, when the split within the Roman Church known as the Great Schism produced two popes and one new wine region. One pope remained in Rome, and the other established himself in 1309 at Avignon, a papal territory in the southern Rhône valley. This created new demand for wine there, not so much because of sacramental requirements as because the establishment of the papal residence was accompanied by the influx of a huge bureaucracy of prelates and officials, all of whom drank generous amounts of wine. (Currently, Vatican City has the highest per capita wine consumption rate in the world, an achievement that seems to have long historical roots.) Such was the devotion of many members of the pope's retinue to the wines of

Beaune that they were later said to have resisted returning to Rome for fear of being unable to get supplies there.[12]

The papal court also required different (and less expensive) wine, a need that stimulated the expansion of vineyards near the pope's new country residence outside Avignon. This region became known as Châteauneuf-du-Pape (New castle of the pope). There is some question whether it was the first or second of the Avignon popes who ordered the planting of a vineyard next to the papal summer palace to the north of the city, but at the time, little importance seems to have been attached to the wine's pontifical connections, and it was called simply *vin d'Avignon*.

Relatively little is known of the medieval wine trade in France's Mediterranean regions, now generally known as Provence and Languedoc-Roussillon. Although they were especially suitable for wine production, they did not participate to the extent that they left the records we often rely on for information on viticultural developments. The broad Mediterranean region was locally well provided with wine, making long-distance commerce unnecessary, and the North African coast was dominated by Muslims, who generally did not drink wine. From time to time, wine from Languedoc was recorded in royal cellars in northern France, but it is quite possible that France's Mediterranean vineyards went into decline after the Black Death. Around Béziers, an important Languedoc wine town, 40 percent of the fields were in vines in 1353, 33 percent in 1378, and only 6 percent in 1400. More than a century later, in 1520, the percentage had risen to 20, but that was still only half the 1353 percentage.[13]

In contrast, medieval Bordeaux entered a time of prosperity and became the center of France's most important wine trade. In 1000, most of the wine referred to as "Bordeaux" came from the broader region of Gascony rather than the more limited territory (the département of Gironde) that the Bordeaux appellation occupies today. A great deal of present-day Bordeaux's vineyard area was planted between 1200 and 1750, and much of the wine identified with Bordeaux in the Middle Ages came from regions such as Gaillac, Moissac, and Cahors, up the Garonne, Tarn, and Lot Rivers.

In the early 1100s, viticulture in the district of Bordeaux was largely confined to the gravel soils around the town itself, but as a major wine trade with England developed, the area under vines expanded. Even so, throughout the medieval period the core of Bordeaux's vineyards remained restricted to a band four to five kilometers (2.5 to 3 miles) wide around the town walls. In these extramural areas, vines were planted intensively and viticulture was virtually the only form of agriculture. The great majority of these vineyards were owned by people who lived in the town, many in the parishes that were closest to their vineyards. Vineyard workers also lived in the town, and extra labor could be drawn from the urban population (about thirty thousand by the mid-1300s) when it was needed, especially during the harvest. Much of the wine from these vineyards was destined for export, but Bordeaux's vignerons also provided wine for local consumption.

The intensive viticulture (almost monoculture) that surrounded the town of Bordeaux ended where it encountered the villages in the town's hinterland, at which points vines were planted along with other crops (generally taking up no more than a fifth of the land) or not at all. Vineyards were planted almost randomly in this area, in communes such as Pessac, Talence, and Mérignac (now the location of Bordeaux's airport) but not in others. Vines also grew in the *palus,* the marshland that occupied much of the Bordeaux region, especially near the Garonne River. The palus to the north of Bordeaux, between the town walls and the Les Chartrons district, was drained and reclaimed, then successfully planted with vines. Les Chartrons, on the left bank of the Garonne River, soon became the center of Bordeaux's wine trade and the site of many *chais,* warehouses for storing wine before it was shipped. Similarly, some areas of the palus on the other side of the Garonne were drained and planted with vines. Farther to the west, south, and north of Bordeaux, however, vineyards were scattered and sparse.

In the densely planted area around Bordeaux, vineyards were very small, usually less than a fifth of a hectare (half an acre) each. This seems to have been common throughout France, perhaps because high-yielding varieties could be profitable for a vigneron who cultivated even such a small parcel of land. Extrapolating from later practices, we can say that vineyards grew more than one variety of grape and that vines were planted densely and randomly, rather like trees in a forest and certainly not in the neat, regularly spaced rows that are now the rule. This was likely the result of propagating new vines by *provignage:* burying the canes of an existing vine and allowing them to grow their own root system, so that a new vine grew close to the parent. Sometimes the connecting cane between the two was cut, but it was not necessary to do so. If the method was continued over time, a parcel of vines would be filled with many generations that traced their origins back to a small number of vines. Some of Bordeaux's vineyards were surrounded by hedges or marked off by ditches, but most were not, and Bordeaux's medieval viticultural landscape must have had an open and rural appearance quite different from today's.

Through to the fifteenth century, then, viticulture in Bordeaux was for the most part geographically restricted to the immediate environs of the town of Bordeaux itself. Some of the smaller communities nearby, such as

Saint-Émilion, Libourne, Bourg, and Blaye, also had vineyards in their close environs, but their extent was much more limited. The tightly planted vineyards that encircled Bordeaux might well have been the largest continuous area planted with vines in France. There were some efforts (such as draining the palus) to extend viticulture even farther, but the entrepreneurial vignerons of Bordeaux ran into resistance when they tried to push it into parts of Bordeaux where cereals were the main crop. Grapes might have been an increasingly valuable source of income, but grain was the single most important component in the daily diet of the mass of the population. It was not until the early eighteenth century that much of the rest of the present Bordeaux region (especially the Médoc district) was planted with vines.

The vineyards around Bordeaux might have been extensive in contemporary French terms, but they could not produce enough wine for both local consumption and the substantial wine trade that developed from the early 1200s. More important sources of wines lay farther inland, up the valleys of the Garonne, Tarn, and Lot Rivers, in what was known as the Haut-Pays, "High Country." From locations as distant as Gaillac, Moissac, and Cahors (which continue to produce notable and distinctive wines), barrels were shipped to Bordeaux for export as Gascon wine—although it was sometimes known as "Bordeaux wine" because it was shipped on from there. Most of this wine was red, but some was white: Scottish financial records from 1460 show the arrival of "five pipes [barrels] of Gascon wine, one white and four red."[14]

A name that was even more common was *clairet* or *cleret*, which was anglicized as *claret* in England in the sixteenth century.[15] *Claret* became the English term used widely and generically until the late twentieth century to refer to the red wines of Bordeaux. From the nineteenth century, Bordeaux reds were definitely red, but in their medieval form clairets lay somewhere between rosé and light red in color; they were not intensely red, and they were certainly not dark red or the color of wines that were sometimes referred to as "black." Called *vinum clarum* (clear wine) in medieval Latin documents, clairet was distinguished from *vinum rubeum purum*, "pure ruby-colored wine"—what we know generically as red wine. *Purum* signifies that the wine had not been diluted with water, and the fact that this word was not added to *vinum clarum* raises the possibility that some clairets were sometimes diluted in that way. The "clearness" implied by *clairet* suggests a degree of transparency rather than density in the appearance of the wine,[16] and that was one of its important characteristics.

Clairet was by far the most common style of wine made in Bordeaux: a study of wine making in the estates owned by the archbishopric of Bordeaux at the end of the Middle Ages concluded that 87 percent was clairet and 13 percent was red.[17] Although clairet became closely identified with Bordeaux, the same style of wine was made in many other regions—quite possibly everywhere in France that dark-skinned grapes were grown, whether Bordeaux, Burgundy, Languedoc, the Rhône valley, or the Paris region. An early sixteenth-century record of the wines held in the cellars of Pierre Le Gendre, the administrator of the king's finances, includes barrels of clairet from Orléans (in the Loire valley), Beaune (in Burgundy), and Montmartre (in the Paris region), along with others of no specified provenance but variously described as *gros clairet* (of higher quality), *clairet nouveau* (less than a year old), or simply "clairet." More than four-fifths of the wine in these cellars was clairet.[18] Clairet was the default nonwhite wine of France until the end of the seventeenth century: the main wine styles were white and clairet, with wines described as "red" appearing only occasionally and in certain regions. Marcel Lachiver suggests that "the producers [of red wine] could not or did not want to make wine in the dominant way" and instead produced their wine by deliberately or accidentally exposing the juice to longer skin contact than needed for clairet or by using only dark-skinned grapes.[19]

The same methods used to produce clairet wines in Bordeaux seem to have been employed throughout France.[20] Whole bunches of dark- and light-skinned grapes of several varieties were crushed by foot in a vat, and the juice was fermented on the stems, skins, and seeds. Fermentation (without temperature control, of course) began quickly—in a matter of hours in warm conditions. If grape varieties such as syrah, grenache, or malbec were used, the juice took on a pink color in as short a time as ten hours, but enough color was achieved within twenty-four hours no matter what the varieties. As soon as the juice was a satisfactory color—as with rosé wines today, color depth and tone were critical characteristics of clairet—the wine was racked into barrels to complete its fermentation. The whole process was very compact, and there are records of wine being made—from grapes being tipped into the crushing vat to wine being sealed in a barrel and readied for sale—in as short a time as eight days.

The pink or light red of clairet was undoubtedly influenced by the use of both dark- and light-skinned grapes; wines at this time were field blends, representing the grape varieties as they grew in the vineyards, rather than the result of careful blending in the winery. There was no specified range or depth of color that clairet had to show, but the agronomist Olivier de Serres wrote in 1600 that it came in two principal hues. The first was *rubis oriental*, a red in the spectrum of the rising sun, and the second was *œil de perdrix* (partridge eye), a pale pink said to be reminiscent of the eye of a dying partridge. Serres also wrote that clairet was "hyacinth tending to orange," with "hyacinth" presumably referring to a pink variety of the flower. (He noted that many Greek wines of his time were somewhat orange too.) Of the broad range of colors for clairet, Serres observed that the differences "are easier to discern than it is to judge which is the more exquisite."[21] Clearly, not all clairets were the same color, or even close to being the same, but limpidity was essential to distinguish them from red wines.

The wine left at the bottom of the fermentation vat after the clairet was removed, together with wine pressed from the solids, was darker and denser in color and no doubt more flavorful and more tannic, with perhaps some bitterness if the seeds were crushed. It became red wine that could be consumed as it was or used to give more color to clairets judged to be too light. Color was evidently very important, and many records refer to clairet being topped up with red wine specifically to deepen it. It is possible that color was not only important in itself but also an indicator of the style of the wine: the darker and denser the color, the stronger the aromas and flavors. The archbishop of Bordeaux's cellar master added red wine to clairet to give it not just more color but also more "strength."[22]

Some batches of wine were left longer on their skins, so as to make a darker, more tannic wine, although because many of these wines are also described as sweet, they cannot have been fermented dry. Medieval wine drinkers might have preferred to drink the clairet style, which Lachiver suggests combined the best qualities of both white and red wines and helped the digestion of meat-heavy diets. The acidity of clairet was partly achieved by harvesting the grapes when the earliest-ripening varieties were ripe, so that the blend included varieties that were underripe to one degree or another. But as we shall see, medieval physicians found a role for sweeter and stronger wines as therapies for many illnesses and physical problems.

White wine was also made, either with light-skinned grapes or by using dark-skinned varieties and removing the juice from the skins before they gave it any color. Another wine, known as *breuvage* or *piquette*, was made by adding water to the solid matter left over after wine making. This produced wine with a color even lighter than that of clairet and certainly with less flavor and strength (between 2 and 3 percent alcohol) than those of clairet or red wine.

Piquette was not taxed, but regular wines were more and more subject to taxes and duties during the Middle Ages. The town council of Bordeaux levied a tax on all wine sold there, and the English government imposed a duty on all wines passing through the port of Bordeaux. The port at Libourne was built in the mid-1200s as a counterpart to Bordeaux simply as a means of taxing wine: wine shipped down the Dordogne River from vineyards around towns such as Saint-Émilion and Bergerac bypassed the port of Bordeaux because the Dordogne joins the Gironde estuary north of the city. By compelling those wines to pass by officials stationed at Libourne, the government was able to tax them.

"High Country" wine was important to sustain Bordeaux's burgeoning wine trade. In 1308–9, for example, 130 vignerons from Moissac shipped a total of 3,500 tuns (252-liter, or 67-gallon, barrels) of wine down the Garonne River to Bordeaux—some 882,000 liters (233,000 gallons).[23] But Bordeaux's producers adopted restrictive policies to protect their own wine. They were able to do so because they not only produced wine but also controlled warehousing and shipping from the city's port. Under these regulations, which were applied in the early 1200s even though not given royal approval until 1373, High Country wines could not be brought into Bordeaux for shipping before Saint Martin's Day (11 November). This meant that wines from the vineyards closest to Bordeaux had no competition early in the harvest year, and in general it was not until they had been sold that the High Country wines were allowed on to the Bordeaux market. In practice, however, many communities obtained exemptions, and in poor harvest years, wine from the High Country was needed sooner, so as to fill orders from English and northern European clients.

Bordeaux's wine trade with England, the single most important relationship of this sort in medieval Europe, was facilitated by political events. In 1152, Eleanor of Aquitaine (which included Gascony and thus Bordeaux, as well as Poitou) married Henry, Duke of Normandy and Count of Anjou; it was more a dynastic alliance than a personal relationship. Two years later, Henry became King Henry II of England, so the same crown ruled England, Normandy, and Aquitaine. It was an unstable arrangement, however, marked by family conflict on a grand military scale, and Eleanor favored La Rochelle over Bordeaux, ignoring the persistent complaints of Bordeaux's winegrowers that punitive taxes were harming sales of their quality Gascon wines. It was not until Eleanor's youngest son, John, became the king of England that Bordeaux was able to emerge from the shadow of La Rochelle, and even then, dynastic considerations were uppermost. In 1203, John agreed to lower the taxes on Gascon wine entering England in exchange for Bordeaux's providing ships and other support for his war against the king of France.

La Rochelle and Poitou protested against this arrangement which gave Bordeaux a commercial edge, and in 1204 John granted them the privileges he had extended to Bordeaux. In principle, the wine regions of western France were now in a position to compete equally for the important English market, but once again, dynastic events proved critical. As a reward for

MAP 2.1. Main wine trade routes from Bordeaux, thirteenth and fourteenth centuries

resisting an attack of the king of Castile, King John placed an order for Bordeaux wine, a conspicuous and valuable sign of support for the region's exporters. Even more important, however, was the loss of La Rochelle to the king of France in 1224, which eliminated Bordeaux's main competition for easy access to the English market.

With privileged access to England once again, Bordeaux's wine merchants sent hundreds of ships every October on the minimum weeklong voyage along the Atlantic coast and through the English Channel to London and other English ports, as well as to northern France, Ireland, and ports on the North Sea and in the Baltic region (see map 2.1). At a time when wine was unstable and lasted scarcely a year, young Gascon wine was highly prized at its destinations, and it fetched good prices. Further shipments were made the following spring, when weather permitted, but the older wine, although only six or eight months old, was considered inferior, and it sold for less.

Toward the end of summer, as this French wine was starting to fade in availability or quality (or both) and before the arrival of the next vintage in October, wines arrived in England from Mediterranean sources such as Cyprus, Corfu, Greece, and Italy. These were sweeter and much higher in alcohol than the French wines, making them more durable and giving them the stamina to survive the long summer voyage across the Mediterranean, through the Strait of Gibraltar, and up the Atlantic coast to England and northern Europe.

But Bordeaux's exports to England were far more important, and each year hundreds of the city's merchants accompanied their wine to London, where many of them had established cellars on the banks of the river Thames near the wharves where the wine was unloaded from their ships. Other merchants from Bordeaux fanned out through England and other parts of northern Europe, selling their wines in towns and at fairs. The English government gave Gascon wine merchants advantages over other wine importers: from 1280 it extended the period they could stay in England from forty days to three months, exempted them from the most onerous English levies on their wine, and imposed a duty of only two shillings a barrel, much less than the tax on wine from other regions. These favorable terms supported massive exports: between the 1305–6 and 1329–30 export years (twelve months starting in October), shipments from Bordeaux averaged up to one hundred thousand tuns of wine, about twenty-five million liters (6.6 million gallons), annually.

Bordeaux's advantaged status lasted until the mid-1300s, when pressure from English wine merchants forced the king of England to repeal some of its privileges. At the same time, more and more English merchants began to travel to Bordeaux to buy wine there,[24] and by the 1340s they had almost completely replaced their Gascon counterparts. The Hundred Years' War reduced exports later in the century: only twenty-eight thousand tuns (7.6 million liters, or 2 million gallons) were shipped in 1369–70 and a mere nine thousand (2.3 million liters, or 610,000 gallons) in 1380–81.[25] These included wines from Bordeaux and the High Country. The English had a virtual monopoly on the trade until the French captured Bordeaux in 1451, and the city (and its wine) was so important that an English expeditionary army recaptured and held it for a few months, during which time it shipped nine thousand tuns of wine to England. With the final annexation of Bordeaux by the French in 1453, the terms of the wine trade with England changed and the volumes exported fluctuated dramatically, but claret remained a core wine preference of the English upper classes. The English kings were regular and mostly loyal clients during much of this period. In 1243 alone, Henry III bought 1,445 barrels (364,000 liters, or 96,000 gallons) of Gascon wine.

Wine from Bordeaux was also exported to important urban markets in northern Europe and to towns on the Baltic Sea. These population centers were also supplied by a wine trade route than ran down the Rhine to the North Sea and served northern Germany, the Low Countries, England, Scandinavia, and the Baltic Sea area. In eastern Europe, Kraków, a Polish city home to a royal court and a wealthy merchant elite, became not only a good market for wine but also an ideal transshipment point. Wines arrived there from Germany and the Mediterranean region for forwarding to markets in eastern Europe, in Russia, and around the Baltic Sea, but apart from some periodic deliveries from Burgundy, they rarely included wines from France.[26]

Although there are few useful statistics on French wine production in this period, it clearly increased dramatically so as to serve the growing domestic population and export markets, particularly the swelling urban markets of northern Europe. This phenomenon was not confined to France, as there was a burst of vine planting from 1000 to 1200 throughout Europe. Vineyards proliferated in the Rhineland, Swabia, Franconia, and Thuringia, and by the early 1300s, vines were planted as far east as the farthest frontiers of Hungary, including in the Tokay region, which later produced an iconic sweet wine. In England, the Domesday Book, an agricultural census taken in 1086, lists only forty-two vineyards, but two centuries later there were more than thirteen hundred. In some areas, such as northern Italy, vineyards increased to provide wine for the burgeoning cities nearby, for instance Venice, Milan, Florence, and Genoa.[27]

In France, landowners cleared forests and drained marshes to plant vines and converted poor arable land to viticulture. The growth of Paris's population (which is estimated to have more than doubled, from 110,000 in 1200 to 280,000 in 1400) stimulated viticulture along the Seine, Marne, and Yonne Rivers. Meanwhile, the expansion of cities that lacked adequate nearby sources of wine—such as London in England; Ghent, Bruges, and Brussels in the Low Countries; and cities on the Baltic coast—spurred growth in the vine-growing regions from which they imported wine, including the Bordeaux area.

Beyond the wine trade out of Bordeaux, a number of wine routes were established in medieval France—although we must remember that most of France's vineyards produced wine for quite local consumption. Even so, the wine trade could be profitable, and vignerons around Paris began to send their wine to England in the eleventh century. These wines were called *vins de France* because they came from the Île-de-France region, and even though a distinction was made between them and wine from France more generally, "vin de France" was used to refer to both until the 1700s. Wines from the vineyards around Paris were sent down the Seine River to Rouen, where textile merchants handled onward shipping to England and the Low Countries.[28]

Auxerre, on the Yonne River, was the center of another wine trading route. This one involved wines from vineyards near the town itself and from Chablis and other districts of Burgundy as far south as Beaune. Barrels of wine from Burgundy had to be brought by land to the Yonne, which sustained an important wine trade, carrying wine to the Seine River. The white wines from Auxerre were highly valued for their color and flavor, and some were off-loaded in Paris, where they sold for almost twice the price of wines from the Île-de-France, while most of them continued to Rouen for shipping to the Low Countries. By the 1490s, some thirty thousand *muids* (280-liter, or 74-gallon, barrels) of wine were being shipped annually down the Yonne—8.4 million liters (2.2 million gallons) a year.[29]

In regions where there was no efficient water route, wine had to be transported overland. Some wine from the Paris region went by cart to Flanders, but it took four horses to pull a four-wheeled cart loaded with four barrels holding a total of eleven thousand liters (2,900 gallons) of wine, and there were sometimes months-long delays because of shortages of horses or carts.[30] Wine often spoiled while waiting or spilled when barrels (without steel hoops until the 1700s) split as they were jolted along rough tracks.

As the wine trade developed, regulations were developed and wine began to be taxed as it moved across political frontiers and was brought into urban markets. The wine consumed in Paris was taxed as it passed through the gates in the city walls or as it arrived at designated wharves on the Seine. Some rules were designed to control quality at the point of production, like regulations dealing with pruning, vine care, and harvesting in Burgundy. A council of city representatives and vine growers there also decreed the date (called the *ban de vendange*) when the Burgundy harvest could begin, a measure which ensured that grapes were picked when they were ripe and also stopped vignerons from entering vineyards and stealing grapes from vines they did not own. Other regulations tried to prevent adulteration by merchants and retailers.

There was probably a broad continuity of church and secular ownership of vineyards throughout the Middle Ages, but many religious houses produced only enough wine for their own needs. These varied from order to order, but in-house consumption could be significant. At the monastery of Cluny, in Burgundy, a small meal called the *mixtum,* consisting of bread and a glass of wine, was available to start the day, and main meals (including those during times of penance) were served with half a pint of undiluted wine. On feast days, *pigmentum*—warm wine flavored with honey, pepper, and cinnamon—was served.[31] At times the monks of Cluny were criticized for what was perceived as a lavish diet.

If many monasteries produced wine mainly for their own use, the general rise in production must have involved an extraordinary increase in the output of wineries owned by private individuals. However, just as in the early Middle Ages, so in this period many secular owners transferred vineyards to the church in the expectation of tangible or intangible benefits. From the twelfth century, the Crusades proved to be a boon to monasteries because many knights gave land to the church so that, if they died while they were away, prayers would be said for their souls. Almost every house in the important Cistercian order received at least one vineyard during the 1100s. In 1157, for example, a widow and her six sons gave a monastery about 1.5 hectares (3.7 acres) of vines so that the monks would pray for their dead husband and father.[32]

Dozens of such gifts to the Cistercians' founding abbey in Cîteaux, in Burgundy, meant that by the mid-fourteenth century the order had accumulated hundreds of hectares of vineyards in what are now some of the most prestigious communes of the region, including Beaune, Pommard, Vosne, Nuits, and Corton. By 1336, the Cistercians owned fifty hectares (124 acres) of vines in the commune of Vougeot alone, at the time the largest single area of vines in Burgundy. They developed a reputation for fastidious work in the vineyards and the cellar and gained not only land but fame and privileges. In 1171, Pope Alexander III exempted them from paying the tithe (a church tax) on their vineyards, and he later threatened to excommunicate anyone who challenged the exemption, which suggests that other wine producers objected to the favorable treatment that the Cistercians were receiving. Also in 1171, the duke of Burgundy freed the Cistercians from paying any of the dues that would normally have been levied on the transportation and sale of their produce.[33]

This sort of encouragement led the Cistercians to expand rapidly—into a veritable empire of four hundred houses within fifty years of the order's founding—and they planted vineyards in all their locations, even though many houses made enough wine only for their own Communions and consumption. Yet others became significant commercial producers, like the founding house in Cîteaux and Kloster Eberbach in the Rhine district, founded by monks from Burgundy who discovered that the Rhine valley's climate was exceptionally suitable for white wine production. By 1500, Kloster Eberbach owned nearly seven hundred hectares (1,730 acres) of vines, the largest vineyard estate in Europe.

Although wine was readily available in regions of viticulture, many poor people could not afford it, even in the diluted form of piquette. They drank water, and there is little sense in the Middle Ages that this was thought problematic. By the seventeenth century it was common for physicians to recommend against drinking water: many sources of flowing water and much well water was polluted, and fermented beverages such as wine and beer were far safer to drink. But in the Middle Ages there seems to have been a general acceptance that water was perfectly safe for the purpose of hydration. Various authorities casually mention drinking water, but because it was consumed from wells, springs, lakes, and rivers, it was not recorded in the same way as beverages that had to be produced and paid for. Moreover, when priests ordered clergy and laypeople to follow diets of bread and water for weeks at a time as penance for their sins, they intended to restrict them to the minimum necessary to stay alive, not to make them risk death by drinking something dangerous. During the Black Death, it was alleged that Jews had poisoned wells to cause the fatal outbreaks of the plague,[34] and this is evidence not only of virulent anti-Semitism (Jews were killed in some parts of France and Germany because of these allegations) but also of water consumption. Water has a long association with wine in France, and it is a topic that we will return to in later chapters. But even where water was approved for hydration, wine was thought to have positive properties for health, giving it a dual function as a healthy way of hydrating.

For the most part, the diets of the homeless, the transient, and even the working poor are lost to us, but there is occasional evidence for the strata above them. In Montaillou, in the foothills of the Pyrenees, peasants drank wine as part of their daily diet. The village's 250 inhabitants supported a wine seller, who made the rounds of the houses, selling wine brought by mule from Pamiers, some sixty kilometers (thirty-seven miles) away, but it was noted that the community's shepherds drank only sour wine and some milk regularly, and people reserved good wine for festive occasions.[35] The citizens of Montaillou lived in a region then without vineyards; because they drank wine that had to be transported at considerable cost over long distances, they drank regularly but sparingly.

In contrast, people who lived in wine-producing areas had ready access to less-expensive wine, and they could therefore drink more generous volumes on a daily basis. The townsfolk of Bordeaux, for example, consumed wine from the encircling vineyards and wine shipped downriver from the High Country, but there is no evidence that they drank wine from outside Gascony. Even then, such was the importance of the wine trade that people in Bordeaux might sometimes go without or drink less wine to maximize the volume available for export.[36] The wine commonly drunk in Bordeaux was clairet, which seems to have been consumed at all levels of society, from manual workers to the city's elites. In April 1445, one merchant, Guilhem Forthon, owned thirty barrels of clairet, of which fifteen were new wine (from the 1444 vintage), nine old (from 1443), and the rest of unspecified age. One of the canons of Bordeaux's cathedral, Eymeric de Caumont, owned twenty-six and a half barrels of old clairet. It is doubtful if clairet much more than a year old was still in good condition, but sensory tolerance was undoubtedly different in the fifteenth century than it is today. Even so, there is a record of "a barrel of old wine that has gone bad."[37] Inventories from medieval Bordeaux also record red and white wines, but in far smaller volumes than clairet. Among the poorer inhabitants of the city, piquette was widely consumed, but this was the only social marker represented by wine.

Farther east and north, in wine-producing Lorraine, wine was consumed in households as grand as that of the duke of Lorraine and as modest as those of peasants who made it for their own consumption. In the late 1400s, the duke's household went through seven thousand liters (1,850 gallons) of wine a month, the equivalent of about three hundred standard bottles a day, but we do not know how many people shared this wine or how it was distributed—who drank more, who drank less. When the duke traveled, he provided two or three liters (0.5 to 0.8 gallons) of wine a day for each person in his retinue. His kitchen also used wine in the preparation of food, and in 1481 alone, some 468 liters (124 gallons) were designated "for cooking his lordship's fish."[38]

Lower down the social scale, men and women received wine as gifts and as part of their wages and pensions. In 1499 the nursing nuns of Nancy were given 1,874 liters (495 gallons) of wine, and in 1502 the Minor Brothers received 2,342 (619 gallons) liters of wine "to assist them to live." Wine was included in the annuities that the dukes of Lorraine provided to reward men and women for their services in positions as varied as valets, falconers, trumpeters, and midwives. Meanwhile, all kinds of artisans—masons, carpenters, and cartwrights, among others—received wine, along with beer and other foodstuffs, as part of their wages. When the belfry of the church in Bonlieu-en-Forez, in the Loire valley, was being built, the workers were provided with eggs, meat, rye bread, beans for soup, and "plenty of wine."[39] Beer was also provided as part of the wages in many regions of Europe. It accounted for a significant proportion of the daily calories of sailors while they were at sea.[40]

Although most of the wine consumed on a daily basis—light-bodied, low-alcohol, and fairly acidic clairet—must have been mediocre, there was some differentiation in wine quality at the higher levels of medieval French society. In Bordeaux, for example, some better-off landowners looked for wine from particular sites. In 1488, Johana de Bordeu asked one of her tenants for four barrels of wine from a specific vineyard in Léognan (now part of the prestigious Pessac-Léognan appellation in the Graves region). It is not clear if this wine stood out because of its peculiar blend of varieties, the quality of its grapes, or the skill of its maker. Records show many references to wine from the Graves area, which developed an early reputation for producing quality wines.[41]

Wine consumption in the royal courts of England, Scotland, and other European countries also helped boost the demand for French wine, especially from Bordeaux. In 1243, Henry III of England spent more than £2,300 on his 1,445 barrels of wine. Some was of poor quality, but more than two-thirds was considered high standard and cost more than £2 a barrel. When Henry's daughter Margaret married Alexander III of Scotland in 1251, the guests went through 96,500 liters (25,500 gallons) of wine. It washed down the 1,300 deer, 7,000 hens, 170 boars, 60,000 herrings, and 68,500 loaves of bread that the wedding party and their guests consumed.[42] In one year, Alexander had to pledge all his revenues from the port of Berwick to guarantee payment of the £2,197 he owed a Bordeaux merchant for more than one hundred thousand liters (26,400 gallons) of wine.[43]

The medieval English nobility also supported the wine trade based in Bordeaux. The earl of Northumberland's household consumed 125,000 liters (33,000 gallons) of ale and more than 7,000 liters (1,850 gallons) of wine in one year, although we do not know the number of his family or staff. In 1419, Dame Alice de Bryene's household, which brewed its own ale for domestic consumption, went through twelve hundred liters (317 gallons) of red wine and nearly five hundred liters (132 gallons) of white. On the clerical side of the social ledger, the consumption of one hundred barrels of wine accompanied the installation of the archbishop of York in 1464.[44]

Wine was also supplied to soldiers while they were on duty or in battle. The Bayeux Tapestry, which depicts the Norman invasion of England in 1066, shows a wagon loaded with a cask of wine—"carrum cum vino," the text explains—among the military and other supplies that the Norman army brought ashore. We should assume that this single barrel was one of many that accompanied the Norman army of invasion. Some of this wine would have been destined for Duke William's table, but much more would have been used as rations for the soldiers, as wine and ale were regularly supplied as military rations at this time. During 1406, the six men responsible for guarding the Château de Custines in Lorraine were supplied with two liters (half a gallon) of wine a day—more than might be thought desirable for men who had to remain alert, even with alcohol levels lower than those of modern wines. Wine was also brought along when armies were on the move, as the Normans demonstrated in 1066. A French plan of campaign from 1327 provided about half a liter (0.13 gallons) of wine a day for ordinary soldiers, along with 107 grams (0.24 pounds) of meat and a kilogram (2.2 pounds) of grain.[45] On the apparently rare occasions when medieval armies lived off the land rather than being provided with food and drink from a supply train, it is reasonable to assume they seized whatever wine was stored in the cellars of the localities they passed through or invaded.

More generalized rates of consumption of wine in France during the Middle Ages must remain uncertain. One compilation of estimates of per capita consumption shows a range from 183 to 781 liters (48 to 206 gallons) a year, which is equivalent to average daily consumption ranging from half a liter to just over two liters (0.13 to 0.5 gallons).[46] The low volume was for a Burgundian monk in the early fourteenth century (with an added liter on feast days), and the high figure was for the six soldiers on sentry duty at the Château de Custines. Between these extremes, we find such rates as 220 liters (58 gallons) of wine a year (just over half a liter a day) for students at a papal school near Aix-en-Provence, 365 liters (96 gallons) a year (a liter, or a quarter of a gallon, a day) for a chambermaid in the town of Vernines, in the Auvergne region, and 420 liters (111 gallons) a year for the caretaker of royal property in Gardanne, in Provence. Another compilation shows daily wine rations ranging from 0.5 to 2.5 liters (0.13 to 0.66 gallons), some stratified by rank and gender: in the Hôtel-Dieu of Paris in the fifteenth century, inmates received water and about half a liter (0.13 gallons) of wine a day, nursing nuns half a liter of wine, and novices a quarter of a liter (0.07 gallons) of wine, while monks received a full liter (0.26).[47]

These examples are widely scattered throughout France and over time. If they demonstrate anything, it is that medieval France had no such thing as a general per capita consumption rate of wine. There is a wide variation in volumes consumed in these examples and usually no evident correlation with gender, class, occupation, or the context in which the wine was consumed. On the other hand, these examples demonstrate an important point that must be borne in mind as we discuss wine consumption at later periods, when more accurate per capita assessments are available: per capita rates are of limited value in understanding patterns of wine consumption.

Per capita consumption is obtained by dividing the total volume of wine available to a population by the size of that population: if a town of ten thousand inhabitants imported and consumed a million liters (264,172 gallons) of wine a year, its annual per capita consumption would be one hundred liters (26.4 gallons). As a concrete example, Marcel Lachiver suggests that the 750,000 inhabitants of Brittany in the late 1400s consumed twenty-five million liters (6.6 million gallons) of wine each year, an average of thirty-three liters (8.7 gallons) per capita. But we must remember that not everyone drank the same amount of wine. For physiological and cultural reasons, adults have historically drunk more wine (and other alcoholic beverages) than children, and men have drunk more than women. The very poor might not have drunk wine at all—wine cost money, while water was free—and some people who could afford to buy wine might have chosen not to.

Some calculations of per capita consumption take one of these qualifications into account by using as their base not the total population but only adults, or men and women of legal drinking age or over a specified age. Needless to say, calculations of per capita consumption using different base populations give very different results. Removing women and children from Brittany's drinking population in the late 1400s, Lachiver suggests that men living near the coast (where wine was more accessible) drank about one hundred liters (26.4 gallons) a year, three times the general per capita figure.[48] Yet before eliminating children from populations when calculating the consumption of wine (or beer) in the Middle Ages, we have to bear in mind that childhood is culturally defined and that in the medieval and following periods, children in Europe assumed adult obligations (especially work) at much lower ages than is common in Western societies today. Young people were expected to work from the age of twelve or thirteen, if not before, and to be performing at adult levels by their midteens—well before young people can legally drink in all but a few modern societies. It is quite possible, then, that people in the past whom we might consider children were consuming alcohol in the same way as adults.

That said, most calculations of per capita consumption of wine use total populations. But in doing so, they tell us the average volume of wine available to each person—children, women, and men—not how the wine was distributed. It is quite common for a small percentage of adult males to consume a high percentage of wine. This does not mean we should ignore per capita rates of alcohol consumption, but we should treat them as what they really are: per capita rates of alcohol availability. We should bear in mind that they conceal rates of heavy and light drinking and of abstinence.

It is also important to remember that the level of alcohol in wine has generally risen over time. Wine made from dried grapes in ancient France, following the Roman example, might have had relatively elevated alcohol, because drying increased the ratio of sugar to water and raised the potential alcohol level of the finished wine (which might have been diluted back to a lower level of alcohol before being consumed). But from the early medieval period until the twentieth century, there are few references to this practice in France, and most wine probably contained between 8 and 10 percent alcohol in the Middle Ages. (An exception is *vin cuit*, which is made in Provence by heating and reducing grape juice before fermenting it, thus concentrating the sugar content.) This is significantly lower than the 13 to 14 percent that is common today, and it means that in terms of total alcohol intake, drinking a liter of wine a day in the 1200s was not the same as doing so in the 2000s. Moreover, the far more active work patterns and lifestyles of most Europeans in the 1200s, compared to the 2000s, meant that alcoh consumption had different physiological effects. In short, calculations of per capita wine "consumption" at various historical periods are useful pieces of information, but the more they are understood in their contexts, the more qualified their usefulness becomes.[49]

The upper classes of medieval France might have drunk more wine than their social inferiors, but did they drink better? One of the trends that emerged in the Middle Ages was a sense of connoisseurship, meaning that certain products began to acquire a degree of cultural cachet for their perceived quality. Applied to wine, this was not entirely new, because Greek and Roman writers had drawn up lists of wines they considered a cut above the rest. We might expect wine to have attracted this sort of differentiation earlier than beer: until the later Middle Ages, people had a limited range of beers to choose from, as they were not transported over significant distances and people drank what was brewed locally. Even then, there were very likely preferred brewers, especially in larger towns where numerous brewers competed with one another. Better-off wine consumers in key markets, like London, Antwerp, and Paris, were more fortunate, in that they could regularly choose among wines from many parts of Europe, and connoisseurship of wine of seems to have become more systematic in the Middle Ages. English and northern European consumers gave high marks to the body and light color of the claret from Bordeaux that they consumed in such vast volumes.

In France, a ranking of European wines by quality was to be found in a fictitious "Battle of the Wines," which was the subject of two poems in the thirteenth and fourteenth centuries. Each gives an account of a wine tasting—essentially a forerunner of modern wine competitions—organized by King Philip Augustus of France. As if to emphasize the association between wine and the church, the king was said to have nominated an English priest to judge the wines. This priest wore his stole as he tasted them, so that he could "excommunicate" any that he found unacceptable. The wines judged to be the best were to be given not medals but ecclesiastical and secular titles, ranging from a single pope to several peers.[50]

In the earlier of the two poems, the wines are all white and mainly French (particularly from the north of France, where white wine was more common than red), although there are some representatives of other parts of Europe and the Mediterranean area. Of the seventy wines mentioned by name, only two were from the Bordeaux region, six from Anjou-Poitou, two from Burgundy, and four from Languedoc. The handful from outside France included wines from Mosel and Spain and also one from Cyprus, and it was this last wine that the priest-judge thought was the best of all:

> The king crowned the wines judged good
> To each with a title he honored
> A pope he made of the Cypriot wine
> For like a star in the heavens it shone.[51]

In all, twenty wines were honored for their quality. The runner-up was named a cardinal, while others were named kings, counts, and peers. Eight wines, all from regions in the north of France, such as Brittany and Normandy, were excommunicated. Some were faulted because of their effects on consumers: a wine from Chalons, in Champagne, caused flatulence and itching, while one from Étampes, near Paris, brought on itching and cramps.

It is quite possible that some of the excommunicated wines had spoiled, because spoilage was a constant problem facing anyone (such as tavern keepers, wine merchants, and better-off consumers) who stored substantial volumes of wine. One fourteenth-century writer, Pierre de Crescens, warned wine drinkers of the practice of some tavern keepers and merchants of giving customers salted nuts and cheese before letting them try the wine, so that they would be less able to detect poor wine.[52]

Many ways of fixing spoiled wine were suggested. One popular late fourteenth-century work, Le ménagier de Paris, advised a young wife on such diverse subjects as obeying her husband, hiring servants, training dogs, ridding hawks of lice, and correcting bad wine. Wine that had gone sour could be made drinkable by adding a basket of fresh grapes to the barrel; wine that smelled bad could be improved by the addition of elder wood and powdered cardamom; muddy wine could be clarified by hanging in it bags containing the whites of eggs that had been boiled and then fried; unwanted color in white wine could be removed by adding holly leaves to the barrel; bitter wine could be softened by adding hot boiled corn or, if for some reason that failed, a basketful of sand that had been well washed in water drawn from the Seine River.[53] Some of these remedies might have worked; egg whites (raw, not cooked) are sometimes used today for fining (clarifying) wine. As for the rest, their effectiveness is a matter of conjecture.

We can never taste medieval wines, but we can experience them through the words left to us in medical and other scientific works, literary sources, and records of consumption. There seems to have been a broad distinction between two types of wine: those that were sweet and strong, and those—mainly clairets—that were more acidic and lower in alcohol.[54] This distinction was important within the context of the understanding of the human body and health that medieval physicians inherited from the Greeks and Romans, notably Hippocrates and Galen. This "humoral" understanding of the body underlay the medical approach to wine in France through to the eighteenth century, and it is therefore important to the history of French wine.

In brief, the humoral theory states that four bodily fluids, or humors—blood, phlegm, yellow bile, and black bile—in an individual's body determine his or her temperament and health. When the natural relationship among these humors was disturbed, people became ill, but they could be cured by measures that brought the humors back into equilibrium. Each of the humors was attributed qualities on two continua: moist-dry and cold-warm. Blood was warm and moist, yellow bile was warm and dry, black bile was cold and dry, and phlegm was cold and moist.

Physicians also believed that the relationships among the humors varied according to demographic, cultural, and environmental criteria, with gender, age, geography, and the season determining or heavily influencing an individual's humoral makeup. Men tended to be warmer and drier than women, children were warmer than adults, and older people were cool and got cooler and drier as they approached the ultimate coldness of death. The physician's challenges were to maintain these natural relationships and, in the case of illness—which was a sign that the proper relationship was impaired—to bring the humors back into equilibrium. Thus a patient who had a fever and was sweating was diagnosed as too hot and too moist and needed a cure that reduced both heat and moistness.

Even though physicians used medicines, diet was the most common means that they employed to ensure well-being and to cure illness. Physicians considered all foods and beverages to have properties that related to human health. This went well beyond general notions that some foods are "good for you" and others not. All foods and beverages were assigned humoral qualities: some were considered warm, while others were considered cold. It was not that the foods themselves were thought to have these properties, but it was believed that when they were consumed, the body processed them to enhance one of the humors, thus increasing its influence over the body. Thus a physician would prescribe foods that produced "warmth" when a patient's body was inappropriately influenced by cold humors.

Michele Savonarola, the fourteenth-century Florentine physician whose works were influential throughout Europe and translated into French, attributed different levels of heat to wine: "small wines" were warm in the first (lowest) degree, slightly stronger wines were warm in the second degree, and wines made from certain grape varieties (probably including grenache and malvasia) were warm in the third degree. The only warmer beverages were spirits (eaux-de-vie) that were made by distilling wine.[55] Because wine was more or less "warm," physicians warned that young people, who were already predominantly "hot," should not drink it. On the other hand, they recommended wine for older people, because its "heat" counteracted the natural cooling tendency of their bodies. But by the Middle Ages, some physicians made a distinction between sweet and strong (higher alcohol) wines, which were considered very warm and nutritious, and clairet, whose acidity and lower alcohol were thought to be less "warm" and nutritious but were believed to sharpen the appetite and thereby feed the body indirectly.

Physicians also warned against consuming too much strong wine, as it could raise the temperature of the body to a dangerous level and activate "passions." There was a particular concern about activating sexual passions, and sweet wine and meat were items of the diet that physicians worried about for their ability to arouse dangerously erotic feelings. Medieval pilgrims to the Holy Land were advised against drinking any strong wines they might come across, "because they tempt you to coitus, from which you must abstain."[56] For this very reason, on the other hand, strong wine might be used to aid conception: one recommended dish was a pâté made from the meat of male and female pigeons, seasoned with pepper and ginger and steeped in strong wine.

Most of the wine produced in medieval France was clairet and thus closer to the acidic, low-alcohol end of the spectrum, and it is quite possible that this reflected relatively low demand for stronger and sweeter wines because of the medical advice to consume it only in small quantities. Strong sweet wine was also more expensive than lighter wine, although it is not clear whether that reflected higher costs of production or its cultural value. For a number of reasons, these stronger wines represented a style that was culturally distinct, as well as sensorially different, from the great bulk of the wine produced in medieval France.

Beyond calibrating the humors, medieval physicians employed wine to treat a wide range of specific illnesses and conditions. Henri de Mondeville, a fourteenth-century French surgeon, stressed its benefits for the blood, although he pointed out that one should use the best wine one could find— light, white, or rosé, with a good aroma and pleasant flavor. In a secular restatement of the doctrine of transubstantiation, Mondeville wrote that wine was the best beverage for generating blood, for it entered the bloodstream directly and was immediately transformed into blood. But he added that he could also see the benefits of drinking both wine and milk. People who drank only wine had a reddish complexion, and those who drank only milk were pale, but a proper balance of the two beverages made for the ideal complexion: pale with rosy cheeks.[57]

French medical treatises of this period prescribed wine as a base for medicines, usually boiled so as to dissolve the other ingredients more effectively. Wine was also a means of facilitating the absorption of other medicaments: a common recommendation was to take a specific potion in the evening with some warm wine. A paralyzed patient should be fed ground aloe wood in white wine; to treat an edema, roots of irises and lilies should be mashed in a mortar and drunk with wine; someone suffering from angina should dry and pulverize the white excrement of a dog and drink it in warm white wine. Wine could also be used in a vaporized form: anyone suffering from dysentery should heat a tile until it was red, place it in a basin and cover it with wine, put the basin under a chair with a hole in the seat, and then sit bare bottomed in the chair and absorb the fumes.[58] Wine was also advised for washing the skin before applying poultices. French physicians used other liquids, including milk, vinegar, oil, and urine, as medicines, but wine was by far the most commonly employed. There was no end to the ailments and conditions that wine could cure or relieve: seasickness, childbirth, inflammation of the arms, abscesses, melancholy, and constipation—for these and myriad other problems, there was a recommended treatment that involved wine. Wine might also be chosen because it was suitable for a particular time of the year. Physicians suggested drinking weaker wines during summer and adding water to them if the temperature was very hot. In winter, stronger and sweeter wines were advised, especially if one was going out in the morning of a cold, misty day.

Wine was also widely used in cooking. The ancient French might have been beer drinkers, but by the Middle Ages, beer and ale had no place in French cookery and were condemned as having a "foreign" flavor.[59] The earliest known Anglo-Norman culinary collections (from the late thirteenth and early fourteenth centuries) include wine in many recipes, and one has a recipe for spiced wine called "claree."[60] *Le ménagier de Paris* mentions wine 120 times in its eighty pages devoted to recipes; it is used in sauces and soups, for cooking fish, and for roasting meat. In the *Viandier de Taillevent*, an important collection of recipes also from the fourteenth century, wine appears in dish after dish. A recipe for mustard sauce calls for red wine, while one for marjoram sauce uses white; stewed poultry is prepared with "a great quantity of white wine," and a recipe for wild boar includes clairet.[61] Additionally, wine came to be, among the better-off in medieval France, the default beverage to consume with a meal. Not only was a beverage helpful for swallowing food, but wine was reputed to be excellent for the digestion.

Wine also remained important in religious terms, although there was a radical shift in its relationship to Communion during the Middle Ages. For the first thousand years of Christianity, the faithful who took Communion received both bread and wine (known as "Communion in both kinds"). Only red wine could be used, not only because it resembled the blood of Christ more than white wine did, but also to avoid any confusion between wine and water;[62] Communion wine was often diluted with water, and diluted white wine must have looked very watery. During the twelfth and thirteenth centuries, however, Communion wine was gradually withdrawn from the laity. Several thirteenth-century church councils decreed that Communion in one kind (bread alone) was all that was required for lay Christians and that priests should receive the wine on behalf of their lay congregations. For a while, priests could choose either form of Communion, but in the fourteenth century, Communion in one kind was made mandatory for the laity, and in 1415 the Council of Constance ruled that Communion in both kinds was a heresy.

This did not reflect a shortage of wine but was partly the church's response to a heretical doctrine stating that both the bread and the wine were absolutely necessary for salvation. There were also practical issues to consider. In the thirteenth century, Thomas Aquinas wrote about the fear that Communion wine would be spilled while the chalice was being passed from person to person; at the same time, the practice began of placing the bread on a communicant's tongue to avoid crumbs falling to the floor. There were also difficulties assuring the delivery of wine to some of the farthest reaches of Christendom where the climate made viticulture impossible. Protestants restored Communion wine to the laity in the 1500s, but lay Catholics could not receive Communion wine until the 1960s, when Communion in two kinds was permitted at the discretion of individual bishops. For almost a thousand years when Communion in one kind was practiced universally, the only wine required for Communion in the dominant Christian denomination of France was enough for the priest to sip.

The religious meaning attached to wine probably made excessive wine consumption and drunkenness that much more distressing. Drunkenness was associated with immorality, blasphemy, and lack of self-control, but it was also condemned as dangerous to health. The thirteenth-century physician Adam de Crémone wrote that "if it is taken to excess, [wine] harms the liver, the brain, and the nerves, [and] it brings about paralysis, shaking, convulsions, apoplexy, and sudden death."[63] Excessive drinking was a problem among the French clergy. On a thirteenth-century visitation to parts of northern France, church officials found many priests in breach of the rules governing alcohol: the priest in Saint-Rémy was notorious for drunkenness and for frequenting the local tavern, where he had got into fights on several occasions; the priest at Gilemerville had occasionally lost his clothes in taverns (possibly by gambling, or perhaps in other circumstances); the priest in Pierrepont was habitually drunk; the priest in Grandcourt was notorious for his excessive drinking; the priest in Panliu was not only well known as a drunk but also sold wine and often got his parishioners inebriated.[64]

Excessive drinking by laypeople was no less problematic, and authorities in many places attempted to rein in unacceptable behavior by regulating drinking. Some tried to limit drinking hours, as with the 1350 royal decree requiring Paris innkeepers not to allow new customers into their inns after the bells of Notre-Dame Cathedral had rung out the curfew hour. But such regulations should not make us forget that drinking wine, for hydration or for pleasure (or for pleasant hydration), was fundamentally a social activity in medieval France. It was problematic at times, but it is likely that affording and obtaining wine, not the amount consumed, was more often the problem.

In general terms, the Middle Ages saw the emergence of a wine industry in France. Although most French wine was made by vignerons farming small vineyards and making wine for their own consumption and the local market, big volumes of wine were systematically shipped within France and from France to foreign markets. Regulations and taxes began to be applied, and the spread of vineyards and the increased production they imply suggest that wine was consumed far more broadly, in geographic and social terms, than before. The medieval period thus set in place the foundations of the modern French wine industry, which were built on during the early modern period.

3. New Wines, New Regions

1500–1700

Between 1519 and the 1560s, Spanish missionaries planted vineyards throughout Latin America, from Mexico almost as far as Patagonia, thus founding several important modern wine industries. In the early 1600s, the English government encouraged settlers to cultivate vines in colonies along the eastern seaboard of North America. In the 1650s, the Dutch government helped settlers at the Cape Colony plant the vineyards that grew into South Africa's wine industry. The Spanish wanted local wine (and later, brandy) to supply their mining and other settlements throughout Latin America; the English wanted to start a wine industry in North America to end their dependence on imports from France; and the Dutch wanted wine supplies at the Cape to provision their ships plying the long-distance spice trade route between Europe and Asia.

France, in contrast, did not try to extend wine production to any of its overseas territories, even though some seemed suitable: in 1535, the explorer Jacques Cartier optimistically gave the name Île de Bacchus to an island (now called Île d'Orléans) in the Saint Lawrence River because of the large number of wild grapes he found growing there. This was treated more as a curiosity than as an opportunity when the French settled New France (now Québec), because, unlike the other imperial powers, the French government saw no reason to encourage the extension of viticulture and wine production outside the home country.

Nonetheless, many French vignerons were active in colonial wine ventures in various parts of the world. Most were French Protestants, known as "Huguenots," who had been vignerons in southern and southwestern France, although some came from other regions: many of the Huguenots in Meaux, near Paris, were vignerons.[1] From the early sixteenth century, hundreds of thousands of Huguenots left France to escape persecution, and the number increased when King Louis XIV adopted repressive policies against them in 1685. Displaced Huguenots settled in northern Florida in the 1560s and were reported to have made twenty barrels of wine from native grapes, although Thomas Pinney doubts that they did.[2] In the 1670s in Pennsylvania, William Penn reported drinking wine reminiscent of good claret but made from native grape varieties by a Huguenot, and Penn recruited Huguenot vignerons to his colony. In 1700 a large group of Huguenots settled in Virginia, and in 1702 they produced wine from native grapes that was described as "pleasant, strong, and full body'd."[3] Later, in the mid-1700s, Huguenots settled and planted vineyards in a community in South Carolina they named New Bordeaux; fifteen vignerons are recorded among the eighty-five adults there whose occupations are known.[4] Farther afield, nearly two hundred Huguenots arrived in 1688 at the Dutch colony at the Cape and were granted land for vineyards. They are credited with introducing the chenin blanc variety, which eventually became South Africa's signature white grape. Their settlement at Franschhoek (Afrikaans for "French corner") near Cape Town is now a wine appellation.

Frenchmen (women were not identified as vignerons, even though they undoubtedly cultivated vines and made wine) seem to have been widely assumed to have viticultural skills, and colonial authorities looked to them for help with wine ventures. In 1622, for example, King James I of England ordered all householders in Jamestown, in the Colony of Virginia, to receive a manual telling them how to cultivate vines. It was written by Jean Bonoeil, a Frenchman and a gardener at Oatlands Palace, in Surrey, who clearly fancied himself as having a good eye for vineyard sites he had never seen. Bonoeil was probably a Huguenot from Languedoc, as he refers to that region frequently in his short manual, which undoubtedly reflects what he had observed there before moving to England. Although written for settlers in Virginia, it was effectively a guide to viticulture and wine making in southern France.

Bonoeil wrote that he had been told "there is a great abundance of vines in Virginia, and many of them well loaden with grapes. . . . Moreover they avouch it is a better Country than Languedock, which is one of the fruitfullest Provinces in all France."[5] Much of his advice echoes French descriptions of vineyard and wine making practices at the time, but some of his suggestions were different. For instance, rather than planting vines haphazardly, the common practice in France, Bonoeil proposed the modern system of planting them equally spaced and in straight rows. On the other hand, he suggested propagation by provignage, which generally led to irregularly spaced vines, and he recommended training vines up trees or poles.

Bonoeil's description of wine making was also fairly conventional, but although he endorsed the French practice of blending varieties as they were interplanted in the vineyard (that is, making field blends), he seems to have favored the separation of light- from dark-skinned grapes. The exception was for claret, the lighter and more transparent red wine: "Whoever will have his wine all Claret, let him gather all his grapes at once, the white and the black, and put them all together in one vessel, and let them work [ferment] together." To make red or white wine, on the other hand, only dark- or light-skinned grapes, respectively, should be used, a practice at odds with those recommended by most other French writers until the eighteenth century. Finally, Bonoeil advised, in this manual designed for settlers in Virginia, using native grapes for wine. He suggested that they be boiled in water, then pressed, and the juice, water, and skins fermented together. After seven or eight days, the liquid could be put in barrels, and the result would be a "meane small wine." "I have oftentimes seen such Wine made reasonable good for the houshold," Bonoeil wrote. "And by this means every man may presently have Wine in Virginia to drink."[6]

It is striking that foreigners—especially English and Dutch—so often drew on French viticultural expertise. This was still true in the eighteenth century, when a book on viticulture and wine making for the New Bordeaux settlement in South Carolina declared that it followed "the most approved methods in the most celebrated wine-countries in France."[7] Perhaps this is only to be expected, as England and the Netherlands were key markets for French wine. But in a broader sense, between 1500 and 1700, a number of developments enhanced France's reputation for making superior wine: the clearer identification of regions, subregions, and even individual estates as sources of superior wine; the production of new wine styles, such as sweeter white wines and sparkling wines; and the creation of France's brandy industry. Together these represented important changes for French wine.

Reliable figures on the total land under vines in France are not available until the nineteenth century, and we can only estimate trends at earlier periods. It is clear that land used for viticulture shrank between 1350 and 1400, when the Black Death reduced France's population by a quarter to a third, leaving a smaller labor force to work the vineyards and lower demand for all commodities, including wine. Thousands of vineyards throughout France were abandoned and might not have returned to production for a century or more. In part because of the Hundred Years' War (1337–1453), the number of inhabitants in France recovered only slowly, reaching about fifteen million by 1500. From then, however, it began to rise more rapidly, to 16 million in 1550 and 18.5 million in 1600 before reaching about 22 million in 1700, so there was a 50 percent increase in the two centuries that this chapter covers. Needless to say, a steadily growing population meant increased demand for food and drink, and that provided the motivation not only to replant abandoned vineyards but also to extend viticulture into new areas.

The rebounding market is visible in export figures, which rose substantially between the early 1500s and the early 1600s. Bordeaux's annual exports in the early 1500s seem to have averaged twenty to thirty thousand barrels, rising to eighty thousand in exceptional years, but by the 1640s about sixty thousand barrels was a common annual number.[8] The single most important market was England, although the fluctuating relations between France and England complicated trade. In 1495, the privileges that English merchants had enjoyed in Bordeaux in the 1300s were reinstated, and various treaties signed early in King Henry VIII's reign facilitated trade. There were periods of war (such as in 1513, 1522–23, and 1542) and longer periods of uneasy peace, but the Bordeaux trade was seriously hobbled only when, in 1531, Henry prohibited the importation into England of wine before 2 February each year.[9] This was a direct threat to clairet, which was shipped in November soon after fermentation and often went off in a few months, and it heralded the beginning of a gradual shift in English imports from claret to fuller-bodied, deeper-colored, and longer-lasting red wines. Examples of this style were being made in Bordeaux's Graves district, and in the late 1520s they were fetching higher prices in London than any other wines. Henry VIII bought red wine from Graves at more than £5 a barrel,[10] and perhaps he wanted to share the pleasure with his subjects by denying them claret.

Despite these problems with exporting to England, clairet remained France's most common nonwhite wine, and the shift to darker, fuller-bodied red wines was only gradual. In Olivier de Serres's treatise on wine, published in 1600, clairet is the default wine, and there is no hint that this style was in decline. Clairet was the dominant style of red wine in many areas of southwest France that shipped through Bordeaux, including Bergerac and some of the regions closer to the Pyrenees. But it was Bordeaux that prospered, not least because wines from farther afield were not permitted into the city before December and (unlike wines from Bordeaux) were taxed as they were exported.

Although Bordeaux was by far France's preeminent wine-exporting port, Nantes (at the mouth of the Loire River) became increasingly important during the 1500s as the vineyards around the city and upstream, especially between Angers and Saumur, expanded. Some eighteen thousand nine-hundred-liter (238-gallon) barrels of wine from the Nantes region and from upstream vineyards were shipped through Nantes each year in the mid-1550s. Perhaps a fifth of this wine was consumed in the Nantes region itself, with the rest destined primarily for England. Scotland, northern France, and the Netherlands were also important customers, and smaller numbers of barrels were shipped to Ireland, Spain, Portugal, and Germany. Production increased rapidly along the Loire valley in the 1560s and 1570s, and in 1570–72 more than thirty-two thousand barrels (about thirty million liters, or eight million gallons) of wine were shipped each year from vineyards along the Loire River alone, almost double the number of twenty years earlier.[11] This trade declined when the Wars of Religion disrupted it, and it is likely that production also declined at that time, because the region could not absorb that much wine.

In the northeast, the vineyards of Alsace covered more and more land. During the 1500s, there were reports of some of the grape varieties that are still its most important: riesling, pinot blanc, pinot gris, and pinot noir. Quality seems to have been matched by quantity, and Alsace exported much of its wine. In 1548, the German geographer Sebastien Münster noted that "the good wine that grows in this land of Alsace is continuously transported by carts and sometimes also by water to Switzerland, Swabia, Bavaria, Lorraine, and lower Germany and sometimes to England."[12] In 1584, Michel de Montaigne was traveling near Mulhouse and wrote, "The next day in the morning we came across a fine, broad plain, flanked on its left side by slopes covered with vines that were beautiful and very well cultivated, and so extensive that the Gascons [from the Bordeaux region] who were there said they had never seen the equal."[13]

New vineyards were also planted in Lorraine, which, although no longer a major French wine region, was a significant producer in the early modern period. In the mid-1530s, Duke Antoine planted vines along the Moselle River in the district of Custines, a few kilometers north of Nancy. The first vines were brought from Burgundy, and in 1598 Duke Charles III followed the best Burgundy tradition and ordered the pulling out of all gamay vines. In the early 1600s, ten thousand vines were brought from Ay, in Champagne. Lorraine's vineyards were owned by both the church and secular proprietors. Stretching intermittently across a hundred kilometers (sixty-two miles) along the Moselle and at most three or four kilometers (1.9 or 2.5 miles) wide, this wine region was not massive, but it expanded significantly during the 1500s.[14]

So it was in the Rhône valley. Around Lyon, the area in vines increased from 600 to 750 hectares (1,483 to 1,853 acres) between 1493 and 1518, but even by the end of the 1500s the wines of the northern Rhône valley had made little impact on the major markets of France. They did, however, supply regional markets, including the major city, Lyon. Citizens of Lyon could also buy wines imported from Spain and elsewhere. In 1573, the geographer Nicolas de Nicolay noted with disapproval these "strong white and red wines, which are superfluous and not necessary, serving only to foolishly cost this realm twenty or thirty thousand livres a year."[15] Although Burgundy and Beaune (then thought of as different wine regions) were producing notable wines that sold well in Paris, the wine regions to the immediate south, Beaujolais and the Rhône valley, had still to make their mark, which they did during the 1600s.[16]

Viticulture also began to revive in Languedoc-Roussillon. At the end of the 1400s, vineyards around Béziers had shrunk to a mere 6 percent of cultivated fields (down from 40 percent at the time when the Black Death struck), and land planted with vines had returned to wasteland. But by 1520, when the population began to recover, vineyards had rebounded to 20 percent. As production expanded, exports began to rise, and some wine was shipped to nearby Italian markets such as Genoa, Pisa, and Livorno (Leghorn) from Frontignan, Aigues-Mortes, and other French Mediterranean ports.[17]

A range of styles—white and red, sweet and dry—was made in Languedoc-Roussillon. The Swiss physician Félix Platter studied in Montpellier in the 1550s, and in 1553 he visited his master's vineyard: "The vineyard was very vigorous and the vines laden with fat, red grapes. They grow virtually no white grapes, except for muscat, which is golden and exquisite." Platter noted a few vines of another white grape variety, which he said produced grapes "as fat and fleshy as plums," but he did not provide a name. He later noted that his master harvested the grapes on 13 September, which accorded with the contemporaneous Languedoc practice of harvesting by mid-September, whatever the weather or ripeness of the grapes.[18]

Platter also recorded the wine provided at mealtimes in his master's house, where he boarded: "Wine is at one's discretion; it is dark red and one drinks it well diluted with water. The serving woman first pours the quantity of water that you want, then adds the wine. If you don't drink it all, she throws away what is left. This wine does not last more than a year and turns to vinegar."[19] Perhaps diluting wine was common in the town; Platter observed later, "I never saw a man drunk in Montpellier, with the exception of Germans."[20]

If the 1500s were a period of recovery after the Black Death, the seventeenth century saw French wine take great strides forward. In western France, Dutch participation in viticulture, wine production, and the wine trade proved to be the single most important influence on change. The

Dutch merchant fleet was the world's biggest in the seventeenth century, and the Netherlands (known as "the United Provinces" after gaining independence in the 1580s) had good access to the Atlantic Ocean and the North and Baltic Seas. Dutch ships carried goods produced in many countries and became the major means of shipping wine from Bordeaux to England and northern Europe. The French-Dutch alliance during the Thirty Years' War (1618–48), reinforced by a trade agreement in 1635, gave Dutch merchants open access to Bordeaux, and they replaced many of the English wine merchants who had formerly resided there. By the 1640s, Dutch merchants were shipping some sixty thousand nine-hundred-liter (238-gallon) barrels of wine annually, double or triple the number of a century earlier.[21]

The core period of Dutch influence on Bordeaux's wine industry, from about 1635 to 1672, saw important transformations in the region's vineyards, wine styles, and production. But the dominant position of the Dutch was contested by French merchants who alleged that they engaged in corrupt business and wine-making practices. Two merchants, (Henri de?) Canasilles of Bordeaux and Jean Eon of Nantes, wrote that while French merchants were scrupulously "honorable" intermediaries in their dealings with producers and clients, both buying and selling at "just prices," Dutch merchants underpaid producers and overcharged their clients. Canasilles suggested that Dutch merchants made a profit of 1.8 million livres a year on the wine they shipped from Bordeaux. That figure is probably too high,[22] but it is indicative of the French merchants' portrayal of the Dutch interlopers as crass capitalists who were interested only in making money and had no respect for the moral relationships that bound vignerons, merchants, and consumers.

French merchants also charged that the Dutch often misrepresented inferior wines as coming from more prestigious areas and were given to adding brandy, spices, roots, and leaves to wines to give them more flavor and body and to enable them to withstand shipping and aging better.[23] These allegations, which combined adulteration (adding unacceptable ingredients) and counterfeiting (misrepresenting provenance and character), were part of a long discourse in the history of French wine. From the Middle Ages to the twentieth century, French producers and merchants can be found arguing for regulations to protect them from their compatriots or foreigners—Dutch and German merchants were common targets—who had gained an unfair commercial advantage through practices such as adulterating, blending, and misrepresenting French wines.

Dutch business practices might have been deplored, but no one criticized another sphere of activity where the Dutch were prominent: reclaiming

Bordeaux's marshland (known as *palus,* Latin for "swamp") and making it suitable for viticulture. Much of the Netherlands itself was reclaimed from marshlands and the sea during the Middle Ages, and networks of dikes protected its integrity. (Because of their marshy landscape and supposedly amphibious lives, the English at this time referred to the Dutch as "frogs," a term that transferred to the French only in the nineteenth century.)[24] Dutch engineers began to drain land along the banks of the major rivers and the marshland of the Médoc region in the early 1600s, thus opening up new areas for viticulture in Bordeaux. The Médoc was soon recognized as an excellent site for ripening dark grape varieties, and it was extensively planted between the mid-seventeenth and mid-eighteenth centuries, a development that makes this period formative for the shape of modern Bordeaux.

Not only did the area under vines expand, but vineyards were no longer confined to the environs of Bordeaux and other towns: viticulture began to spread into rural, previously uncultivated districts. Vineyards were looked after by sharecroppers, who received payment in money and wine. At La Tour, which the powerful and noble Mullet family owned, the cultivator received thirteen 225-liter (60-gallon) barrels of wine annually in the 1630s.[25] Moreover, it seems that some of the new vineyards were planted in rows, as there are records of oxen being used to plow in them, a technique virtually impossible where vines were planted haphazardly.

As Dutch merchants dominated Bordeaux's international wine trade, which was far more important to the city than local or regional markets, they were able to influence production, quality, and even the styles of wine that were produced. The tastes in wine of the Dutch and their northern European clients began to diverge from those of the English: while the English continued to prefer the lighter clarets, the Dutch opted for deeper-colored, fuller-bodied reds and dry and sweeter whites, many made from the muscat variety.

Dutch merchants bought the fuller-bodied and darker wines of Cahors and other High Country districts, but by the middle of the seventeenth century they had become such important customers that Bordeaux's vignerons were planting and vinifying to suit their tastes. Many areas with reclaimed alluvial soils proved especially suitable for red wines of this style, and the result was the beginning of significant red wine production in the Médoc region, with the deeply colored, richly flavored, and tannic petit verdot variety playing an important role.[26] On the Gironde's right bank, red wine became the dominant style in districts such as Saint-Émilion and Fronsac.

Other districts switched from making red wine to white so as to fill the order books of their Dutch clients. Some white varieties, notably muscat, made aromatic and fruity wines, but more defined sweetness could be achieved simply by stopping fermentation before all the sugar in the must was converted to alcohol; the result was a low-alcohol, sweet white wine. Alternatively, white grapes could be left on the vine well beyond the usual harvest date, shriveling as their water evaporated and their ratio of sugar to water rose. When these grapes were late-harvested and fermented, they produced wines with high levels of residual sugar. Yet other wines were sweetened by the addition of sugar after fermentation, but this was probably a rare practice: sugar had been introduced to France in the 1300s, but it was still an expensive luxury three centuries later. On the other hand, some English (and perhaps other) wine drinkers began to add sugar to their wine, as they did to coffee and tea. All this speaks to a growing demand for sweetness in wines in the seventeenth century. Among the districts that began to produce white wine was Sauternes, in the Graves region, which the Dutch had identified as a locality where the harvest could be delayed well into the autumn so as to maximize the sugar content of the grapes. It was in the period of Dutch hegemony, specifically in the 1660s, that Sauternes began to produce the sweet white wine for which it became famous.

Preferences in styles of wine were clear in the prices that merchants paid. In 1647, the Jurade de Bordeaux, the city's town council, held an assembly of representatives of the region's wine districts, together with Dutch and English wine agents. This assembly set the minimum and maximum prices for wine (see table 3.1) based on recent trends, and even though it includes only about thirty districts, this is the first known of the many classifications of Bordeaux wines that appeared from the seventeenth to the twentieth century. The Jurade's 1647 classification was also notable in that, by defining the price range of wines from each district, it implicitly rejected the operation of a free market in wine. Perhaps this was a response to concerns about the allegedly profiteering practices of Dutch merchants. The classification is also an early example of treating price as an index of quality, which continued up to and after the 1855 Bordeaux Classification. Although a classification is expected to reflect quality, price was taken as a surrogate for quality, on the ground that the more that well-off (and supposedly discriminating) consumers were prepared to pay for a wine, the higher its quality must be.

There was sometimes a considerable range between minimum and maximum prices and also some overlap of ranges. A barrel of Saint–Macaire that sold for its maximum price (ninety livres) was more expensive than a barrel

TABLE 3.1 Legal prices for Bordeaux wines, 1647 (livres per nine-hundred-liter barrel)

District	Price range (minimum to maximum)	Price average
Graves and Médoc	78–100	89
Entre-deux-Mers	60–75	68
Côtes	72–84	78
Palus	90–105	98
Libourne and Fronsadais	54–66	60
Guîtres and Coutras	54–66	60
Bourg	66–78	72
Blaye	54–72	63
Saint-Macaire and its region	72–90	81
Langon, Beaumes, and Sauternes	84–105	95
Barsac and Preignac	84–100	92
Pujols and Fargues	84–100	92
Cérons and Podensac	72–90	81
Castres and Portets	60–75	68
Saint-Émilion	60–78	69
Castillon	60–66	63
Rions and Cadillac	72–84	78
Sainte-Croix-du-Mont	72–90	81
Benauge	54–60	57

SOURCE: Jean-Claude Hinnewinkel, "Vignes et vins de la Porte de l'Entre-deux-Mers: La fin d'une longue histoire?," paper presented at "La rive droite de Bordeaux," thirteenth "L'Entre-deux-Mers et son identité" conference, 2011, posted 23 January 2013, https://halshs.archives-ouvertes.fr/halshs-00780053.

of Sauternes that sold for its minimum price (eighty-four livres), even though Sauternes was clearly valued higher on average. Taking the average of the minimum and maximum prices (not done in the original document but shown in table 3.1) gives us a clearer idea of the wines' rankings, even though it is not necessarily an accurate representation of prices paid. Wines from the palus of Médoc were clearly ranked the highest, at ninety-eight livres a barrel, and three other districts averaged more than ninety livres: Langon, Beaumes, and Sauternes; Barsac and Preignac; and Pujols and Fargues. Four districts sold their wine for an average of eighty to eighty-nine livres, three for between seventy and seventy-nine livres, seven for between sixty and sixty-nine livres, and one for fifty-seven livres. The over-all average of averages was seventy-six livres a barrel, so palus wines sold for about 30 percent more than the average of these highly regarded wines.

The Dutch not only extended Bordeaux's area under vines and shipped the region's wines internationally but also introduced techniques to stabilize wine so that it lasted longer. This was sometimes achieved by adding brandy (effective, although considered adulteration by local merchants), but more important, the Dutch began to burn sulfur in barrels before filling them with wine. This prevented the wines from continuing to ferment (and thus losing more of their residual sugar) while they were being shipped. On the negative side, it was necessary to keep these wines in the barrel longer before releasing them for sale, to allow the odors from the sulfur to dissipate.

The Dutch also accelerated the emergence of France's brandy industry—an integral part of France's wine history because wine is distilled to make brandy. Until the sixteenth century, grapes, when they were not eaten fresh or as raisins, had been used solely to make wine that was consumed as a fermented beverage. During the Middle Ages, some wine had been distilled to make what was called "aqua vita" or "eau-de-vie" (water of life), but distilling was a rare, small-scale, and sometimes clandestine activity almost always carried out by monks and nuns in religious houses or by apothecaries and perfume makers. Distilled liquids were used as the basis for medicines or consumed strictly for medical purposes, but because of its similarity to alchemy, distilling was banned for some time during the Middle Ages. In 1380, King Charles V of France made it a capital crime to own distilling equipment.[27]

In the sixteenth century, however, distilled spirits entered the commercial mainstream of alcoholic beverages and began to enter the bloodstreams of Europeans. Throughout much of northern Europe, Protestant churches closed religious houses and released their inhabitants from their vows. The Reformation thus released thousands of wine makers, brewers, and distillers, all former clergy, into the labor pool wherever Protestantism was successful. This is not to say that the production of alcoholic beverages in general necessarily increased, because the market did not expand, but it might well have done so in the specific case of distilled spirits. Protestantism did not succeed in France, but the 1500s saw an increase in the production of eau-de-vie there, which was undoubtedly beneficial to grape growers: distillation was an effective way of dealing with harvests that produced too much wine for demand and of making some return on wines of poor quality that could not be sold for drinking and would spoil after a few months.

Although by the seventeenth century several regions in western France were producing both wine and eau-de-vie, there was not necessarily competition between the two products. Until eau-de-vie became an industry in its own right, it was largely made from wine that could not be sold, so distilling helped vignerons deal with the periodic problem of oversupply. Nor did distilling initially entail any changes to grape varieties or viticultural practices, although this changed when vineyards were dedicated to make wine for distilling. Even in the earlier period, however, eau-de-vie had several commercial advantages over wine. Distilling eliminates much of the water in wine and concentrates the alcohol. This gave the spirits trade an advantage over wine because, on a per-unit-of-alcohol basis, the costs were much lower for shipping spirits than for shipping wine. For consumers, spirits provided a different but palpable benefit: an immediate feeling of warmth that wine and beer lacked. Perhaps this quality explains the popularity of spirits in the cooler, northern regions of Europe.

But the savings on transporting eau-de-vie rather than wine could be realized only if the wine was distilled before being shipped. Stills were set up in Bordeaux, but it made little sense to distill wine of good quality that fetched good prices when all that was needed was the alcohol, so entrepreneurs looked for regions that produced poor-quality wine. By the mid-1600s, two regions stood out for eau-de-vie production. The Charente region to the north of Bordeaux made mediocre wine and was well furnished with forests that could supply the wood needed to fuel the stills. Here the Dutch encouraged the cultivation of grapes specifically for distilling instead of relying on wine available because it was too poor to sell or because a big harvest produced a glut on the market. The first commercial stills in Charente were set up in 1624, and the next year eau-de-vie was shipped from the port of La Rochelle, which quickly became its main point of export. In England and northern Europe, this eau-de-vie became known as "brandy," from the Dutch *brandewijn*, meaning "burned wine," a reference to the fire under the wine-filled still pot.

By 1640, brandy was being taxed, a sure sign of its growing importance, and by the 1660s, Charente, which includes the area of Cognac, which later gave its name to a distinct brandy, was the center of a massive distilling industry. Dutch merchants were the main shippers, taking brandy (along with wool and salt) to England and to ports on the North and Baltic Seas such as Danzig (now Gdańsk), Riga, and Königsberg (now Kaliningrad). Merchant and naval ships quickly adopted brandy as their alcohol of choice because it occupied less space and stayed good for far longer than wine, and it soon became popular at many social levels in the Netherlands, England, and other northern European countries. In 1673, England imported some 7,300 hogsheads (239-liter, or 39-gallon, barrels) of French brandy, more than 175,000 liters (46,000 gallons),[28] but two years later that had shot up to 4.5 million liters (1.2 million gallons), and in 1689 England imported almost 9 million liters (2.4 million gallons). It was the scale of these imports from Catholic France that persuaded England's new Protestant monarch, King William III, to relax the regulations against domestic distilling, which led to the so-called gin craze in London and other cities in the first decades of the eighteenth century.[29]

South of Bordeaux, the Armagnac region began to make eau-de-vie in commercial volumes in the 1650s. Although supporters of Armagnac have long argued that a distilling industry was in place there before in Cognac, François Brumont makes a convincing argument for later distilling in Armagnac. During the seventeenth century, this region produced wine that was sold locally and in the nearby Basque country, with small volumes shipped from Bayonne to northern France, the Netherlands, and England. In the first half of the seventeenth century, the wines of Tursan were well regarded in the Netherlands, where they fetched prices more than 50 percent higher than those of the most common wines from Bordeaux.[30] But much of the wine was unremarkable, and in the 1600s, Dutch and other merchants established distilleries to turn unsellable wine into eau-de-vie that was eventually known as armagnac.

Significant volumes of eau-de-vie from Armagnac were not exported until the second half of the seventeenth century. The records are patchy, but they show, for example, 15 barrels of eau-de-vie exported from Bayonne in 1628–29, 358 in 1649, 97 in 1650, 2 in 1656, 905 in 1657, and 520 in 1661.[31] These big annual fluctuations speak to variations in the size and quality of the harvest and suggest that eau-de-vie was still, at midcentury, an opportunistic product that was a means of dealing with excess wine—an adjunct to the wine industry rather than an industry in its own right. But signs of institutionalization began to appear. Barrel sizes were standardized in the 1650s and 1660s and prices were fixed, sometimes reflecting the prevailing price of eau-de-vie on the Bordeaux market. As for the destination of armagnac at this time, more than 90 percent of the barrels shipped north went to the Netherlands, while smaller volumes were sold in Spain and other nearby regions. Some was taken on board boats that headed to the cod fisheries off Newfoundland, for consumption after being diluted with water; eight half barrels were loaded aboard one fishing boat and sixteen half barrels aboard another in 1659.[32]

So quickly did the demand for brandy grow that wine makers in other parts of France and Europe began to distill their own unsellable wines. In Languedoc and elsewhere, producers distilled wine that was so poor that it would otherwise have been sold as vinegar within six months of the harvest. Brandy was a common drink in Languedoc from the 1660s onward, and the port of Sète, built in 1670, became a major export point for the region's distilled alcohol: in 1699 it handled a million liters (264,000 gallons) of brandy, about 1.3 million modern bottles.[33]

Eau-de-vie was also the base for a number of new drinks produced by the addition of ingredients that easily dissolved in the alcohol. In the sixteenth century, a monk at the Benedictine Fécamp Abbey, in Normandy, added honey and herbs to eau-de-vie, resulting in a liqueur that became known as "Benedictine." Early in the seventeenth century, an infusion of what was said to be more than a hundred herbs in eau-de-vie was created by Carthusian monks in Paris and given the name "Chartreuse." These were only two of what became scores of liqueurs, representing various combinations of herbs, spices, and other ingredients infused in distilled wine.

But despite the clear benefits that Dutch merchants and technical expertise brought to France's wine and distilling industries, there was growing resentment in the English and French governments at the Dutch commercial success. Wishing to thoroughly integrate themselves into Bordeaux's wine economy, hundreds of Dutch families had become naturalized citizens of the city so that they could benefit from the commercial privileges that accompanied citizenship. There were persistent complaints from French commentators that wine was being made to order for foreigners, and there were concerns in some regions about the effects on wood supplies of cutting down trees to fuel brandy stills. Distillers were in competition for wood with the French navy and merchant marine, which needed hundreds of thousands of trees for their shipbuilding programs.

Limits were placed on the activities of Dutch merchants and entrepreneurs as the French and English saw Dutch commercial power as a threat and began to adopt policies to protect their own merchant fleets. In England, a series of Navigation Acts made it difficult for any but English ships to import goods. For their part, the French embarked on a rapid shipbuilding program in the mid-1600s to create a merchant fleet that could compete with the Dutch. In the 1660s, Jean-Baptiste Colbert, Louis XIV's finance minister, imposed punitive tariffs on foreign merchants, which harmed Bordeaux's wine exports and led to open conflict between it and the royal government.

The important Dutch influence on the wine industries of Bordeaux and other regions ended after some forty years when France went to war against the United Provinces in 1672. While France was at war with the Netherlands, English ships carried French wine and brandy, first to English ports, then to the Netherlands and other northern European markets. In the first year of hostilities, English ships carried 7,315 barrels of Bordeaux brandy, more than double the 3,000 barrels they had taken in 1669. But while the Dutch were at war with France, they looked farther afield for wine and brandy. Dutch merchants established themselves in Porto and began to ship white wines from around Lisbon and northern Portugal and the full-bodied red wines of Madeira and the Douro valley. In Spain they sourced white wines from Jerez and red wines from Málaga, Alicante, and the Canary Islands. In the Mediterranean region they bought wines from Greece and Crete and some even some eau-de-vie from Béziers, in Languedoc.

When the French and the Dutch signed a peace treaty in 1678, it included clauses that normalized and improved the conditions of trade between their countries. But when the English were refused the same conditions of trade with France, the English government banned the importation of French wine and turned to Portugal for supplies. Portuguese producers could not supply the volume that the English had been importing from Bordeaux, so Bordeaux wine was shipped to Portugal and then redirected to England. In this way, England imported fifty-two thousand barrels of supposed Portuguese wine in 1682, but when the embargo against French wine ended in 1685, imports from Portugal—now genuine Portuguese wine—fell to a mere twelve hundred barrels, while imports from France totaled fifty-four thousand.[34]

In 1688, soon after Louis XIV had begun a new phase of oppressing France's Huguenot population, the Dutch Protestant prince Wilhelm of Orange took the throne of England as King William III and another phase in the history of French wine exports began when war broke out between France and an alliance of England and the Netherlands. Hostilities continued intermittently until 1713, and neutral Portuguese ships replaced English ships in carrying French wine and brandy to England and the Netherlands. The English and the Dutch imposed a blockade on French commerce, making it necessary for them to find alternative sources of wine. English merchants became more active in Portugal's Douro valley, where they favored the bigger red wines and, more important, became significant players in the development of another fortified wine: port. For England, the wine trade with Portugal effectively replaced the trade in French wine, and it was cemented by the 1703 Methuen Treaty, which guaranteed that Portuguese wine would always be levied a lower duty than French wine.

Exports from Bordeaux continued at a reduced scale from 1688 to 1691 and continued at all largely because Louis Bazin de Bezons, the intendant (royal representative) in Bordeaux, protected the city's Dutch, English, and Jewish wine merchants from Louis XIV's oppressive laws against Jews (1684) and Protestants (1685). With Dutch and English merchants far less active in Bordeaux and other ports of the region, local merchants reorganized; the chamber of commerce of Bordeaux, the association of wine merchants that was later responsible for drawing up the 1855 Bordeaux Classification, was formed in 1705.

Other French wine regions followed different trajectories during the 1600s. Spanish forces ravaged much of Alsace, Champagne, and Burgundy in 1636, part of the Thirty Years' War (1618–48). Occupation armies drank the wine in the cellars, while vineyards that armies did not destroy as they made their way across hostile countryside suffered decades of neglect during the drawn-out conflict. Vineyards were typically grown right up to city walls, and invading armies ripped out vines so as to put pressure on towns under siege. Equipment such as presses, barrels, and barges were also destroyed, and many skilled vineyard workers were dispersed or lost their lives, meaning that wine production recovered only slowly when peace was restored.

Vineyard losses were significant. Some 1,300 hectares (3,200 acres) of land around Ammerschwihr, in Alsace, were under viticulture before the Thirty Years' War, but only 200 hectares (500 acres) after it. Land suitable for vines lost its value to the point that in Riquewihr, where notable rieslings are now produced, an arpent (about a third of a hectare, or five-sixths of an acre) of vines could be traded for a horse.[35] The slow recovery of Alsatian viticulture was also due to the loss of markets. Even though Lorraine, Germany, and Switzerland reopened trade with Alsace when the war ended, their populations had been ruined. When the Dutch Wars broke out in 1672, Alsace lost its markets not only in the Netherlands but also in England and Scandinavia.[36] On the more positive side, the devastation of Alsace's vineyards allowed for widespread replanting with what turned out to be the productive and profitable riesling variety.

The development of Burgundy in this period is complicated by the fact that as far as wine was concerned, the region was defined far more expansively in geographical terms than it is today. Modern Burgundy runs from Auxerre almost as far as Lyon, and its main subregions include (from north to south) Chablis, the Côtes d'Or, de Nuits, de Beaune, and Chalonnaise, the Mâconnais, and Beaujolais. But this long, narrow region was only the core of a much larger wine region that was recognized as Burgundy in the early modern period, and viticulture there expanded in the late 1400s and throughout the 1500s. Notarial records from the 1580s document the efforts of vignerons in Savigny-lès-Beaune and Mavilly to recover and plant land,[37] and the seigneurs of Chassagne planted the vineyard of Montrachet at the end of the fifteenth century.

Burgundy also suffered during the Thirty Years' War, but planting began soon after it was over, and in 1660 the Parlement (a royal law court that also had administrative functions) of Dijon was clearly concerned at the spread of vineyards at the cost of arable land. It issued an edict forbidding "all planting of vines in land where grain is cultivated" and authorized the planting of vines "only on the slopes." In 1666, Claude Bouchu, the intendant in Burgundy, reported on the spread of vineyards and complained that fine wines were suffering from competition from vast volumes of ordinary wines.[38] At the same time, a number of vineyards in what are now prestigious communes passed from church ownership into the hands of some of Burgundy's most powerful noble families, who thus gained control of vines in Gevrey, Fixin, and Aloxe, among others.

Despite the successive bans on gamay, the variety was still quite widely planted on the slopes and plains of Burgundy, and it was prolific in Beaujolais, where vineyards expanded during the 1600s. As late as 1573, the geographer Nicolas de Nicolay noted that Beaujolais was far more sparsely planted with vines than the region around Lyon and that only eight of its parishes had vineyards. But by 1669, vines were being cultivated in forty parishes and vineyards had spread into rural areas in Beaujolais, even though most were still concentrated around small villages. Some of these (such as Morgon, Brouilly, Fleurie, and Chiroubles) became cru Beaujolais appellations in the twentieth century. Still, the region had to contend with the fact that it had no large urban market. Some of its wine was sold in Lyon, but protectionist policies of Dijon's city government effectively ruled out that town as a market for the wines of Beaujolais (and the Rhône valley). Moreover, the grape variety widely planted in Beaujolais was (as it still is) gamay, the variety expelled from the rest of Burgundy. In 1620, the administrators of Mâcon, to the north, forbade the growing of gamay in their vineyards and complained that the vignerons of Beaujolais were making wine harmful to human health by using the variety.[39]

The Rhône valley suffered difficulties in getting its wines to market, as the authorities in Burgundy stood in the way of transporting them to Paris. This is not to say that none of its wines found their way to important markets: the wines of Condrieu seem to have gained a reputation, and in 1680 a high rate of tax was imposed on them in Paris, evidence that they were perceived as able to sustain a price increase. The administrators of Lyon used wine to reward people who helped the city. In 1620 it paid to ship three barrels of muscat wine to Paris, where the councillor Philippe Sève would distribute it to the "lords and other men who are favoring the said town

[Lyon]." That same year, Lyon also paid for "wine offered to maréchal de Lesdiguières and to MM. de Guise, de Bution and de Montmorency."[40]

As Languedoc-Roussillon recovered from the Wars of Religion, land was cleared and vineyards were planted in the poor soils that could support no other crop. While some were owned by wealthy bourgeois who hired labor, many Languedoc vineyards were cultivated by impoverished vignerons on the *complant* system, in which a landowner gave a peasant a piece of unimproved land to clear, plant, and cultivate for five years, after which it was divided equally between them. The advantage to the landowner was that, although he received no rent for five years and then ended up with only half the land, that half was worth much more than the initial piece of uncultivated land. The advantage to the vigneron was obvious: by cultivating rent-free land for five years, he gained land and a living. Most of these Languedoc vineyards were planted with the terret and piquepoul varieties.

As in Beaujolais and the Rhône valley, access to markets limited the expansion of viticulture in Languedoc-Roussillon. Muscat from the region was well known and exported to many parts of Europe, but the rest of its wine was mediocre. Some was exported to Italian ports such as Genoa and Livorno and some to Spain, but those regions were well supplied by their own or local vineyards and could absorb only limited volumes of imported wine. It was possible for wines from Languedoc-Roussillon to wend their way by rivers to Bordeaux for export, but in 1500, to reduce competition with its own wines, Bordeaux restricted the timing of shipments of Languedoc-Roussillon wine (as it already did with High Country wine).[41] The opening of the Canal du Midi (then known as the Canal des Deux Mers) in 1682 made it far easier to send Languedoc wines to Bordeaux for onward shipping, but the merchants of that city held to their centuries-old protectionist policies. There was a glut of wine in Bordeaux when the canal opened, following big harvests from 1678 to 1682, and the city's intendant noted that "most wines are not sold. . . . There is too much wine in this region."[42] Although Bordeaux suspended its restrictive policies for four years in the 1690s when harvests were disastrous, and although some Dutch ships carried Languedoc-Roussillon wine through the Strait of Gibraltar to northern Europe, viticulture in Languedoc-Roussillon languished. Distillers bought much of the wine that the region's vignerons could not otherwise sell, and Sète became a major export point for eau-de-vie.

It is clear that the difficulties of accessing markets limited the development of some French wine regions until the nineteenth century. Languedoc-Roussillon was an obvious example: it was a region with a climate well suited to viticulture but poorly located in terms of markets. It exported some wine to ports on Italy's Ligurian coast, but the Mediterranean area was well supplied with wines from the Italian peninsula, Sicily, Spain, and Greece. Transporting wine overland to French urban markets was prohibitively expensive (unless it was in such demand that the sale price could cover the cost of shipping), and although a combination of land, rivers, and small canals could be employed to get wine to Paris, the route was tortuous, long, and not inexpensive. The Canal du Midi, an efficient route to Bordeaux, from which wine could be shipped around the coast and then up the Seine River to Paris, was effectively blocked by the taxes imposed at Bordeaux.

Restrictive practices such as Bordeaux's were the rule rather than the exception in early modern France, and they added a political dimension to the geographical barriers to the wine trade. In eastern France, Dijon kept wines from Mâcon, Beaujolais, and the Rhône valley from its market, while Lyon discriminated against wines from Burgundy, Beaune, and Mâcon, and the authorities in Mâcon levied a heavy tax on wines from Beaujolais that were transported across its territory. Other trade barriers included duties that had to be paid as goods crossed provincial boundaries within France or entered many towns and cities. All of these were suppressed in the decades just before or during the French Revolution, which reduced the costs of moving wine from one part of France to another. But transportation costs were not significantly reduced until the mid-1800s, when railroads and improved canal networks enabled the producers of Languedoc-Roussillon and other regions to ship their wine to the population centers of northern France.

Physical and fiscal obstacles to trade slowed the development of some wine regions but did not paralyze them. A few Paris wine merchants bought wine from Mâcon and Beaujolais, using oxen-drawn carts to haul the two-hundred- and four-hundred-liter (53- and 106-gallon) barrels to the Loire River, where they were shipped by barge to a tributary of the Seine River and then to Paris. This was a long journey, taking forty-five to fifty days, and it added measurably to the price of the wine in Paris. Yet even though the volume of wine shipped that way was substantial in absolute terms, the contribution of these regions to the thirsty Paris market was marginal: in 1700 they contributed perhaps 2.4 million of the 60 million liters (0.6 million of the 19 million gallons) of wine brought into the city that year.[43]

As Thomas Brennan has shown, the domestic wine trade of early modern France was highly formalized. From the medieval period, a number of wine towns appointed brokers, known as courtiers, who were a sort of wine police responsible for overseeing quality, the fulfillment of contracts, and the general operation of the wine trade in their districts.[44] In Beaune, for example, the brokers' tasks included certifying wine quality by putting the town's mark on approved barrels and facilitating the work of visiting merchants. But in the late 1500s, the monarchy tried to undermine the independence of wine towns by creating royal wine brokers and mandating their use by merchants. Another purpose, as of many royal policies at this time, was to make money: royal brokers bought their position, and there was a fee to use them. A number of towns paid the crown to allow them to retain control of their municipal brokers: Reims paid 150,000 livres in 1691, and Burgundy paid 200,000 livres the following year. Over time, brokering wine became a private business in many parts of France, so merchants looking for wine could choose their own broker. Brokers succeeded by knowing the wine business in their localities, being reliable guides to quality wine, and giving good service to their clients.

Various other attempts by the royal government to raise money from the wine trade included fining unofficial brokers. Such moves were an indication that the wine trade was a profitable business by the seventeenth century—or at least was believed by the royal government to be so profitable that it could be squeezed for money. In the case of fining unofficial wine brokers, the government cast its definition so wide that it included many ordinary wine merchants. Wine-producing regions opposed all of these measures, on the grounds that they would ruin the wine trade. The head of the company that owned the right to sales taxes in Champagne complained that fining unofficial brokers would "suddenly stop the commerce of wines in this province."[45]

The situation was complicated because in some towns, individuals carried out functions that blurred the distinction between merchants and brokers—between those who bought and sold wine and those who were merely intermediaries between merchants and producers. A list of brokers subject to the royal tax indicates the relative importance of the centers of the French wine trade. Bordeaux and its environs were responsible for a quarter of the national total, while the broad Loire region was assessed for a third. Burgundy paid a sixth, while the Paris region paid a tenth. Four towns—Bordeaux, Nantes, Reims, and Beaune—had nearly a third of France's wine brokers, and they paid two-thirds of the total tax. This distribution confirms that Bordeaux, the Loire valley, Champagne, and Burgundy were the major wine producing and trading regions of early modern France. It also highlights the relatively marginal positions of Alsace, the Rhône valley, and Languedoc-Roussillon at the time. The official brokerage system, whether under the control of town authorities or the state, ended in 1706, and from that time, French wine merchants and *négociants* (men who bought and blended finished wine and often sold it under their own name) operated as private entrepreneurs.

The royal government's attempts to profit from the wine business were part of a broader policy of taxing commodities. In the 1540s, a modest royal duty of five sous per muid (a 288-liter, or 76-gallon, barrel) was imposed on all wine entering Paris, and in the 1560s it was extended to all walled towns in France. Despite its initial term of six years, the duty was maintained until the French Revolution at ever-rising rates; by 1663 it had reached sixteen sous at Chartres.[46] Towns fought constantly with the royal government over wine taxes, while officials struggled to get citizens to pay the taxes and duties on wine to which they were subject. There are records of innkeepers who had several cellars, one to show the tax inspectors and others for actual use; of citizens whose wine cellars never changed, no matter how much they consumed; of merchants and tavern keepers who bought their wine "in the fields"—clandestinely from peasants rather than at markets watched over by tax officials. These officials had the right to demand the keys to cellars, to stop traffic and inspect goods on roads and waterways, and to oversee the loading and unloading of all means of transportation. Such powers brought producers into constant conflict with the state. It did not help that the nobility and the clergy were exempt from many of these taxes—they could, for example, sell their own wine retail without paying taxes that amounted sometimes to an eighth, sometimes to a quarter, of its value.[47]

While producers throughout France struggled with the demands of the government, some regions began to produce new styles of wine. We have noted the shifts from clairet to fuller-bodied and deeper-hued reds and from dry to sweet whites that took place in western and southwestern France during the seventeenth century, but in other regions a dramatically different style appeared on the market: sparkling wine. It can be made by various methods, but the original created bubbles when fermentation continued after wine had been sealed in a bottle. Fermentation not only turns sugar into alcohol but also generates carbon dioxide, and while this escapes when fermentation takes place in an open vat, it cannot escape from an airtight container, such as a sealed bottle. Instead, the carbon dioxide dissolves in the wine, and when the bottle is opened, the gas emerges in the form of small bubbles.

For a century and a half starting in the 1820s, the invention of sparkling wine was attributed to a monk, Pierre Pérignon (often known as "Dom Pérignon"), who was the cellar master at the Abbey Saint-Pierre d'Hautvillers, near Épernay in Champagne, during the 1660s. As the story was often told, he was blind and possessed extraordinary senses of smell and taste, and he developed bubbles in wine by accident. On drinking sparkling wine for the first time, he is said to have exclaimed, "I am drinking the stars!" It is generally agreed that much of the story is fiction. Although Pérignon existed and was the cellar master at the monastery, the claim that he invented sparkling wine—and not just sparkling wine, but champagne itself—is generally attributed to Jean-Baptiste Grossard, who was later a monk at the same monastery before it was shut down during the French Revolution. In the 1820s, he made up the story that Pérignon had invented sparkling wine, as a way of embellishing the reputation of the church, and it was widely accepted as true until the late twentieth century.[48]

Just how sparkling wine was first made is unclear, but it might well have been that some wine was bottled when its fermentation was apparently complete but had in fact stalled because the cellar temperature had dropped below the tolerance of the yeasts. Warmer temperatures in the spring would have reactivated the yeasts, which would have completed the fermentation in the sealed bottle. The carbon dioxide generated by the restarted fermentation would have dissolved in the wine and appeared as bubbles when the bottle was opened. But this explanation does not explain how the process could have been replicated. Seventeenth-century wine makers did not know that yeasts were responsible for fermentation, and the same sequence of temperatures would not have occurred every year.

Rather than Pérignon being the inventor of sparkling wine, a stronger case can be made for Christopher Merret, an English scientist who in the 1660s—while Pérignon was at his monastery—presented a paper on wine to the Royal Society in London. It includes a demonstration that adding sugar to wine in a bottle which is then sealed produces a second fermentation that results in bubbles when the bottle is opened. It is possible that Merret discovered this by chance because the English had begun to add sugar to their wine. The travel writer Fynes Moryson noted in 1617, "Gentlemen carouse only with wine, with which many mix sugar. . . . And because the taste of the English is thus delighted with sweetness, the wines in taverns (for I speak not of merchants' or gentlemen's cellars) are commonly mixed at the filling thereof, to make them pleasant."[49] It is possible that some wine merchants or consumers decided to add sugar to bottles of wine as they were filled from a barrel, and found sparkling rather than sweet wine on opening them. This is a more plausible, if prosaic, explanation that the romantic story of the monk in his cellar.

It is not clear where sparkling wine was first produced commercially. As early as 1531—almost a century and a half before Dom Pérignon's work—Benedictine monks at the Abbey of Saint-Hilaire, near Limoux in Languedoc, wrote about blanquette de Limoux, which seems to have been a sparkling white wine that had undergone a restarted fermentation in a bottle. There are suggestions that Dom Pérignon visited the Abbey of Saint-Hilaire while on a pilgrimage and learned the technique of making sparkling wine while there. A little to the north, in Gaillac and in Die, wines were made that were effervescent, if not sparkling, although the imprecision of the records makes it impossible to distinguish between *mousseux, pétillant, perlant,* and the various other degrees of sparkling available today. Gaillac is said to have produced sparkling wine during the Middle Ages. Some of the production methods are still known by names that give an impression of a long history, such as *méthode ancestrale* and *méthode rurale.* The *méthode champenoise* was known as *méthode traditionelle* the moment it was developed, an excellent example of the creation of an instant tradition.

In the still-wine culture of France during the seventeenth century, bubbles might well have been considered a flaw that needed correcting rather than an exciting innovation. But as the history of champagne shows—no matter who first made sparkling wine, or where, Champagne was the first region to popularize it—sparkling wine quickly became popular. The rarity of sparkling wine made it both desirable and expensive, and it was soon a sign of a luxurious and wealthy lifestyle in both England and France. The English diarist Samuel Pepys noted that in March 1679 he traveled through Hyde Park in his carriage, "the first time this year, taking two bottles of champagne in my way." Jolting the bottles in a horse-drawn carriage with steel-rimmed wheels was probably not the best way to ensure the survival of the wine, but Pepys makes no mention of disaster.

New styles of wine, such as full-bodied reds, sweet whites, sparkling wines, and distilled wines (eaux-de-vie), contributed to a significant broadening of the beverages available to the French and other Europeans by the middle of the 1600s. Nonalcoholic drinks added to the list, as this period saw the growing popularity of tea, coffee, and chocolate (which was consumed only as a drink until the nineteenth century). At first these caffeinated beverages were not considered very different from alcoholic beverages, as both had a stimulating effect when consumed in small quantities. The custom began in many parts of Europe of having a shot of either eau-de-vie or coffee (and sometimes both) to start the workday.

As far as wine is concerned, the seventeenth century was both innovative, and in this sense positive, and difficult, as international relations and war interfered with the increasingly important French export wine trade. At the end of the century, weather eclipsed political problems: for four years, from 1691 to 1694, cold temperatures, incessant rain, flooding, wet springs and summers, and frequent hailstorms ruined harvests of all kinds in many parts of France. Poor grain harvests led to widespread malnutrition and millions of deaths; it is estimated that during the harsh winter of 1693–94, which followed a disastrously poor harvest, about 5 percent of France's inhabitants died. The wars that preceded the 1690s amplified the effects of this weather; food had been requisitioned for the armies (France's numbered four hundred thousand soldiers), which interfered with normal patterns of civilian supplies, while increased taxes to pay for the wars left peasants unable to buy seed for sowing.[50]

Reports of poor grape harvests flowed in from many regions. The intendant in Limoges wrote in the fall of 1692 that the weather was so cold and wet "that the vines have suffered a great deal, and are currently suffering, such that there will be very little wine." In October of the same year, his counterpart in Limoux wrote that frost had had such an effect on the vines "that it looked as if fire has passed through them." In 1693, the intendant in Auvergne noted that "the vines which seemed to be promising are completely lost following these latest frosts. There is no chance that the grapes will ripen."[51] As far as Bordeaux was concerned, four successive grape harvests were so small and the wine they produced so poor that the Baron de Margaux reported in 1693 that he had wine worth 120,000 livres in his cellars but had not sold any for four years.[52] The authorities in Bordeaux suspended their restrictive policies so that wine could be brought from Languedoc-Roussillon through the Canal du Midi to supply both Bordeaux and the French fleet based at Brouage, along the Atlantic coast.

Despite periodic setbacks such as this, France's wine production not only grew overall but began to diversify in quality. There had always been better wines and worse wines, but in the second half of the 1600s, some of France's regions reinforced their reputations for producing superior wines. Holding wines from specific regions in high esteem was not new. Roman writers had praised wines from districts such as Bordeaux, Gaillac, and Vienne, and the medieval "Battle of the Wines" had shown that some regions produced better wines than others. But these were assessments by individuals, and what made the early modern period different was a consensus that three French regions stood out from the rest: Bordeaux, Burgundy, and Champagne. This judgment was largely based on the prices that wines from these regions fetched on markets in France and abroad in comparison with the wines of other French regions. Relative price was not simply a matter of more or less money: it indicated willingness to pay, and the assumption was that the more that people were prepared to pay, the better the quality of the wine must be. Additionally, at the higher end of the price range, it was wealthier and therefore more powerful and prestigious consumers who were prepared to pay more for wine, and these consumers were the arbiters of taste in wine, just as in food, art, and behavior generally.[53]

Henri Enjalbert sees a "revolution" in Bordeaux in the late 1600s as the region transformed from a producer predominantly of clairet to a producer of a more diverse range of wine: ordinary red wines, high-quality reds, dry white wines, sweet whites, and wines for distilling into brandy. Production rose, and these wines were produced for northern Europe in volumes far greater than had been sold in England. Finally, a tier of great wines (*grands vins*) appeared as Bordeaux's wines developed a stratification of quality that replaced the former pattern of "uniform and banal" production.[54] Although Enjalbert's characterization of the transformations in Bordeaux downplays the range of styles and quality that had existed there before, we can see the reputation of certain of Bordeaux's districts, as well as individual estates, rise above the rest in this period. In this sense we are observing the beginnings of the classification systems that were codified—some might say ossified—in the nineteenth century; the consensus of late seventeenth- and early eighteenth-century elite French wine drinkers has lasted for more than three hundred years.

Not only were regions singled out as superior, but so were specific estates. In the early 1700s, when the earl of Bristol recorded purchases of French wine, he mentioned districts such as Langon and Avignon and estates such as Haut-Brion and Margaux. Haut-Brion, which was classified as a First Growth (premier cru) in 1855, was one of the first estates to be singled out: in 1660, King Charles II's cellar master bought 169 bottles of "Hobriono" for £180 and 60 bottles of other Graves wines for £32.[55] The price difference—slightly more than £1 a bottle for Haut-Brion and half that for the generic Graves wines—is significant. Three years later, Pepys famously recorded that he went to the Royal Oak Tavern "and here drank a sort of French wine, called Ho Bryan, that hath a good and most particular taste that I never met with."[56] We do not know which vintage of Haut-Brion Pepys tasted (vintage year was seldom mentioned at this time, unless it was a particularly awful year), nor do we know what made the wine stand out. Perhaps Pepys had drunk only claret from Bordeaux until this time and found himself confronted by a darker, full-bodied red.

Haut-Brion became very popular in London, in part because the owner of the estate, the wealthy and noble Arnaud de Pontac, opened a high-end tavern called Pontac's Head there in 1666. It was not an auspicious year, with the Great Fire and outbreaks of plague, but his two wines—one called "Haut-Brion," from the thirty-eight-hectare (ninety-four-acre) estate in Graves, and the other "Pontac," from his vineyard at Pez (now Château de

Pez in Saint-Estèphe)—caught on among well-off drinkers, who regularly paid up to three times as much for Haut-Brion as for ordinary claret. The philosopher John Locke pointed to demand pushing up prices: "A tun of the best wine at Bourdeaux, which is that of Médoc or Pontac, is worth . . . 80 or 100 crowns. For this the English may thank their own folly; for, whereas some years since the same wine was sold for 50 or 60 crowns per tun, the fashionable sending over of orders to have the best wine sent them at any rate, they have, by striving who should get it, brought it to that price."[57]

Haut-Brion was the cult wine of England at this time. In 1677, Locke made a visit (almost a pilgrimage) to the estate and described its soil as "white sand mixed with a little gravel, which one would think would bear nothing." But he was assured by wine merchants in Bordeaux that "there was such a particularity in the soil . . . that the wine growing in the very next vineyards, where there was only a ditch between, and the soil, to appearance, perfectly the same, was by no means so good." As a good philosopher, Locke speculated as to what might make the Haut-Brion estate distinctive, and he noted that the vineyard's slope and exposure to the sun set it off from its neighbors. He was also told that the "older the vineyard, the fewer the grapes, but the better the wine,"[58] so it is likely that the Haut-Brion wines on sale at the time would today be labeled "vieilles vignes."

Beyond the major shifts in style and the vagaries of trade relations, there were broad continuities in France's wine culture in this period. Again, we do not have reliable statistics on wine consumption or different drinking patterns by region, class, or gender. One thing we can be sure of is that consumption must have fluctuated according to the availability of wine as politics, wars, and climatic events affected production and commerce. Wine was like grain in this respect: if vines were destroyed by invading troops during the Thirty Years' War, so were fields of cereals; and when rain, freezing temperatures, and hail destroyed vines in the early 1690s, they also wiped out the grain. As people starved—and died of the diseases to which malnutrition made them more vulnerable—it was their whole diet that they were deprived of: bread and wine.

Specific examples of wine consumption in the early modern period have a wide range, with no consistent pattern or centralizing tendency (see table 3.2). Marcel Lachiver calculates that around 1550, the inhabitants of Lyon (male and female, adults and children) had access to an average of two hundred liters (fifty-three gallons) a year.[59] We can assume that children did not drink, that women drank less than men, and that the poor, who could make up a quarter or more of the population (depending on the state of the economy), drank only a little wine and mostly diluted wine or water. The

TABLE 3.2 Annual per capita consumption of wine (liters)

Nantes, 1500	100–120
Nantes, seventeenth century	110–200
Paris, 1637	155
Lyon, 1680	200
Lyon, late seventeenth century	274

SOURCE: A. Lynn Martin, *Alcohol, Violence, and Disorder in Traditional Europe* (Kirksville, MO: Truman State University Press, 2009), 55, table 3.5.

TABLE 3.3 Annual per capita payments and rations in wine (liters)

Fishermen, Grand Banks, sixteenth century	910–1,095
Apothecary and assistants, at court, Paris, 1555	680
Laundress and assistants, at court, Paris, 1555	272
Worker on cathedral, Toul, 1580	456
Construction worker on château, Murol, 1591	365
Monk, Saint-Germain-des-Prés, seventeenth century	438

SOURCE: A. Lynn Martin, *Alcohol, Violence, and Disorder in Traditional Europe* (Kirksville, MO: Truman State University Press, 2009), 57, table 3.8.

adult men of Lyon must, then, have had access to at least six hundred liters (159 gallons) a year on average, almost two liters (half a gallon) a day. Perhaps it was heavy drinking by some sections of the male population that led Lyon's town council to forbid residents to sit at taverns while drinking wine. Only travelers and visitors could sit, and the rule seems to have been designed to encourage tavern patrons to keep their drinking sessions short. If impressions count for anything, the rule failed: an Italian visiting Lyon in 1664 claimed that its three thousand citizens "drink more wine than is consumed in a dozen Italian towns combined; there is a bar in almost every house."[60]

As table 3.3 shows, employers provided wine as part payment for a wide range of services or as rations in the army, in the navy, on board merchant ships and fishing boats, and in religious houses. Other examples can easily be added. The monks at Montbéliard, in the Jura, went through wine at rates that varied from 584 to 840 liters (154 to 222 gallons) a year (1.6 to 2.3 liters, or 0.42 to 0.61 gallons, a day) between 1519 and 1530.[61] Although it is risky to generalize from these examples, it is striking that wine provided as payment or rations was consistently more generous, usually far more generous, than the per capita volumes estimated for whole towns. This is undoubtedly the simple effect of eliminating the nondrinking and little-drinking sections of the population, notably children, women, and the poor. Among men who did drink wine, perhaps two hundred to four hundred liters (53 to 106 gallons) a year (half a liter to a liter, or an eighth to a quarter of a gallon, a day) is a reasonable estimate of consumption.

Beyond being part of the daily diet, wine retained its position in Christian rituals, but Protestants challenged the Catholic practice of Communion in one kind, whereby the lay congregation received only bread and the priest took the wine on behalf of all; the Catholic church had declared it a heresy to say that lay Christians should receive Communion wine. Jean Calvin, the French-born Protestant theologian, wrote that by adopting Communion in one kind, the church had "stolen or snatched [wine] from the greater part of God's people ... [and] given a special property to a few shaven and anointed men."[62] Protestants promptly restored wine to the laity, and although that made little additional demand on supplies, it returned wine to the position it had occupied in the early church.

Protestants might well have been viewed in France as a threat to wine, even though the French state remained resolutely Catholic and Huguenots accounted for only about 5 percent of the population. A common Protestant allegation was that the Catholic church had tolerated immorality of all kinds, including excessive wine consumption and drunkenness. Fornication, adultery, blasphemy, and other sins were bad enough, but drunkenness had a special place, then and later, because it was seen as a condition that led men and women into other forms of immorality. Protestants were particularly critical of the Catholic clergy, whom they portrayed as lazy, impious, wine-soaked fornicators. With a few minor exceptions, Protestants did not promote abstinence but encouraged moderation, and they put in place laws to ensure that people did not drink to excess. Calvin regarded public drinking as especially problematic and instituted rules for taverns in Geneva in the 1540s that give us an idea of the behavior expected of Huguenots in France. He started by placing French-language Bibles in Geneva's taverns, a precursor to the distribution of Bibles in hotel rooms by the Gideons International and an act that blurred what had been a stark distinction between the tavern and the church. Medieval and early modern writers often complained that men opted to attend the tavern rather than the church, and in many places taverns were ordered closed during church services. Under Calvin's regulations, patrons of Geneva's taverns who swore or blasphemed—in other words, who behaved as men did in taverns—did so in the presence of the Bible. Calvin went further and attacked widely accepted notions of sociability by decreeing, "There is to be no treating of one another to drinks, under penalty of three sous." As for being drunk, a first offense was punished by a fine of three sous, a second by a fine of five sous, and a third by a fine of ten sous and a period of imprisonment.[63]

French Catholics, males especially, who heard of these rules could be excused for thinking that Calvinism was bad news for wine and for wine-centered sociability. In Dijon, the largest town in Burgundy and not too far from Geneva, vignerons clearly rejected Calvinism. In its 1561 mayoral elections, 93 percent of vignerons supported a fervent Catholic candidate, and he won thanks to their support: 58 percent of his votes were cast by vignerons.[64] In the sixteenth century, vineyards extended right to the walls of Dijon, and its vignerons tended to live in the city rather than outside on their estates. They were, moreover, a considerable part of Dijon's population, accounting for between a fifth and a quarter of households in the 1500s. Not only were vignerons numerous, but they were quite well off and politically active, and what is notable about their political activity is that it was geared to supporting rigorous Catholicism over the newly arrived Protestantism.

Dijon's was not an isolated case. Vigneron support for the existing church against Protestant encroachment seems to have been general throughout France. Vignerons were conspicuous by their absence from Protestant movements in communities as widely dispersed as Rouen, Amiens, and Troyes in the north and Béziers, Montpellier, Toulouse, and Bordeaux in the south and west. Dijon is in the east. This is far from saying that no vignerons supported Protestantism, for we know that many Huguenot emigrants were vignerons, but they were a small minority of the hundreds of thousands of French vignerons.

It is possible that vignerons felt a special connection to Christianity. They worked with the vines and made the wine, which were such rich themes throughout the Bible, and wine makers in Dijon referred to the words of Christ: "I am the true vine, and my Father is the wine maker. . . . I am the vine, and you the branches. He who dwells in me, as I dwell in him, bears much fruit; for apart from me you can do nothing."[65] There was a belief that God favored or punished vignerons according to their virtue. A late sixteenth-century anonymous work from Burgundy, the *Monologue of the Worthy Vigneron*, notes that "it is when our vines are frozen in winter or hailed upon in summer, or when by some other means we harvest very little wine, that God has means enough to punish our past sins." On the other hand, "God protects the noble vigneron."[66]

Biblical references were common to both Catholics and Protestants, and it is possible that the high profile of wine in doctrine and ritual gave vignerons a special status among the faithful. (One could even argue that the Catholic doctrine of reserving wine for the priest alone in Communion elevated the status of wine.) Perhaps this tight vigneron-wine-God nexus made most vignerons more conservative doctrinally. God protected the vines of virtuous vignerons from drought, lice, and insects, and it was proper that the vignerons of Dijon repaid this by ridding the city of Protestants. They frequently referred to Protestants as insects or vermin attacking the holy church, as if they were the insects and vermin with which vignerons had to contend in their vineyards.[67]

Yet Protestant and Catholic positions on the secular consumption of wine (or beer, cider, mead, or any other alcoholic beverage) were essentially the same. Wine was a gift of God, was healthy, and had medicinal value, and Calvin approved of a priest providing it "for the weaker brethren, and those who without it cannot attain bodily health."[68] But consumption of wine had to be moderate, which seems to have meant that it could be used as a medicine or for hydration but not for pleasure. Consuming any more than strictly necessary was excessive and sinful, even if the drinker did not become drunk. Drunkenness was definitely a sin, and despite Protestant allegations, Catholic writers routinely condemned excess in both eating and drinking as harmful to the body, soul, and society.

But the cure for drunkenness, even persistent drunkenness (the concept of alcoholism had not yet been developed), was moderation, not abstinence, and wine was probably part of the daily diet for many French men, especially in wine-producing areas, where it was relatively inexpensive. But it is likely to have been more widely consumed in cities than in rural areas, and ironically, it seems that many small-scale vignerons drank little of their own production. The economics of vine growing dictated that peasants had to sell all the wine they could in order to purchase the essentials—notably grain—that they did not produce because they practiced viticulture.

The social spread of wine is suggested by the way it began to appear in proverbs, which are frequently expressions of common attitudes toward everyday experiences. French proverbs captured the prevailing sense that wine should be consumed in moderate quantities. "Eat bread as long as it lasts, but drink wine moderately," one advises. Drunkenness threatened order: "Whoever surrenders to too much wine retains little wisdom." Other proverbs express the long-standing anxiety about women drinking wine, such as "A drunk woman is not the mistress of her body." Proverbs also reveal a number of drinking preferences. Red wine was favored over white, and Greek wine retained its good reputation, as in the saying "Of all the wine, the Greek is divine." Its association with royalty placed wine at the top of the hierarchy of drinks, at whose bottom was water: "Drink wine like a king, water like a bull." Wine produces happiness: "Water makes you cry, wine makes you sing." And it is best drunk in company: "Wine without a friend is like life without a witness."[69]

Those whose employers did not provide them with wine and who could not afford to buy it in bulk had several alternatives for obtaining small quantities. Until 1759, the owners of vineyards who lived in cities were permitted to sell wine at their door, as long as the purchaser did not step inside and create the possibility of consuming it on the spot. Wine was available in taverns, of course, and inns were also an option, but French law prohibited innkeepers from selling to anyone who lived in their town; inns were exclusively for travelers. This restriction, which dated back to the Middle Ages, was renewed by the Parlement of Paris in 1579, which suggests that it was widely ignored. It continued to be flouted, and the availability of inns as outlets for wine can only have reinforced the spread of wine consumption.

As we have seen, a more systematic sense of wine connoisseurship developed in this period. It was perhaps related to the possibility of keeping wine in bottles, which reduced the chances of deterioration: in a barrel, wine was exposed to more and more air as its level fell. By the end of the seventeenth century, the word *bouteille* (bottle) had taken on a definitive meaning in French, and bottles were widely used for wine, even though it was forbidden to sell wine in bottles. Bottle owners could have them filled from barrels for storage in their cellars, but in practice bottles were generally used to hold only the best wines; wine for daily drinking was stored in barrels. The cellar belonging to Anne Robert Jacques Turgot, the French economist and politician, included only one barrel of wine (from Joigny, in the Yonne region) but 4,185 bottles of wine, from Burgundy, Champagne, Roussillon, Bordeaux, and several regions in Spain and elsewhere.[70]

Increasing appreciation of wine was also due to a heightened awareness of the distinctions not only among wines of different regions but also among wines of the same region, and even—as the case of Haut-Brion indicates—awareness of individual estates. Until the seventeenth century, wine drinkers referred to wines as coming from broad regions rather than from specific localities. For the most part, clarets were clarets, and burgundies were burgundies. If Beaune was singled out, it was because Beaune was considered a region in its own right, separate from Burgundy. It is hardly surprising that the great majority of French wines were not identified in narrower terms. Right through this period, and long after it, for that matter, the wines that reached consumers were blended with little regard to provenance or grape variety. Wines sold retail in taverns or wholesale by the barrel were seldom produced by individual vignerons but rather blends created by merchants. One vigneron's light wine might be mixed with another's full bodied, some brandy might be added to raise the alcohol level and give the wine some durability, and other ingredients might be included according to the merchant's recipe. Or a merchant might simply water down his wine (see figure 3.1). Whatever the process, and even if a merchant shipped a barrel of wine without altering it, no customer had (or expected to have) confidence that the wine purchased represented a particular estate, vineyard, or grape variety. The originality and commercial success of Pontac and his estate-identified Haut-Brion lay in his departure from this practice.

A number of signs suggest a growing interest in wine during the 1600s. British travelers in Europe commented frequently, and for the most part positively, on food and wine to be found in France, Italy, and elsewhere. Many of them were on the Grand Tour, designed to give well-off young Englishmen an appreciation of the history and culture of Europe. Some were more attracted by other diversions offered in foreign places, and a number cited wine in their published accounts of their travels. The exiled John Evelyn noted wines and vineyards as he traveled through France and Italy, although some of his comments are rather eccentric. Visiting Orléans in 1644, he wrote, "The wine of this place is so strong, that the King's cup bearers are, as I was assured, sworn never to give the King any of it: but it is a very noble liquor, and much of it is transported into other countries." He noted that Orléans was popular with Germans, but the English "make no long sojourn here, except such as can drink and debauch." Near Tours he was invited to a vineyard "which was so artificially planted and supported with arched poles, that stooping down one might see from end to end, a very great length, under the vines, the bunches hanging down in abundance."[71] It is noteworthy that Evelyn thought vines trellised and in rows were "artificially planted"; this supports the argument that most vineyards were planted haphazardly.

Thought was also given to the temperature at which wine should be drunk. In sixteenth-century France, it was often warmed, and King Francis I's doctor Jean-Baptiste Bruyère-Champier noted that this practice was common to all social classes and seasons. "Some put their cups or bottles near the fire," he wrote, "others warm the water with which the wine is diluted; some toss toasted bread into their drink; certain others heat up iron blades, and the elegant and wealthy gold blades, which they dip in their cups, while the poor plunge therein burning sticks from the fire."[72] While

FIGURE 3.1.   An innkeeper adds water to his wine while his wife distracts his customer, a baker's son. Engraving by Jacques Lagniet, 1660 (Wellcome Library no. 25927i). Courtesy of the Wellcome Library, London.

Bruyère-Champier did not approve of warming wine, he was firmer in his disapproval of drinking wine straight from a cool cellar; the temperature of such wine would damage the throat, chest, lungs, stomach, and intestines, corrupt the liver, and cause incurable illnesses, even rapid death. He advised anyone with a cool cellar to take the wine out a few hours before drinking it so that it could warm in the ambient air. (No distinction was made between red and white wines.) Here was early advice to bring wine to room temperature, although that in itself varies widely by location and season.

But a consensus was far off, and a few decades later another physician advised just the opposite. Laurent Jaubert wrote that it was necessary, particularly for a young person with hot blood, to counter the warmth of the atmosphere with a drink of cool wine. If no cellar was available, the wine could be cooled in a fountain or a stream.[73] The custom of drinking chilled wine in the summer became widespread in France during the sixteenth century, and eventually the French adopted Spanish and Italian practice and cooled their wines with snow and ice.

In medical writing, wine maintained its strong position as a source of nutrition and a basic therapy. A number of physicians began to make increasingly stark distinctions among kinds of wine, in terms of not only their properties of sweetness and dryness or color and depth (perhaps a reflection of the greater diversity of styles then available) but the classes of people that would benefit from them. Doctors drew upon the humoral theory and beliefs that people of different social classes or occupations were biologically different. Olivier de Serres wrote in 1600 that "good, full-bodied red and black wines" were "appropriate for working people . . . and greatly sought after by them as much as white and clairet wines are by people of leisure."[74]

This was not simply a matter of taste, as Jean Liebault, a French physician, explained a few years later: "Red wine nourishes more than white or clairet, and it is more suitable for those who work hard[,] because work and vigorous exercise neutralize any of the disadvantages that red wine has." As for black (dark red) wine, "it is best for vignerons and farmers[,] because once digested by the activity of the stomach and work, it gives more solid and plentiful nourishment and makes the man stronger in his work."[75] Liebault linked social class and wine type even more closely than Serres did. Even if these full-bodied, earthy wines had the effect of weighing on drinkers and making their blood "thick, melancholic, and slow-flowing," there was no cause for concern, because peasants were reputed to be earthy, crude, thick, and slow anyway. But the same wine would have terrible effects on nobles, bourgeois, and the clergy, whose work required them to be lively and spiritual. Such men would suffer obstructions of the liver and spleen, loss of appetite, and rawness in the stomach. There was a medical consensus that light red or white wines were more suitable for better-off consumers because such beverages passed easily from the stomach to the liver, producing rich blood and rejuvenating the heart and the brain.

Medical ideas of the health properties of wine entered popular consciousness and were embodied in proverbs.[76] Some express the good effects of wine throughout the year: "In summer when it's hot and in winter when it's cold, wine gives you energy." Wine was excellent for the digestion: "If you don't drink wine after raw vegetables, you risk being ill." Many proverbs reflect contemporaneous concern about pears, which were reputed to be very difficult to digest. One saying advises, "After pear, drink wine," while a Breton proverb direly predicts that "if pears are not followed by wine, they will be followed by the priest." Pears were regarded as not only hard to digest but also essentially feminine. As such, they needed to be balanced by "masculine" wine.

What about water? In the 1580s, Michel de Montaigne stopped at the hot springs of Plombières, in Lorraine, but he did more than bathe: "M. Montaigne drank the water for eleven days: nine glasses a day for eight days, and seven glasses a day for three, and bathed five times. He did this every day before dinner [lunch]. There was no other effect than urinating. His appetite was good, [and] his sleeping and digestion showed nothing out of the ordinary for drinking this beverage."[77] What is notable here (apart from the daily volume of water that Montaigne consumed) is the implication that drinking water might have negative effects. It suggests that by this time, water might not have been consumed as a default beverage but was being treated with some caution.

It is suggestive of the significance of wine in the French diet at this period that in times of great hardship, alternatives to it were suggested. One doctor advised that "in place of wine, because it is expensive for the poor, one should drink beer, cider, perry [pear-based cider]." Elsewhere it was suggested that bodies weakened by famine should not be subjected to the harshness of beer and that a weak solution of wine was beneficial. Some doctors recommended using piquette (thin wine) as the basis of gruels that also would include nuts, herbs, or spinach.[78]

Wine was so central to the diet of the sick that when in 1670 Louis XIV founded Les Invalides, the military hospital in Paris, he exempted it from paying taxes on the first fifty thousand liters (thirteen thousand gallons) each year.[79] Wine was regularly distributed to the patients, and such was the level of consumption that the exemption was progressively raised, until by 1705 it was set at eight hundred thousand liters (two hundred thousand gallons) a year. Officers were given a daily ration of 1.25 liters (0.33 gallons) of wine, a quarter liter being brought to their rooms each morning and a half liter served at lunch and dinner. Noncommissioned officers and ordinary soldiers had a smaller ration, half of what the superior officers received at each meal. Rations were doubled at the evening meal on certain festivals, such as Mardi Gras. Wine was also dispensed to employees of the hospital, and some was used in cooking. In February 1710, when there was a daily average of 2,500 resident patients, Les Invalides went through 460,000 liters (120,000 gallons) of wine, a daily average of 6.5 liters (1.7 gallons) per patient. The staff consumed some wine, but even if there were as many employees as patients, this volume seems well in excess of requirements. Wine was clearly intrinsic to the care of military patients, and when some soldiers were sent from Les Invalides for a two-month thermal treatment, special provision was made for them to take wine along because there was none in the hospital at which they would stay.

In addition to consuming their rations, some pensioners who were residents of Les Invalides got more wine in local bars, and there are ample records of drunkenness leading to violence, blasphemy, and offences against public morality. Officers found drunk were arrested and deprived of wine for eight days. Soldiers who had been convicted eight times were sent to prison for a year. Deprivation of wine was clearly a major punishment, and it was also the penalty for writing obscenities on walls, throwing refuse, urine, or water out the hospital windows, not respecting the rules regarding cleanness, and having a fire or a candle lit at night after the beating of the retreat.

Over time, medical writers who drew attention to the harmful effects of alcohol challenged the panegyrics on the benefits of wine. One of the earliest criticisms of wine as a healthy beverage was published in the late sixteenth century by a partisan of another fermented beverage who was tired of wine's privileged position in medical writing. Julien le Paulmier, the author of a number of medical works, was clearly a loyal inhabitant of Normandy, a province where viticulture was marginal but that became famous for its apple cider and later for the apple-based spirit calvados.

A pall had been cast over the cider industry by the allegation that drinking cider caused leprosy, which was more common in Normandy than elsewhere in France. Le Paulmier set out to correct the bad press that cider had received and to show that it was superior to wine in every respect. Describing wine as one might a dangerous drug that should be carefully controlled by professionals, he noted that it possessed excellent qualities but could be dangerous if not used with judgment and discretion. It could cause "an infinity of illnesses and indispositions," because patients did not know what sort of wine to drink, how much to dilute it, or how to suit it to the climate, season, and individual needs.[80]

The point of this treatise was not simply to highlight the problems with wine but to show the superiority of cider, which, Le Paulmier insisted, had all the benefits attributed to wine but none of the disadvantages. Cider was good for the digestion and the blood; it was warm, but moderately so, so that the best and strongest cider rarely exceeded the first level of warmth, while the strongest wines reached the top of the third level. Le Paulmier's ultimate claim for cider was straightforward: "A man who drinks cider lives longer than a man who drinks wine."

This was a voice in the wilderness of Normandy, where vines grew so poorly that attempts to cultivate them were eventually abandoned. Elsewhere the consensus remained strong that wine was not only a healthy beverage but also enjoyable to drink. The emergence of fine wines, like Arnaud de Pontac's Haut-Brion, and of growing awareness of the characteristics that specific grapes, localities, and producers imparted led in the early modern period to a stark divergence between the mass of wine consumers, for whom wine was merely part of the daily diet, and connoisseurs, for whom it was also an aesthetic experience. In the following centuries, connoisseurship played an increasingly important role.

4. Enlightenment and Revolution

1700–1800

As the eighteenth century opened, a burst of vine planting throughout France suggested that vignerons and landowners were generally optimistic about the future for wine sales. As if to justify that optimism, in Bordeaux at least, the all-important English market was opened to French wine again in 1697, after years of on and off trade relations between France and England. But politics and weather soon punctured the optimism. In 1703, the English market was closed again (for seven years this time) as hostilities broke out once more between the two countries. To add insult to embargo, England signed a trade agreement that gave Portuguese wine preferential tariffs, disadvantaging future imports from France. Six years later, a vicious winter not only killed vines all over France and virtually wiped out the 1709 harvest but also ruined much of the wine from the 1708 vintage that was still stored in cellars.

The interruption in exports to England was easier to deal with than the weather, as it seems that Bordeaux's producers found an ingenious way to evade the trade embargo: by allowing their wine to be "confiscated" and then sold, with some of the proceeds being returned to them. Ships laden with top-quality Bordeaux wine would sail close to the English coast, where English privateers could "seize" their freight. This wine was auctioned in London, with most of the proceeds going to the privateers, a small payment going to the owner of the tavern where the auction was held, and the rest going to the crown. The seizure of French goods was not uncommon, but so much expensive Bordeaux wine was captured this way—and these were the very wines that were popular among the English elite—that it is reasonable to suppose that the shippers and the privateers had conspired to return some of the proceeds to Bordeaux.[1]

Bordeaux's wine was becoming popular among the well-off in many parts of Europe, but England's was by far the most important market in the early 1700s, as we can gauge by the success with which the seized wine was sold. In May 1705, for example, 200 barrels of Haut-Brion and Pontac wine were auctioned, and in the following month, 250 barrels of Haut-Brion and Margaux. Soon after, 288 barrels of Haut-Brion, Pontac, and Margaux went under the hammer. These premium wines sold for more than twice the price per barrel of ordinary claret, and the proceeds of these three lots was more than £40,000. If only a third of that ended up in Bordeaux, it still would have been a substantial sum, and probably more than the shippers would have received otherwise.

The wine was purchased by London wine merchants, who then sold it to private clients. One was John Hervey, Earl of Bristol, whose accounts for the period 1703–10 (when French wine could not legally be imported into England) include £27 10s. "for a hogshead of Margoose [Margaux] claret" in December 1703, £16 10s. "for 3 chests of wine from Avignon" (perhaps Châteauneuf-du-Pape) in June 1704, £80 "for 3 hogsheads of wine, 2 of Obrian [Haut-Brion] and 1 of white Langoon [Langon]" in July 1705, and £56 "for 2 hogsheads of Obrian wine" in May 1707.[2]

When the trade embargo was lifted in 1710, France's wine producers were unable to take immediate advantage of the commercial opportunities. In January 1709, heavy snow fell over much of France, and then temperatures plummeted to well below normal, reaching −16 degrees Celsius (3.2 degrees Fahrenheit) in Montpellier, −18 (−0.4 degrees Fahrenheit) in Marseille, and −24 (−11 degrees Fahrenheit) in Bordeaux. Reports from Bordeaux record ships frozen in the rivers, ink frozen in inkwells, wine frozen in bottles, and (perhaps exaggerations) water freezing in the air as it was poured from pitcher to glass and birds eating one another.[3] Then temperatures rose, melting the snow and ice and causing floods, before plummeting even lower than before. Such cold and fluctuating temperatures killed vines throughout the country, effectively ruining the 1709 vintage. René Lehoreau, a priest in Angers, wrote that "two-thirds of the vines died, including the old ones. . . . Quite honestly, in the whole of our Anjou, we produced 80 barrels of wine, and that wine was not drinkable because the grapes were unripe. . . . I speak from experience, having harvested from my own vines only enough wine to fill a nutshell."[4] Not only was the 1709 harvest ruined, but so was much of the previous year's as it sat in barrels only two or three months after fermentation. The temperature in many cellars fell precipitously, freezing the wine, which burst the barrels as it expanded, then froze in red or yellow shards that protruded between the staves.

There were shortages of wine everywhere between 1708 and 1710. The Abbey of Saint-Denis near Paris produced about 35,000 liters (9,000 gallons) of wine in each of 1706 and 1707, but only 7,500 liters (1,980 gallons) survived from 1708, and the 1709 vintage produced a mere 3,750 liters (990 gallons). Damage to vineyards varied enormously from place to place throughout France. Vines in low-lying areas fared worse than those on slopes; some vines were killed outright and had to be pulled out, while others were affected only above ground and recovered. The vines planted in the spring of 1709 to replace those killed during the winter were not productive for two or three years; although the 1710 vintage at the Abbey of Saint-Denis was bigger than the previous two, it was only 8,300 liters (2,200 gallons), but the following harvest rebounded to nearly 45,000 liters (12,000 gallons).[5] The vineyards of Champagne returned to full production that year too: in October 1711, the maréchal de Montesquiou placed an order for wine and noted, with a refined appreciation of the relationship of supply to demand, "It is said that there is a lot [of wine] this year, and that it will be inexpensive. I am sure you will do your best."[6]

Following the disastrous winter of early 1709, the prices of wine and other produce (especially grain, the core of the peasant diet) shot up. Many small-scale vignerons were ruined, having lost the vines that provided their livelihood and being unable to afford food at now elevated prices. A harvest like 1709's was disastrous for vignerons who lived from year to year and could not simply absorb the loss. Lacking capital to buy vines, many of these poor vignerons were unable to participate in the orgy of planting that began in the spring of 1709. As wealthier landowners took advantage of the high prices that wine was fetching, they replaced dead vines soon enough, but planting continued into the 1720s and into areas where vines had not been cultivated before. In 1724, Claude Boucher, the intendant of Bordeaux, noted, more in alarm than in approval, that "for ten leagues [about forty kilometers or twenty-five miles] around Bordeaux you see nothing but vines. The same mania has taken hold in the rest of the region."[7] This was the moment when Bordeaux's vineyards began to spread well beyond the vicinity of the city itself.

Concerned about the encroachment of vines on land used for cereals, authorities throughout France stepped in. The Parlement of Metz, in Lorraine, was the first to act when in 1722 it ordered the ripping out of vines planted since 1700 in locations where vines had not been planted before. In Bordeaux in 1724, new plantings were forbidden and all vines planted since 1709 ordered pulled out—although exemptions were made for those that were planted in districts traditionally planted with vines or in some of the best sites in the Médoc area, which was then being developed for viticulture. In Burgundy, the Parlement of Dijon considered a similar policy in 1725 but decided to wait for the king to act with a national policy, while in Besançon in 1731 the Parlement ordered recent plantings grubbed up. In the tiny province of Béarn, in the foothills of the Pyrenees, peasants fearing a shortage of grain protested in 1725 against the planting of vine-yards on parts of the higher land that had been used for other crops. The authorities agreed with them and in 1727 forbade the planting of vines on land suitable for cereals and ordered all vines planted since October 1714 to be pulled out.[8]

Despite such attempts to rein in vine planting, vineyards expanded eve-rywhere and wine production rose. In 1724, the vineyards around Paris pro-duced more that 8.5 million liters (2.2 million gallons) of wine, twice the annual average of the preceding ten years. Finally, in 1731, the government of Louis XV forbade the planting of any new vineyards anywhere in France without the express consent of the king. The government feared that there would be grain shortages if viticulture took over too much arable and graz-ing land and that an oversupply of wine would depress prices and cause hardship to the millions of peasants who made their living, wholly or in part, from wine. In Languedoc, the land in question was scrubland (known as "garrigue") used as rough pasture for the sheep that supplied the wool industry.

As sensible as the royal policy seemed—although it might have been motivated as much by fear of grain riots and social unrest as by solicitude for the well-being of the king's often unruly subjects—it was opposed by those who wanted to take advantage of the financial opportunities that viti-culture offered. One was the political philosopher Montesquieu, who owned vineyards in the Graves and Entre-deux-Mers districts of Bordeaux and who in 1725 bought ten hectares (twenty-five acres) of land in Pessac, near the Haut-Brion estate. He opposed the royal ban on planting because it denied landowners the right to cultivate their land as they wished and pre-vented them from benefiting from the demand for wine.[9] In the end, though, the various edicts forbidding the planting of vines were widely ignored. There was no point in fining impoverished small-scale vignerons when they planted illegally, and when better-off landowners wanted to plant vines, even in places where vines had not grown before, they had only to purchase a privilege (license) from the royal bureaucracy. In 1756, an inquiry showed that land under vines had increased without causing a grain shortage, and in 1758 the royal government annulled its 1731 edict, opening the way to the untrammeled expansion of France's vineyards.

Indirectly, the disastrous winter of early 1709 transformed France's wine landscape, as it led to a rapid extension of land under vines. The country's population substantially increased during the 1700s—rising to twenty-eight million in 1789, a 30 percent gain from 1720—and this meant increased demand for food and drink. When it came to wine, the options facing producers were to raise yields or to plant more land with vines, and France's vignerons did both. The poorer, small-scale producers, who made the bulk of France's wine and whose customers were more sensitive to price than to quality, began to plant heavy-cropping varieties like gamay and gouais blanc. Yields on poor land cultivated by small-scale vignerons for the local market were only about twenty hectoliters per hectare (214 gallons per acre), but fertilized and well-tended vineyards could produce a lot more, like the thirty-four hectoliters per hectare (363 gallons per acre) in Argenteuil, north of Paris, in the 1760s. By the early 1780s, thanks to planting with generous-cropping varieties, the vineyards around Paris were yielding fifty to sixty hectoliters per hectare (535 to 641 gallons per acre), while 1785, the year of a massive but poor-quality vintage, they produced an astonishing 150 hectoliters per hectare (1,604 gallons per acre).[10] A harvest this abundant must have well exceeded the capacity of vats and barrels and stretched vignerons' ingenuity to the limit.

Increasing yields to produce enough poor-quality wine for the growing population of common people was one thing, but there was also increasing demand for quality wines, especially from the expanding middle classes of France's towns and cities. Quality wines became known as "bourgeois wines" or "good vigneron wines," and there was a growing awareness that some regions or estates consistently produced them. There were several classifications of Bordeaux wines in the eighteenth century, precursors of the famous 1855 Bordeaux Classification. Like it, they were based on the prices that specific wines fetched, but price implied quality: it was assumed that the more that discerning buyers were willing to pay, the better the wine must be. A 1745 classification placed Margaux, Lafite, and Haut-Brion at the top, followed by estates such as Calon-Ségur, Rausan-Segla, and d'Issan.[11]

Wines of mediocre quality were called "small-vigneron wines" or simply "wines for drinking" (*vins de boisson*), perhaps to distinguish them from quality wines that a consumer might appreciate for a brief moment before drinking them. Not only did bourgeois consumers want wines that were different from the common wine popular among peasants and manual workers, but many had developed an appreciation of quality wines that separated them from the masses, who guzzled wine as they gobbled food without reflecting too much on its character and style. Wine was, then, a commodity that marked social distinctions, and the demand for quality wines gave better-off producers the opportunity to plant more carefully: to plant varieties that gave quality over quantity, and in locations where they would produce the best wine.

In 1787, the gap between these two broad categories was described thus, in respect of wine from Champagne: "Vines in general ... have worth and quality only inasmuch as they are made with pinot grapes, and one finds them only among bourgeois, or the well-off individual who prefers quality to quantity; the vigneron, on the contrary, as everywhere else, has filled his vineyards with gros plant [gouais blanc], which, being less susceptible to frost, always produces a lot of wine that is hard, cold, and disagreeable to the taste."[12] In the 1730s or 1740s, gamay was reintroduced to Burgundy because it had done so well in the Rhône valley, producing not only a lot of wine but wine of excellent quality. Although it made "flat and bitter" wine with no aroma when planted in Burgundy, some vignerons there embraced it because its yield was four times that of pinot noir. One quality-conscious vigneron was quoted as saying, "Gamay will kill Burgundy."[13] In some districts, there were conflicts between vignerons looking for volume and those seeking quality. In Bar-le-Duc, in Lorraine, the town council demanded that gamay and other high-yielding varieties be ripped out and replaced by "the small pinot noir, whose production is low in terms of quantity, but is far superior to other varieties in terms of quality."[14]

Concern about the effects on quality of some high-cropping varieties drew more attention to grape varieties, whose names at that time varied according to region. This is still the case, but less so: the variety known as "chardonnay" (in Burgundy), for example, is called "auvernat" in Orléans and "gamay blanc" in Jura, while "malbec" (in Bordeaux) is "cot" in Cahors and "agreste" in Lorraine. The authoritative guide to wine grapes lists a dozen French synonyms for "chenin blanc" and twice that number for "cabernet franc."[15] Confusion over names and the eighteenth-century passion for categorizing led to several attempts to standardize the names of grape varieties. In 1771, the botanist Abbé François Rozier established a vineyard near Béziers with the aim of collecting vines from all over France so as to compare and categorize them. In the same decade, the intendant of the Bordeaux area sponsored a vineyard just outside the city in which to plant vines from the Paris region and other parts of France. Again, the purpose was to categorize the vines and "to judge if there are really as many different species as is imagined."[16]

Until a more standardized system of naming was adopted in the twentieth century, writers used many names to discuss grape varieties and their most suitable soil types. In the mid-1700s, a dictionary of agriculture listed eleven main families of grapes (including chardonnay, muscat, malvaisie, and pinot) and scores of individual varieties, together with comments on their best growing conditions, susceptibility to frost, size of bunches and grapes, and suitability for making wine.[17] Many are described as providing heavy crops or making "a lot of wine," which suggests that volume was an advantage, while others are said to be good to eat and to make good wine. A typical entry is that for "morillon noir" (pinot noir): "Called *pineau* in Burgundy, and *auvernas* in Orléans because the plant comes from Auvergne, it is very mild, sweet, black, is excellent to eat, grows in all kinds of soils, and is known to make the best wine in the areas around Paris."[18]

The same source suggests that, when grown in heavier soils, pinot noir on its own cannot produce wine with enough body and needs to be blended with tressot, a black variety that is now almost extinct.[19] But the Burgundy agronomist Edme Beguillet denounced this notion as "an incorrect observation on pinot, because the whole slope of Burgundy [presumably the Côte d'Or] is planted only with pinot, which makes excellent wines without being blended with other grapes." He noted that pinot grows best in stony or light, sandy soils and conceded that when grown in heavy soil, it makes wine that might require the addition of small quantities of other varieties. But, he added, it was better to use heavy soils for growing cereals; if vines had to be grown there, it was better to plant "gamays and other sorts of grapes that yield a lot, but which make detestable wines."[20] Centuries after the dukes of Burgundy had tried to exile gamay, the prejudice against it was alive and well.

During the eighteenth century, most French vineyards continued to grow a range of grape varieties, which were interplanted and harvested together, so wines were generally field blends—mixes of grape varieties in the proportions that grew in the vineyards, rather than blends assembled from varietal wines that had fermented separately. Around Nantes, for example, vineyards were a mix of folle-blanche (known locally as "grosplant") and melon de Bourgogne.[21] In Burgundy through to the mid-1800s, some pinot noir vineyards included a small percentage of both chardonnay and pinot gris.[22] These field blends need not have been chaotic or random, although some undoubtedly were. The mid-eighteenth-century guide to grape varieties made it clear that different varieties should be carefully selected and interplanted so as to make more balanced wines: "When one wishes to plant vines in ... heavy soil, one need only make provision for morillons, otherwise known as 'pinot blanc' and 'noir,' but more of the latter than the former, interspersed with tressot, otherwise known as 'Burgundy grapes.'" This is a recommendation for planting three varieties in different proportions to produce a multivarietal, field-blend wine. A vigneron wanting to make a deep-colored red wine should be sure to include some noirant (now called "teinturier," a dark-fleshed variety), which "serves only to cover the wine so as to darken it; that is why a little of it is planted in each vineyard." So successful at this was the teinturier grape (whose name means "dyer" in French) that it was also recommended for dyeing linen.[23]

Interplanting varieties (*multi-encépagement*) made some sense, because by including varieties with different characteristics—lesser or greater resistance to frost or certain diseases, for example—a vigneron with a small vineyard would have a greater chance of having some grapes to harvest, no matter what weather, vine diseases, or pests afflicted it. But the practice was challenged. Representing the system that would become the standard, Beguillet argued that each grape variety should be planted in a distinct parcel or vineyard. He wrote that the common practice of mixing varieties in a single vineyard was bad, because different varieties ripen at different times; if a vigneron picked the grapes when the earliest varieties were ready, those of the later-ripening varieties would be green and would make for an acidic wine, but if the vigneron harvested when the later-ripening grapes were mature, the earlier-ripened ones would be overripe or rotten. The solution was to separate the varieties and harvest each when it was ripe. Beguillet criticized vignerons resistant to reorganizing their vineyards this way as "too lazy" to want to change old routines.[24]

The separation of grape varieties in vineyards was not generally practiced in France until widespread replanting was needed following the phylloxera crisis of the late 1800s, but it was more or less practiced in some regions and on some estates during the eighteenth century. The Côte d'Or was often described (as by Beguillet) as being planted with a single variety, pinot noir, although there is reason to believe that many pinot noir vineyards also included other varieties. A 1750 vine census of the Weinbach estate, owned by the Capuchin religious order, in Kientzheim, in Alsace, shows a total of more than seventeen thousand vines. They included 7,700 räuschling, 3,000 roter traminer (savagnin rose), 3,000 muscat, 2,000 pinot noir, 700 riesling, 500 tokay, and 500 chasselas. Such a count surely could not have been made if the varieties had not been segregated.

The cost of replanting in this way was a deterrent to the great majority of French wine producers, small-scale vignerons who farmed a hectare or two (2.5 to 5 acres) at most and who interspersed not only grape varieties but also grape vines with other crops. Although all vines eventually had to be replaced, when they were old and began to bear less and less fruit, vignerons did so on a vine-by-vine basis rather than replant a complete vineyard and have no income from it until the new vines began to produce. Grapes were important because a peasant could support a family on half a hectare (1.2 acres) of vines, far less land than was needed for cereals. But other crops provided food for family consumption or sale, and they were some insurance against a poor grape harvest.

Much of the vineyard expansion in the 1700s was carried out by wealthier proprietors who had the means to purchase land and to experiment with grape varieties. In Bordeaux, nobles were prominent in planting the Médoc district, and in 1744 the subdelegate of Bordeaux wrote that more than half of his jurisdiction was planted in vines, 90 percent of the land being owned by nobles and wealthy bourgeois.[25] Over time, the dominance of wealthy landowners in Bordeaux increased because they had a competitive advantage over peasants. Until the late 1700s, wine was taxed when it was brought into the city, but residents were exempted, and nobles and well-off bourgeois (many of whom lived in a manner that was materially indistinguishable from that of nobles) generally had residences in the city as well as in the country. The shift in the class balance of landownership in the eighteenth century laid the foundation for the aristocratic image of Bordeaux, with the grand châteaux that came to define its identity in the 1800s. Wealthy proprietors had the means to make higher-quality wines, which demanded low-yielding vines, careful grape selection, and better barrels, all of which raised the costs of production.

Wine was, in fact, the main source of income for many of Bordeaux's noble families. In 1755, sixty-eight noble magistrates earned almost three-quarters of their landed income this way. Even a small property could sustain a family well, if the wine fetched the high prices of many top Bordeaux wines. The *conseiller royal* Castelnau had only ten hectares (twenty-five acres) of vines, which produced twenty-five barrels of wine a year, but each barrel sold for 900 livres in 1755, giving him 22,500 livres. There were taxes and other expenses to be paid, of course, but workers' wage rates scarcely changed between 1750 and the 1770s, and nobles were exempt from many taxes. Castelnau's income from wine was twice what was required for a comfortable living that included summer and winter residences, four to six servants, a coach, quality clothes, good food and wine, entertainment, and travel. Others did even better. The comte de Ségur, who owned the Lafite and Latour properties, drew an annual income from them of between 100,000 and 180,000 livres, although he reported less to the tax authorities.[26]

Although Bordeaux was distinctive in that nobles and very wealthy landowners carried out much of its vineyard expansion, it shared with the rest of France the general expansion of viticulture during the 1700s. Land under vines increased by nearly 50 percent around Ammerschwir, in Alsace, from 321 hectares (793 acres) in 1721 to 465 (1,169 acres) in 1762, and overall it doubled in Alsace during the century. Trends like this were accelerated by government policies adopted in the 1760s that encouraged the clearing of land that had not been cultivated for at least forty years. Forests were exempted (to protect trees needed for shipbuilding), but various tax concessions (such as freedom from state taxes for fifteen years) were offered as inducements to clear land for agriculture so as to expand the national economy and provide for France's rapidly growing population.

Not all the newly cleared land was planted in vines, of course, but much of it was. A "fever" of planting gripped Champagne from the 1760s, under the pressure of demand from the Parisian market.[27] In Languedoc, more than four thousand hectares (ten thousand acres) of land were cleared between 1773 and 1777, and another thirty-five thousand (86,500 acres) in the following ten years. These figures do not take into account clearances by peasants who seized land.[28] When weather or disease destroyed vineyards, they were replanted. In Cahors, a bourgeois landowner noted in 1787, "We have planted half the plot of land at Arnisac . . . which had been uncultivated for twenty years since the old vines were entirely wiped out by the extraordinary cold of the years 1765 and 1767."[29] All kinds of land were planted with vines: stony, gravelly, and clayey soils, slopes and plains, hitherto uncultivated land, garrigue, and arable land. In 1787, the English agronomist Arthur Young, who traveled throughout France in 1787, 1788, and 1789, remarked that he saw "in every part of France . . . new vineyards already planted, or begun to be planted, on corn lands."[30]

The size and quality of harvests depends largely on the weather during each growing season, and the eighteenth century provided a vast range of conditions. After the disastrous winter of early 1709, harvests were generally good for more than half a century, from 1710 to 1766, with exceptions in specific regions. As the Cahors producer noted, 1765 was a very cold year there, while the combination of a harsh winter and a summer drought did nothing for the 1754 vintage in the vineyards around La Rochelle. But apart from sporadic and regional setbacks such as these, wine production must have more than kept up with population growth in France. The regular and plentiful supply of relatively affordable wine in these decades very likely reinforced the place of wine in the daily diet of many French people, making shortages and price increases that much less tolerable.

And shortages and price increases there were from 1767 to 1778, when a succession of cold springs and wet summers resulted in three poor and eight very poor vintages. Annual production in the vineyards around Paris dropped to half what it had been in the 1750s. One Besançon grower noted during the harvest of 1771, "The vines are producing virtually nothing, as much because of the awful winter followed by the heavy rains that ruined the grapes that had so much promise as because of the dry July that damaged them even further."[31] Other growers reported frozen grapes and grapes so green that they were difficult to crush. The price of wine rose as supply foundered and demand increased, driven by the growing population. In Argenteuil, the price of wine that had been stable at thirty-five to forty livres a barrel for the more than five decades between 1711 and 1766 rose to an average of sixty-six livres for the period 1767–77 and reached ninety-three livres in 1778.[32]

From the late 1770s until the French Revolution in 1789, there were several abundant and good-quality harvests, and prices began to fall back to their pre-1767 levels. But the biggest harvest of all, the vintage of 1785, was also the worst, as it followed weeks of heavy rains. The vines sagged under bunches of big grapes swollen with water, many suffering from gray rot, so the wine of 1785 was widely decried for its bad flavor and lack of color. Together, abundance and poor quality depressed prices to levels seldom seen in the eighteenth century. In Argenteuil, wine could be had for fifteen livres, less than the price of the barrel it was stored in, and much of it soon went bad and had to be poured away.[33]

The harvests following this disastrous year were generally poor. There was a cold spring and a lot of summer rain in 1786 in Champagne, so the grapes rotted on the vine. The following year, Young was traveling through Beauvais and remarked on "the melancholy spectacle of the vintage of 1787, which I saw there in the midst of incessant rains."[34] Although the 1788 harvest was good, a very cold winter in 1788–89, followed by late frosts, a dry spring, and heavy summer rain, ruined the 1789 crop and in some regions killed most of the vines.[35] Just as the French Revolution began, in the summer of 1789, vignerons faced reduced incomes for the next few years, and consumers (always keenly aware of the size and quality of grain and grape harvests and their effects on supply and prices) anticipated paying more for their wine.

The run of good harvests and low prices for more than half the century must have reinforced the place of wine in diets even in rural parts of the north where viticulture was marginal and beer and cider were widely consumed. A 1767 work notes that cider was easily produced in Normandy but that a long fermentation would compensate for the greenness of the grapes grown there and produce a drinkable wine. The result would not be fine wine; it could not be exported, and rich people would not seek it out, but it would be acceptable and do no harm.[36] We do not know how much or how often people drank wine, but there is good reason to believe that men, at least, did so on a regular basis; they gathered at public drinking places to drink and to do business, play games, and gamble.[37] Wine seems to have been fundamental to the diets of millions of common people in France, although not as fundamental as grain; there are plenty of documented grain and bread riots during times of shortage and high prices, but no one has yet documented a riot generated by a shortage of wine. Violence targeting the taxes applied to wine is a different story, as we shall see.

This is not to say that wine was not implicated in violence, for one of the concerns of the authorities was alcohol-induced social disorder. In his 1707 *Traité de la police*, Nicolas de la Mare wrote that taverns were commendable, as they sold wine to be taken home and drunk "with the family at regular meals," but cabarets (places where food and drink were served) were a problem, because their patrons too often drank too much: "What happens there degenerates into debauchery and drunkenness . . . without mentioning how much men of honor risk their reputation and others the ruin of their health and of their families."[38] Violence was a not uncommon occurrence in public drinking places, as court records before and during the Revolution show,[39] even though they were predominantly peaceful and were vital to sociability among peasants and urban workers and artisans.

It was the same with drinking at home—largely congenial and harmonious but sometimes fueling arguments and domestic violence. Defendants in divorce cases in France during the 1790s argued that their responsibility was diminished when they were "seized by wine." One told a court that "he admits having ill-treated his wife . . . that the abuse, harsh words, and threats he directed at her . . . often occurred when he was drunk." Women plaintiffs complained that men often returned home drunk and assaulted them, and many women associated the worst episodes of ill treatment with religious holidays, such as Easter and Pentecost, when men drank all day. On the other hand, one woman complained to a divorce court that "her husband gets drunk every day and profits from his drunkenness to abuse her."[40] Of course, excessive and problematic drinking was far more likely to be recorded than the amicable sharing of wine that was the rule.

Two examples from Languedoc capture the range of consumption. In 1761, the marquis de Londres received wine deliveries every three or four days and drank wine with all his meals, but at the very moderate rate of about half a bottle a day.[41] In contrast, Arthur Young noted more generous rations in 1787: "I met with labourers in Languedoc, who drank each three bottles of strong wine a day; and I saw, amongst the poor, in every part of the kingdom, an appearance of a pretty regular consumption, either of wine or cyder; and recourse was not had to water, but in case of failing crops."[42]

The French were certainly drinking more French wine than the English, because although French wine regained access to the important English market for most of the eighteenth century, between the wars of the early 1700s and the French Revolution, it was not as popular as it had been. There was strong demand in England for full-bodied French reds rather than the lighter clarets that had been popular for centuries, and it is likely that the English preferred stronger-flavored beverages of all kinds in the eighteenth century. Portugal replaced France as England's main supplier of wine when a 1703 trade agreement guaranteed that Portuguese wines would always pay less duty in England than French ones, and port, a sweet wine fortified with eau-de-vie, became very popular.

The French wines imported into England were predominantly luxury wines, from Bordeaux estates such as Haut-Brion, Margaux, Latour, and Lafite. Even when they cost more because of the higher duty levied on them, they sold well. Perhaps it is indicative of the positive view of French wines that the only comment on wine in an eighteenth-century French phrase book for English travelers is the complimentary "There's [i.e., this is] excellent wine." In contrast, for beer the book suggests phrases such as "It is full of dregs" and "This beer is dead," while comments relating to food include "This bread is moldy," "This meat is raw," and "This makes me vomit."[43] Arthur Young did not hesitate to pass judgment on the wines he tasted. Although some were "excrable," he was complimentary about most of what he drank and was especially keen on the three- and ten-year-old wines he tasted at Cahors: "Both excellent, full-bodied, great spirit, without being fiery, and to my palate much better than our ports." He ordered a barrel of wine from the vigneron, but when it arrived in England it was bad.[44]

Thomas Jefferson, the future U.S. president, visited several French wine regions (including Burgundy, the Rhône valley, Provence, Bordeaux, and the Loire valley) in 1787 while he was the ambassador to France, and made many observations on viticulture and wines. On the whole, he focused on districts already well known for their wines. In Burgundy he praised wines from Volnay, Beaune, Chambertin, and Vougeot. In Bordeaux he identified the usual quartet of estates (Lafite, Latour, Haut-Brion, and Margaux) as the best but recommended not drinking wines from any of these four until they were three or four years old.[45]

When Jefferson returned to the United States, he imported French wines and perhaps boosted their popularity among better-off wine drinkers of the new republic. The decrease in exports to England certainly made it necessary for French wine producers to open up markets elsewhere. Bordeaux, by far the most important French exporting region, began to ship more wine to towns and cities on the North and Baltic Seas, such as Bremen, Hamburg, and Danzig (now Gdańsk), and by the 1780s these markets were taking half the wine that it exported.[46] Also of growing importance was the bilateral trade with France's colonies in the Caribbean, which shipped sugar back to Bordeaux after off-loading its wine. Champagne began to export greater volumes of sparkling wine in the eighteenth century, although they did not reach important levels until the nineteenth. In the 1770s, Philippe Clicquot, a successful exporter of many commodities, calculated that the wealthy clients in Venice who bought his woolen textiles would also purchase his high-quality sparkling wine. He made his first sales of white champagne in Venice in 1772 and added rosé three years later. In the following few years, most of his exports were to Italy, Germany, and Switzerland, but he also sold to customers as far afield as Kraków, Vienna, Moscow, and Saint Petersburg.[47]

In southwest France, the province of Béarn (which then included what are now the Béarn, Vic-Bilh, and Jurançon appellations) went to extraordinary lengths to secure export markets for its quality wines. During the 1600s, Dutch merchants had regularly visited there to buy red and white wines directly from vignerons and to oversee the loading of barrels on to their ships. In the eighteenth century, the trade grew to the point that they began to employ agents, but the absence of personal supervision soon gave rise to problems. It was one thing when carters taking barrels to the ports siphoned off wine and replaced it with water or stones, but outright fraud was much more worrying. The practice developed of stopping fermentation with sulfur, resulting in a sweeter, richer wine with a very smooth texture, but the effect was only temporary, so buyers soon found themselves with a wine unlike what they had tasted and purchased. And some of Béarn's full-bodied and higher-alcohol wines were blended with light, low-alcohol wines from neighboring provinces such as Armagnac and Bigorre, then sold as if they were authentic Béarn wines.[48]

For decades, the authorities tried in vain to stop these practices. In 1776, they considered an ambitious plan to create a wine export office whose agents would visit vignerons, taste their wines, stamp approved barrels with the region's coat of arms, and oversee shipping, but the project was too expensive. A couple of years later, they asked the French consuls in Amsterdam, Rotterdam, Hamburg, and other markets to request local merchants to resume dealing directly with Béarnais vignerons. They were horrified to learn from the consuls that in northern Europe the name "Béarn" was no longer associated with any wine and that their wine had become an anonymous component of a regional blend known as "ordinary wine of Bayonne" (because that was where it was shipped from) which arrived there in huge volumes: more than twenty-six thousand barrels a year in the late 1770s.

Béarn mounted a very modern-looking trade mission to its historic northern European markets to reestablish "the reputation that the quality of our wines deserves." In 1779, a ship set sail for Hamburg (ironically, from Bayonne) with fifty-two barriques of Béarnais wine: forty-six from the very good 1778 vintage (sixteen white and thirty red; one-third from Vic-Bilh and the rest from Jurançon) and six from older vintages. The reception in Hamburg was disappointing: better-off consumers were firmly wedded to wines from Bordeaux, and the merchants supplying the mass market needed a lot of cheap wine for blending. When local négociants tasted the Béarnais wines, they liked the new whites, thought the new reds lacked enough color, and said the older wines were not old enough.[49]

But in Stralsund (now in Germany, then in Swedish Pomerania) there was much more interest, and an agreement was reached to establish trade between both regions. A private company was established in 1780 with the mission of increasing the consumption of Béarnais wine abroad. Investors, who paid for shares in money or wine, included vignerons, négociants, lawyers, civic leaders, and nobles, and the royal government promised commercial support if needed. All seemed very promising, but within two years the company was dissolved; many investors had not paid for their shares, the English navy was blockading the Atlantic coast because France was assisting the Americans in their War of Independence, the French tax agency had seized hundreds of barrels of wine, and payments from Stralsund were late. The vignerons of Béarn looked to sales within France, but nearby Bordeaux was out of the question and the distance to markets like Rouen and Paris, together with internal duties and excises, added costs that made the price of their wine too high. Little wonder that the grievances drawn up by these vignerons on the eve of the French Revolution called on the government to eliminate the taxes and duties on wine.

The example of Béarn highlights the commitment to quality that was geographically widespread, even if only a small percentage of French producers embraced it. The general improvement in quality wines during the eighteenth century drew on the research and experiments of scientists— botanists, agronomists, and chemists, among them—who embodied the spirit of the Enlightenment. From the middle of the century there was a marked increase in the number of books and pamphlets devoted to viticulture and wine making. The Academy of Bordeaux encouraged the writing of treatises on these subjects and in 1756 invited contributions on the theme "What is the best way of making, clarifying, and conserving wines? Is the method of clarifying them without eggs as good as or better than using eggs?"[50] At the same time, the Academy of Dijon took up the question of the quality of Burgundy wines, and in 1777 a correspondent suggested that it sponsor a competition to identify the best ways to promote the trade in wines of superior quality.[51] A work on methods of fermentation won a prize offered in 1766 by the Royal Society of Agriculture of Limoges.[52]

New techniques included chaptalization, adding sugar to must before fermentation to increase the alcohol content of the finished wine. First published in 1765, the article on wine in the *Encyclopédie*, a compendium of contemporary knowledge, refers to the use of sugar, and a succession of French scientists proposed adding sugar, honey, or sugar syrup as a means of starting fermentation as quickly as possible. The chemist Pierre-Joseph Macquer added sugar to the sour juice of underripe grapes from the poor 1776 harvest and declared that the resulting wine tasted as good as any other from that vintage (a low bar): there was nothing syrupy about it, he wrote, and no sensory evidence that the juice had been artificially sweetened.[53]

Bordeaux, Champagne, and Burgundy were the key regions for quality wines, but they operated in quite different markets outside their own territories. Bordeaux's most prestigious wines sold on the English market, as did Champagne's, while Burgundy's top-tier wines became more popular among the expanding bourgeoisie of Paris. But whereas Londoners were willing to pay twice and more the cost of ordinary wines for Bordeaux's luxury wines, in Paris the wines from prestigious sites such as Clos de Vougeot, Chambertin, Beaune, and Nuits sold for only about 50 percent more than ordinary wines, and those from Romanée and Montrachet fetched about a third more.[54]

It was only the better-off producers who could afford to make quality wine. Only they could weather the two or three years of no or little fruit when new varieties were planted or vineyards were replanted, and only they could afford the sugar—a luxury commodity at the time—to chaptalize their wines. Only they could afford to select only healthy, ripe grapes for their wine and discard berries that were unripe or rotten, as Young saw producers do in Champagne. This is not to say that modest, small-scale vignerons could not make quality wine, but they were greatly disadvantaged. Even if they did improve the quality of their wine, it is unlikely that it would have fetched higher prices, as it was sold locally. Except in terms of the scale of production, there were probably very few eighteenth-century equivalents of modern *garagistes* (artisanal producers of highly reputed wines), and there are no records of small-scale vignerons in remote hamlets producing cult wines in the eighteenth century.

It is likely that most made wine in the way that one report from Toulouse describes: the vines were not well planted or pruned, and the soil was cultivated only twice a year; the grapes were often picked too early and crushed by foot in large vats, with the juice left for months in the open air and then poured into dirty and usually unseasoned casks; the resulting wine was generally too acidic to compete with those from nearby Gaillac, Montpellier, or Bordeaux, and so it was sold locally.[55] This not only illustrates the gap between common and quality wines but should serve as a warning to modern marketers who think of promoting their wines as being made according to "traditional" methods. These were the traditional methods, and although French wine makers gradually began to abandon them in the eighteenth century, they seem to have been common practice until the late nineteenth.

One practice that largely disappeared from French wine making in the eighteenth century was treating wine with lead, which adds sweetness and inhibits the growth of some bacteria. Lead had been added to wine from classical times, and it was still done here and there in the 1700s, even though the dangers were known and the practice forbidden. Some wine makers of Poitou were said to add lead oxide to sweeten their wines and make them more competitive with the sweet whites of the Loire valley. In 1750, Paris authorities discovered that thirty thousand barrels of spoiled wine had been brought into the city, ostensibly to be turned into vinegar. Suspicious of this volume, officials investigated and found that the wine was being treated with yellow oxide of lead to sweeten it for sale as wine rather than as vinegar.[56]

It is impossible to know how widespread wine fraud was in the eighteenth century, but with quality generally low and very variable, consumers must have been used to some foul-tasting beverages passing as wine. Officials probably had more success rooting out fraud in the cities than in the country. In 1751, for example, a Paris wine merchant, Étienne Corrot, was convicted of selling various concoctions, including one of water, pear cider, grape skins left over from wine making, and brandy. He was sentenced to pay damages of three thousand livres and a fine of five hundred livres, to have the contents of the barrels poured into the street in front of his shop, and then to see his barrels burned and bottles smashed. His shop was to be boarded up for a year, and Corrot himself was banned for life

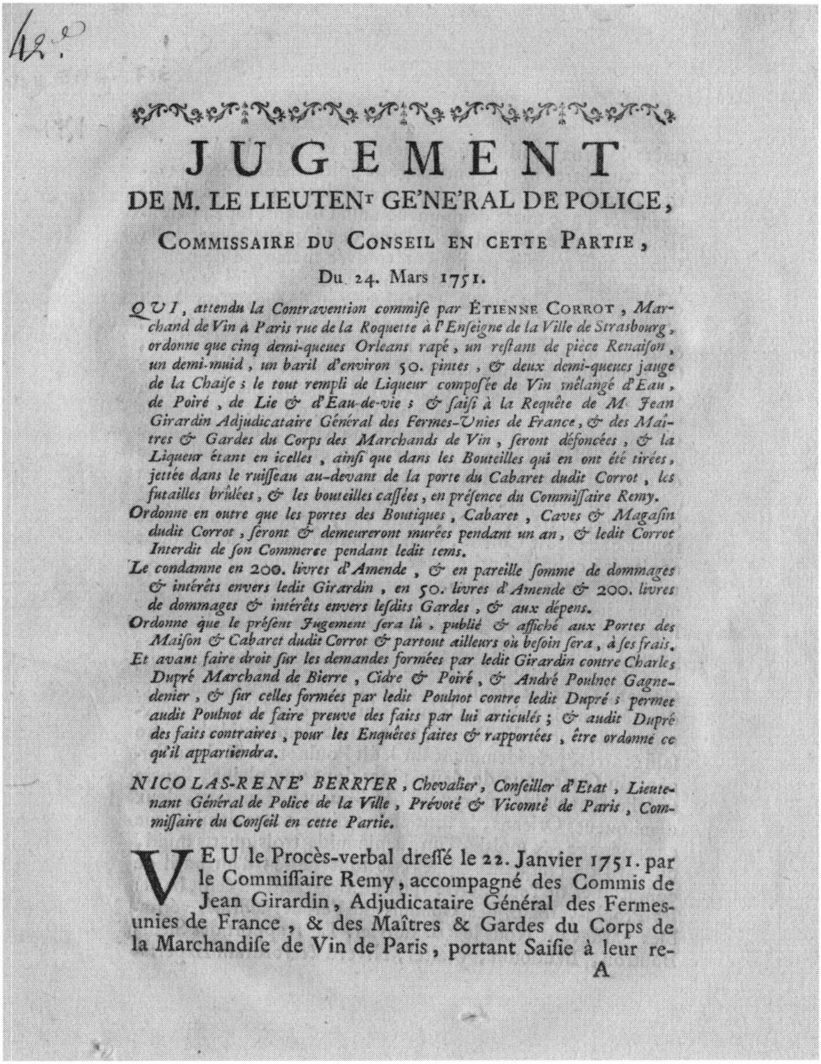

4₂.º

JUGEMENT
DE M. LE LIEUTENᵀ GE'NE'RAL DE POLICE,
COMMISSAIRE DU CONSEIL EN CETTE PARTIE,
Du 24. Mars 1751.

Q U I, attendu la Contravention commife par ÉTIENNE CORROT *, Marchand de Vin à Paris rue de la Roquette à l'Enfeigne de la Ville de Strasbourg, ordonne que cinq demi-queues Orleans rapé, un reftant de piece Renaifon, un demi-muid, un baril d'environ 50. pintes, & deux demi-queues jauge de la Chaife ; le tout rempli de Liqueur compofée de Vin mêlangé d'Eau, de Poiré, de Lie & d'Eau-de-vie ; & faifi à la Requête de M. Jean Girardin Adjudicataire Général des Fermes-Unies de France, & des Maîtres & Gardes du Corps des Marchands de Vin, feront défoncées, & la Liqueur étant en icelles, ainfi que dans les Bouteilles qui en ont été tirées, jettée dans le ruiffeau au-devant de la porte du Cabaret dudit Corrot, les futailles brûlées, & les bouteilles caffées, en préfence du Commiffaire Remy.*
Ordonne en outre que les portes des Boutiques, Cabaret, Caves & Magafin dudit Corrot, feront & demeureront murées pendant un an, & ledit Corrot Interdit de fon Commerce pendant ledit tems.
Le condamne en 200. livres d'Amende, & en pareille fomme de dommages & intérêts envers ledit Girardin, en 50. livres d'Amende & 200. livres de dommages & intérêts envers lefdits Gardes, & aux dépens.
Ordonne que le préfent Jugement fera lû, publié & affiché aux Portes des Maifon & Cabaret dudit Corrot & partout ailleurs où befoin fera, à fes frais.
Et avant faire droit fur les demandes formées par ledit Girardin contre Charles Dupré Marchand de Bierre, Cidre & Poiré, & André Poulnot Gagnedenier, & fur celles formées par ledit Poulnot contre ledit Dupré ; permet audit Poulnot de faire preuve des faits par lui articulés ; & audit Dupré des faits contraires, pour les Enquêtes faites & rapportées, être ordonné ce qu'il appartiendra.

NICOLAS-RENE' BERRYER, Chevalier, Confeiller d'Etat, Lieutenant Général de Police de la Ville, Prévoté & Vicomté de Paris, Commiffaire du Confeil en cette Partie.

VEU le Procès-verbal dreffé le 22. Janvier 1751. par le Commiffaire Remy, accompagné des Commis de Jean Girardin, Adjudicataire Général des Fermesunies de France, & des Maîtres & Gardes du Corps de la Marchandife de Vin de Paris, portant Saifie à leur re-
A

FIGURE 4.1. *Jugement de M. le lieutenant général de police:* a 1751 judgment against Étienne Corrot, a Paris wine merchant, for adulterating wine. (In the author's possession.)

from working as a wine merchant or being employed by a wine merchant (see figure 4.1).[57] This suggests a serious approach to wine fraud, but Corrot's mixture was not far from the one in a method proposed to make "a drink that tastes like wine": dry thirty pounds (fourteen kilograms) of grapes in the sun, put them in a barrel, fill it with water and a good amount of brandy, and then let this mix ferment for twenty-four hours with the bung out before sealing the barrel. "At the end of six weeks, you will have a recognizable drink, with a pleasant flavor."[58]

Some of the counterfeit "wines," adulterated with lead and such harmful additives that one physician said, "Of which I do not wish to speak," were dangerous to the consumer. This placed them at odds with real wine not only because they were fake but also because wine was widely believed to be healthy. Wine hydrated more safely than much of the available water, it was considered beneficial for the digestion, blood, and memory, and many believed that it "opens the way to fine thoughts." This was truer of red wine than white, as red wine was suitable for people of all temperaments.[59] On the other hand, wine was not healthy when consumed to excess, and it was also implicated in gout, a condition much discussed in eighteenth century.

Champagne had a particular status in discussions of health. It was commonly believed that champagne, no matter how much one consumed, would lead to a kind of euphoria rather than to intoxication. Just as the wine sparkled, so it was particularly suited to those with a lively spirit—nobles in particular—instead of people (peasants, artisans) who were dull and stolid.[60] It was also widely believed that champagne did not cause gout and that the condition was far less common in Champagne than in the rest of the kingdom. But a royal physician contested this in 1777, writing, "If all the gout sufferers in Paris, where wine from Champagne is more fashionable than ever, were to be truthful, they would admit that when they drank wine from Champagne, especially to excess, they never failed to have an attack of gout that was more painful and lasted longer than at other times."[61] But not all champagnes were equally problematic: "Under the general name of 'champagne wine,'" he wrote, "there are some that strongly dispose toward gout, some that do so moderately, and others that do not do so at all."[62]

Gout inducing or not, wine fascinated more and more bourgeois and nobles in this period, and they began to keep wine cellars and record their contents. Voltaire, who hosted sumptuous dinners on his estate at Ferney, bought large volumes of wine in barrels and bottled it on arrival; his accounts show orders for thousands of bottles and corks. His favorite wine was beaujolais, but his orders also included burgundies and Spanish wine from Málaga. Perhaps it is not surprising that the nonconforming Voltaire used his burgundy to top up his barrels of beaujolais—that is, used pinot noir, the pride of Burgundy's vignerons, to top up wine made from gamay, the grape variety they scorned.[63] The cellar of the duke of Tavanes was mainly stocked with hundreds of bottles of wines from Beaune and Médoc, but he also had wines from Cyprus and Hungary.[64] Claude Philippe Fyot de la Marche, the first president of the Parlement of Dijon, seems to have been loyal to his locality: most of his fine wines were burgundies from estates such as Chambertin, Clos de Vougeot, and Montrachet. Between February and June 1761, his household went through 760 bottles of wine (571 described as "ordinary" and 189 as "fine"), as well as 113 bottles of beer and 19 bottles of liqueur.[65]

Some collections of wine were truly impressive in size and scope. The duke of Penthièvre had a cellar of nearly three thousand bottles in 1772, as befitted one of the wealthiest men in France. About half his wine was French, with a marked preference for wines from Burgundy (20 percent of the bottles) over Champagne (7 percent) and Bordeaux (6 percent). The rest of the duke's wine was from Spain, Italy, Cyprus, and Germany. In the course of 1772 he consumed 660 bottles, but it is noteworthy that 300 held wines from Volnay, in Burgundy, even though those represented only one in six of the total cellar. His other favorite regions that year included Málaga (153 bottles drunk) and Cyprus. A broad geographical range was characteristic of the wines kept in the cellars of the elites of Paris in the 1780s. About two-thirds of these wines were French, and the rest were from Spain, Portugal, Italy, Hungary, Germany, Cyprus, and even South Africa.[66]

It is likely that very few eighteenth-century wines, made in France or anywhere else, aged well. Although wealthier wine drinkers kept cellars, they must have consumed their wines quite quickly. The *Encyclopédie* notes, "With respect to age, wine is either old or new or middle-aged. For us, new wine is that which has aged two or three months, old is that which has aged a year, and middle-aged wine is that which, having aged four months, has not yet aged a year."[67] Storage in infected and dirty barrels would have accelerated the deterioration of wine, almost all of which was stored and shipped in barrels of varying sizes. By 1700, some of France's most prestigious wines were exported in bottles sealed with corks, but in 1728 a law banned the importation into Britain of wine in bottles. Apart from the sparkling wine of Champagne, it had to be shipped in barrels and bottled only when it was sold to individual customers—a procedure that opened the door to adulteration and fraud by wine merchants.[68]

Yet the expansion of wine connoisseurship speaks to the idea that wines were to be contemplated and appreciated for their characters and qualities. This is not to say that the common people guzzled their wine unthinkingly, but they had access to wine of only poor to mediocre quality. They were very likely happy to drink whatever wine they could afford, because if they could not afford wine (or beer or cider) they had no choice but to drink water, which by the 1700s was widely thought to be unhealthy, if not outright dangerous. They drank wine with or without a modicum of sensory enjoyment, as a food, and because it was considered healthy, but quality cannot have been an overriding concern. Voltaire might have enjoyed his beaujolais, but he cultivated his own vineyard at Ferney, on the border with Geneva, and gave his servants homemade wine, which he described as "my own bad wine, which is by no means unwholesome." Little wonder that, as he complained, they stole his good wine from time to time.[69]

Any wine consumed by the poor, who made up a third or more of France's population, must have been thin, flavorless, and acidic. In 1794, the Paris authorities took samples of wine from sixty-eight cabarets and taverns and declared that only eight could reasonably be described as wine. While it is true that the revolutionary period brought particular challenges and hardships, it is likely that much of the wine that circulated before the Revolution was equally suspect. It is also likely that advances in making top-tier wines in the eighteenth century led to a wider gap than ever before between the best of wines and the worst of wines.

Poor-quality wine was in great demand by the mass of peasants and urban workers. It was generally safer to drink than the water that was available, and even if it was thin and often oxidized, it contained enough alcohol—7 or 8 percent seems to have been common—to liven the day and create a mood of sociability or help deaden the chronic misery of everyday life. We do not know how much wine rural and urban workers drank, any more than we know the drinking patterns of the better-off, and estimates of consumption in all but the recent past must be treated with caution. As we have noted, even accurate figures of the total amount of wine available to a population of a known size do not reveal how the wine was distributed.

That said, some sixty million to eighty million liters (sixteen million to twenty-one million gallons) of wine were taxed as they entered Paris each year in the late eighteenth century, enough for every man, woman, and child to have two or three liters (0.5 or 0.8 gallons) of wine a week. It is thought that up to half as much again was smuggled in, and if we add that and remove children under about fifteen years of age from the drinking population, it is likely that each adult in Paris had access to about nine liters (2.4 gallons) of wine each week. If men drank twice as much as women, they would have had access to about twelve liters (3.2 gallons) a week, almost two liters a day. Some men would have drunk less than that, some more. It is a sizable volume, but we should remember that the alcohol level of the wine was often less than half that of modern wine.

These figures underscore the importance of wine as an everyday beverage and of its place in the daily diets of men in particular. The people of

Paris drank their wine at a thousand cafés and cabarets, chafing at a price that included taxes on production and the customs duties that were charged as the wine came through the city gates or was unloaded from barges on the Seine River. These taxes had been light when they were first applied, centuries earlier, but by the late 1700s they effectively tripled the price of wine. Moreover, a standard duty was levied on wine by the barrel regardless of quality or value, so in relation to price, inexpensive, low-quality wine was taxed more heavily than more expensive, better wine. In response, Parisians devised many subterfuges for smuggling wine into their city. In addition to the unimaginative ploy of hiding barrels of wine under other produce on wagons, they drilled holes through the thick city walls, lined them with wood, iron, lead, or leather, and poured wine through them from the outside into buckets inside the wall. The authorities regularly detected these channels, but as one was closed, another was drilled to replace it.

A legal way of avoiding customs duties was to drink at the *guinguettes* (bars serving wine and food) outside the city walls, where the wine was cheaper because it was not subject to the duties imposed at the city gates (see figure 4.2). Guinguettes, especially popular on Sundays, came into their own in the mid-1700s and were idealized by Étienne Chevalier, a vigneron who was a member of the first revolutionary legislature in 1789: "Wine is the basis of survival of the poor citizen of Paris. When bread, meat, and other foods are too expensive, he turns to wine; he nourishes and consoles himself with it. How many poor families go and eat at the guinguette in winter! There they find honest and inexpensive wine."[70] There was widespread dismay when, in 1784, the government announced plans to extend the perimeter of Paris's walls, which would bring the existing guinguettes into the taxed zone and raise the price of their wine. New guinguettes would spring up outside the new walls, of course, but they would be even farther away from the workers who lived in the center of Paris.

Construction of the new walls began in 1785, and by 1788 officials had discovered and closed eighty wine conduits drilled through them. Soon the people of Paris took firmer action: for four days beginning on 11 July 1789, they burned the customs barriers at the city gates where the detested duties on wine and other goods were levied and collected. This violence was not random or wanton but carefully directed at targets defined as oppressive. The burning of the customs booths preceded the storming of the Bastille on 14 July, and it is arguably the better candidate for the event marking the beginning of the French Revolution (1789–99).

The Revolution was an important phase in the history of French wine: the revolutionary governments oversaw a massive transfer of vineyard

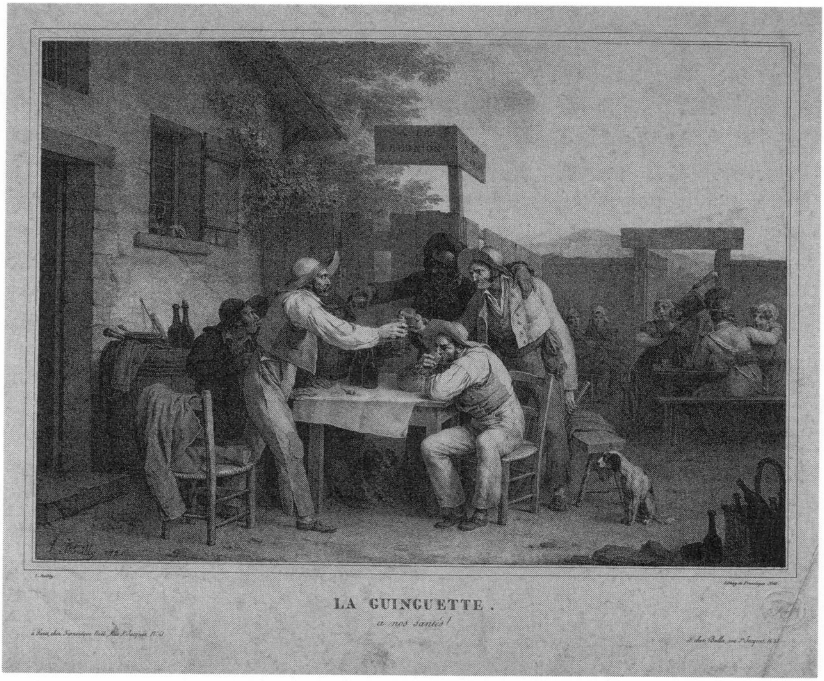

LA GUINGUETTE.
à nos santés!

FIGURE 4.2.   "À nos santés!" (To our health!) Men drinking wine at a guinguette. Lithograph by Francisque Noël after Louis-Léopold Boilly, 1826 (Wellcome Library no. 26926i). Courtesy of the Wellcome Library, London.

ownership, promoted quality, and encouraged consumption. As Noelle Plack has pointed out, wine was embedded in the revolutionary rhetoric of liberty and equality, and the common people came to regard a regular supply at reasonable prices as one measure of the success of the Revolution. At the core of the popular grievances against the ancien régime were the taxes levied on basic necessities, and the taxes on wine were often highlighted. It was all well and good for revolutionary politicians to talk about liberty and equality, but removing the taxes on wine represented liberty and equality in a material sense, liberty and equality that could be tasted.[71]

The grievance lists drawn up throughout France in 1789 show widespread detestation of taxes of all kinds, including those on wine. The inhabitants of Menetou, near Sancerre, complained that the tax on wine was "perhaps the most harmful to all people and the least profitable to the king," while another grievance list noted that it was even impossible for a charitable person to send a bottle of wine to the home of an "unfortunate" person without some zealous official trying to tax it. The burden of taxes on wine was said to lead to evasion and its consequences: "How many clandestine wineshops there are in the country! Often they are the refuge of that sort of people who, having lost their minds through drinking so much wine, are reduced to a level below animals ... from which follow assaults, violence, loss of health, changes in character, and scorn for decent people."[72] Farther west, near Nantes, residents of Saint-Philbert-de-Grand-Lieu complained about restrictions on planting vines and deriving the greatest financial benefit from their land.[73]

Yet although the Revolution fostered wine production, its early years were disappointing for French wine drinkers. The government badly needed the tax revenues from wine and other goods, and existing taxes remained temporarily in force. The new walls around Paris, with customs barriers at more than fifty gates, were completed in 1790. But there was constant pressure on the government to abolish these taxes, not only because they made wine and other necessities so expensive but also because they were seen as unfair. As the deputy Étienne Chevalier said, "It is deplorable that in a free nation, the poor should pay as much tax for their mediocre wines as the rich pay for their bottles of burgundy and champagne."[74]

In 1791, the revolutionary government abolished all indirect taxes, including those on wine. As soon as the policy went into effect, at midnight on 1 May, a convoy of hundreds of carts rolled into Paris carrying an estimated two million liters (half a million gallons) of wine. Patriotic Parisians partied all night with wine that sold at three sous a *pinte* (almost a liter, or about a quart). Huge volumes of brandy were sold off in the same way, and similar scenes played out throughout France. Wine remained far less expensive during the Revolution than it had been before, even though prices rose in the 1790s, largely because of poor harvests. And although the impoverished government reintroduced indirect taxes in 1798, they were on the order of 3 or 4 percent, far lower than at any time before the Revolution.

It is likely that the consumption of wine rose during the Revolution, not only because prices were lower but also because there was an increase in supply. Figures can be only estimates, but it seems that land under vines rose modestly from 1.58 million hectares (3.9 million acres) in 1788 to 1.68 million (4.15 million acres) in 1808, and annual wine production rose from 27.2 million hectoliters (719 million gallons) before the Revolution to an average of 36.8 million (972 million gallons) in the period 1805–12, an increase of a third in about twenty years.[75] If production so outpaced vineyard expansion, overall yields per hectare must have risen significantly—from seventeen to twenty-two hectoliters per hectare (182 to 235 gallons per acre), if these figures are right. As production rose much more rapidly than population and as exports dwindled during the Revolution, there must have been plenty of wine available for France's citizenry. Margaret Darrow notes that while the authorities in Montauban were concerned about shortages of bread and meat in 1793, "they rarely expressed any anxiety about wine shortages. Instead, their fears were exactly the opposite; it was an overabundance of cheap alcohol that occasioned disorder." In light of this, they limited the times and locations where wine could be served and forbade its sale to prostitutes, vagabonds, soldiers, and strangers.[76]

The expansion of viticulture during the decade of the French Revolution is difficult to gauge because many statistics compare 1789 with various dates in the early nineteenth century, and we have no clear sense of whether it happened more or less evenly during the whole period or was concentrated in the 1790s or afterward. On the other hand, the administrative districts known as départements were created early in the Revolution, and their administrations quickly became adept at collecting statistical information. In Aude, which became one of France's biggest wine-producing départements, cultivated land was estimated to have increased by a fifth between 1789 and 1800, and most was planted in vines. The inspector of forests wrote in 1802, "The only sector of agriculture which seems to have prospered is wine-growing; the area has considerably increased over the past ten years, and the consumption of local wines has replaced foreign imports." The new vineyards were planted on land cleared of garrigue, low-lying scrub that includes wild lavender, thyme, sage, and rosemary. As the historian Peter McPhee has written, during the Revolution, many of Languedoc-Roussillon's communities started on the road to becoming the wine villages of the nineteenth century, where inhabitants depended on wine for their survival.[77] This reliance on a single crop was attended with risks, as they discovered during the phylloxera crisis less than a century later.

Land under vines increased elsewhere in Languedoc-Roussillon too. An official reported in 1792 that much of the land left uncultivated around Narbonne before the Revolution had already been planted with vines. Later statistics show that Narbonne's vineyard area had grown from 10,111 hectares (24,985 acres) in 1788 to 15,790 (39,018 acres) in 1812, an increase of more than 50 percent.[78] Although the timing of the increase is not clear, the 1792 report suggests that it was well under way in the early 1790s. Information even less nuanced by period shows that in the département of Gard, the amount of land planted in vines rose from 51,151 hectares (126,397 acres) in 1788 to 71,583 (176,885 acres) in 1808, a 40 percent increase, and by 1800 wine was Gard's main product.[79] To the north and east of Corbières, most districts saw an increase in viticulture, and over the longer period from 1789 to 1829, the surface devoted to it increased by some 250 percent.[80] In other regions, however, expansion was much more modest. In Burgundy, for example, the area in vines rose about 16 percent in forty years, from 17,658 hectares (43,634 acres) in 1786–88 to 20,548 (50,775 acres) in 1826–28.[81]

Land under vines expanded during the 1790s partly because revolutionary reforms did away with many of the restrictions on the way that peasants used their land. Most communities had common lands, often forests or land difficult to cultivate but a shared resource where peasants could graze their livestock. A 1793 agrarian reform allowed the inhabitants of a community to divide the common land among themselves and to cultivate their new properties individually. Although only a small percentage of communities in southern France seem to have privatized their common lands in this way, those that did planted them with vines.[82] A great deal more land was simply appropriated by peasants in what McPhee calls "a viticultural revolution from below."[83] This was an important shift from the earlier part of the century, when the expansion of viticulture seems to have been driven more by better-off landowners, who could afford to buy land and plant vines.

The Revolution also did away with other constraints, such as the periodic royal and provincial bans on planting vines when this seemed to threaten the grain supply, and the myriad taxes peasants had to pay on their wine production. Before the Revolution, peasants throughout France were forbidden to own grape presses, so those who wished to make wine had to use their seigneur's and pay for the privilege with from 5 to as much as 30 percent of the wine produced. Using the seigneur's press was expensive, and he had priority in its use—enabling him to press his grapes at optimum ripeness and forcing peasants to press either early, when their grapes were not fully ripe, or late, when their grapes were overripe or rotten.

The Revolution thus not only opened the way for an expansion of viticulture and wine production but also witnessed a massive transfer of land ownership. In 1790, the French state assumed responsibility for the costs of running the church, and because the church therefore no longer needed the land that had provided most of its income, the state confiscated all church-owned land, including any owned by religious orders (which were abolished). These policies had a dramatic impact on viticulture because religious orders, cathedrals, and other church entities owned vineyards, often significant in area, throughout France. This was especially true in Burgundy, where the Abbey of Cîteaux alone owned more than two thousand hectares (five thousand acres) of land, most under vines and including the forty-five hectares (111 acres) of Clos de Vougeot. Later in the 1790s, property (including vineyards) owned by *émigrés* (opponents of the Revolution who left France to live abroad) was also confiscated and sold.

The confiscated land was sold to pay off the monarchy's debts, and the sales produced an unprecedented change of land ownership in a short period. Because the aim was to raise as much money as possible, land was sold by auction, which favored better-off citizens. In Beaune during February and March 1791, hundreds of vineyards belonging to the Abbey of Cîteaux, the Cathedral of Autun, the Collégiale of Beaune, and other church entities were auctioned, most in parcels of less than a hectare (2.5 acres).[84] Bourgeois and wealthy peasants bought the majority. On a single day in March 1795, at an auction in Burgundy, one man bought ten parcels of land planted with vines in Gevrey-Chambertin. The buyer, Jean Aubert, was described as a "cultivateur vigneron" living in Dijon. Clearly well-to-do, he paid a total of 6,625 livres for the vineyards in a district considered one of the best in Burgundy.[85] More impressive were the purchases of Jean Foccard, a Paris banker who in 1791 spent more than a million livres to buy the Clos de Vougeot and other vineyards in prestigious districts such as Vosne-Romanée, Richebourg, Chambolle-Musigny, and Morey-Saint-Denis. Another Paris financier paid more than a million livres for the Abbey of Cîteaux and its surrounding vineyards.[86] Any vineyards that vignerons of modest means were able to buy were small and of poor quality, despite attempts during the more radical phase of the Revolution to help poorer peasants acquire land to support themselves.

In addition to Clos de Vougeot, other prestigious vineyards went under the hammer. One was La Romanée, seized from the last prince of Conti and auctioned in July 1794. The catalog description suggests the awe in which its wine was held in this period, when it commanded five or six times the price of other distinguished wines from the Côte de Nuits. The vineyard is described as "famed for the excellent quality of its wine," with a location "the most advantageous for the perfect ripening of the grapes; higher to the west than to the east, it receives the first rays of the sun in all seasons, being thus imbued with the impetus of the greatest heat of the day." The wine was "the most excellent of all those of the Côte d'Or and even of all the vineyards of the French Republic," and "its brilliant and velvety color, its ardor, and its scent charm all the senses." If well kept, it was at its best in its eighth or tenth year, when "it is then a balm for the elderly, the feeble, and the disabled, and will restore life to the dying."[87]

This description was written during the most radical phase of the Revolution, which might explain why it presents the wine as a potential benefit to the elderly and disadvantaged rather than a luxury for the wealthy few. The vineyard's new owner, Nicolas Defer of Paris, was a military engineer who, ironically, was working on ways to pipe potable water to the capital. He died soon after buying La Romanée, and after the Revolution was over, the next owner added "Conti" to its name.

The fragmented ownership patterns of many of Burgundy's vineyards today can in part be traced to the Revolution. Not only was the confiscated land auctioned off in small parcels, but a 1793 law mandated equal inheritance among all children regardless of gender and age (a policy often incorrectly attributed to Napoleon), thus potentially subdividing family-owned land at each generation. Equal inheritance of this sort had been the rule in some parts of France before the Revolution. Remarking on "the smallness of the vineyards," Arthur Young wrote in 1789 that "the universal [sic] practice of dividing [land] between the children multiplies these little farms to such a degree, that a family depends upon a spot of land for support that cannot possibly yield it."[88] The Revolution generalized this practice, and it underlies the complicated ownership patterns of many of modern Burgundy's vineyards; many vineyards have several proprietors, each owning so many rows of vines.

Although Burgundy was especially important, these land sales took place throughout France, their significance depending on the extent of church-owned vineyards in the area. In 1791, Jean-Rémy Moët, the head of the champagne house founded in 1743 (whose family later joined with Pierre-Gabriel Chandon to form Moët et Chandon), bought 5.4 hectares (13.3 acres) of vineyards that had belonged to the Abbeys of Châlons and Épernay. They accounted for a quarter of his vineyards when he died in 1832.[89]

If political calculations partly underlay the new patterns of vineyard ownership in France—it was expected that people who gained land during the Revolution would support the Revolution—wine itself was a politically charged commodity, as one revolutionary print suggests. It depicts three figures, who represent the three estates of France—the clergy, the nobility, and the commoners—toasting the new regime with wine. But it is clearly not the same wine for each. The priest holds a glass with a round, bulblike bowl, appropriate for wine from Burgundy, where the church owned the most vineyards; the noble holds a flute, typically used for champagne, an expensive and aristocratic wine; and the commoner holds a goblet of the kind used for ordinary wine. If the Revolution temporarily brought different social groups together, they were still differentiated by wine, as much as by their clothing and their political beliefs.[90]

It was ordinary wine that flowed freely in revolutionary festivities or from revolutionary fountains of wine. *La Marseillaise,* the revolutionary marching song that became France's national anthem, was at times a drinking song, with its second line, "Le jour de gloire est arrivé" (The day of glory has arrived) rewritten as "Le jour de boire est arrivé" (The day of drinking has arrived). Most of the wine was red, and we can see in the common wine of the Revolution a precursor of pinard, the red wine that sustained French soldiers during World War I. Wine was the drink of choice in the hundreds of cafés and cabarets of Paris, and it lubricated formal and informal patriotic festivities of all kinds. In 1794, neighbors in a working-class district of Paris celebrated three marriages by making toasts in a wine-shop to the couples and to the Convention (the new revolutionary legislature) and by shouting, "Death to the tyrants! Long live Liberty and Equality!" A police observer noted that "in their wine they spoke with a religious respect for the Convention."[91]

Like powdered wigs and frock coats, luxury wines became regarded by more radical revolutionaries as symbolic of counterrevolution. In 1794, during the Terror, the government instructed local authorities to draw up inventories of the fine wines in the houses of individuals identified as enemies of the Revolution—those who had emigrated or been convicted of political crimes. "Liqueurs, foreign wines, and fine wines of all kinds" that "the desire for luxury of their former owners had brought together" were to be listed so that they might be "used advantageously in exchange for basic necessities."[92]

This did not mean that revolutionary governments wished to condemn the common people to a perpetual diet of poor wine. Works on viticulture and wine making continued to be published throughout the Revolution, and in 1795 (after the Terror) yet another Bordeaux classification was drawn up.[93] The revolutionaries chose "Vendémiaire," the time of the grape harvest, as the name of the first month of the republican calendar (used in France from 1793 to 1805) because it spanned the period from late September to late October of the Gregorian calendar. Prizes recognized achievements in viticulture. In 1799, eight of the ten awarded to vignerons in Savigny, in Burgundy, were given for achievements such as having "vines perfectly cultivated with no diseased plants and with an abundant crop" or being "an excellent grower, hard-working and choosing his vines well" or "a good grower and a good son, taking care of his very old father who was one of the best vignerons in Savigny."[94] Even Bacchus was recognized: a 1794–95 circular praised him as the god "who instructed his contemporaries in the arts of planting vines and harvesting."[95]

Equality did not mean that all wines were equal, and when price controls were placed on wine and other basic necessities, they took into account quality and reputation. In 1793 in the district of Beaune, top-quality reds from Volnay and Pommard were priced at 560 to 570 livres a *queue* (a barrel of 456 liters, or 120 gallons), while wines of Savigny were capped at 340 livres and those from Monthelie at 250 livres. The maximum prices for passe-tout-grains (a blend of gamay and pinot noir) and gamay, both considered inferior wines, were only 200 and 180 livres a queue, respectively.[96]

Ordinary wine of mediocre quality was the common currency of the Revolution, and successive governments ordered it in vast volumes for the armies and military hospitals during the wars that France waged from 1792. In that year, for example, the nuns of Sainte-Marthe in Orgelet, in the Jura département, were expelled from the hospital they ran, which was converted into a military hospital, whose patients were supplied with wine. In August 1794, seven carts were dispatched to bring eighty barrels of wine to the hospital from the cellar of an émigré. Even though an officer of health found sixteen of the barrels "full of bad wine and running the risk of spoiling," the hospital was well supplied for a time.[97] Demand for plenty of ordinary wine might well have encouraged vignerons to plant higher-cropping varieties. In Eure-et-Loir, pinot noir was widely planted in 1789, but by the early 1800s, not only had vineyard area increased by a quarter but pinot noir had been replaced by pinot meunier, "which produced a lot of mediocre wine."[98]

The French Revolution was generally a positive period for wine. Restrictions on planting were removed, and land under vines expanded; taxes were lowered, and the retail price of wine fell; quality was encouraged. There were, of course, winners and losers. Religious entities, like cathedrals and monasteries, lost their vineyards, but many more individuals were able to buy them; no vineyards were abandoned as a result of the confiscation of church lands. Wealthy émigrés and other enemies of the Revolution lost their cellars, but soldiers gained a wine ration. Most regions flourished, even if a few suffered: some of the vineyards near Nantes were in the battle zones of the Vendée uprising and civil war between 1793 and 1795, and damage to the vines and the requisitioning of local wine for the army interrupted their production. Yet as complicated a picture as this is, the Revolution and the decades that preceded it put in place some of the key conditions for the expansion of the French wine industry in the nineteenth century.

5. Stability and Growth

1800–1870

In his pioneering popular history of wine, Hugh Johnson bravely declares that "the Golden Age of wine-growing in Bordeaux and Burgundy in the 19th century is no fable."[1] The insistence that it was "no fable" suggests that Johnson anticipated objections to calling the period a "Golden Age"— as well he might, when we consider the adulteration, interregional blending, and misrepresentation of provenance that were widespread in Bordeaux and Burgundy at the time. But golden age or not, the period from the end of the French Revolution to the arrival of the deadly phylloxera vine aphid in the 1860s was transformative, and not only for Bordeaux and Burgundy. Champagne began to take on its modern form, a railroad network helped create a coherent national wine market in France for the first time, and the 1855 Bordeaux Classification formalized the idea of wine quality.

Land under vines in France increased substantially between 1789 and 1810–30 (the date depends on who kept the statistics), but we cannot say with any certainty whether the increase was steady over the whole period or concentrated in the Revolutionary decade (1789–99), the Napoleonic period (1799–1815), or the longer, post-Napoleonic era. Undoubtedly, the pace of planting varied from region to region. The Revolution removed many of the obstacles to viticulture and wine production, and although Napoleon's foreign policies made some international trade difficult, his government encouraged viticulture and promoted quality, while the following period did little to hinder wine production and fostered international trade.

There was a steady increase in the area under vines between 1800 and 1870, although the figures vary for the earlier parts of the period, when statistics were gathered less systematically. One source gives 1,674,489 hectares (4,137,752 acres) of vines throughout France in 1806 and 1,736,689 hectares (4,291,452 acres) in 1823, an increase of 4 percent,[2] while others suggest a slightly higher rate of increase. Around 1830, however, the number of hectares planted with vines throughout France began to exceed two million (five million acres), and by 1870, just as phylloxera was beginning to make an impact, France had 2,275,000 hectares (5,622,000 acres) of vineyards. The total area under vines peaked in 1874, at 2,465,000 hectares (6,091,000 acres)—three times France's viticultural area today. Some regions forged ahead more rapidly than others. Between 1808 and the 1870s, vineyard area almost tripled in the département of Hérault and almost doubled in the Rhône valley, but it increased by a more modest 40 percent in Bordeaux and 33 percent in Burgundy.[3]

National wine production also increased, as we would expect, rising from an annual average of 3.7 billion liters (980 million gallons) in the first decade of the 1800s to 5 billion (1.3 billion gallons) in the 1870s. Again, there were big regional variations. Hérault increased its production dramatically, from about 140 million liters (37 million gallons) in the early 1800s to 650 million (172 million gallons) in 1862 and nearly a billion (2.6 million gallons) by the 1870s, while Bordeaux's production rose more sedately, from 250 million to 300 million liters (66 million to 79 million gallons), and Burgundy's from 63 million to 88 million (17 million to 23 million gallons).[4] On a national basis, yields did not change much from 1800 to 1870—they ranged between twenty and twenty-two hectoliters per hectare (214 and 235 gallons per acre)—but there were marked variations by region. In Languedoc they rose from eighteen to twenty-eight hectoliters per hectare (192 to 299 gallons per acre), while in southwest France they declined and did not exceed twenty hectoliters per hectare over the whole period.

Following the example of the Revolution, Napoleon's government not only focused on quantity but also promoted the production of quality wine and encouraged the modernization of the industry. One of Napoleon's ministers was Jean-Antoine Chaptal, a chemist who was fascinated by viticulture and wine making and became an important commentator on both. He is best known for promoting the addition of sugar to grape juice before fermentation so as to raise its potential alcohol level; this is now commonly known as chaptalization, even though it was practiced long before Chaptal began to advocate it. Adding sugar was at the core of a booklet that Chaptal, as the minister of the interior, somewhat immodestly sent to all France's prefects (the representatives of the central government, one in each département) in 1801, urging them to distribute it to the vignerons in their jurisdiction. Titled *The Art of Making Wine, According to the Method of Chaptal,* the slim book was priced by the dozen for this purpose and was

written by Antoine-Alexis Cadet-de-Vaux, also a chemist, who summa-
rized what Chaptal had written (at much greater length) earlier that year in
his *Theory and Practice of Vine Cultivation*. Perhaps Chaptal had been
inspired to write this two-volume work by a sense that with the end of the
Revolution, political stability might usher in a period of growth and
improvement in France's wine industry. It was certainly more stable for
Chaptal himself: he had been arrested in 1793 after writing an ill-advised
political piece, and he spent the rest of the Revolution lying low in
Montpellier, among the vineyards of Languedoc. But he held a number of
high positions in Napoleon's governments and was eventually made a
noble. His name is one of the seventy-two inscribed in gold on the Eiffel
Tower to honor renowned French scientists and engineers.

Cadet-de-Vaux's book is an easy-to-read summary of best practices at
the beginning of the century—easy to read, but prevailing literacy rates
made it unlikely that more than a minority of vignerons would have been
able read it. Even so, its information would have circulated as vignerons
met to socialize and drink together and to discuss their work. The book is
significant not only for what it advocates but also for what it implies or
states explicitly about common wine-making techniques in France at the
beginning of the nineteenth century.

Although much of the advice might seem fairly conventional, we should
assume that Chaptal and Cadet-de-Vaux wanted it disseminated because it
was not general practice at the time. Cadet-de-Vaux wrote in his introduction addressed "to vignerons" that although making wine was one of the
first skills (*arts*) mastered by humans, "it is still in its infancy. . . . It is
scarcely a century since perceptible progress has been made in the famous
estates; in these vineyards where nature contributes a lot to the good quality of the wines, skill has a smaller role to play."[5] If that was so, then vignerons whose vineyards were in less favored locations needed to work that
much harder: "It is not nature that makes wine, it is skill; nature furnishes
the material, just as it provides stone for building, but it is the architect who
draws up the plans, it is the workers who construct the building."[6] In wine
making, nature provided the grapes, Chaptal was the architect, and vignerons were the workers.

Chaptal's basic message, channeled through Cadet-de-Vaux, was that
wine making could and should trump nature: "There are no years so bad,
there are no vineyards so mediocre, that one cannot, with the help of this
skill, make wine of good quality. Where nature does little, skill has a lot to
contribute."[7] This promise of being able to make good wine year after year,
no matter what the weather or the state of their vineyards, might have

sounded too good to be true, but it would have been music to the ears of the hundreds of thousands of small-scale vignerons who eked out a living in the face of poor terrain, mediocre grape varieties, and periodic weather disasters. Further into the book, Cadet-de-Vaux qualifies the role of the wine maker and his own ambition to make "very good" wine from his own mediocre vineyard near Paris: "This 'very good' is relative, because nature plays a big role in the quality of wine, and all the skill imaginable will not make a Volnay wine from a Surenne wine."[8] (The references are to Volnay in Burgundy and Surenne in the Paris region.)

Some of Cadet-de-Vaux's advice relates to safety. He spends four pages warning of "carbon gas" (carbon dioxide) poisoning during fermentation, which makes one wonder how many French vignerons died of asphyxiation each year. He recommends lighting a candle as a guide; if it goes out, the vigneron should open the doors and windows of the fermentation room or cellar and exit immediately. There is a page of instructions on how to deal with anyone who has lost consciousness because of carbon dioxide poisoning.

As for wine making, vignerons should harvest grapes that were fully ripe (unless they were intended for sparkling wine), separate out green or rotten grapes for making into their own wine (an indication that vignerons should waste no grapes), and destem the grapes if they wanted a more delicate or early-drinking wine. If it had rained during the harvest and the grapes held too much water, a vigneron could boil the must (grape juice) to concentrate it, but adding sugar or honey was preferable. Fermentation vats were to be washed with warm water and a lime solution, which would not only clean the vats but also reduce acidity in wines that were hard, bitter, and slow to mature. If fermentation was slow to begin, one or two buckets of boiling must stirred into the base must could accelerate it. The must should be tightly covered during fermentation. Contrary to modern methods of periodically stirring the fermenting must or punching down the floating skins to maximize contact between juice and skin, the advice here is not to touch the wine once fermentation began: "The cover in place, the vigneron respects his harvest, and does not disturb the fermentation. He closes the doors and windows of his winery, and reenters only to empty the vat."[9] (The result would have been lighter-colored, less-concentrated red wines.)

To highlight the good sense of following these procedures, Cadet-de-Vaux describes the wrong procedures, which he implies were common in "small vineyards": picking grapes before they were ripe; crushing ripe, green, and rotten grapes together; crushing too many grapes at a time so that some remained intact; failing to cover the must while it was fermenting; and stirring the fermenting must one or more times a day. The result would be part wine and part vinegar and would smell of balsamic and eau-de-vie. This was the wine making that had to be eliminated: "Where there is more education and more intelligence there is less prejudice and less resistance to learning. A man who learns does better than one who blindly follows a routine."[10] The bad wines that resulted from these practices were "what most vignerons make of a present that nature gives man to lighten his burden, strengthen him when he is ill, and sometimes help him forget the troubles of his life."[11] That was the point: most French vignerons, especially small-scale producers, were following outmoded practices that produced wine that was poor when it was not outright bad.

It remained only to consider the style of wine, and here Cadet-de-Vaux focuses on its *vinosité*, alcohol strength. "The more alcohol a wine has," he writes, "the better it is, the better it lasts, and the better it sells."[12] Not surprisingly, the recommended way to increase alcohol is to add sugar to the must before it ferments. It is not necessary to add sugar when the grapes have developed enough on their own, but adding some will produce "wines as robust as those of Burgundy, even those of Languedoc." Cadet-de-Vaux stresses that adding sugar simply compensates for what nature has provided in too small quantities: "The grape has ripened perfectly? The wines of your vineyard have good alcohol and last well? Don't add sugar. . . . If, in contrast, the worst year has given you a sour grape . . . add to the must four or five pounds of sugar per barrel, and you will get quality wine that will age well."[13]

Cadet-de-Vaux also offers advice about other additives, although he argues that sugar is not one, because it is naturally present in the grape. Fermented as recommended, wine should develop good color, which should not need deepening through the use of wild fruit such as elderberries, which was forbidden in any case. Similarly, adding alcohol afterward—fortifying the wine—was "a veritable fraud"[14] that was totally different from adding sugar so that the must would naturally increase its alcohol level. Yet surprisingly, Cadet-de-Vaux suggests that if the finished wine lacks the bouquet of similar-styled wines, a handful or two of dried peach or almond blossoms or elderberry flowers will rectify it.[15]

In his summary of Chaptal's method, Cadet-de-Vaux provides several accounts of making wine from his own "mediocre" vineyard in Franconville, northwest of Paris. He notes that his fermentation was much shorter than his neighboring vignerons' (only sixty-eight hours, in contrast to their ten to twelve days) and that by following Chaptal's recommendations he produced a wine that astonished the local inhabitants: "All refused to believe that this was a wine from our district."[16] Rather than sell it immediately, he decided to age it as long as a wine from Burgundy, and it was eventually priced at twenty francs more a barrel than other local wines, and half that price again outside the district. In blind tastings that included vignerons and négociants, Cadet-de-Vaux's white wines were judged superior to those of Burgundy. To this account of his own experience, Cadet-de-Vaux adds letters from vignerons, all praising the results they achieved by using Chaptal's method.

Cadet-de-Vaux's summary of Chaptal—which Chaptal endorsed—deals only with making wine and does not mention viticulture. Indeed, it implies, even states explicitly, that grape quality is unimportant, because wine making can override any shortcomings. But Chaptal deals with viticulture extensively in his book, which is an important guide to the state of vineyards in late eighteenth- and early nineteenth-century France. He was in no doubt that a guide to viticulture and wine making was needed and that French wine was in a parlous state: "How is it that a great number of wines of France, once renowned, have fallen into discredit? Why are these wines of such mediocre quality when other regions have gained or kept the reputation they have earned?"

His answer is that France's vignerons had blindly followed historic routines instead of looking after their vines properly, had planted varieties in unsuitable soil and climatic conditions, had selected high-yielding varieties rather than those that gave better wine, and did not know how to make wine.[17] He paints a depressing picture of the average small-scale vigneron: "These unfortunate vignerons . . . are the most overworked class in the most difficult part of agriculture, exhausted by fatigue by the time they reach forty years of age, and succumbing soon after, under the weight of a life of excessive labor."[18] Arguing for top-down change, Chaptal writes that these vignerons will not read his work and that it is to "well-off proprietors, to them alone, that is reserved the honor of this great restoration" of France's vineyards and wine, if only they will accept the challenge.[19] Small-scale vignerons could not read, but they could follow examples. The timing was good for a book like this, published in the midst of viticultural expansion.

Chaptal deals extensively and dispassionately with issues such as vine spacing, pruning, cultivation, and the economics of wine production, but he takes up some issues with fervency. One is the then common practice of interplanting grape varieties and harvesting and fermenting them together. Chaptal refers to these field blends as "monstrous mixtures of grapes of all species, all types, all varieties, such as you see in nearly all the vineyards in France—because there are only a few exceptions in the best vineyards of Champagne and Burgundy—and which leave the wine with no distinctive flavor. . . . They remove from the wine all its character while giving none to it."[20] Vignerons, he adds, should plant their vines in rows so as to clearly separate the varieties.

This was a serious indictment of the quality of not only the mass of French wine but also most of the country's prestigious wines. Although there is a grudging concession to Champagne and Burgundy, Bordeaux is implicitly lumped in with regions not noted for anything but poor wine. Chaptal's advice is to separate white and dark grape varieties in distinct parcels or vineyards, and although he concedes that some interplanting is acceptable, he cautions that a vigneron should avoid too many varieties. One or two of each color should be dominant, and any additional varieties planted to contribute particular character to the wine should be of the same quality and should ripen at the same time as the dominant varieties.

Chaptal is also adamant that grape varieties be carefully selected to suit the soil and climatic conditions, and he gives example of vignerons (with "more zeal than intelligence") who had planted Burgundy vines near Paris and Champagne vines in Lorraine in the expectation that their wines would rise to the quality of those of the originating regions. His advice is to buy vines locally and carefully: many sellers deliberately or unintentionally misrepresent grape varieties, and once a vine no longer carries fruit and has lost its leaves, the variety is difficult to verify. Chaptal does not join in the conventional denunciation of gamay, which, he writes, was planted in two-thirds of France's vineyards. He points out that although it was unsuited to Burgundy, it performed well in the Rhône valley, where it was planted along both sides of the river "because it produces abundantly and they make excellent wine from its juice."[21]

Although he clearly believed that Burgundy made better wine, Chaptal focuses particularly on Bordeaux: of the four Bordeaux estates widely considered preeminent (Haut-Brion, Margaux, Lafite, and Latour), he thought that Haut-Brion was the only one making wine that approached the quality of Burgundy's best. He valued the wines of the Graves district, followed by those from Bourg and Blaye, on the right bank of the Gironde estuary. Saint-Émilion produced wines with more power and aroma that those from Graves, and Entre-deux-Mers made wine of good quality from vineyards where white and dark grapes were interspersed. Among Bordeaux's white wines, Chaptal points out, wines from Barsac were much in demand by merchants, not (as we might think) because of their intrinsic quality but because they were "more suitable than any other to strengthen the light white wines with which they blend very well."[22]

Chaptal's assessment of the wines of various regions is careful and measured, and he ridicules the outrageous claims made for some. The wines of Burgundy were said to be healthier than any other, and the wine from Nuits, in particular, was reputed to be without equal as a medicine, such that no one could drink too much of it. It was prescribed by Louis XIV's physicians when he was ill in 1680. If that was an unfounded claim, so was the belief that drinking the wine of Joigny, in the Yonne region, would produce male children. Chaptal scoffs at the assertion that proof lay in the local population, where there were half as many boys again as girls.

He also broaches the topic of *goût de terroir*, a concept that has bedevilled wine writers. The question is whether the flavors and textures of a particular wine reflect the place where its grapes grew—some modern writers argue, for example, that "minerality" derives from underlying limestone. Chaptal was in no doubt that this sort of transfer from soil to wine takes place, but he makes a distinction between *goût naturel* and *goût artificiel*. The former results from the dissolution or evaporation of minerals and metals in the soil of certain vineyards and is expressed in the wine as aromas and flavors such as flint, truffles, violets, and raspberries, all positive attributes. Artificial goût de terroir, on the other hand, comes from external sources, including the odor of improperly prepared fertilizer, human excrement (this is not explained), and smoke. Chaptal notes that in Beaune, burning leaves or straw was forbidden during the two weeks before harvest so that the odor of smoke would not contaminate the delicate aromas and flavors of the local wine.[23]

Chaptal's work was designed to improve the quality of French wine, but it is unlikely to have resulted in much, or any, change in the practices in the great majority of France's vineyards and wineries. Quality might well have improved on some estates where proprietors could afford to replant and restructure vineyards and adopt different practices in the winery, such as keeping barrels clean. But the expense of innovations put them out of the reach of most of the million and more small-scale vignerons, who, even if they did undertake them, could not pass the additional costs on to their customers. There was, quite simply, a robust and reliable market for the kinds of wine that Chaptal deplored, and there is certainly no evidence of consumer dissatisfaction with the quality of the wine that was widely available. Napoleon's government also required volumes of ordinary wine for state purposes, notably for a daily quarter-liter (quarter-quart) wine ration (with occasional servings of brandy) for the soldiers of the imperial army.

The Napoleonic Wars ended in 1815, and the years on either side were cool, with the first full year of peace bringing disastrous grape, cereal, and other harvests to France. In what became known as the Year without a Summer, temperatures during the 1816 growing season dropped well below normal, harvests failed, and there was widespread famine. In Pauillac, in Bordeaux, the 1816 harvest began on 28 October, the latest of the whole nineteenth century. As grapes failed to ripen fully, some vignerons tested Chaptal's dictum that good wine could be made in any climatic conditions. At Latour the wine maker added five or six pounds of sugar to each 225-liter (60-gallon) barrel, but the result was not what he wanted, and he later wondered if fifteen or twenty pounds might have been better. He noted that he had come to believe "that when nature refuses to give the raw material for quality wine, skill can do little to make up for it; it only ever achieves mediocrity."[24]

Despite such setbacks, the planting of vineyards continued, especially in Languedoc, but there was some contraction in the north and around Paris. By 1830, France had about two million hectares (five million acres) of vineyards, by far the largest area in Europe devoted to viticulture. (By comparison, Austria had 625,000 hectares, or 1.5 million acres, Hungary 550,000, or 1.4 million, Italy 430,000, or 1 million, and Spain 400,000, or 990,000.) Production in France was in the range of 3.5 to 4 billion liters (925 million to 1 billion gallons) per year, giving an average yield of only twenty hectoliters per hectare (214 gallons per acre), low by modern standards, even for high-quality wine, but all that could be coaxed from the vines given that many were planted in marginal conditions. There was no incentive to increase yields, because prices remained low. Between 1820 and 1850, the price of wine paid to producers fell by a quarter compared to 1800–1820, even though consumer prices rose because of the taxes applied to wine.

Exports rose after the Napoleonic period, and by 1828 France was shipping 120 million liters (32 million gallons) of wine a year, the most important markets (each taking more than ten million liters, or 2.5 million gallons) being Sweden and Norway, Germany, Switzerland, and Mexico. Most of this was mediocre wine. The better wine, only a small percentage of which was exported in bottles, made up only sixty-five thousand liters (seventeen thousand gallons) of the 120 million, and a third of it went to England or to the English colonies in India.[25]

The notion of a golden age of anything suggests that it reached a peak in qualitative terms, and to speak of French wines in this way implies that they achieved levels of quality that were not only unprecedented but also not matched since. Quite clearly, it is a problematic term. It obviously does not refer to the broad and deep rivers of inexpensive wine that flowed from Languedoc-Roussillon to the cities of northern France, nor to the wine produced in the extensive vineyards around Paris; rather, as Hugh Johnson uses the phrase, it refers mainly to the wines produced by the small and

ACTUALITES.

NOUVELLES VINICOLES.
Le vin est très faible .... dans les collèges !.....la comète n'y a pas encore fait sentir son influence.

FIGURE 5.1. "Nouvelles vinicoles: Le vin est très faible . . . dans les collèges! . . . la comête n'y a pas encore fait sentir son influence." (Vinicultural news: The wine is very weak . . . in the schools! . . . the comet has not yet made its influence felt.) Ordinary French wine was thin and low in alcohol, but comets were believed to produce excellent vintages (called "Comet Vintages") the year they appeared. The reference here is to 1858's Donati's comet, one of the most brilliant of the nineteenth century. *Le Charivari*, 1858. (In the author's possession).

prestigious estates of Bordeaux, Burgundy, Champagne, and perhaps a handful of other districts. Even so, it is difficult to gauge the quality of these wines at the time. The small number of people able to afford them might have praised them to the skies—particularly in years when comets appeared (see figure 5.1)—but what does that tell us about their quality?

One way of explaining the sense that some French wines of this period were superior to those that preceded them and those that followed is to note that the middle decades of the nineteenth century were relatively calm for the French wine industry. France was at peace for more than half a century between the end of the Napoleonic Wars in 1815 and the Franco-Prussian War of 1870–71. While it had brief phases of political turmoil in 1830 and 1848, its economy grew steadily in this period, and the wealthier strata of the middle classes, an important market for premium wines, expanded apace. Industrialization and the growth of the state throughout much of Europe and North America increased the size of the better-off and wealthy middle classes there too and thus broadened and deepened the potential markets for the exports of high-quality wine, which was an important marker of social status.

Bordeaux exported its prestigious wines to England and northern Europe again and now also to the United States. Exports were largely to merchants rather than individual clients, and the wine was shipped in barrels and bottled at its destination. A little was sent already bottled, but labels were rare; the bottles went in numbered wood cases, with a manifest indicating the provenance of the wine in each case. It was partly due to the predominance of shipping in bulk, which continued well into the 1900s, that falsification was so widespread. Bulk wines went through the hands of merchants who were often tempted to "improve" a wine or adjust it to the known preferences of a client by adding a little (or more) of a different wine. We should note that although we may refer to these practices as "falsification" or "fraud," they were not seen as extraordinary at the time, when there was a much more relaxed view of place of origin. The English wine commentator Cyrus Redding noted quite matter-of-factly in 1851 that Bordeaux exports exceeded production by about a third: "This is drawn by the merchants from Spain, and from other departments of France, such as the Lot, Lot and Garonne, Haute Garonne, and others, and is mingled with the genuine wines of the Bordelais for the foreign market."[26]

As French wine production rose during the mid-1800s, wine regions in the New World began to make their presence known. Vineyards were planted in California after the gold rush subsided, and when the transcontinental railroad was built in the 1860s, California wines were shipped to the large urban markets in the east. The Australian wine industry also began to take off, as did Chile's. Individual New World wines, many of them fortified and made in styles similar to sherry and port, began to interest British and other European consumers. Constantia, a sweet wine made near Cape Town from chenin blanc grapes, became popular as an alternative to the sweet wines of Sauternes.

But these were the early days of New World wines, and French commentators gave no hint that they might in any way rival the quality and established supremacy of French wines. One French writer who surveyed the world of wine slightly later in the century sniffed that Australia produced wines "burdened with the most pretentious names and generally of very mediocre quality."[27] He might have been thinking of the Tahbilk winery in Victoria, which had changed its name to Château Tahbilk in 1878. As for the burgeoning American wine industry, the same writer noted that the wine making there "leaves much to be desired" despite serious attempts to improve it. He acknowledged that some white wines from Ohio and some sweet fortified wines from California "are not without some good qualities and even an agreeable bouquet,"[28] but he wrote off American wine as largely of poor quality.

If some French writers commented on the wines of other countries, many French and non-French writers had a lot to say about French wine in the early and middle decades of the nineteenth century. The very fact that so many books on French wine were published in the 1840s and 1850s speaks to widening awareness of its quality. These books went through numerous editions, suggesting a demand for information among wine consumers, even if only a small percentage of them. They were not always unqualified in their praise of French wine, but the very fact that they gave it so much attention attests to its standing at the time.

Two writers set the new tone and standard of wine writing: Redding, an English journalist, and André Jullien, a French wine merchant. In 1816, Jullien published a wide-ranging book, *A Description of All the Known Wine Regions*, that deals mainly with the wine regions of France but also Europe more generally and other parts of the world. Jullien's breadth was astonishing, and he provided information designed to assist wine drinkers to develop their cellars and help producers to make their wines.

In 1833, the English equivalent of Jullien's work, Redding's *A History and Description of Modern Wines*, was first published. This too is a global survey of wines, but Redding also devotes chapters to practical matters such as conservation and adulteration. According to him, adulteration and deception were widespread among the wines imported to England. This applied particularly to fortified wines, whose alcohol strength could mask adulteration and deceive even very experienced tastes, but also to top-quality table wines. Yet Redding thought that wine connoisseurs would quickly see through counterfeits: "Any attempt to fabricate Romanée-Conti would not thus easily answer, because the fineness, delicacy, and perfume of this wine are not to be copied." It was an optimistic view, based on the assumptions that anyone who bought a fake Romanée-Conti had tasted the genuine article before and could therefore tell the difference and that the cultivated palates of the mid-nineteenth century were particularly keen.

Redding blamed the English for the extent of fraud among French and other foreign wines: they so much preferred spirits and fortified wines to "pure" wines, he wrote, that their palates were dulled to the point where they could hardly tell genuine wine from the fraudulent beverages they were sold. "The cuticle on the hand of a blacksmith is hardened by the hot iron, and cannot distinguish objects by the sense of feeling; in the same manner the stomach of the spirit drinker is lost to the healthy freshness of wine, being too cold and unseasoned for his seared stomach, while adulterations or coarse mixtures of the grape remain undiscovered." Even so, English drinkers might have drunk French wine because they believed it was good for them. In a series of articles published in a medical journal in the 1860s and then in a best-selling book, the English physician Robert Druitt argued for the particular health benefits of French wine. Much more than wine from Spain or Portugal, he wrote, French wines (especially from Bordeaux or Burgundy) were ideal for children, the old, the sick, and anyone who needed to use their brain.[29]

The growth of consumer-centred wine writing signaled a more sophisticated and educated approach to wine drinking among the European middle and upper classes. Guides such as Jullien's and Redding's were not written for peasants and urban workers. These large social groups might have consumed vast volumes of wine, but they bought at the inexpensive end of the price spectrum and invariably only enough for their immediate requirements. They no more had cellars full of aging wine than they had savings accounts or pension plans.

Many guides focused on the quality wines of France, not the common wine produced throughout the country by small-scale vignerons for local consumption. This was largely anonymous wine, of varying quality, sold in bulk, and drunk as part of the working-class diet. Most of it has escaped the historical record. In contrast, the names of wines from prestigious regions and estates were becoming well known to well-off wine consumers. By the early 1800s, three of France's regions had consolidated their reputations as producers of excellent wine. Champagne had given its name to a distinctive style of wine that was becoming associated with celebrations and luxury. Burgundy had gained a reputation for fine wines, particularly red, but it was still largely in the shadow of Bordeaux, which could trace its reputation back much further, to the exports of wine to England in the Middle Ages. Over time, the wine producers of Bordeaux carefully managed their reputation and image and strategically developed markets in France, in Europe, and in the wider world. The popularity of fine clarets among better-off English consumers, whose manners and behavior were widely admired, helped to develop markets in places as diverse as Germany and the United States.

There was, in the nineteenth century, the same fixation on Bordeaux as persists today, when each vintage is pored over and evaluated, commune by commune, château by château. Many books discussed the merits of the grape varieties that went into clairet, but unlike today, when only six varieties are permitted (and of those, one is not used and two are little used in blends), nineteenth-century producers drew on a wider range. In the 1853 edition of his judicious and balanced book on Médoc, William Franck describes wine made from cabernet (he does not distinguish between sauvignon and franc) as fine, agreeable, and with a rich bouquet but not deep in color, and wine made from carmenère as similar but with more color. These were the only varieties planted in some "privileged" vineyards, he notes. Wine made from malbec was very ripe, had good color but not much body, and soon went bitter if not kept in a cool cellar. Franck lists petit verdot yet has nothing to say about the wine, but he thought that wine from gros verdot was very delicate, with beautiful color and a rich bouquet, and lasted well when the grapes ripened completely (which he says is rare). He notes that cabernet, carmenère, malbec, and gros verdot made the best wine in Médoc: "blended with wise intelligence, the product is among the most distinguished wines." As for merlot, now a permitted variety but grown primarily in appellations across the river from Médoc, Franck thought it was less delicate than malbec but made good wine when blended with verdot or cabernet.

Other varieties grown in Médoc in the nineteenth century were mancin/ sumansingue, which made "a lot of inferior wine"; teinturier/alicante, which had deep color and was blended to give color but had to be used sparingly, lest it pass on its "disagreeable" flavor; pelouville/pelouye, which made common, pale wine; petite-chalosse noire, hung to dry out after the harvest, for making a dessert wine the following spring; cruchinet, which made a common wine that kept well; cioutat; pied de perdrix, which made very ordinary wine; and balouzat, which produced mediocre wine, with good body, deep color, and a distinctive flavor that was not absolutely disagreeable.[30]

Franck also classifies the estates in Médoc, in what he calls "the most delicate part of my work."[31] He is at pains to point out that a ranking should not be regarded as definitive: vintage is always important, and there are times when wines not included in classifications are better than those that do appear. With that in mind, he lists five categories by cru and includes the usual four estates in his premier cru: Margaux, Lafite, Latour, and Haut-Brion.

As we have seen, the 1855 Bordeaux Classification was not the first, and in fact, by 1855 the division of Médoc's wines into five categories of cru— what became known as "growths" in English—was standard. Since the seventeenth century, minimum and maximum wine prices in Bordeaux's various districts had been set annually in light of supply, demand, and quality. They were not arrived at arbitrarily but were based on the prices suggested by vignerons at an assembly after the harvest. Buyers then negotiated with producers to determine the precise price they would pay within the parameters established for the region. Between the 1600s and the mid-1800s there were dozens of classifications, some from official bodies, others from individual commentators.

Dewey Markham Jr. has collected these classifications in one place where they can be compared easily,[32] and what is striking is the similarity among so many of them, especially when it comes to identifying the top tier—the small group that was soon referred to as premier cru, or First Growth wines. The reason is largely that the rankings were based on the prices of the wines from specific districts, and later from specific estates or châteaux, and the relative prices (unlike the actual prices) changed little over time. Margaux, Latour, Lafite, and Haut-Brion are listed as the only premiers crus in various classifications of 1815, 1816, 1829, 1832, 1833, 1834, 1842, 1851, and other years. Prior rankings might well have influenced each classifier, and it certainly would have taken courage to modify the top tier once it had consistently included the same four properties for many years. But this consistency also reflects the consistency in the pricing structure in which these properties fetched the highest prices.

That is the important point about many of these classifications: they were not intended to be direct and explicit guides to quality, except insofar as it could be argued that discerning consumers judged with their wallets and were willing to pay more for wines of higher quality than for wines of lesser quality. To this extent, and as long as one knew the rules, it was easy enough to draw up a classification if the prices in a given year were known. Anyone who bought these wines because of their ranking in the classification thus relied on the wisdom—or foolishness—of the existing and earlier markets.

Other classifications were based on impressions of quality. Franck, a wine merchant who drew up a classification in 1824, introduced his list with the observation that "we have drawn up, and submit to enlightened judges, the attempt at classification that you can read below." The suggestion is that he is presenting a classification based on quality rather than derived mechanistically from prices and that others might disagree with it. He identifies the usual four estates as First Growths, noting that the wines of this quartet fetched between 1,800 and 2,400 francs a barrel, sometimes going as high as 3,500 francs, and he establishes a base of 2,400 francs for First Growth wines. Second Growth wines sold for about three hundred francs less and Third Growths for three hundred less again.[33] Franck presents the price information descriptively, not prescriptively, in the sense that price determines rank but the relationship of price to perceived quality is clear. No expensive wine is found among the Fourth Growths, no relatively inexpensive wine among the Firsts or Seconds.

To say that the many classifications were based on price is not to say that there was no change over time. There were shifts in ranking within the growths and also some movements between growths, although few affected the First Growth wines, as they were the key to the whole pricing structure. Cos-d'Esternel was often listed as a Fourth Growth in the 1700s, but in the early 1800s its owner Louis-Joseph-Gaspard d'Estournel worked to improve the quality and reputation of his wine so as to raise its value on the market. It eventually achieved Second Growth status. The best-known promotion is that of Château Mouton Rothschild from the top of the Second Growths to a coveted First Growth as recently as 1973, but the process began in the 1850s. In 1851 the manager of the property (then called Brane-Mouton) acknowledged that "if Lafite sells for a given price, Mouton is worth a given proportion." But between 1851 and 1853 the owners began to ask for and receive higher and higher prices, which narrowed, then closed the gap with Lafite. In 1853, when Baron Nathaniel de Rothschild bought the Mouton property, the opening price of the wine—five thousand francs—was the same as Lafite's. The correspondence of rank and price was broken.[34]

There are more differences among the classifications when it comes to the Third, Fourth, and Fifth Growths—although some schemes comprise only Four Growths, and classifications vary in the number of properties they deem worthy of listing. Beaucaillou is a Second Growth in one, a Third Growth in another; La Tour-Carnet and Langoa-Barton are variously Third or Fourth Growths; Calon Ségur is relegated to Fourth from Third. There is no clear pattern and no complete consensus on the allocation of estates to growths or the ordering of estates within growths, but it must be said that these many classifications have more commonalities than differences. The disagreements involve a minority of estates and relatively narrow ranges of ranking.[35]

But however the various classifications were constructed, they were designed not as consumer guides to quality per se but as aids to help the wine trade set prices. Once the prices of the top-tier wines were established, those below them fell into place. If First Growths were priced at 2,400 francs, the top Second Growths were at 2,100 and the rest at 1,900 to 2,000; the top Third Growths would be at 1,700 to 1,900 francs, and so on. The actual prices varied by vintage. In 1816, which produced terrible quality, First Growths sold for 500 francs, Second for 450, Third for 400, and Fourth and Fifth for 380 and up.[36] The classifications, in short, were designed primarily as guides to prices and only indirectly reflected the quality of the wines produced by the listed estates. Merchants in the high end of the Bordeaux wine trade employed them, and they carried over to the 1855 classification.

The Bordeaux Classification of 1855, then, was not generated solely from assessments that year but was simply another iteration of a schema that had existed for decades. It stands out from earlier and later classifications not because it is so different from them but simply because it became the best known and the point of reference for quality Bordeaux wine ever since. This particular classification emerged when France's départements were requested to come up with exhibits for the 1855 Universal Exposition in Paris, which was designed to show the world the variety and quality of the nation's industrial, agricultural, and cultural products. A committee in each département decided what it might highlight. In its first six meetings in 1854, the committee of Bordeaux's Gironde département focused on industries, such as shipbuilding and rope making, and the arts. Wine was not mentioned once.[37] Perhaps its composition explains the bias: the ten members included Bordeaux's mayor, a shipbuilder, a cabinetmaker, and professors of physics and design; only one, a merchant, had any connection to wine. That Bordeaux's famous wine might be a fit product to represent Gironde at the exhibition seems to have occurred to them only when the committee was contacted by its counterpart in the département of Côte-d'Or, asking if Bordeaux wanted to participate with Burgundy and Champagne in a joint display of quality wines—and that was six months after they had started discussions and only twelve months before the exhibition was due to open.

When polled, Bordeaux's wine producers were enthusiastic about the idea of showing their wine in Paris, and the matter was referred to the Bordeaux chamber of commerce, made up of wine merchants, which set up a four-man committee. It was headed by the chamber's president, Lodi-Martin Duffour-Dubergier, the owner of the Smith-Haut-Laffite estate in Graves and Gironville in Médoc. Although apparently modest about his own wines, he was a booster of Bordeaux's: "For me, the touchstone of civilization is the wine of Bordeaux!"[38] But the chamber of commerce was afraid of having wines chosen for display by competition, in case the judges arrived at a ranking that differed from that of the classification used by Bordeaux's wine merchants—in which, as we have seen, rank correlates with price. It would be difficult if wine judges in Paris rated less expensive wines higher than expensive ones. Of the exposition's wine judges, the committee asked, "Who imagines that their opinion regarding a wine is authoritative? . . . Mistakes are regrettable . . . but how much more harmful would the consequences be were they to come from a jury called to deliver its verdict before the whole world?"

To avoid a quality-based ranking decided by tasting, the Bordeaux committee argued that the display should include bottles from each commune in the département but the label should show only the name of the commune and perhaps the vintage, not the name of the property or producer. The committee's justification was that, while vignerons worked hard in the vineyard and winery, "it is nature alone" that makes the wine. "Thus, what right has the proprietor to a reward, an honor? None, we think." A different rule would apply to the classified wines, which could show the names of the estate and commune but not the name of the proprietor, "in order to avoid any individual competition and all conflicts of self-esteem."[39] What sounds like a less than visually captivating display of bottles of wine, their labels conveying little useful information, was to be accompanied by a chart of the classification, along with the price of each wine and the growing conditions. As a final note, the board proposed that once the exposition was over, the bottles of wine be donated to the General Hospital of Paris, where, presumably, patients could accelerate their recovery by drinking some of the world's finest wines. The Gironde committee accepted these proposals and stressed that the display should be a collective representation of Bordeaux's vinous richness and should avoid disturbing the order of quality that had been established as the basis of the region's wine trade.

In early 1855, the chamber of commerce invited the mayor of each of Bordeaux's more than four hundred communes to put together a case of six bottles "from good years . . . [and] capable of giving the most favorable and exact impression of your commune's production." They were not to have labels; the chamber would apply a standard label that highlighted the name of the chamber of commerce and showed the identity of the commune. In reality, the communes could have sent six bottles of any mediocre wine, and no one—the chamber of commerce or spectators at the exposition—would have been any the wiser. Only a connoisseur who was a patient in the General Hospital might later have noticed. The chamber also wrote to the owners of sixty to seventy estates whose names appeared on most of the classifications, inviting them to send six bottles of their wine—also unlabeled, but in these cases the chamber would add the name of the estate to the label. The chamber of commerce made arrangements to receive as many as three thousand bottles of wine, but in the end, even after a deadline extension, only a quarter of the communes and half of the classified estates responded. Fewer than seven hundred bottles were available for the exposition.

At this point there was still no 1855 classification, and there never would have been one had the organizers of the Paris Exposition not decided to prepare a map of the Bordeaux vineyards indicating the location of the classified growths. To do that, they needed a definitive list, which they asked the chamber of commerce to put together. This it did in just two weeks—a period that suggests some consultation but not long enough for an exhaustive investigation that included tastings. The list drew on existing classifications and differs only in detail from those of the previous decade. It includes sixty-eight estates, with fifty-seven red wines divided into five growths, and twenty-one white wines divided into a "Superior First Growth" (Yquem, in Sauternes), First Growths, and Second Growths.

The 1855 classification—which has provided the parameters for discussing, judging, tasting, and buying wines from these districts ever since—thus is largely derivative, was hurriedly constructed, and reflected not quality but current selling prices. The traders noted that First Growth wines sold for 3,000 francs, Second for 2,500 to 2,700, Third for 2,100 to 2,400, Fourth for 1,800 to 2,100, and Fifth for 1,400 to 1,600. This scale implies a ranking of quality: the well-off men of discernment who could afford such wines were trustworthy arbiters of taste in the mid-nineteenth century, and what they were willing to pay expressed the relative quality of wines.

As for the exposition, it provided little but grief for the organizers of Bordeaux's wine presentation. They had wanted not to mention owners' names, explicitly so as to avoid competition and jealousy but probably more to prevent buyers going directly to the owners and bypassing the agents. But the owner of the Lafite estate asked to use the estate's own labels on the bottles to be displayed. When the chamber of commerce rejected his request, he appealed directly to the head of the Imperial Commission for the Exposition, Jérôme Napoleon (the brother of Emperor Louis Napoleon), who agreed that the wines from classified growths ought to bear their own labels and show the name of the owner. This was just what the chamber of commerce did not want, as it wished to minimize the importance of the estates and maximize the role of the merchants. But it had to follow the instructions of Jérôme Napoleon.

This dispute highlighted the tension between producers and agents. Until the late 1800s, wines even in highly reputed Bordeaux districts were identified as much by the agent as by the producer—just as wines in Burgundy were known by négociants' names, and most producers in Champagne sold their wines to the big houses. In Bordeaux, producers would sell to more than one agent, and each merchant would manipulate the wine according to the preferences of his clients.

It was also common for wines to be "improved" by wines from outside regions. Syrah was often added to the red wines of Bordeaux, a practice known as hermitaging because the syrah variety was known at the time as hermitage, after the Hermitage district in the northern Rhône valley, where it was (and is) notably grown. Other French reds were given more body by the addition of wine made from the bobal variety in Valencia, Spain. Much of the prestigious wine that ostensibly came from Bordeaux was, then, the work of agents rather than wine makers, and many of these wines were multiregional blends. One agent advised his son, "One thing that must not be lost sight of in making up the wines is that they will come into competition with those of other houses. We must not depend on our name, but on the superior quality of our wine." As Markham notes, "The reference to 'our wine' was entirely accurate."[40]

The wines in the 1855 Bordeaux Classification were only a few of the highly reputed wines of France in the mid-1800s, but quality wines of this sort represented a very small percentage of French wines. Most, by far, were made from relatively high-cropping varieties and were inexpensive and mediocre. Most came from Languedoc-Roussillon, which in the 1850s produced half of the country's wine, and the building of the railroad network in the 1840s and 1850s gave production there a boost. By 1860, all the major wine towns in Languedoc-Roussillon were linked by rail to the million inhabitants of Paris, France's most important wine market, and to the other urban markets of northern France. The advent of the railroad made transporting wine more rapid (which was important to minimize spoilage), eventually less expensive, and often less complicated than it was on other transportation routes, which involved both land and water segments.

Time and convenience were important, but transportation cost was critical to the price of wine at its destination market, and in 1858 an agreement between the government and the largest railroad companies reduced the cost of transporting wine to a fraction of what it had been. The cost to send a seven-hundred-liter (185-gallon) barrel of wine from Montpellier to the important Lyon market was slashed from fifty to seven francs. Within a few decades the railroad companies constructed tanker-cars to carry wine in bulk in massive wooden barrels that held sixteen thousand liters (4,227 gallons), and later twenty thousand and thirty thousand (5,283 and 7,925 gallons). But in the early years of the railroad, wine was carried on rails as it had been for centuries on barges, carts, and ships: in the barrels of varying sizes that it had finished fermenting and been stored in. When wine from the provinces arrived in Paris, it was stored in massive purpose-built warehouses in Bercy, now a suburb of the capital. This depot covered 140,000 square meters (1.5 million square feet) and comprised fourteen galleries that could hold two hundred thousand barrels at a time.

Railroads did not immediately replace water as the principal medium of transportation; although shipping by train was faster and more efficient, it was not initially less expensive than waterborne shipping. During the nineteenth century, France's extensive system of canals expanded fourfold, and to that must be added its thousands of kilometers of navigable rivers. The coastal traffic was also significant, and wine was shipped from the south of France, notably through Sète, to ports on the Atlantic coast and even up the Seine River as far as Rouen, where it could be loaded on barges for transportation to Paris. Needless to say, when Algerian wine became an important component of France's wine production, beginning in the 1880s, it was shipped across the Mediterranean. The railroads, then, were an integral part of a wider network of transportation routes although they provided a more direct route to the important northern destinations. They mostly radiated from Paris to the provinces, reflecting the centralized administrative structure of France, while most canals and rivers tended to link provincial centers and markets.

Not only did wine flow more freely throughout France during the nineteenth century, but the steady increase in supply and the stagnation of France's population growth meant there was often an oversupply that led to lower prices, until the shortages that accompanied the phylloxera crisis pushed prices up again. The relationship of supply and demand was one thing, but taxation also came into play, because wine was again subject to higher taxes from 1816 onward. Before the French Revolution, taxes and duties of various kinds—taxes on production, duties levied as wine crossed internal provincial borders and as it was brought through town and city gates—hindered trade and consumption. These levies, which were built into the retail price of wine, were suppressed by 1791, and although a wine tax was reimposed in 1798, it was far lower than those levied before the Revolution. In 1816, however, the new royal government placed new taxes on wine, and they rose in the following decades. By the 1840s, producers were complaining that the taxes were greater than the cost of their wine. In 1843 a vigneron from Roanne noted that he was unable to sell wine to his Paris customers who were "middling or lower in wealth" when it was valued at ten francs for one hundred liters (twenty-six gallons) but the tax was more than twice that, twenty-three francs.[41]

The railroads benefited Languedoc-Roussillon from the point of view of sales and Paris from the perspective of consumption, but all of France's wine regions gained from the creation of a national market for wine during the nineteenth century. For the most part, however, this national market consisted of wine producers selling their wines in Paris and other northern cities; there was relatively little trade in wine among regions where wine production was significant. Then as now, it was far easier to buy wines from Burgundy in Dijon, wines from Bordeaux in the city of Bordeaux, and wines from the Loire valley in Nantes than to purchase wines from other French regions in these places. But the urban markets of the north and northeast—regions where viticulture was often marginal—were open to wines from all of France, and vineyards in some of the northern regions began to decline in the face of competition. In the 1870s and 1880s, phylloxera all but destroyed the nearby vineyards that had supplied Paris with inexpensive wine for centuries (see the following chapter), but they had begun to contract in the decades before, under the impact of wines arriving from the south. The département of Seine-et-Oise had 734,000 hectares (1.81 million acres) of vines in 1852 but only 434,000 (1.07 million acres) in 1862, a loss of 40 percent in a decade. By the 1870s it was down to 201,000 hectares (497,000 acres). The winners from the advent of the railroad were the producers of high-volume, inexpensive wines in the south of France, which overwhelmed the historic suppliers of the Paris and other urban markets, and the producers of higher-quality wines that now reached the better-off consumers in these markets more efficiently.

As demand for wine from the south grew, the four most important southern wine-producing départements saw their vineyard areas expand steadily, from 294,000 hectares (726,000 acres) in 1852 to 393,000 (971,000 acres) in 1862, an increase of a third in just ten years. Another ten years later, they had grown to more than 450,000 hectares (1.1 million acres). Production increased even more rapidly, thanks to vignerons raising yields to produce more and more wine. The same four départements produced 790 million liters (210 million gallons) of wine annually in the early 1850s and 1.5 billion liters (400 million gallons) a year in the early 1870s: an increase in production of almost 100 percent against an increase in viticultural land of about 50 percent. Languedoc was not the only wine region to expand at this time, nor was it only the production of mediocre, inexpensive wines that increased: the growth of France's urban middle class of people in business, the professions, and the bureaucracy also broadened the demand for better wines.

Although overall wine production increased, from the mid-1800s France's vineyards were struck by a series of disasters. Phylloxera was by far the worst, but it was preceded in the 1840s by powdery mildew (oidium), a fungus native to North America. Its symptoms are powdery-looking spores that infect grapes, preventing them from coloring properly and growing to full size. Not only does powdery mildew reduce yields, but the affected fruit has characteristic off-flavors, and while it did relatively little damage to indigenous grapes in North America, it was devastating to *Vitis vinifera* varieties. French vineyards were widely affected in the 1850s, and the vintage of 1854 was disastrous, less than half the harvest of the preceding year and very likely the smallest since 1788. Only after that experience did French winegrowers begin to apply sulfur as a fungicide.

These setbacks apart, the overall trend was of increased production, but the growth of domestic demand for wine was not the result of a rapidly growing population. France had one of nineteenth-century Europe's slowest population growth rates, only 40 percent between 1800 and 1900, compared to 150 percent in both Germany and Great Britain. France's population grew more slowly than its national wine production, so we might expect per capita wine consumption to have increased—which it did, rising from fifty-one liters (thirteen gallons) per person in 1848 to eighty (twenty-one gallons) in 1880.[42]

There were significant regional variations. In Hérault, which produced more wine than any other département, per capita consumption was a staggering 250 liters (66 gallons) in 1840, 407 (108 gallons) in 1859, and 457 (121 gallons) in 1873.[43] (From that point it declined to under 200 liters, or 53 gallons, largely because phylloxera reduced the availability of wine.) What we do not know is whether and how consumption patterns differed in Hérault from those in other regions. In a region with a dense concentration of vignerons and a high percentage of the labor force engaged in the wine industry, there might well have been a lower rate of nondrinking and a broader constituency of heavier consumers. In contrast, in Normandy and Brittany, wine consumption was low: in the département of Finistère, per capita wine consumption was only twelve liters (three gallons) in 1840 and twice that by the beginning of the 1900s. Wine consumption was also low in some northern areas where beer was the more popular beverage.

As we have noted several times, per capita wine consumption is a very imperfect guide to consumption, because it tells us only how much wine was available, on average, to each person in the population; it does not tell us about actual consumption patterns, because it conceals widespread abstention or virtual abstention from wine (especially among the poor and children), low rates of consumption (among many women), and heavy drinking (among some categories of men). Even so, any significant increase in per capita production, such as the nearly 60 percent in the thirty-two years between 1848 and 1880, meant a considerably greater volume of wine for France's various categories of wine drinkers to avail themselves of. Quite possibly, the arrival of less-expensive Languedoc-Roussillon wine in northern urban markets, thanks to the efficiencies of the railroad, also broadened the consumption of wine by making it available to more people in the poorer social strata.

Attitudes to drinking were highly diversified by class, and there was much hand-wringing among middle-class observers to whom drinking by the poor represented a real threat to the social and moral order. On the whole, though, middle-class commentators were more concerned about spirits than wine (or beer). In 1840, the French economist Eugène Buret wrote in his book on the working classes of England and France that French workers were like "savages" in the way they took to alcohol (by which he meant distilled spirits): "To the savage, intoxication is supreme felicity, to the destitute of the great cities it is an invincible passion, an indulgence which they cannot do without and purchase regardless of its price at the expense of health and life itself."[44] But wine was part of the working-class diet, and because it was believed to be nutritious and healthy, the critics of working-class drinking tended to turn a blind eye to its intoxicating effects. Wine was to the French what beer was to the British; in 1834, the British government passed legislation that made beer far more widely available than it had been, the main purpose being to deter workers from drinking distilled spirits.[45]

Wine was part of the daily diet of the mass of French workers, both urban and rural, although bread had primacy: a report on food supplies in Paris in 1816 notes that "the excessively high price of wine has reduced its consumption. . . . The working class needs all the more bread in order to feed itself."[46] Among the heaviest drinkers were vignerons and other vineyard and winery workers, undoubtedly because they had ready access to what seemed unlimited supplies at no observable cost. As Didier Nourrisson observes, there was no meal at a winery that did not have a pitcher of wine on the table. In Champagne, the first meal of the day (at 5 AM in summer and 6 AM in winter) was a piece of bread with a glass or two of wine. The midday meal, the snack at 4 PM, and supper were all accompanied by wine, which the workers helped themselves to on the understanding that each was entitled to a liter or two (a quarter or half of a gallon) a day. At harvest time the wages posted for workers included wine. For a male not being boarded, the rate was five francs and three liters (0.8 gallons) of wine for an eight-hour day; for a woman not being boarded, three francs and a liter (0.3 gallons); for men and women being boarded, pay was three francs fifty centimes and two francs seventy-five centimes, respectively, with wine freely available.[47]

The long period from the end of the French Revolution to the arrival of the deadly phylloxera in the 1860s presents us with a mixed image of French wine. If Chaptal's observations were accurate, the great majority of France's vineyards were unsuited to make anything more than poor wine and common wine-making practices did nothing to improve the finished result. We must acknowledge, of course, that most, perhaps nearly all, of the wine was sold in bulk and that appreciations of quality should be understood in the context of nineteenth-century consumers' requirements and expectations. There was a tier of quality wine, and it might well have expanded to provide for the growing middle classes of the time, but there is little to suggest that widespread changes in viticulture or wine making occurred in the first two-thirds of the 1800s. Arguably, there was little incentive to make changes, nearly all of which would have involved either expense (replanting and restructuring vineyards) or modifying vineyard and winery practices that had been handed down from generation to generation of vignerons.

Honoré de Balzac put the prevailing attitude into the mouth of a vigneron in *Lost Illusions*, serialized between 1837 and 1843, in the middle of this phase of the history of French wine: "The bourgeois—I mean Monsieur le Marquis, Monsieur le Comte, monsieur this, that, and the other—claim that I make junk instead of wine. . . . Listen, these gentlemen harvest seven, sometimes eight barrels to the hectare, and sell them at sixty francs a barrel, which makes at the most four hundred francs a hectare in a good year. Me, I harvest twenty barrels at thirty francs, total six hundred francs. So who are the fools? Quality, quality! What use is quality to me? They can keep their quality, the marquis and all. For me, quality is cash."[48] Small-scale vignerons might not have prospered like this, but wine continued to sell well and consumption rose, and under these circumstances it is not surprising that most vignerons—making wine for sale in bulk in their local market—simply stayed the course. It would take an earthquake to disturb this slowly changing landscape, and that earthquake was phylloxera.

6. Phylloxera and Renewal

1870–1914

The last three decades of the nineteenth century were pivotal in the long-term history of French wine. The idea that the middle of the century was a golden age might be more than a little shaky, but there is no doubt that France dominated the world of wine at that time. Yet by the 1880s, its wine industry was in disarray: land under vines had shrunk dramatically, the production of fine and ordinary wines had plummeted, the bottom had fallen out of exports, and vignerons had left the countryside in droves. As France's wine drinkers found French wine in short supply, many took to wine from other countries, to "wines" made from various products, and to other beverages. Consumers outside France looked for wine from other sources. When France's wine production began to rebound in the 1890s, an excess of supply and widespread fraud led to social turmoil in a number of regions. By the time World War I broke out, the apparent heyday of French wine in the mid-1800s was but a faint memory.

The immediate cause of the problems that beset French wine was a tiny yellow aphid called phylloxera, which had a deadly effect on the country's vineyards.[1] Phylloxera feeds on the roots of *Vitis vinifera* vines, gradually cutting off the flow of water and nutrients that the vines need to stay alive. The first aboveground symptom is the drying and discoloring of leaves, and once phylloxera (which means "dry leaf") has attacked a vine, it will die unless action is quickly taken. Phylloxera is native to the eastern regions of North America, where two forms of it attack indigenous varieties of vines (from species such as *Vitis riparia* and *Vitis labrusca*). The underground form of phylloxera lives on the roots of the vine and kills some American varieties, but most are somewhat or totally resistant to it. The aerial form of the aphid attacks the leaves, but even though they might develop reddish galls (bubble-like swellings), the vines survive and continue to produce grapes.

Vitis vinifera varieties growing in Europe had never been exposed to phylloxera and had no immunity to it. It is quite possible that many of the vines that Europeans planted in North America from the seventeenth century onward failed as much on account of phylloxera as because of the climate. If the late nineteenth-century experience in France is a guide, phylloxera would have attacked the roots of the transplanted *Vitis vinifera* vines with deadly effect. But this was not a French or European problem until phylloxera crossed the Atlantic.

Although European vines were regularly brought to the Americas from the 1500s, starting with the Spanish varieties that were successfully planted throughout Latin America (where phylloxera did not then exist), the reverse traffic was more sporadic. There was no incentive to plant American varieties in Europe, as experience had shown that they generally made mediocre or unpalatable wine. But after American vines became the basis of a wine industry in America's Midwest starting in the early 1800s, European viticulturists were intrigued by their potential, and during the mid-1800s thousands of cuttings were brought to Europe for experimental purposes. It was an example of the global exchange of plant life of all kinds at a time when there was no awareness of the dangers this traffic posed to indigenous flora and there were no quarantine restrictions.

Between 1858 and 1862, large numbers of indigenous American vines were distributed to scientific establishments, nurseries, and vineyards in England, France, Germany, Spain, and Portugal. In France they were planted in several regions, including Bordeaux, the Rhône valley, and Languedoc-Roussillon, generally in existing vineyards among *Vitis vinifera* vines. In 1863 there were reports of vines dying in the southern Rhône valley and in the département of Gard, in Languedoc. Three years later, leaves on vines in a vineyard near Arles began to turn red in the middle of the growing season. In all these cases it was noted that affected vines seemed to infect their neighbors, as dying and dead vines formed radiating circles with the first dead vine at their center. By the spring of the following year, 1867, many of the vines in the Arles vineyard were dead, and by that year's harvest five hectares (twelve acres) were dying or dead. Soon after, dying and dead vines were reported in other localities in the southern Rhône valley, and vines in Bordeaux's Entre-deux-Mers district began to die.

With the benefit of hindsight, we know that these afflicted vines in the south and southwest were the first signs of a broad catastrophe that enveloped France's vineyards during the next thirty years. But at first there was no sense of urgency. The dying and dead vines represented only a few score of France's more than two million hectares (five million acres) of vineyards, the affected areas were scattered, and there seemed no pattern. The losses had a negligible impact on grape harvests in the 1860s, and harvest size varied from year to year in any case. The great majority of France's vignerons were unconcerned, because their vines were not affected. Rumors of problems in far-off vineyards were probably common, and vignerons could write off distant misfortunes as due to bad vineyard practices, localized outbreaks of plant disease, the vagaries of climate, or sheer bad luck. Needless to say, their counterparts with affected vineyards and their neighbors were not so blasé; by 1868, vignerons in various places in southern France could see expanding areas of dead vines, and producers in Entre-deux-Mers saw the first vines start to die.

That year, scientists in Hérault, one of the départements most affected, set up a three-man commission to investigate the problem. At first it could find nothing distinctive about the dead vines that gave any indication of cause of death. The reason was that phylloxera attack the roots, and when a vine is dead and their food supply is gone, the aphids migrate to a new food source, the roots of a neighboring vine. That meant that when scientists dug up dead vines to examine their roots, there were no aphids to be seen. It was only when someone thought to dig up a still-healthy vine that was growing close to affected vines that phylloxera was discovered. Jules-Émile Planchon, who was a member of the Hérault commission and became the main figure in the long struggle to find a remedy for phylloxera, later wrote, "Suddenly under the magnifying lens . . . appeared an insect, a plant louse of yellowish color, tight on the wood, sucking the sap. One looked more attentively; it is not one, it is not ten, but hundreds, thousands. . . . During three days we found—at every place the malady had attacked—these innumerable insects. At Saint-Rémy, at Gravaison, at Châteauneuf-du-Pape, at Orange."[2] He recognized the insect as related to the phylloxera aphid that attacked oak trees. To this variety that fed on vines, he prophetically added the qualifier *vastatrix*—"devastator."

The discovery and identification of phylloxera might be thought to have been a breakthrough, enabling scientists to focus on ways to eliminate or neutralize the aphids. Planchon and his colleagues showed aphid-infested roots to local vignerons, who clearly thought this was the beginning of the end of their problem. Planchon quoted them as exclaiming, "Ah! There's the enemy. It's good, we will make it perish. Courage, our vines can be reborn, our ruin is no longer certain, at last we can defend ourselves."[3] But it took almost a decade before there was a consensus, among scientists and vignerons alike, that phylloxera was the direct cause of the devastation in France's vineyards, and almost another decade to begin to apply the remedy systematically.

There was also the question of where phylloxera had come from. At first there was no thought of implicating the imported American vines, because they thrived in vineyards as their *Vitis vinifera* neighbors died. The leaves of some American vines showed galls that were symptomatic of phylloxera, yet the different sites of attack—leaves of American vines, roots of European—seemed to implicate a different insect in each case. But when Planchon and a colleague put phylloxera-infected leaves from American vines into pots growing *Vitis vinifera* vines, the aphids migrated within two days from the leaves to the roots, where they began to feed on the sap of the healthy vines, showing the same appearance and behavior as the aphids found on other vines. This was proof that the insect known in America as *Pemphigus vitifolii* and the insect identified in France as phylloxera were one and the same. This finding indicated that the infection had probably spread from the American vines. It also suggested the solution that was eventually adopted: reversing Planchon's experimental grafting of American vines on to European roots, instead grafting European vines on to the phylloxera-resistant roots of American varieties.

Although there was soon a consensus that American vines had been the carriers of phylloxera, French scientists spent years debating its actual role in the deaths of vines.[4] On one side were those who argued that phylloxera was, quite simply, the direct cause of the vine deaths. On the other side were scientists who favored a more complex explanation: that one thing or another—harsh winters and poor soil were suggested—had weakened the affected vines, which had made them vulnerable to phylloxera. These different understandings implied different solutions. If phylloxera was the direct and sole cause of the vine deaths, it was necessary to find some way to deal with it. But if phylloxera infestation was merely an effect of other problems, then solving them would deal indirectly with it.

It was not until the mid-1870s that there was general agreement among French scientists that it was phylloxera that was killing vines. A number of findings supported this conclusion. One was that flooding an affected vineyard and drowning the aphids arrested the death of vines. Another was an observation that phylloxera was rarely found on the roots of vines growing in very sandy soils, and vines planted in those conditions were spared the mortality rates of vines growing in other types of soil. It was clear that even if there were conditions that predisposed vines to attack by phylloxera, the presence or absence of phylloxera made the critical difference between a vine that died and one that did not.

Years that might have been devoted to finding a remedy were consumed by the debate on the actual role of phylloxera. The French government was involved only marginally at first, because the first years of the phylloxera crisis coincided with the run-up to the Franco-Prussian War of 1870–71, the short war itself (which entailed Prussian/German occupation of Champagne and the capture of Paris), and then the consequences of defeat, including the loss of Alsace and Lorraine to Germany. Just before the Prussian army placed Paris under siege in 1870, the National Assembly relocated to Bordeaux, where phylloxera was already beginning to kill vines. The government set up a national phylloxera commission that year, whose first actions were to offer a twenty-thousand-franc reward for a remedy and to recommend that each département set up a committee to study and take precautions against phylloxera. But there was still no sense of urgency. In 1870 only a few regions were affected, total vine losses were small, and there was no inkling that the problem would spread. Unaffected départements saw no reason to act quickly. It took four years for Côte-d'Or, where most of the grapes for Burgundy's fine wines were grown, to set up a committee, and many other départements did so only when their vineyards were attacked.

During the early 1870s, as phylloxera spread farther through southern France and Bordeaux, a number of methods to control it were tried, the most successful being sand, water, and chemicals.[5] Vines growing in sandy soils were less likely to be affected, and experiments showed that the aphid was especially averse to soils that were about 75 percent fine sand. Some vignerons with vines in other types of soil excavated around the roots of their vines and packed them with sand. Others planted vines in nearby sandy soils, and by the early 1880s, vineyards occupied all the sandy areas along the Mediterranean. Because sand lacks nutrients, it was necessary to fertilize these vines with phosphates and nitrates. Even though some sandy soils did not resist phylloxera permanently, they gave some districts a breathing space. In the Rhône delta, sandy areas close to the river were cleared of scrub and planted with vines,[6] while in Saint-Laurent, a coastal town near Perpignan, the sandy soils delayed the arrival of phylloxera until 1885, when the grafting solution was well understood.[7]

A second approach was flooding vineyards during winter in order to drown the aphids, but there were limitations to its effectiveness. The first was obvious: it was possible to flood vineyards on flat terrain but impossible on slopes. Second, there had to be a nearby supply of suitable water. But not all water was equally effective (stagnant water with low oxygen levels was best), flooding demanded immense volumes (nearly twenty thousand cubic meters per hectare, or almost three hundred thousand cubic feet per acre, in one documented case), and considerable pumping capacity was required. The soil had to hold the water long enough to drown the aphids—

up to forty days was recommended—so well-drained vineyards were not candidates for the procedure, and walls had to be built around the vines to contain the water. Flooding vineyards at least once a year was advised. The practical issues and the expense ruled out flooding for small-scale vignerons, and it was used in only a small proportion of vineyards, covering perhaps forty thousand hectares (one hundred thousand acres) of France's more than two million (five million acres).

A third method was to inject pesticides into the soil. The treatments involved carbon disulfide, a toxic and flammable liquid, and the more effective salts of potassium thiocarbonate. The drawback of the latter was that they needed to be dissolved in large volumes of water. Both killed phylloxera, but they did not prevent reinfestation, and vineyards needed to be treated annually and sometimes twice a year. Again, soil type was important, as the liquid had to percolate easily through the area of the root system to kill all the aphids. The treatment was expensive, particularly for small-scale vignerons; even though subsidies were provided when vignerons formed syndicates, the areas treated were limited.

These chemicals could not be used on vines that grew among other crops, as they did in many small properties, because they killed everything except grapevines—and even then, many grapevines did not survive treatment by the chemicals. For that reason alone, many vignerons rejected the chemical solution. Some in the département of Aude argued that they would rather take their chances with phylloxera and get another two or three harvests of grapes than risk having their vines killed by chemicals: "We are all equal before the scourge, and we see little need to kill our vines or let them be killed in order to save those of our neighbors."[8]

Finally, there was the more mundane method of controlling phylloxera: ripping the vines out of infected vineyards, leaving the land fallow for up to ten years until the aphids had disappeared, and then replanting with new vines. But this was impossible for small-scale vignerons, who lived from harvest to harvest and had no savings to fall back on. Their vines were often planted in stony soils or on slopes that were unsuitable for anything but vines, so they would be unable to plant cereals, vegetables, or any other crop to tide them over until they could plant vines again. They could not survive without income during that time, and there was no guarantee that phylloxera would not return.

While these methods of controlling phylloxera were being tried, some scientists and vignerons worked another angle. In case it took decades to solve the problem—or worse, in case it could not be solved and France's *Vitis vinifera* vineyards were doomed—it made sense to experiment with phylloxera-resistant American vine varieties as self-producers, to make wines suitable either for blending with *Vitis vinifera* grapes or for drinking as varietal wines. A prominent voice in the defense of these wines was Margaret, Duchess of Fitz-James, who owned vineyards in Languedoc and wrote that wine produced by vignerons in that region from some varieties native to the southern United States "resembles French wine; its color, its degree of alcohol, varies around Narbonne from the richest, most full-bodied to the most delicate of rosés."[9] But the director of the British Royal Gardens at Kew reported a different opinion when he visited Bordeaux in 1899 and tasted wines made from the American jacquez and herbemont varieties: "These wines were far from palatable, being exceedingly acid, with a peculiar mawkish flavour." They might replace "the coarser kind of vin ordinaire [common wine] or vin du midi [southern French wine]" or might be used for blending, he wrote, but the vines would be better used as rootstock for grafting.[10] Despite the unpromising results, American vines were widely planted in France, and it is not often realized how important they were to French vineyards through to the 1930s.

A good deal of research was also devoted to creating hybrids of American and *Vitis vinifera* vines—hybrids whose essential trait had to be resistance to phylloxera but that would also grow well in French climatic and soil conditions, produce good yields, and make wine that was acceptable to the French palate. Alexis Millardet, a noted botanist, declared that new hybrid varieties meeting those requirements "will be the solution par excellence to the phylloxera problem."[11] A vigneron from Pierrefeu, in the département of Var, reported that a hybrid of mourvèdre and a *Vitis rupestris* variety "makes good fruit, not in great quantity, and a wine of deeper color than jacquez." If it could be made more productive, he added, it would be a direct producer to recommend.[12]

While these various methods of dealing with phylloxera did not meet with total failure, their limited success made them unattractive to vignerons wanting a quick, reliable, and permanent solution. There was only one option, the one that the national commission had resisted for years: grafting European vines on to the rootstock of American vines to produce a vine with roots that were resistant to phylloxera and a *Vitis vinifera* upper section that would produce grapes in the usual way. Although the roots are merely a conduit for water and nutrients from the soil, there were concerns that the wine from such vines would have the flavor of the American varieties that the roots came from. American wines made from some indigenous varieties had a distinctive flavor often referred to as "foxy"[13] and were generally regarded in France as far inferior to any French wine.

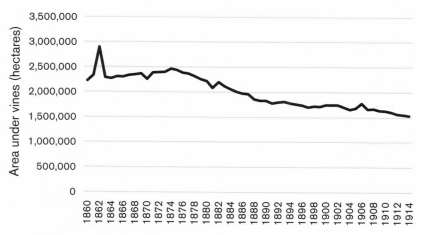

DIAGRAM 6.1. Area under vines, France, 1860–1914

As the respective merits and disadvantages of these solutions were being debated and tried in the 1870s, phylloxera broke out of the southern regions where it had been confined for a decade and began to kill vines in a much wider area of central France (see map 6.1). By 1878, nearly half France's départements were affected, with 370,000 hectares (915,000 acres) of vines dead and another 250,000 hectares (620,000 acres) dying—more than a quarter of the national vineyard area. All varieties were affected, and even those with harder wood, such as cabernet sauvignon, could not resist the aphid. But the pace and scale of the disaster varied from region to region, and because France's vignerons were directly affected at different times and confronted varying levels of destruction, they did not develop a consensus on what they were facing. Vines began to die in Entre-deux-Mers in 1867, and one hundred communities in Bordeaux were affected by 1872; by 1876 phylloxera had spread to both banks of the Garonne River, and four years later 100,000 of Bordeaux's 170,000 hectares (250,000 of 420,000 acres) of vineyards were dead or dying.[14] In the Loire valley's Muscadet region, in contrast, there was no sign of phylloxera until 1884.[15]

The national phylloxera commission faced a situation demanding urgent and decisive action in the late 1870s, but it still hesitated. While acknowledging that phylloxera was the problem, the commissioners could not bring themselves to admit that most of France's vineyards would have to be replanted with vines grafted on to American rootstock. The idea that American vines, the cause of the disaster, should be planted throughout

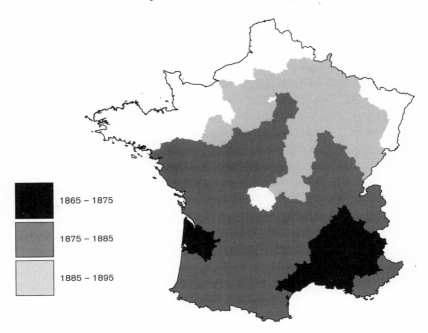

1865 – 1875

1875 – 1885

1885 – 1895

MAP 6.1. Progress of phylloxera in France, 1865–1895

France was repugnant to them in principle, and there was residual concern that wine from grafted vines would carry the flavor of the American varieties. An overriding impulse was simple resistance to change. Grafting and replanting meant doing things differently, and the commission—conscious of the reputation of France's fine wines—insisted that vineyard practices ought to follow "tradition," with long-planted varieties being cultivated in traditional ways. Tradition did not include grafting vines on to American rootstock.

Laws passed in 1878 and 1879 reflected the commission's ambivalence. In the south of France, where damage to vineyards was most extensive, grafted vines could be planted; in a broad central zone, where phylloxera infestation was patchy and moderate, grafted vines were prohibited and chemicals were to be used to eradicate the aphids; in the north, which was still unaffected by phylloxera, nothing was to be done and grafting on to American rootstock was strictly prohibited. These were entirely reactive measures that dealt effectively only with highly affected regions and did not envisage the further spread of phylloxera. The commission hoped to stabilize the status quo of 1879 by banning the movement of American vine

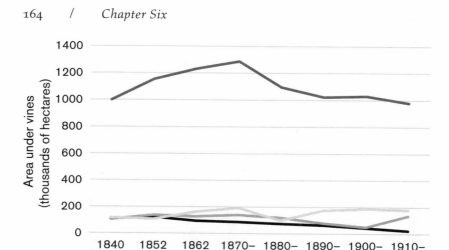

DIAGRAM 6.2.   Area under vines, selected regions, 1840–1919

material, establishing cordons sanitaires between the zones, and providing for regular inspections of vineyards, gardens, and plant nurseries. In 1880 the rules were extended to Algeria, which was then phylloxera free: no vines could be sent there from any phylloxera-affected area of metropolitan France.

Underlying the commission's plan was a ranking of the importance of French wine regions. France's most prestigious regions were Bordeaux, Burgundy, and Champagne, and in the late 1870s, Bordeaux was seriously affected by phylloxera, Burgundy lightly affected, and Champagne not affected at all. But all three were grouped in regions where grafting on to American vines was prohibited, thereby allowing their vineyards to retain their 100 percent French (*Vitis vinifera*) character. This was especially beneficial to Bordeaux's reputation but harmful to its continued production, as it delayed the grafting that was eventually needed. There was far greater readiness to allow grafting in the south, as that region was simply the source of huge volumes of ordinary wine and the appearance of breaking with tradition there was less important. From this perspective, it was a stroke of good luck that phylloxera first appeared in the south and not in one of the regions that had made French wine famous.

The policies adopted in the late 1870s failed: phylloxera bred prolifically and overcame any obstacle placed in the way of its migration. By 1884, within five years of these laws being passed, another 250,000 hectares

(620,000 acres) of vines died and hundreds of thousands more began to show evidence of phylloxera. Eventually, land planted with vines in France decreased by almost a third, from 2,300,000 hectares (5,700,000 acres) before the outbreak of phylloxera to 1,730,000 hectares (4,270,000 acres) in 1900,[16] and even then, not all of this area was in full production. The country's wine production always fluctuated annually, depending on weather, diseases, and pests, but it declined steadily in this period. Throughout the 1860s and 1870s it generally lay between five and six billion liters (1.3 and 1.6 billion gallons) a year. In the 1880s it settled at a little more than half that—about three billion liters (0.8 billion gallons) annually—and production did not recover until the early 1900s. As we would expect, the effects varied from region to region. Hérault had some 220,000 hectares (540,000 acres) of vines in 1872, the largest area of vineyards of any département, but ten years later was left with only 90,000 hectares (222,000 acres). Gard lost more than four-fifths of the 88,000 hectares (217,000 acres) of vines that it boasted before phylloxera struck. Vaucluse lost a third of its 28,000 hectares (69,000 acres) during the 1870s. France's two main brandy-producing départements, Charente and Charente-Inférieure (now Charente-Maritime), lost 205,000 of their 265,000 hectares (507,000 of 655,000 acres) between 1875 and 1889.[17]

Alsace followed a completely different trajectory. After the German victory in 1871, it was annexed to Germany and became a German wine region. But its immense potential—it would have provided two-fifths of Germany's wine at the time—alarmed producers in other parts of Germany, who successfully disabled their new rivals. Alsace's vignerons were compelled to rip out and burn all their vines and then wait ten years before replanting. Even then, the vineyards were established on the plains rather than on the hillsides that had produced fine wines before the arrival of phylloxera, and instead of the riesling vines that had brought Alsace fame, producers were permitted to use only hybrids. Alsace went from making distinctive and some fine wines to producing cheap wine that was blended with German wine and labeled as coming from the Rhine valley. In 1909, producers there were permitted to add sugar and raise the alcohol content. But by the time Alsace rejoined France in 1918, its wines were far inferior to those that the region had produced before Germany annexed it.[18]

The results of phylloxera elsewhere in France were no less catastrophic on a number of levels because of the importance of wine to France's economy and culture. It provided a living for millions of vignerons, vineyard workers, winery hands, and their families, as well as for people employed in barrel-making, bottle-production, and other associated industries; it contributed to national revenue through taxes; it was an important export; and it was an important part of the French diet and was widely considered a healthy beverage. It was also an important element of France's cultural identity. These considerations gave urgency to finding a remedy for phylloxera, and as an added inducement, the government in 1884 raised the reward for a solution from twenty thousand to three hundred thousand francs.

Yet attitudes toward phylloxera among scientists, government officials, and vignerons remained mixed. Some scientists and officials were unable or unwilling to accept that grafting on to American vines, which were the cause of the catastrophe, could be the solution. The attitudes of vignerons—especially small-scale vignerons, who made up the majority of wine producers in France—were largely conditioned by their personal experience and the limited range of actions they were financially able to undertake. Their attitudes varied from simple denial that phylloxera was a problem—or that it even existed—through frequent reluctance to report affected vines, to resistance to chemical treatments. In Champagne, one of the last regions to be affected (as late as 1890), vignerons voiced sentiments such as "the existence of the phylloxera is not sufficiently proved" and "the phylloxera doesn't exist, it's an imaginary malady."[19] In Burgundy, vignerons delayed reporting sick vines, hoping that a change in the weather would fix things. When a team of workers arrived in Chenôve, near Marsannay, to treat vineyards with chemicals, a crowd of vignerons drove them out, shouting "that they were scoundrels, more to be feared than the phylloxera."[20]

Finally, at an international congress on phylloxera held in Bordeaux in 1881, grafting *Vitis vinifera* on to American vines was accepted as the best solution. Grafting was not simply a matter of attaching, say, a merlot vine to the root of any American vine, as not all indigenous American vines were completely resistant to phylloxera. French scientists, including Planchon, made several trips to the United States to classify indigenous varieties and to assess their resistance, and they put hundreds from several species into three categories: those never attacked by phylloxera, those generally resistant to phylloxera, and those totally resistant. Thousands of combinations of American and *Vitis vinifera* varieties were made, and each was planted in a number of vineyards in different regions of France to test its resistance to phylloxera and suitability for specific soil types and climatic conditions. By the mid-1880s, it was determined that the most resistant vines were from the *Vitis rupestris* and *Vitis riparia* species, and replanting on to their rootstock began. There were still some setbacks, as when scattered examples of grafted vines died after a few years, reviving doubts about this method of dealing with phylloxera, but by 1887 suitable rootstocks had been identified for almost all of France's wine regions and soil types.

The white, chalky soils of parts of southwest France, especially in the brandy-producing Charente region, where the Cognac district is located, presented particular problems. No American vines seemed to survive in those conditions, and unless a suitable variety could be identified, vast areas of vineyards would have to be abandoned. Pierre Viala, a professor of viticulture at Montpellier, traveled to the United States to try to find vines growing in soils similar to Charente's and identified such a species, called berlandieri, that grew well in Texas. When Millardet and his colleagues created a hybrid from it and a *Vitis vinifera* vine in 1896, the new variety provided roots suitable for grafting. Finding a suitable rootstock for Charente completed this stage of dealing with the phylloxera crisis, but even so, two-thirds of that region's vineyard area was never replanted.

A vine-grafting industry arose as soon as the procedure and the varieties were approved (see figure 6.1). Many new nurseries were established, most using women and teenagers to do the repetitive work of cutting, notching, and tying root to vine; they were said to be more adept than men, and they were certainly cheaper. Replanting began quickly, and by 1900 more than two-thirds of the vines growing in France had American roots. Owners of small vineyards were initially slow to participate, not least because of the expense and the disruption to production caused by pulling out and replacing vines. Fears that American rootstocks would pass on undesirable flavors to the European vines proved unfounded, but some regions held out against the program anyway. Burgundy forbade the use of American vines for grafting until 1887, when widespread grafting by winegrowers forced the regional authorities to capitulate.

From the first signs of phylloxera in the mid-1860s to the determination of how best to respond, two decades passed. Because of the need to propagate hundreds of millions of vines for rootstock, replanting took years; the renewal of vineyards was still going on in Champagne when World War I broke out, and it had to be suspended for four years because some vineyards were in the battle zones. Once grafted vines were planted, it was a few years before they came into full production, and in the meantime there was a shortage of French wine for the home and export markets. The initial decline was slow and uneven during the 1870s, mirroring the advance of phylloxera, but production hit an extended low in the 1880s. It then rose gradually from the end of the 1880s, as replanting began, and by 1900 much of the replanting project was complete (see diagram 6.3).

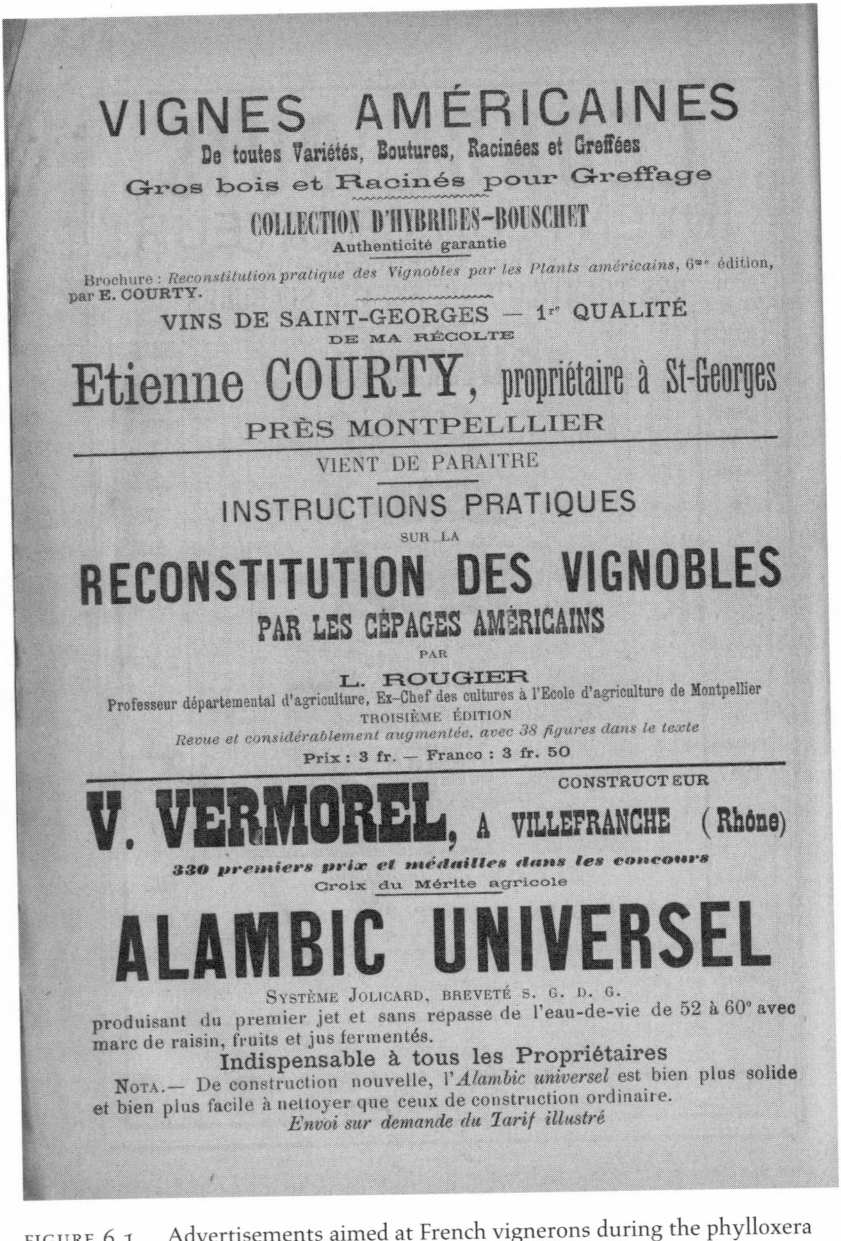

VIGNES AMÉRICAINES
De toutes Variétés, Boutures, Racinées et Greffées
Gros bois et Racinés pour Greffage
COLLECTION D'HYBRIDES-BOUSCHET
Authenticité garantie
Brochure : *Reconstitution pratique des Vignobles par les Plants américains*, 6me édition, par E. COURTY.
VINS DE SAINT-GEORGES — 1r QUALITÉ
DE MA RÉCOLTE
Etienne COURTY, propriétaire à St-Georges
PRÈS MONTPELLLIER

VIENT DE PARAITRE
INSTRUCTIONS PRATIQUES
SUR LA
RECONSTITUTION DES VIGNOBLES
PAR LES CÉPAGES AMÉRICAINS
PAR
L. ROUGIER
Professeur départemental d'agriculture, Ex-Chef des cultures à l'Ecole d'agriculture de Montpellier
TROISIÈME ÉDITION
Revue et considérablement augmentée, avec 38 figures dans le texte
Prix : 3 fr. — Franco : 3 fr. 50

V. VERMOREL, CONSTRUCTEUR A VILLEFRANCHE (Rhône)
330 premiers prix et médailles dans les concours
Croix du Mérite agricole
ALAMBIC UNIVERSEL
Système Jolicard, breveté s. g. d. g.
produisant du premier jet et sans repasse de l'eau-de-vie de 52 à 60° avec marc de raisin, fruits et jus fermentés.
Indispensable à tous les Propriétaires
Nota.— De construction nouvelle, l'*Alambic universel* est bien plus solide et bien plus facile à nettoyer que ceux de construction ordinaire.
Envoi sur demande du Tarif illustré

FIGURE 6.1. Advertisements aimed at French vignerons during the phylloxera crisis: indigenous American vines, instructions on planting American varieties, and distilling equipment. *Progrès agricole et viticole,* October 1891. (In the author's possession).

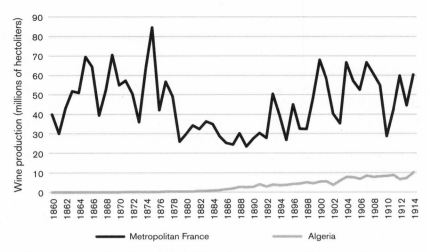

DIAGRAM 6.3.   Wine production, Metropolitan France and Algeria, 1860–1914

While wine production was low and before replacement vines became fully productive, French wine merchants imported wine from other European countries, often blending it with French wine. By the 1880s, hundreds of millions of liters from Italy, Spain, and Portugal were being imported, much of it in the form of full-bodied reds. France had historically been a wine-exporting country, but from the 1880s until World War I it was a net importer. In the second half of the 1880s, when the proportion of French vineyards out of production was at its highest, imports totaled more than a billion liters (264 million gallons), four times the 239 million liters (63 million gallons) of exports. Even after the worst effects of the phylloxera crisis had ebbed, in 1910–14 imports were four times greater than exports.[21]

The French also began to expand viticulture in Algeria and to a lesser extent Tunisia, even though their populations were predominantly Muslims, for whom alcohol of any sort was anathema. In the late 1870s the French government called on Algeria to "bring relief to this viticultural, agricultural, and commercial disaster. It has been decided to plant vines everywhere the soil seems suitable."[22] The département of Hérault arranged for some vignerons to relocate to Algeria, those who were "reduced to misery, and who were basing all their hopes for making a living on being able to use their skills in our African colony." They were given loans to cover their moving expenses, and the governor of Algeria offered each of the families thirty hectares (seventy-four acres) of land where vines were known to grow well.[23] The offer was later made to vignerons throughout

France, and about ten thousand (most from Languedoc-Roussillon, Provence, and the Rhône valley) responded. It was a large number but a tiny proportion of France's million-plus vignerons, most of whom pinned their hopes on staying put and surviving the crisis somehow. With help from banks, the new arrivals boosted Algeria's vineyards from seventeen thousand hectares (forty-two thousand acres) in 1878 to more than sixty thousand (148,000 acres) in 1885, and soon they were shipping millions of liters of wine to metropolitan France (the territory of France in continental Europe). A smaller number of vignerons moved to Corsica, but the island's wine production paled against Algeria's.

Much of Algeria's wine was ordinary, inexpensive, and made from varieties such as grenache, carignan, and mourvèdre. In 1881 a Nantes négociant wrote ambivalently to an Algerian producer, "We have received your sample of red wine. . . . It is very similar to Bordeaux, but we found a little touch of heat and sharpness, which were perhaps caused by shipping." Pointing out that ordinary Bordeaux wines were in very short supply, he added that were the Algerian wines to succeed, "they will be in great demand."[24] This was the beginning of a brisk commerce between Algerian producers and French merchants, which lasted until the 1960s (see figure 6.2). Although most of the wine was mediocre, some Algerians aspired to make better wines. In 1885 the Société d'Agriculture d'Algérie recommended using only lower-yield varieties such as carignan, mourvèdre, and alicante to make wines of higher quality. It recommended against grenache because its color was unstable and it gave a rancio flavor, and suggested cinsault be used mainly for rosé wines. But the great thirst in metropolitan France encouraged quantity more than quality, and for the first half of the 1880s, millions of barrels of wine were shipped from ports big and small along the Algerian coast. Even the lack of a port was no obstacle. Barrels were sometimes rolled down beaches and loaded on to small boats in the surf or lashed together and floated out to ships in deeper water. Once in metropolitan France, Algerian wines were blended with inexpensive wines from the south and sold at much lower prices than unblended wines of similar quality and alcoholic strength.

Algeria's wine industry seemed to be booming when, in 1885, phylloxera was discovered in vines near Tlemcen in the northwest and then near Sidi Bel Abbès in the northeast. In the next year it was reported in several other regions. It is not known how phylloxera reached Algeria, but it was most likely on American vines, which were acquired illicitly in breach of the 1880 quarantine and often planted in gardens. In any case, even though phylloxera arrived just as the grafting question was being resolved in

FIGURE 6.2. Letter from an Algerian wine producer to a French customer, 12 January 1912. (In the author's possession.)

metropolitan France, there was a vigorous debate among Algerian vignerons about the best way to deal with it. These recent arrivals, we should remember, had faced phylloxera before but had left metropolitan France before the consensus on grafting was reached there. It was almost as if nothing had been learned. The Algerian authorities adopted a literal scorched-earth policy: they employed soldiers to pull out and burn affected vines, then turn over the soil and douse it with boiling water before soaking it with gasoline and covering it with piles of straw, which were set ablaze. Phylloxera persisted, but it was not until the 1890s that the governor authorized, region by region, the grafting of *Vitis vinifera* vines on to American rootstock.

Unlike metropolitan France, Algeria did not see wine production decline as a result of phylloxera, because planting outpaced vine death, even before the grafting program began in the 1890s. Land under vines rose from 60,000 hectares (148,000 acres) in 1885 to 100,000 (247,000 acres) in 1890 and to 150,000 (371,000 acres) by the end of the century. Production also rose: by 1885 more than one hundred million liters (twenty-six million gallons) of wine were produced annually, and by 1900 more than five hundred million (132 million gallons). Bigger yields in the replanted vineyards also made up for losses to phylloxera: between 1885 and 1900, when production rose five-fold, the area under vines increased at only half that rate, suggesting that yields had more than doubled.[25] Metropolitan French consumers—at least those who drank inexpensive, ordinary wine—continued to rely on the annual arrival of millions of liters of Algerian wine until the 1960s.

Phylloxera had a number of long-term effects, one of which was the transformation of France's vineyards. It was not only that most vines in France were now on American rootstocks and that hybrid and American varieties were common but also that the scale and character of viticulture had changed. France entered the phylloxera crisis in the mid-1860s with 2.3 million hectares (5.7 million acres) of land under vines. That area fluctuated throughout the 1870s, 1880s, and 1890s as vines died, were ripped out, and were replaced. We must also remember that total vineyard area does not provide an accurate guide to production, as phylloxera-affected and newly planted vineyards were not fully producing. The latter is always true, of course, as all vineyards have to be replanted at one time or another, but there was more volatility in the phylloxera period. By the eve of World War I, when the situation had stabilized, the area under vines in France had settled at about 1.5 million hectares (3.7 million acres),[26] a third less than before phylloxera.

The reason for the decline of viticultural area between 1865 and 1914 is that many vineyards were not replanted. In the north of France especially, many vineyards had been in areas not climatically suited for vines and had produced wines of very poor quality. With the growth of a wine market in which fuller-bodied and higher-alcohol wines (including Algerian blends) could be easily be shipped in bulk from the south of France and sold at affordable prices throughout the country, these poorer wines became uncompetitive. So it was that the five départements around Paris had a combined 33,516 hectares (82,820 acres) of vines in 1862 but fewer than 10,000 (25,000 acres) in 1900–1909. Vineyards in the area had a long history because of their proximity to the huge Paris market in times when transportation was difficult and expensive. They had already started to decline when railroads enabled wine from more distant regions to be sent to Paris efficiently and cheaply. The costs of replanting after phylloxera reduced their competitiveness even more. In other regions the decision was made to abandon viticulture almost entirely. The center-west of France lost more than half of its land under vines: 440,000 hectares (1.1 million acres) were planted with vines in 1862 but only 217,000 (536,000 acres) by 1900.[27]

In contrast, some regions of southern France saw an increase in land under vines. The four départements of Languedoc-Roussillon had accounted for a sixth of France's total vineyard area in 1875 but made up more than a quarter of it in 1900. On the other hand, Provence lost about a quarter of its vineyard area. Overall, the center of gravity of French wine production shifted south as vines were replanted, and phylloxera thus intensified a trend that was already under way before the 1860s.

Increased yields more than compensated for the loss of land under vines, as many vineyards were replanted with higher-cropping varieties and vignerons began to use more fertilizer and adopt other vineyard practices to improve productivity. In global terms, the 2.3 million hectares (5.7 million acres) of vines in 1865 gave 69.5 million hectoliters (1.84 billion gallons) of wine, an average of thirty hectoliters per hectare (321 gallons per acre), but in 1914, 1.5 million hectares (3.7 million acres) produced 60.3 million hectoliters (1.59 billion gallons), an average of forty hectoliters per hectare (428 gallons per acre). Yields varied regionally and annually, of course, but there was a clear and steady increase. In the 1880s some 3.4 billion liters (0.9 billion gallons) of wine were available on the French market each year, but in 1900 the market was flooded with more than 7.1 billion liters (1.9 billion gallons). At the same time, the French population grew very sluggishly, so there was twice as much wine available on a per capita basis in 1900.

There was also a change in patterns of planting. Before phylloxera struck, most of France's vineyards still had a range of grape varieties, as they had for centuries; most wines were field blends rather than varietal wines or multivarietal blends assembled in the winery. There seems to have been a gradual shift before phylloxera toward planting parcels and even whole vineyards with vines of a single variety, but it was concentrated among producers of quality wines who wanted to pick grapes when they were uniformly ripe—which is easier when vines are separated by variety rather than grown in vineyards with both earlier- and later-ripening varieties. Vineyards that were replanted were more likely to be planted with grape varieties separated from one another.

Replanted vineyards also looked different. Throughout France, vines were now planted in rows rather than randomly. This allowed vignerons to use horses (and later machinery) in the vineyards. Vines were spaced more widely too rather than being planted close together. Although a number of départements in the northeast had densities of more than twenty thousand vines per hectare (eight thousand per acre), the southern and Atlantic regions seldom had even half that, and some had fewer than five thousand vines per hectare (two thousand per acre). Although in principle reducing density would reduce yield per hectare, vines that were less crowded were generally healthier and more productive.

The legacy of phylloxera was social as well as viticultural, as it wiped out many small-scale vignerons who lived from harvest to harvest and had neither savings nor the ability to get bank loans. Thousands of vigneron families left the land entirely, joining the migration of hundreds of thousands of other rural dwellers as they fled the countryside, where there was a general agricultural depression in the late 1800s. In Bordeaux, the countryside and villages lost eighteen thousand and the towns gained twenty-two thousand people between the 1901 and 1906 censuses; Bordeaux's population alone rose by four thousand. Most of the migrants were young people, especially women, looking for work in the city. Not only that, but Bordeaux's rural birthrate fell, as couples matched family size to their reduced incomes, and deaths began to outnumber births.[28] Throughout almost all the viticultural zones of Bordeaux, from Médoc to Bourg to Sauternes, population decline reflected the depressed state of the wine industry. Those who remained experienced degraded standards of living, so much so that children born during phylloxera years in the main wine-producing départements of France were malnourished: although the height of French males rose gradually during the nineteenth century, boys born to viticultural families in years when phylloxera reduced their parents' incomes were half a centimeter to a centimeter (0.2 to 0.4 inches) shorter than boys born in unaffected départements.[29]

One way or another, phylloxera also had a major impact on the wine consumption patterns of the French from the 1870s to the early 1900s. Clearly, they were able to drink less wine from metropolitan France, and even though they drank some blended with wine from Algeria, Italy, and Spain, annual consumption on a per capita basis fell from 148 liters (39 gallons) in the late 1860s to 93–104 liters (25–27 gallons) during the 1880s before rising to 108–22 liters (29–32 gallons) in the following decade. In the three years before World War I, average annual consumption was 128 liters (34 gallons) per person, closer to the prephylloxera rate. There were, of course, big regional variations. One estimate put consumption in the département of Hérault at 457 liters (121 gallons) a year in 1873, 184 (49 gallons) in 1885, and 193 (51 gallons) in 1904—levels far higher than the national average.[30]

A relaxation of licensing laws and resulting increase in licensed drinking places after 1880 aided the postphylloxera rebound in consumption. There were 425,000 licensed cafés, cabarets, guinguettes, taverns, and bars throughout France's cities, towns, and rural villages in 1897, 464,000 in 1901, and 483,000 in 1913. On the eve of the war, there was one public drinking place for every eighty-two inhabitants, or one for every thirty-five adult men.[31] There was probably increased demand in the growing urban populations, as middle-class consumers looked for good, affordable wine, while industrial workers drank cheaper wine of poorer quality.

Paris workers drank wine as part of their daily diet—it was one of their gastronomic trilogy, which also included bread and meat—and between 1870 and 1914 they devoted 12 to 18 percent of their budgets to it.[32] Starting in the 1870s they also began to drink more brandy—a shot with or instead of breakfast was especially popular—but although beer also gained in popularity, wine remained the beverage of choice. Increased consumption of wine was part of a general improvement in working-class diets. In 1885 the president of the Paris carpenters' association told an inquiry, "Before . . . we spent twenty-five sous [there were twenty sous in a franc] at the maximum for our evening meal; today the workers spend three francs or three francs fifty, and then there is the wine at noon. . . . Bread is a better buy today, and [where] we used to drink a *demi-setier* [quarter liter], now they drink a liter [of wine]."[33]

The French sociologist Frédéric Le Play studied family budgets around 1870 and provided concrete examples of wine consumption at various levels of French society. A master bleacher living in Paris spent three hundred francs a year on alcohol, almost all of it on wine from Burgundy. "The wine, purchased in barrels, is put in bottles by the head of the family. The whole family drinks wine at the midday and evening meals; it observes . . . no days of abstinence." Another Parisian family, its head a carpenter, consumed ninety liters (twenty-four gallons) of wine a year (in baskets of ten one-liter, or quarter-gallon, bottles), together with some bottles of brandy. The southern French families whom Le Play studied drank only wine. A family of peasants in Béarn drank wine from Gers, but only on special occasions and at times of hard labor, such as during the harvest. The family of a soap maker of lower Provence consumed 320 liters (85 gallons) of wine a year from their own vines and also fortified a little of their wine with brandy.[34] Examples like these indicate a wide range of consumption patterns and remind us of the limited usefulness of per capita generalizations.

If some French men and women consumed less wine than the average, others consumed more, and heavy, regular drinking—often generically referred to as "alcoholism" at the time—was a growing concern in France. Despite the prevailing belief that wine could not cause alcoholism, some patients confined to asylums as alcoholics insisted that they drank only or mainly wine, and men and women working in the wine trades (such as café owners) were overrepresented among patients diagnosed as alcoholics. Many claimed that they drank no more than a liter (0.26 gallons) of wine a day (which physicians recommended as the maximum for manual laborers by World War I), sometimes diluted with water.[35]

As we can see, there was a lot of volatility in per capita consumption rates, only some of it (like the big drop in the 1880s) attributable to supply. Prices did not automatically reflect the relationship of supply to demand, and diminished supply did not consistently lead to the rise in prices that might have been expected. It is possible that the anti-alcohol ideas current in the late 1800s reduced demand somewhat, but temperance movements gained far less traction in France than in regions such as Scandinavia and North America.[36] Temperance campaigners were especially active in France starting in the 1870s, just as phylloxera began to have an effect on wine production, and they took advantage of the raft of dubious beverages that filled the market during the wine shortage to convince some consumers that drinking "alcohol" (meaning spirits and excluding wine) was dangerous.

This was a major difference between France and countries where temperance and prohibition movements influenced policy: most French temperance advocates echoed the mainstream French medical and political fiction that the alcohol in wine was quite unlike the alcohol in distilled spirits. While spirits were said to be dangerous to health and a menace to society, wine was portrayed as a healthy beverage that benefited individuals and society and was a bulwark against alcoholism. No one was more widely quoted at this time than Louis Pasteur, the renowned French chemist whose research on fermentation in the 1850s and 1860s had long-term implications for wine making. But he was no dispassionate scientist. He promoted wines from his native Jura region (and often used Jura wines in his experiments) and supported wine consumption generally. His declaration that "wine is the healthiest and most hygienic of drinks" was continually disseminated by the wine industry to counter claims that it was harmful.[37] Pasteur's endorsement lay behind the French government's decisions to define wine, beer, and cider as "hygienic" beverages in 1900 and to tax them at a lower rate than distilled spirits.

With few exceptions, the French temperance movement found drinking wine and other fermented beverages acceptable, unlike counterpart movements elsewhere, which condemned all beverages containing alcohol. As for voluntary abstinence from all forms of alcohol, Patricia Prestwich has suggested that the French regarded it as an eccentricity akin to vegetarianism, concern for animal rights, and Protestantism.[38] The main target of French temperance campaigners was distilled spirits, and they were undoubtedly happy to see the production of brandy decline as phylloxera ravaged the vineyards of Charente. But although some of the shortfall was filled by spirits made from potatoes and sugar beets, a more worrying drink was absinthe. It had been made in France from the mid-1800s, but it became much more popular as wine supplies declined: consumption rose from seven hundred thousand liters (two hundred thousand gallons) in 1874 to thirty-six million liters (9.5 million gallons) in 1910. Absinthe was widely regarded as not only an intoxicant but hallucinogenic, and even though it was credited with enhancing artistic creativity, it was also believed to cause insanity. After it was implicated in a murder, absinthe was banned in Switzerland in 1907, and by many countries afterward, including France in 1914.[39]

As wine production decreased under the impact of phylloxera in 1877, Ludger Lunier, the founder of France's main temperance movement, the Société Française de Tempérance, wrote, "Our efforts must then tend to augment the production of wine, to improve and multiply the means of conserving it." It was not wine but wine fraud that was the enemy: "At the same time we must also fight against mixtures and falsifications that, in denaturing wine, render it more dangerous for public health because it is presented to the consumer under a false label."[40]

The widespread adulteration of wine and the fabrication of winelike beverages during this period of shortage had long-term effects on wine regulation in France specifically and Europe more generally. Until the 1870s, various kinds of intervention (such as adding sugar to must, diluting wine with water, and coloring wine with berries) were made, but they were not necessarily considered any more fraudulent than adding seawater, herbs, or spices to wine was among the ancient Romans. The extent of adulteration over time can never be measured, not only because definitions of adulteration have changed but also because the cases that appeared before the authorities undoubtedly represent only a small proportion of such practices.

Many cases came to light during the phylloxera crisis, partly because demand for wine outstripped supply for years on end and many consumers lowered their standards enough to buy all manner of concoctions posing as wine. By this time, advances in food chemistry had enabled scientists to isolate many of the ingredients in foods and beverages and to detect adulteration more accurately. This coincided with the rise of the hygiene movement in France, which promoted health and sanitation and was preoccupied with foods and drinks that were considered "natural"—a complicated concept that still bedevils the wine world, but one that certainly ruled out many additives. The range of such additives varied, however: chaptalizing wine was widespread in the nineteenth century, but some vignerons argued against it, insisting that only wine made from unsugared must was "natural."[41] It is clear too that when French vignerons complained about shady practices, they were thinking not only of foreigners but also of their French colleagues, and that they kept their eyes open for anything that would constitute unfair competition. In short, the demand for wine, opportunities to adulterate, improved technology, greater awareness of dangers to health, and surveillance by peers during the phylloxera crisis combined to favor not only a higher level of adulteration but also a higher level of detection.

Perhaps the most common form of wine adulteration was dilution with water. This was usually not done at the point of production, because producers paid taxes based on the volume of wine they made; it made sense to water down wine after the taxes had been paid, making the additional volume tax free. Adding plaster (gypsum or calcium sulfate) to wine was also widespread, because it produced a brighter and clearer color and elevated acidity, an important preservative. French scientists had determined that two grams of plaster per liter (0.27 ounces per gallon) of wine was not harmful to health, but in the 1880s this maximum was suspended, and in 1891 Bordeaux producers were able to have plastering banned entirely. The reason was that some Bordeaux négociants were blending plastered wines from the Midi (southern France) and Spain into local wines, which were harming Bordeaux's reputation.

Chaptalization, practiced in France since the eighteenth century, became more common at the end of the nineteenth to strengthen otherwise low-alcohol wines. During the 1880s and 1890s, more than a million vignerons, most in Burgundy and the central and northern regions, resorted to chaptalization each year, raising the alcohol level of their wines by 3 to 4 percent. The practice was denounced as unfair competition by producers in the Midi, where the grapes had a higher natural sugar count, which gave their wine a higher potential alcohol level.

The scarcity of French wine during the phylloxera crisis also encouraged the manufacture of wine from other products, such as imported raisins and currants. France had been a minor importer of Greek currants before the 1880s, but during that decade it took almost half of Greece's substantial production.[42] A popular book titled *The Art of Making Wine with Raisins* appeared in 1880 and went through twelve printings in the next six years. The recipe was simple enough: soak one hundred kilograms (220 pounds) of raisins in three hundred liters (eighty gallons) of warm water, let this ferment for about twelve days, and then press the liquid off the pulp. The result was three hundred liters of white "wine" with an alcohol level of 10 or 11 percent, which could be converted to red "wine" by adding thirty liters (eight gallons) of genuine red wine, enough elderberries, or a harmless chemical dye. Bordeaux and Hérault were the major centers of raisin wine production, and Bordeaux became a major port for the arrival of raisins and currants from Greece and Turkey. In 1892, as wine production recovered, under pressure from producers in the Midi, who regarded raisin wine as unfair competition, the French government raised duties on imported raisins and currants so as to price this beverage off the market.

There was also wine known as *deuxième cuvée* (second batch) because it used the marc (the solid residue, mainly skins, left over from wine making) a second time. This residue was mixed with warm water and cane or beet sugar and left to ferment for eight to twelve days, then the color was fixed and tartaric acid was added. Hundreds of millions of liters of deuxième cuvée and raisin wine were made—more than forty million (eleven million gallons) in 1890 alone—and together they accounted for an estimated 6 percent of the wine sold in France in the early 1880s and 10 percent in 1890.[43] These were the mainstream and more acceptable forms of what many regarded as wine fraud; although the Ministry of Justice declared raisin wine fraudulent in 1879, it later published a notice that the beverage was not harmful to health.

But these beverages were harmful to the reputation of French wine, especially of wines from Bordeaux. Vast volumes of Spanish and Portuguese wines were imported through Bordeaux, the region was a major producer of raisin wine, and many wines sold as "from Bordeaux" were international blends. In Britain, the major market for the prestigious and expensive clarets of Bordeaux, the London *Telegraph* noted in 1885, "An immense proportion of the wine sold in England as Claret has nothing to do with the banks of the Garonne, save that harsh, heavy vintages have been brought from Spain and Italy, and dried currants from Greece, there to be manipulated and re-shipped to England and the rest of the World as Lafitte, Larose, St. Julien, and St. Estèphe."[44]

Were all these practices fraudulent? Blending non-French wines with wines from Bordeaux is better thought of as counterfeiting (selling under a misleading label) than adulterating. Of the adulterating practices, some (like plastering, chaptalization, and using raisins) were permitted, to the extent that in the 1880s and 1890s regulations were posted requiring these wines to be appropriately labeled. They were clearly not fraudulent in a legal sense, but various lobby groups, usually regional associations of vignerons, called them fraudulent because they themselves did not follow these practices, which they believed gave others an unfair commercial advantage. This is an important point, as fraud by adulteration is often defined, ahistorically, as any departure from an essentially "natural" form of wine.

By the 1890s, many kinds of wine were available in France. There were French wines, foreign wines, and blends of both. (Blends of wines from Algeria and metropolitan France were technically French.) There were wines from vines growing on their own roots, and wines sourced from grafted vines. There were wines made from *Vitis vinifera* varieties, from indigenous American varieties, and from hybrids and crosses. There were wines made from fresh grapes, from raisins and currants, and from the marc left over from wine making. There were wines that had not been watered down, plastered, or chaptalized, and wines that had been. Despite some labeling rules, few of these were described as anything but "wine." A higher price ought to have indicated that a wine was, at the very least, made from fresh grapes and not stretched with water, but the very existence of so many possibilities in the marketplace gave no grounds for confidence. The decline in demand for luxury wines in this period is probably explained by uncertainty that paying a premium price would get the consumer an authentic wine of superior quality.

Commercial considerations rather than concerns about wine authenticity in itself drove the French government to adopt a series of laws that aimed to define wine.[45] An 1889 law offered a minimal definition of wine as a beverage made solely from fresh grapes. It did not prohibit the production of raisin wine nor prevent producers from calling it "wine," but it required this product to be identified as made from raisins. That satisfied producers of the Midi to some extent. Two years later, the maximum level of plastering was reestablished at two grams per liter (0.27 ounces per gallon). This law affected Midi producers most, as plastering was common there, but it also helped Bordeaux producers in their struggle against some négociants who were blending Bordeaux wine with plastered Midi wine. The same law banned watering down and adding alcohol. Some retailers and merchants tried to get around the ban by clearly marking their wines as being diluted or alcohol enhanced, because French contract law indemnified sellers of any product against legal action if the purchaser was aware of its characteristics. This law, dating from the French Revolution, was changed in 1894 so that the ban on adding water or alcohol could be enforced.

But these laws of 1889 to 1894 posed real problems of enforcement. It was not always clear, for example, who should be charged when wine was found to be diluted: the producer, the négociant, or the retailer. Together with other concerns, such as anxiety in Bordeaux and Champagne that the wines of these regions were being counterfeited on the international market, the general uncertainties surrounding wine prompted the French government to adopt a comprehensive wine law in 1905. It is important to note that French legislators were primarily concerned about ensuring fair competition among producers, not about consumer rights. Although some deputies argued that adulterations were "poisons" that "filled up the insane asylums," the minister of agriculture replied, "We are discussing a law on fraud, not a law on public health. . . . At the same time, I would be pleased if certain provisions of the bill could fight against fraud and also protect public health."[46]

But public health was an issue in the case of many concoctions on the market. Some beverages labeled "wine" contained ingredients such as sulfuric acid and glycerin, and some producers turned to fuchsine (a coal-tar dye) and arsenic to deepen the color of red wines instead of using benign products such as elderberries.[47] A British journal in 1883 noted various procedures that could be carried out to test for harmful substances. If gun cotton (a fluffy white substance and low-level explosive) was stained with red wine and then washed, the color would come out if the wine was "natural" but not if it had mineral dyes. The writer suggested that "by carrying about a supply of gun cotton to test one's vin ordinaire at hotel or restaurant, it would be possible to avoid being poisoned, but one might come within the penal clauses of the Explosives Act."[48]

Phylloxera also had a big effect on France's wine exports. The British market was important, and duties on wine imported there had been lowered in the early 1860s, in principle opening the way for more British to drink more wine. Although Britain had historically imported vast volumes of wine in both fortified and table styles, wine was generally regarded as a luxury product there and annual consumption rates were low, about a bottle and a half for each person in the mid-1800s. But there was a sizable increase in British wine imports after the duties were lowered, and French wine was able to make real gains: its share rose from 8 to 40 percent between the 1850s and the 1880s (mainly at the expense of Portuguese and Spanish wine), and even though it fell as phylloxera reduced production, France supplied more than 30 percent of Britain's wine imports until World War I.[49] For the most part, these were the red wines from Bordeaux that the British called claret, although no consumer could be absolutely certain where they originated: *Ridley's*, the leading British alcohol trade journal, noted in 1891 that "blends with Spanish Red, South of France, and other wines are sold, occasionally under their true designation, but generally under the usurped title of 'Claret.'"[50]

Uncertainty tended to depress demand for higher-priced wines, even those listed in the 1855 Bordeaux Classification, as consumers were hesitant to spend a lot of money for wine of questionable quality and provenance. According to *Ridley's*, the production of First Growth Château Margaux rose from 450 hogsheads (210-liter, or 55-gallon, barrels) of "premier wine" in the early 1880s to 1,200–1,400 hogsheads of "indifferent" or "bad" wine in the early 1900s. In the 1890s, *Ridley's* published a long comment on the reputation of Bordeaux's wine in Britain: "The Public, who unfortunately know more about Growths, than Vintages, receive Circulars offering Château this or Château that at apparently extremely low rates, and on the strength of the name, purchase Wines, which can but prove intensely disappointing. They then are apt to argue that, if wines bearing the names of the best estates of the Médoc be so inferior, then those of lower grade must be bad indeed. Thus their faith in Claret, instead of in the merchant, who has sold it them, is shaken, and an inducement is at hand to try Wine from some other districts."[51]

This seems to lay blame at the door of British wine merchants, some of whom undoubtedly blended prestigious Bordeaux wines with cheaper wines to increase their profits. Some merchants made what were called basis wines from imported must and other substances and blended them with French wine, selling the result as wine from Bordeaux. *Ridley's* noted in 1906 that "people drink so-called 'Claret', composed of one-third of the genuine article and two-thirds of the British imposition, and condemn, not the latter, but Claret."[52] Such practices were possible because the great bulk of wine was shipped and stored in barrels, not in bottles. A handful of Bordeaux producers began to bottle their own wines and use their own labels and branded corks in the 1880s as a way of ensuring that the wine purchased in Britain was the wine that they shipped.

But nothing stopped the slide in claret sales. Between 1877–81 and 1900–1904, quality wine exports from Bordeaux to Britain fell by almost two-thirds. That was a disaster, because Britain took nearly half of Bordeaux's exports at this time. Loss percentages in some other markets were also high—87 and 43 percent in Latin America and Germany, respectively—but the volumes involved were smaller.[53] The reason seems to have been largely a matter of reputation and reliability. Sales to the United States also declined, but more because Americans had tended to drink the more common wines of Bordeaux rather than the higher-end clarets that the British favored. While the limited supplies of the most prestigious clarets held up (undoubtedly with the help of water, foreign wines, and raisin wine), the mass production of the ordinary wines that sold well in the United States declined. At the same time, California was fast becoming the main wine-producing region in North America, and the completion of the transcontinental railroad enabled wine consumers in the major urban markets of the Midwest and East to switch effortlessly from French to American wine. The United States consul in Paris is reported to have recommended that Americans "give up the unwholesome counterfeits of claret that are now produced in France, and drink instead the wines made in the United States, such as catawba."[54]

Faced with widespread reputation problems, many of Bordeaux's producers tried to improve their collective image by adding "Château" to the names of their estates. This became common by the early twentieth century, but when the phylloxera crisis began, almost all estates were known simply by their name, and in the early 1800s many were known only by the name of their owner. In the 1824 edition of his book on Médoc, William Franck lists estates by "Proprietor's Name," and although the 1853 edition lists them by their own names, only two (Margaux and Lafite) are designated as "château."[55] In the 1851 edition of his authoritative 1833 work on wine, Cyrus Redding mentions only one château, Margaux, while the 1855 Bordeaux Classification lists five (First Growths Lafite, Margaux, and Latour, Third Growth d'Issan, and Fourth Growth Beychevelle), and an 1864 English book lists four (Haut-Brion, Lafite, Latour, and Margaux).[56] Margaux was consistently included and might well have been the inspiration for the rest: an anonymous 1745 classification of producers by the price their wine fetched puts Margaux at the top and refers to it simply as "le Château," without the name.[57] By the twentieth century, however, all the estates in the 1855 classification bore the "Château" title, as well as many not in the classification, and they were printing it on their labels.

The significance of the designation is that a château has associations with aristocracy and, through it, connotations of lineage, continuity, age, and permanence. Noble families were commonly assumed to trace their titled ancestors back to the mists of the Middle Ages, even though most nineteenth-century French nobles could trace their nobility no further back than two centuries and most of Bordeaux's châteaux were built in the mid-1800s. Equally important, these associations extended to the château's vines. As one commentary on Château Margaux (which was completed in 1817) noted, "The house is in the image of the vintage. . . . A wine long matured, a house long inhabited: Margaux the vintage and Margaux the château are the products of two equally rare things: *rigor and time*" (italics in the original).[58] Stressing continuity and age was especially important after the disruptions of the phylloxera period, when Bordeaux's sometimes hundred-year-old vines were wiped out and most of the vineyards began to grow young vines on American rootstock. If the château designation failed to overcome the region's reputation for adulterated wine in the short term—*Ridley's* reference to "Château this or Château that" reeks of disdain—it did no harm over the longer term.

Champagne, in contrast, maintained its reputation more consistently than Bordeaux. Small-scale vignerons grew most of the grapes, and although some of them produced champagne under their own names, most sold their wine to the big champagne houses, which could better afford the technology to make sparkling wine. Champagne became heavily dominated and branded by the major houses, and one commentator noted in 1890 that "within ten years we will no longer recognise the name of champagne, but only those of Roederer, Plankaert, Bollinger, without any idea what these wines will be made of."[59] Champagne might be good or bad, but because it was shipped in bottles that were almost totally tamper proof, there was little or no chance that it could be adulterated after it was bottled. Production surged during the nineteenth century, rising from three hundred thousand bottles in 1800 to twenty million in 1850 and reaching thirty-six million in 1883.

As far as selling champagne was concerned, the region did not focus on the vignerons and their vines, as Burgundy did, because most growers sold their wine to the big champagne houses, which blended it with the wines of hundreds of other vignerons. Champagne houses promoted champagne the wine, and their marketing paid little or no attention to regions within Champagne or to Champagne itself; it is likely that many consumers, especially outside France, did not know that Champagne was a place.

Champagne successfully straddled two images in the later 1800s, one aristocratic and exclusive, the other distinctly down-market, but only as far down as the better-off middle classes. The aristocratic image of champagne drew on the royal associations of the region, especially of Reims, which was the city where French kings had been crowned for centuries until the

French Revolution. During the nineteenth century, the clientele of champagne was heavily aristocratic, with steady sales among the titled of Germany, Austria-Hungary, Great Britain, Russia, and other nations. In the late 1890s an advertisement for Laurent-Perrier Sans-Sucre champagne listed some of it consumers, including the kings of Belgium and Greece, the duke of Saxe-Coburg-Gotha, the duchess of Teck, the earl of Durham, the prince of Rohan, Lord Grey of Winton, and an assortment of other nobles, knights, and military leaders. The list was clearly designed to appeal to potential purchasers who were not titled, as the advertisement points out that Laurent-Perrier was available "from all Wine Merchants throughout the World" and announces a competition with prizes valued at £6,000.[60] No self-respecting aristocrat would enter a competition, but an upwardly mobile bourgeois might well.

Champagne's large-scale producers pursued sales wherever they could, and they were among the pioneers of appealing to niche markets. Reflecting its image as a wine for celebrations and good times, champagne labels featured hunting and sports scenes. One, with the name "Grand Vin des cyclistes, fin de siècle," showed a young woman on a bicycle, her hair flying loose in the wind, pursued by two male cyclists. Other labels were designed for champagne to be drunk at baptisms and weddings, while yet others celebrated anniversaries such as Christopher Columbus's arrival in the Americas (1892) and the French Revolution (1889). Nor did champagne producers avoid contemporary politics. One label marking the centennial of the French Revolution showed Marie-Antoinette, which would appeal to conservative drinkers, while another depicted an uplifting republican scene, to appeal to left-wing consumers. During the famous trial of Alfred Dreyfus, a Jewish French artillery officer accused of spying for Germany, one champagne house produced a "Champagne Anti-juif."[61]

Beyond this, as Kolleen Guy has shown, champagne forged an identity with France itself through the idea of terroir. In the nineteenth century, "terroir" was an unstable concept that could simply mean a rural area that was responsible for "the collective character traits of the local inhabitants."[62] Food and drink, especially cheese and wine, were also viewed as deriving their character from the specific localities in which they were produced, and as a national mass market for regional specialities developed in the nineteenth century, French people were able to taste the terroir of places they had never visited. They were metaphorically eating and drinking their country, and there is a mystical quality in the process that echoes the taking of wine and bread in Communion. We are, it should be noted, far away from the common current usage of *terroir*, which refers to the specific ecological characteristics of wine regions (especially soils) that are some-times thought to be perceptible in the flavor and style of the wine the vines there produce.

Producers of sparkling wines in other parts of France began to sell their wines as "champagne" so as to benefit from the premium prices the brand fetched. In 1889, the champagne houses obtained a court ruling that for-bade producers anywhere else in France to label their wines as "champagne" or "vin de Champagne." Yet as worldwide demand for champagne grew beyond the ability of producers to meet it from their phylloxera-dimin-ished vineyards, many champagne houses broke their own law by buying wines from other regions and blending them with wines from Champagne. Fraud became a central issue in Champagne in the early 1900s, especially after the poor harvests of 1908 and 1910.[63] Sales of champagne in Britain declined from thirteen million bottles a year in the 1880s and 1890s to nine million in the years before World War I.

Fraud and misrepresentation remained problems not only in Champagne but throughout France as the nineteenth century turned into the twentieth. The raisin wine of the phylloxera period was disappearing from the market, but fraud was believed to be widespread, and it made exports of French wine difficult. France soon faced a new problem, however: uncontrolled produc-tion. The renewal of its vineyards after phylloxera meant not only planting with grafted vines but also the widespread adoption of different varieties (some higher and some lower yielding), of planting patterns that promoted production, and of the more extensive use of fertilizer. Increased productiv-ity from replanted vineyards more than compensated for the loss of poorly performing land under vines, so yields per hectare rose and France entered a period of wine surplus and declining prices, further stimulated by easier and cheaper transportation. Having survived the ravages of phylloxera, vignerons throughout France expected business to return to normal, but instead they faced a different set of problems.

No vignerons were collectively more desperate than those of Languedoc-Roussillon, where the end of phylloxera and high demand for wine encour-aged the creation of economies largely based on viticulture and related activities: barrel making, fertilizer and sulfur production, and the manufac-ture of equipment used in vineyards and wineries. Hundreds of people were employed in the wine trade in centers such as Béziers and Narbonne. Like any economy based on one commodity, it was highly vulnerable, and in the early years of the twentieth century it began to feel the impact as wine prices declined from about twenty francs a hectoliter in 1899 to less than half that for most of the following decade.

After the short period of prosperity that followed the trials of the phylloxera decades, a depression from 1900 to 1910 pushed the vignerons of Languedoc-Roussillon to take action where the regional and national authorities seemed unwilling. Their target was not overproduction, however, but fraudulent wines that they believed were flooding the market. The protest movement was not confined to small-scale vignerons but also included bigger producers, those with more than forty hectares (ninety-nine acres) of vines, who collectively owned a third of the region's viticultural land. Crossing class and political allegiance, the movement was a broad-based defense of the regional wine industry.[64]

In 1905 the inhabitants of Argeliers, in the département of Aude, led by a local vigneron, Marcelin Albert, signed a petition stating, "The undersigned have determined to pursue their just claims to the very end, to refuse to pay their taxes, and to demand the resignation of the elected officials, and they urge all the communes of the Midi and Algeria to follow their example to the cries of 'Long live natural wine! Down with the poisoners!'"[65] It is notable that this demonstrates no resentment at the substantial wine production of Algeria but instead a sense of solidarity with another French wine region suffering from the effects of fraud. It also entirely ignores the issue of overproduction and lays responsibility for the crisis squarely at the feet of the producers of fraudulent wines.

A commission set up by the government in 1907 declared unambiguously that "the viticultural crisis is not due to overproduction." It pointed out that vineyard area had declined in the late nineteenth century, but it failed to acknowledge that increased yields had more than compensated for that. In the four départements of Languedoc-Roussillon, yields were a third higher than before phylloxera, thanks to replanting predominantly with the aramon variety, which easily gave more than one hundred hectoliters a hectare (1,069 gallons per acre) in some districts.[66] Not only were yields high, but by 1900 Languedoc-Roussillon was responsible for 40 percent of France's wine production, meaning that any notable drop or surge in the size of its harvest would have a meaningful impact on the national supply of wine. Ignoring all this, the commission declared that "the natural production of wine cannot meet the demand for this beverage."[67]

Although overproduction in the region was the most important reason for low prices, the commission and Languedoc-Roussillon's vignerons focused squarely on wine fraud. Quite possibly, after decades when millions of liters of imported wine and various winelike beverages were needed to supply the French market, an oversupply of genuine French wine seemed inconceivable. Acknowledging overproduction would mean having to take action to reduce land under vines—unthinkable to vignerons who had only recently replanted and whose vines were just coming into full production—or to reduce yields, with radical green harvests or by replanting with lower-cropping varieties. For the vignerons of Languedoc-Roussillon, collective destiny and individual well-being were tied inexorably to producing vast volumes of inexpensive wine of mediocre quality, and the solution to their challenges could not compromise that purpose.

Languedoc-Roussillon's vignerons more than achieved their ambitions with abundant harvests from 1905 to 1910 (producing an annual average of more than 6.6 billion liters, or 1.7 billion gallons, compared to 3.5 to 4 billion liters, or 0.92 billion to 1.1 billion gallons, in 1902–3), and in doing so they depressed prices further and deepened their misery. Prices of six or seven francs a hectoliter meant that vignerons were losing money on their vineyards, and many fell into poverty. Sending wives and children out to work was rarely an option, because the region was so dependent on wine that the whole regional economy suffered and there were no jobs available for them. Factories that produced vineyard and winery equipment laid off workers, and as spending power declined there were more and more empty stalls at local markets.

Frustrated at the failure of the government to deal decisively with the crisis that threatened their livelihoods, growers in Languedoc began a series of rallies, each bigger than the one before, throughout Languedoc on successive Sundays from March to June 1907. The first, in Bize, in Aude, attracted six hundred people, and the second, in Narbonne, swelled to eighty thousand. The final two rallies, in Nîmes and Montpellier, saw three hundred thousand and five hundred thousand people demonstrate in the streets.[68] On each occasion Albert addressed the crowd in terms that evoked the French Revolution, calling for a "Committee of Public Safety for the defense of viticulture." By the middle of June, half the mayors of the region's communes had resigned, a challenge to the central government.

The government in Paris tried to appease the vignerons by raising the tax on sugar so as to reduce the profitability of deuxième cuvée wines, which relied on large additions of sugar to compensate for its absence in the second-use marc. But the government also acted forcefully against the protesting vignerons. Arrest warrants were issued for Albert and other leaders of the movement, and troops were dispatched to the troubled region. On 19 June 1907, soldiers in Narbonne fired on protesters, killing five and wounding ten. Learning of this the next day, sympathizers in Perpignan burned down the prefecture (the seat of the national government's representative in each département).[69] But the insurrection did not go much further, because the government was uncertain of the loyalty of locally recruited troops—an infantry regiment at Agde mutinied—and made a number of concessions.

Key among them was the law of 29 June 1907, which was hastily passed to appease the Languedoc vignerons but nonetheless contained provisions that helped solve some of the problems. It required producers to declare the size of their crop and the volume of their wine reserves (including fine wines aging in warehouses and cellars) annually. These declarations would give the authorities information on the volume of wine that would come to market each year. The law also struck at artificial wine by setting limits on the amount of sugar that could be used in making wine and tried to encourage quality by prohibiting the sale of substances designed to improve defective wine. Further legislation in the following months regulated the wine trade and established a central agency for the repression of fraud. In September 1907 an important law defined wine as the exclusive product of "the alcoholic fermentation of fresh grapes or of the juice of fresh grapes."[70] The government thus responded to producers' concerns about quality and fraud without dealing directly with the underlying problem of overproduction.

One important series of regulations concerned delimited regions of production. A 1905 law against fraud made it an offense to falsely portray a commodity as the product of a particular locality so as to increase its value. Starting in 1908, the government established the limits of broad regions that produced distinctive alcoholic beverages, such as Champagne, Cognac, Bordeaux, Banyuls, and Armagnac. This was the beginning of the *appellation d'origine contrôlée* (AOC) system, a complex of rules that eventually regulated the provenance and quality not only of wine but also of commodities such as distilled spirits, cheeses, fruit, and livestock.

But fraud and misrepresentation continued to be both problems and scapegoats for the ongoing problems in the wine industry. Two years after the government began to delimit appellations, the vignerons of Marne declared war on the champagne houses that they accused of fraudulently using wine from other regions of France. Between December 1910 and April 1911, crowds of vignerons stormed one cellar after another where they believed fraud was being perpetrated, and smashed the bottles resting in the riddling racks and along the kilometers of tunnels where wine was being stored before being disgorged. On 17 January, for example, a day when thousands of bottles of wine from the Midi were said to be arriving, a crowd invaded the Perrier champagne house. The vignerons pushed the truck with the bottles of southern wine into the Marne River, then invaded

Perrier's premises and smashed fifteen thousand bottles of wine and barrels holding another two thousand liters (528 gallons).[71] By the end of the wave of disturbances, hundreds of thousands of liters of champagne and base wines had been destroyed and more than thirty-five thousand vines pulled out. Once again, troops were brought in, and parts of Marne were effectively under military control for nine months as soldiers and protesters clashed in the streets of Épernay, Ay, and nearby villages and vineyards.

Although this revolt had clear overtones of a class struggle, one side composed of small-scale vignerons, the other of big champagne houses, the immediate aim of the Marne vignerons was not to transform economic relationships but to end wine fraud. The only champagne houses that they attacked were those they believed to be using wine from outside the Champagne region—although the targets were based on a handwritten list that might not have been wholly accurate. As Kolleen Guy notes, their cause "was quite simple: to protect the connection between 'champagne,' the wine, and 'Champagne,' the land and its terroir."[72] Moreover, the protesters were not only small-scale vignerons and sharecroppers but also more substantial vineyard proprietors; all had an interest in ensuring that champagne was made from only their grapes.

"Fraud" in Champagne was about making wine with grapes grown outside the appellation, and that, of course, raised the issue of the boundaries of Champagne. It might have been expected that any attempts to define delimited wine regions would immediately give rise to complaints from districts that were excluded, and a major problem soon arose in the case of Champagne. The regulations for Champagne were set down in 1905, in 1908, and again in 1911, and all specified that wine sold as "champagne" must be made from grapes grown in designated districts in the département of Marne. They thus excluded producers from the département of Aube entirely. Not only was this an insult, because the chief town of Aube, Troyes, was the historic capital of Champagne, but it also ignored practice: since the 1880s, Aube producers had supplied the champagne houses of Marne with part of their white wine for blending and making into champagne. For several months there was deadlock between partisans of Marne, who wanted it to be the sole source of champagne, and those of Aube, who wanted the boundaries of the Champagne region to include them. The issue was not finally settled until 1927, when the Champagne appellation was defined as including four hundred communes in the départements of Marne, Aisne, and Aube.

The regulatory system that began to emerge in France in the early 1900s, the basis of the comprehensive AOC rules that have governed French wine production since the 1930s, thus arose from the conditions prevailing after phylloxera was brought under control and as producers and the government tried to bring order to an industry and a market in chaos. Politicians in Paris did not simply impose regulations on producers; as we have seen, in a number of cases the direct pressure of producers themselves forced the government into legislative action. Vignerons regarded wine fraud not (or not only) as an issue of quality, reputation, and consumer protection but as unfair competition that was a threat to their very livelihoods. Phylloxera had driven thousands of vignerons out of viticulture, and those who remained were that much more determined to stay.

7. Pinard and Postwar France
1914–1930

France's long wine crisis, which spanned eight decades from the arrival of phylloxera to the end of the Second World War, was a series of disasters and setbacks of many different kinds. France's vineyards did not recover from phylloxera until the early 1900s, and following this natural disaster enhanced by human incompetence, economic problems struck the French wine industry. Then, just as the balance of supply and demand was being restored, World War I broke out, bringing a new set of challenges to the industry. In the decade following the war, exports sagged for reasons as varied as the revolution in Russia and Prohibition in the United States, fraud remained a widespread problem, and attempts to regulate appellations brought chaos to the industry.

When France mobilized for war with Germany in early August 1914, vineyards throughout the country bathed in the warmth of what seemed an ideal summer. Most wine regions had been spared spring frosts, and the weather had been almost perfect from early summer—conditions that promised a plentiful and quality harvest, as long as the autumn held up. But the challenges of late summer and autumn proved not so much climatic as organizational. Although the likelihood of war had been growing for years, French governments had made no plans to maintain, let alone increase, agricultural production during hostilities. France's political and military leaders, like their counterparts throughout Europe, believed that a war would be briskly fought and quickly decided. French vignerons and vineyard workers mobilizing in August 1914 believed the war would be over in time for the harvest in September or October, making them even more optimistic than British soldiers who headed to France thinking they would be home for Christmas. They did not return in time for the harvest, of course, and hundreds of thousands never returned at all.

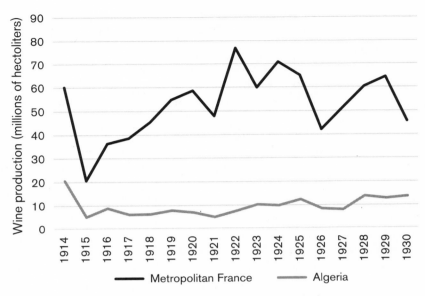

DIAGRAM 7.1. Wine production, Metropolitan France and Algeria, 1914–1930

Like the rest of the agricultural sector, viticulture was struck by an immediate labor shortage in 1914, and that year's harvest was brought in by women and children—many of whom were employed to pick grapes in ordinary years—and men who had been exempted from the first draft because of age or other reasons. Even if many of these grape harvesters were not as skilled or able as the usual workers, accounts stressed the patriotic energy and enthusiasm with which the grapes were picked in 1914. Those who picked the grapes in Champagne needed extra doses of patriotism, as they worked within range of German artillery and snipers. At least twenty children, detailed to pick grapes from the most exposed vines because they were small targets, were killed in the course of the harvest, and many more were wounded.

Vineyard workers throughout the rest of France faced more banal challenges. Horses were widely used in French vineyards, but most were requisitioned for the military, putting additional pressure on grape harvesters. Once the wine was made, it was difficult to get it to any but local markets; railways, which had become vital for moving wine from the south and west of France to Paris and other northern cities, were requisitioned at the outbreak of war, and their transportation of commercial goods was suspended. As the prospects for shipping wine dimmed, wholesale prices plummeted, although they picked up when the suspension on transporting commercial goods by rail was eased and when military wine purchases began in November 1914. But even then, the army requisitioned the bulk of the rail tankers that the wine industry had used. Transportation remained a problem for producers wanting to get their wine to civilian markets throughout the war, as the government regarded civilian wine supplies as a lower priority than supplies for the military.

True to expectations, the 1914 harvest was a bumper crop that produced vast volumes of wine: some six billion liters (1.6 billion gallons) in metro-politan France, almost 50 percent more than the preceding year. In a spirit of patriotism and commercial calculation, Languedoc-Roussillon producers donated twenty million liters (five million gallons) of wine (which was sell-ing at depressed prices) for distribution to military hospitals, where it would boost the morale of the wounded and (given prevailing French med-ical views that wine was healthy and therapeutic) hasten their recovery and recuperation. By the time the wine was shipped, the atrocious battles that had already cost hundreds of thousands of dead and wounded had cooled the optimism of summer, and the conflict on the western front had settled into a drawn-out war of attrition.

Wine was given not only to the wounded in military hospitals, for there was a long tradition of supplying wine to French soldiers, even if not on a systematic basis. During the nineteenth century, the temperance move-ment and the wine industry had called spirits into question, and there were some claims that alcoholic beverages of any kind had negative effects on military discipline and efficiency. Some prominent French military leaders, such as General Joseph Gallieni, were nondrinkers, and some ministers of war had opposed the drinking of wine by soldiers.

In the early 1900s, a number of European armies carried out experi-ments to see how alcohol affected performance. A German survey of sol-diers who fired some thirty-six thousand rounds over sixteen consecutive days compared those who had drunk spirits (presumably a small volume) and those who had not; the results indicated that marksmanship was not affected.[1] The French military command seemed more realistic about the chances of preventing soldiers from drinking. Instead of comparing the effi-ciency of those who drank and those who did not, the French compared the effects of beer and wine. They concluded that wine had less impact than beer on marksmanship, and this confirmed a study of soldiers in Bordeaux who were "less tired and went along the road singing and chanting" after drinking wine but were "sluggish [and] marched with a heavy step" after drinking beer.[2] The decision to allow French soldiers to continue drinking wine was an easy one, and perhaps their commanders thought this might even give their men an advantage if they had to fight beer-drinking German soldiers.

Not only was wine seen as not harmful to military efficiency, but it was considered a positive benefit for soldiers. As we have seen, the weight of opinion in the French medical profession at this time was that wine was a positive component of the daily diet and a powerful tool in the struggle against alcoholism. The few physicians who did express doubts about the health value of wine were blamed for what was believed to be a growing number of French families' opting to drink mineral water rather than wine with their meals; annual production of bottled water in France rose from 30 million to 115 million bottles between 1881 and 1911.[3] Any skepticism about the health benefits of wine was widely contested by the majority of French physicians, who insisted on the centrality of wine in the French diet.

Pierre Viala, the editor of the *Revue de viticulture* and a professor of viticulture at the National Institute of Agronomy, wrote as war dragged on in 1916 that doctors who denied the health benefits of wine were "motivated more by snobbism than by professional duty." The experience of war, he argued, was undercutting their "foreign and anti-French" ideas: "Our soldiers at the front have definitively dealt with [sabré] these ideas that are anti-French both in their conception and in their application."[4] Not only was wine a "food of the first order," Viala wrote, but it was healthy and therapeutic, aided digestion, counteracted parasites, and enlivened the nervous system. "Soldiers who drank wine were less fatigued, had more energy, and were able to carry out more sustained military activity."[5]

Before 1914 there was no regular daily wine ration in the French army, although a quarter liter (about a quarter quart) could be doled out at a commander's discretion on holidays, during major maneuvers, and when activities required strenuous physical effort. But in November 1914, two months into the war, soldiers were allotted a daily ration of a quarter liter of wine, and the government, taking a lesson from the gift of Languedoc wine to military hospitals, appealed for donations of wine for serving soldiers. Again, southern vignerons responded generously (the producers of Hérault alone sent ten million liters, or 2.6 million gallons), giving the popular left-wing singer Gaston Montéhus, who had composed a song to celebrate the 1907 vignerons' rebellion, the occasion to write a hymn to wine. One stanza read,

In drinking this generous wine, they will forget all their misery.
In its warmth they will feel strength, energy, courage.
For wine revives the heart and inspires arms to take up their task.[6]

If the producers of Languedoc-Roussillon intended their gift to be self-serving as well as patriotic, they judged it well, for the government decided early in 1915 to start giving soldiers a more generous wine ration. It varied throughout that year: sometimes a quarter of a liter (0.07 gallons), sometimes a third (0.08 gallons), sometimes a half (0.13 gallons). Additional wine could be distributed to soldiers in demanding circumstances, and soldiers would also get a ration of 125 milliliters (about half a cup) of high-alcohol spirits.[7] These wine purchases placed little pressure on the government at first, because the large 1914 harvest depressed wine prices and caused producers to sell their wines at bargain prices just to reduce their stocks. Moreover, these were not fine wines by any means but of poor or mediocre quality, made from high-yielding grape varies such as aramon and expected to last a year at most. Military needs grew as the armies expanded and wine rations increased, and because wartime harvests after 1914 were modest at best, the pressure of demand on supply began to inflate prices. In 1916, when a small harvest threatened shortages of wine, the government set prices by decree, ostensibly guided by criteria such as region, alcohol strength, and quality, but in reality to its own advantage and often well below market price: wine that could be sold on the open market for 180 to 200 francs per 228-liter (60-gallon) barrel was requisitioned by the army at 112 to 130 francs.[8]

Wine requisitions were supposed to strike all producers and regions proportionately, but in practice almost 90 percent came from five départements: four in Languedoc-Roussillon (Hérault, Aude, Gard, Pyrénées-Orientales) and Gironde, the location of Bordeaux's vineyards. Together, these départements produced 58 percent of the nation's wine, so they were forced to contribute a disproportionate share of the army's wine requirements.[9] They were also the five leading wine-producing départements, and they were well provided with rail links to the population centers of northeastern France, which were important markets in peacetime and close to the battlefronts from 1914. It was clearly more efficient to draw wine from these départements than to requisition small volumes from minor wine-producing départements that were not connected to main railroads. Moreover, the burden of requisitioning fell most heavily on large producers. Those who produced more than ten thousand liters (2,600 gallons) had to turn over a third of their production at fixed prices, while those who produced less than six thousand liters (1,600 gallons) were spared requisitioning demands altogether. Those in between had varying fractions of their production requisitioned.

Wine requisitions rose when the daily military wine ration was increased to half a liter (0.13 gallons), a volume that Viala (and General Joseph Joffre) thought was the absolute minimum a soldier should drink each day to maintain his well-being. In 1918, in response to mutinies the previous year, the ration was raised to three-quarters of a liter (0.2 gallons) and soldiers were allowed to purchase a further quarter liter (0.07 gallons) at subsidized prices. By that time it had become difficult for soldiers to buy additional wine; the merchants and négociants who had worked the war zones in the early years of the war, carrying their alcohol to the trenches in wheelbarrows, were effectively kept away by 1918, as the French commander, General Philippe Pétain, had adopted a more rigorous alcohol policy. But soldiers might also drink more wine as food: a military cookbook includes a "soupe vigneronne," made of a liter (0.26 gallons) of wine, a liter of water, sugar, and crumbled bread. It is said to have been especially appreciated by men during rests on marches during summer.[10]

A liter of wine a day (even at the 10 to 11 percent alcohol level that was common then) seems generous for soldiers on active duty, and one army physician, while noting that wine was "a healthy drink," warned against exceeding the daily ration. He wrote that soldiers "instinctively distrust water," whose dangers were clear, but stressed that a liter of wine a day was "the dose that it is unwise to exceed in any case or under any pretext." At the front, he said, the military authorities were obliged to act against any soldier who was drunk. "More than one has paid dearly for his debauchery. Some have lost their rank or have appeared before a military court for acts committed while drunk; others have died as a result of being so unwise as to get drunk."[11] Nevertheless, the military authorities rarely prosecuted drunkenness unless it was aggravated by another offense, such as theft or insulting an officer.[12] Adam Zietnek argues that the French military authorities tried during the war to identify the volume of wine that was enough to keep soldiers happy and prepare them for combat but not so much that would it lead to indiscipline. The sweet spot, he suggests, lay between half a liter and a liter (0.13 and 0.26 gallons) of wine a day.[13]

The military authorities constantly fought against attempts to smuggle spirits into the war zone, and regulations issued the year before war was declared express their priorities: "In order to prevent cases of drunkenness, the military commission will regulate the consumption of healthy beverages (wine, beer, cider) and forbid the consumption of distilled spirits [*boissons alcooliques*]."[14] While the wine ration seems generous, it was

carefully regulated. An official guide for officers on the minutiae of con-
ducting war and looking after their troops specifies that "wine must be
natural, correct to the taste, clear, and contain 10 to 11 percent alcohol to
guarantee its quality and that it will keep."[15] It also specifies that in certain
conditions, such as during route marches in the heat of the day, soldiers
should fill their canteens with pure water or water fortified with coffee, but
"NEVER WINE OR ALCOHOL."[16] At other times, soldiers were permitted
to add coffee or wine to their water.

French forces at the front (about 2.8 million men at any given time)
consumed 1.2 billion liters (320 million gallons) of wine in 1917 and
1.5 billion liters (400 million gallons) in 1918. The 1918 figure represented
two-fifths of 1917's production. The wine was delivered to war zones by rail
in thousands of tankers, then transferred to 225- or 500-liter (59- or
132-gallon) barrels before being taken close to the front lines by truck or
horse and distributed in buckets to soldiers in the trenches. Virtually all this
wine was red, because it was thought more masculine and more likely than
white to put fire into soldiers' blood and breathe courage into their hearts.
The respective merits of red and white wine were debated in the Chamber
of Deputies in 1916 when one deputy drew attention to a case where white
wine had replaced red wine destined for French troops. The debate hinged
on the respective prices of red and white wine, but some deputies thought
that supplying white wine to troops was scandalous, while others argued
that good white wine was just as beneficial as red.[17] The undersecretary for
supply pointed out that there were indeed problems with the wine supplied
to the army—most was good, but some was mediocre and some was simply
bad—but that he understood that vignerons sometimes did not have
enough red wine and had to use white wine to make up the volume that
they were required to supply. On a number of occasions, he said, he had
pleaded with the courts not to prosecute, especially when it concerned "the
brave women who looked after their vineyards while their husbands were
at the front."[18]

The French common soldier was known as a *poilu* ("hairy man," because
he was often unshaven), and his ordinary red wine of middling quality was
known as "pinard." The origin of *pinard* is uncertain, but the word was
used as early as the 1880s and might well have originated in the Loire valley and derived from *pinot noir*. Even though military wine during the war
came from regions where virtually no pinot noir was grown, this slang
term would have been used by soldiers from the Loire and might have
been adopted by those from other parts of France. Pinard became a cult
commodity, almost a fetish—it was sometimes called Père (Father) Pinard,

sometimes Saint Pinard—among soldiers, who were said to await the arrival of the pinard wagons (*fourgons pinardiers*) with more anticipation than food or letters from home (see figure 7.1). During the parliamentary debate on the virtues of red and white wine, one deputy said that to a soldier, "a glass of wine . . . is a glass of morale."[19] Wartime illustrations often depict poilu and pinard together (see figure 7.2). One cartoon shows a poilu saluting a barrel of pinard as he passes, a wartime poster called on citizens to "save your wine for our poilus" (a way of justifying the shortages of wine for civilian consumption), and hymns were written to pinard. A stanza of one song from 1916 goes:

Love your country, love your flag,
Love your sergeant, love your captain,
Love the adjutant even if he has a filthy mouth,
But that doesn't prevent you from loving pinard![20]

The reason for the association was probably no more complicated than that regular servings of wine provided welcome relief from the discomforts and dangers of life at the front. Over the longer term, drinking pinard while on active service was said to have created a generation of wine drinkers for the postwar decades. Pierre Viala, a tireless advocate for French wine, was confident in 1916 that French soldiers from Normandy and Brittany, where cider was the popular drink, would give it up and remain true to wine after they had experienced its benefits in the trenches. In fact, he was confident that all armies fighting alongside France "will take back to their countries, along with victory, the healthy habit of consuming wine and the appreciation of its value for moral and physical well-being."[21] Ironically, the wine-drinking experience of Australian (and other British Empire) soldiers in France seems to have given the English language the word *plonk*, meaning cheap or poor wine. It is believed to be a corruption of *vin blanc*, which the Australians pronounced "van blonk,"[22] making it probable that Australian soldiers drank wine of a color the French considered inappropriate for fighting men.

At the end of the war a French military newspaper, *L'écho des tranchées*, gave wine some of the credit for victory: "No doubt our brilliant generals and heroic soldiers were the immortal artisans of victory. But would they have been without the pinard that kept them going to the end, that endowed them with spirit, courage, tenacity, and scorn for danger, and made them repeat with unbreakable conviction, 'We will prevail'?"[23] Here was the clinching argument in favor of wine: not only could it save France from alcoholism and social decline, but it had saved the nation from military defeat.

L'ARRIVÉE DU "PINARD" SUR LE FRONT

Le pinard, que les gens de l'arrière appellent « vin », est un produit dont le poilu ne prononce le nom qu'avec respect. Le poilu fait volontiers le sacrifice de quelques rations de vivres, mais pour un empire il ne laisserait perdre un centilitre de ce divin breuvage. Voici, arrêté dans un village reconquis, le bazar ambulant où se débite la précieuse liqueur ; accourus en foule, les troupiers assiègent le fourgon, chacun tendant sa pièce de quarante sous pour en recevoir un litre qu'il emportera avec mille précautions.

Figure 7.1.   "L'arrivée du 'pinard' sur le front" (The arrival of "pinard" at the front). The caption reads in part, "The soldier will gladly sacrifice several food rations, but would not give up a centiliter of this divine liquid for an empire. Here, stopped in a recaptured village, is a mobile canteen where the precious beverage is sold; running in a crowd, the troopers besiege the wagon, each holding out a forty-sou coin to receive a liter that he will carry off with the greatest care." *Le pays de France*, 21 June 1917. (In the author's possession).

Figure 7.2. World War I postcard showing French soldiers celebrating with pinard, their ordinary wine. (In the author's possession.)

Yet it had been far from easy for French producers to meet the demands of the military. The 1914 harvest had been excellent, but the following year's yielded only two billion liters (528 million gallons), which was only a third of its volume and lower than that of the worst grape harvest during the phylloxera crisis. Damp weather had fostered a variety of diseases (including mildew) in vineyards, and there were not enough laborers or chemicals to treat them effectively. Throughout the war, horses, insecticides, fertilizer, and other vineyard resources that had become necessities grew more and more scarce, and although French harvests after 1915 improved, none exceeded two-thirds of 1914's. Algeria's vineyards fared nearly as badly in 1915—five hundred million liters (132 million gallons) of wine were produced, half the volume of 1914—but they picked up in the following years and were able to make up some of the shortfall in metropolitan France. Even so, more than 1.3 billion liters (343 million gallons) of Italian and Spanish wine was needed to supply France's civilian and military demand during the war, and in 1916 the French secured most of Portugal's wine production. The French army even sent officers to Napa Valley in California and Mendoza in Argentina to price wine, but shipping proved both too expensive and too risky, in light of German submarine attacks.

It is difficult to estimate the consumption of wine by civilians during the war, but it must have been considerably less than before and after. In 1917, the military authorities set the civilian wine ration at half a liter (0.13 gallons) for adults and a quarter liter (0.07 gallons) for children. If any community possessed wine in excess of these volumes, the army could requisition it.[24] Supplies of wine to civilians were low and deliveries erratic, prices rose steadily, and while the population not on active duty included the heavy-drinking demographic of older men, women and children dominated it. Women were generally assumed in normal times to drink far less than men, although suspicions were voiced that they got away with drinking more than was commonly thought because they drank privately and at home, unlike men, who drank in public. Married women drank together for mutual comfort while their husbands were at the front, and wartime asylum records contain evidence of problematic wine drinking by women, some of it directly related to the war. One husband said his wife started drinking wine heavily because their only son was at the front. Another patient said she had drunk regularly with her brother, a café owner, and continued on her own after he was mobilized in 1914.[25]

It was not only the commercial-quality wine consumed on a daily basis that wartime challenges affected. High-quality wines were needed for export, but their producers also encountered difficulties. At Bordeaux's Château Latour, the grapes were so poor in 1915 that all the wine was declassified and sold as ordinary red wine so as not to compromise the reputation of the estate.[26] Overall, French exports of wine fell from a steady two hundred to three hundred million liters (fifty-three to seventy-nine million gallons) before 1914 to fewer than fifty million (thirteen million gallons) by 1918. The small volume of French wine exported in bottles— only the more expensive and prestigious wines, while the rest was shipped in barrels at this time—declined by half.[27] By 1917, Britain was importing less than half the still and sparkling wine that it had in 1913. When champagne was in short supply because many vineyards were in battle zones, imports of sparkling wine from Saumur, in the Loire valley, took up some of the slack. "Fancy the [volume] of Saumur reaching half the total of champagne . . . !" the *Wine Trade Review* exclaimed somewhat patronizingly.[28]

Smaller wartime harvests required fewer workers to pick the grapes, and that was just as well, because although the government adopted policies to ensure that vineyards had enough workers, the results fell well short. Refugees from war zones were steered toward agricultural work, including viticulture, but they counted in the thousands and did not come close to matching, in numbers or in skill, the hundreds of thousands of vineyard workers who had been mobilized. Offices were set up on the Italian and

Spanish borders to encourage agricultural laborers to go to France to replace farmworkers serving in the army, but many took advantage of the relaxed entry rules to work in the better-paying industries of northern France instead.

The French government also provided for reserve soldiers who were not at the battlefront to have periodic fifteen-day leaves to work in their fields and vineyards, and even for troops to work on nearby farms, but commanders were often unwilling to release their soldiers for this work. This problem affected the whole spectrum of wine producers, from small vineyards in Languedoc-Roussillon to prestigious estates in Bordeaux and Burgundy. In 1915, the owners of Château Haut-Brion complained that although they had been offered soldiers to help in their vineyards, not one had appeared. In 1916 the government adopted measures "to help the wine-producing population assure a harvest that represents one of the important elements of national wealth." A regulation set out monthlong periods when various regions could expect the grape harvest to take place: from 15 September to 15 October in the Rhône valley, for example, and from 25 September to 25 October in Marne. Vignerons in uniform (as long as they were not performing essential tasks, such as training new recruits) were granted twenty days' leave within these periods to return home to oversee the grape harvest. The regulation also gave them access to horses and donkeys, on the same basis as other farmers, and provided for contingents of prisoners of war to assist in the harvest.[29]

It made sense to use soldiers to help produce wine, as much of it became pinard. Military requisitions took up an increasing proportion of total wine production as the war went on; in 1918 the army requisitioned 40 percent of 1917's wine production. The proportion available to civilians thus declined, and it was not always available in any case, because the railroads gave priority to military goods. At the start of the war, wine prices fell dramatically, because of the size of the 1914 harvest and a decline in consumer buying power. In Nîmes, white wine that sold for thirty-two to thirty-five francs a barrel in 1914 fetched only ten to fifteen francs a year later. The reason, according to one observer, was that demand for wine had collapsed as consumers gave priority to bread, meat, and potatoes.[30] But the harvests from 1915 to 1918 were far smaller than 1914's (they averaged 3.5 billion liters, or 0.92 billion gallons, compared to 1914's 6 billion liters, or 1.6 billion gallons) and could not meet both civilian and military demand, which required imports from Spain, Italy, and Portugal.

Scarcity on the home market led to rising prices: a liter (0.26 gallons) of wine that cost twenty centimes in 1914 fetched one franc ten centimes, more than five times as much, by 1918.[31] It is likely too that increases in the price of wine sold on the civilian market reflected attempts by producers to make up some of the losses brought about by having to sell to the government at its fixed, lower prices. Yet when price controls were introduced for some foods and products in 1916, they included foodstuffs like sugar, potatoes, and milk but not wine. Even though some deputies tried to add wine to the list on the ground that it was as necessary as bread to French people, it remained excluded from the widening list of price-controlled commodities. This is an interesting corrective to the notion that wine was universally considered an integral part of the French diet.

Nonetheless, wine (with beer and cider) was clearly distinguished from distilled spirits in a wartime campaign against alcohol, as it had been for decades. The production of absinthe was banned in the first months of the war, and numerous laws were passed in the following years to reduce the consumption of spirits. Cafés and other drinking places came under tighter regulations, and there was a crackdown on public drunkenness. As in other countries, the motivation was to reduce the effects of drinking on wartime productivity. In 1916 the French premier, Aristide Briand, called for power to suppress distilled spirits completely, and there was some fear that wine might be caught in the net. Instead, the consumption of wine was encouraged for the usual reasons: it was nutritious and healthy, a source of energy, and protection against spirits-generated alcoholism.

If wartime consumption of wine fell on the home front, it held up among serving troops. If, in 1916, a soldier drank the permitted half liter (0.13 gallons) a day every day, he consumed about 180 liters (48 gallons) that year, far more than France's prevailing per capita consumption rate of just over 100 liters (26 gallons). A soldier who drank 1918's permitted ration of a liter (0.26 gallons) a day exceeded it by far more, of course. Civilians had less chance of meeting these levels, not only because they had to pay for their wine but also because it was often in short supply. Moreover, the number of bars and cafés serving wine decreased slightly during and just after the war, from 480,000 in 1914 to 420,000 in 1920, although many of the drinking places that closed were in war zones.[32]

Unlike earlier wars, when invading armies devastated vineyards throughout France, World War I in northern Europe was largely stationary, and the western front scarcely moved for four years after a stalemate was established in December 1914. But some of the most intensive fighting took place in Champagne. German troops occupied both Reims and Épernay for a short time in September 1914 and later shelled them with artillery. First French troops, then German troops, then French troops again billeted in the cellars of the champagne houses, and soldiers of both armies pillaged stocks of champagne.

As the western front stabilized in parallel trenches near the Marne River, thousands of hectares of Champagne's vineyards were effectively put out of commission. When hostilities began, much of Marne's vineyard area was in the process of being replanted to replace vines killed by phylloxera, but this was suspended until the end of the war. Artillery and the movement of troops destroyed some vineyards, but even where vines were not affected, there were few people to tend them and no horses, fertilizer, or other necessities.[33] Replanting vineyards in many parts of Champagne was delayed for some time after the war because of the dangers from the unexploded shells that littered the countryside and from the chemical-filled shells that were leaking toxins into the soil.

Nonetheless, parts of Champagne continued to produce its distinctive wine throughout the war, even though vine growers and harvesters often risked—and sometimes lost—their lives to tend the vines and bring in the grapes. Maurice Pol-Roger, the head of the champagne house bearing his name, who was the mayor of Épernay in 1914, observed later that the grapes were "harvested to the sound of gunfire but to be drunk to the sound of trumpets." The first wartime vintage in Champagne, in fact, is reputed to have been one of the century's greatest, not despite the war but, indirectly, because of it. The harvest was less organized than usual, and amid fears that the Germans would renew their offensive, it was decided to pick some of the grapes earlier than normal. These underripe grapes increased the acidity of the vintage and contributed to the longevity of its champagnes, which were still in good condition a century later. A bottle of 1914 Pol Roger champagne was auctioned in London in 2014 to aid the refurbishment of the Imperial War Museum's First World War galleries.

If World War I was fought for anything, it was for power in Europe and for colonies, but some prominent figures in France's wine industry implied that the French were also fighting to defend their wine. This was more than the perennial association of French wine and French civilization; it was the far more banal claim that the French were defending the reputation of their wine brands from frauds and deceptions committed by Germans. Viala wrote in 1916 that Germans had long sold counterfeit French champagne and cognac and before the war had begun to extend their illicit activities to the great red wines of Burgundy and Bordeaux. According to him, German wine merchants commonly adulterated French cognac with cheap distilled spirits and reexported the resulting concoction (much of it to Germany's colonies in Africa) as authentic cognac.[34]

As for champagne, Viala claimed that Germans had been buying still white wine from Champagne in vast volumes, blending it with inferior wines from Switzerland and the south of France, as well as with apple and pear juice, adding sugar, and then carbonating the result. They then reexported it as genuine champagne, in bottles bearing the labels of well-known champagne houses.[35] Viala asserted that in 1911 Germany had reexported three hundred thousand more bottles of "champagne" than the million bottles it had imported, and in 1912 had exported twenty million bottles that were labeled "champagne" but contained "a mixture of all sorts of sparkling drinks, often simple, sweetened liquids coming from apples purchased from Normandy and carbonated."[36]

It is likely that some of what Viala here referred to as "champagne" were the *tailles*, the second and third pressings of champagne grapes. Tailles, which made inferior but perfectly good wine, were commonly bought by Germans for producing Sekt, the German sparkling wine that did not have to be made from grapes grown in Germany.[37] We should note too that it was common practice until the very late twentieth century (when appellation laws began to be observed internationally) for producers of sparkling wine in many countries to label it "champagne."

Viala argued that it was because they wanted to seize Champagne's vineyards so as to exploit its name on corrupted blends that German armies were careful not to damage vineyards as they invaded Verzy, Verzenay, Épernay, and Avize in 1914. (There are echoes here of Edward Gibbon's claim, two centuries earlier, that the Germanic "Barbarians" invaded the Roman Empire to get their hands on its wine.)[38] But another wartime French writer put a more sinister gloss on the Germans' relationship with Champagne. Alphonse Nicot wrote that many Champagne houses had belonged to Germans, and even though the owners had been interned, a number of the employees had returned to Germany and were now officers in the German army. They "have an intimate knowledge of the neighborhoods of the unfortunate town of Reims, and can indicate to the artillerymen of Wilhelm II the precise places where they ought to aim their cannons."[39]

It was not only champagne that the Germans wanted, Viala wrote; they had turned their attention to France's great red wines, especially Bordeaux's. Germans had bought a number of châteaux—not those of classified growths, but still respectable producers—and also virtually the entire production of some of the best châteaux in excellent vintages. The result was that French consumers often had to go to Hamburg to buy the finest of their own country's wines. Viala predicted that Germans would practice the same counterfeiting with Bordeaux wines as they already had with cognac and champagne. Such fraud would be stopped only "by the victory of our soldiers," which would enable the French to force Germans to observe "honesty in commerce, and the guarantee of origin of products and brands." As we shall see, the Treaty of Versailles, the peace agreement that Germany was forced to sign in 1919, includes a clause requiring German manufacturers and producers to respect French appellations.

It was unthinkable to Viala that the French would lose the war, because that would leave Alsace and its vineyards in Germany and allow Germany to annex not only the neighboring regions of Champagne and Burgundy but also Algeria and France's colonies in North Africa, where there was potential for even more wine production.[40] A German victory would lead to a disastrous wine war between Germany and what was left of France's wine regions and would result in the destruction of French viticulture. Shrewd German wine merchants, Viala noted, knew the "tastes, temperaments, and habits" of consumers and were able to exploit them. He recounted a visit to a restaurant in San Antonio, Texas (during his 1883 trip to look for American vines suitable as rootstock for the Charente region), where all the French wine he ordered was spoiled, as it had been kept in the dining room at temperatures of 30 to 35 degrees Celsius (86 to 95 degrees Fahrenheit). In contrast, a bottle of German wine was in perfect condition, as the German wine merchant had told the restaurant owner to keep it in the cool cellar. Whether Viala was making a point about American stupidity or German cunning (either would resonate with French readers), he used the example to press home the point that the French had not only to stop German wine fraud but also to emulate German commercial know-how.

During the war, France continued to export wine, although in decreasing volumes, because harvests were small and more wine was needed for the domestic market. From a consistent 200 million liters (53 million gallons) and more annually up to 1913, exports steadily shrank from 166 million liters (44 million gallons) in 1914 to less than 50 million (13 million gallons) in 1919. Germany and the Austro-Hungarian Empire ceased to be markets because they were the enemy, but Germany did receive some French wine: vignerons in the districts of Champagne under German occupation were forced to harvest their grapes in 1915, 1916, and 1917 and turn the wine over to the German army. Commercial exports continued to other markets, such as the United States—but contracted there as one state after another adopted prohibition policies. Exports to Britain declined, as many wine-drinking men were officers on active duty in northern France, where they undoubted drank the French wine sold by merchants behind the front lines.

In a spirit of sacrifice and to set an example of sobriety, King George V of Great Britain banned wine—presumably most of it had been French—from the royal family's meals. The wine trade to Russia, which took about 10 percent of champagne exports before 1914, slowed with the outbreak of war. Tsar Nicholas II had imposed prohibition for the duration of hostilities, and the Russian imperial court was declared "dry" to demonstrate its solidarity with the masses. But shipments of wine to Saint Petersburg continued nonetheless: in 1916 a German submarine in the Gulf of Finland torpedoed a ship carrying wine to the Russian imperial court, whose cargo of champagne—Heidsieck Monopole "Goût américain" 1907—was salvaged in 1998. More than two thousand bottles were recovered, and most were found to be in very good condition.[41]

Although wine was treated like a war hero in 1918 for its contributions to the nutrition and morale of French soldiers, it was—like many French war heroes—one of the casualties of the conflict. The French wine industry faced a new world at the end of World War I, as it contemplated the prospect of rebuilding for the second time in three decades. In Champagne the rebuilding took literal form, as a third of the total vineyard area and two-fifths of grand cru vineyards had been destroyed, were no longer productive because they had been neglected for four years, or were affected by phylloxera. In the important Montagne de Reims district, some pinot noir vineyards lost almost half their vines to phylloxera between 1914 and 1918, while others lost a sixth of their vines to other pests and diseases that could not be treated during the war. In Montagne de Reims as a whole, vineyards were reduced from about 1,000 to 650 hectares (2,471 to 1,606 acres) between 1914 and 1918.[42] Widespread replanting on American rootstock was needed, but before that could start, much of Champagne's viticultural land had to be recontoured, because trenches, artillery barrages, and the movement of soldiers, horses, and equipment had torn it up. Only 8,500 hectares (21,000 acres) of land were replanted with vines in the years immediately following the war, so Champagne entered the postwar period in a much reduced state.[43] In the 1920s, the vineyards of Marne covered only half of their area before the arrival of phylloxera.

With Germany's defeat, Alsace and Lorraine returned to France, and both regions were in need of radical viticultural renewal. After these provinces were annexed to Germany in 1871, German wine producers had wanted to avoid competition from them and had successfully lobbied the German government to reduce them to suppliers of mediocre wines for blending purposes. When phylloxera affected Alsace's vineyards, the vines were pulled out and the land left fallow, and when they were replanted it was with hybrid varieties rather than the riesling vines on which Alsace had built its reputation. Restoring the viticultural heritage of Alsace and Lorraine became a patriotic cause. In the early 1920s, a French deputy insisted that Lorraine needed to be strengthened as a bastion against barbarism: "Is the vine not the small daughter of Latin civilization? Is wine not a beneficial influence on our thought? That is why I believe it is a patriotic duty to conserve the integrity of the viticultural inheritance of Lorraine."[44]

Beyond Champagne, Alsace, and Lorraine, the war had affected France's wine regions in a variety of ways. Much of the poorer wine of Languedoc and Bordeaux had been requisitioned, and although producers received low prices for it, at least it did move from the cellars and was not caught up in transportation problems. Some of Burgundy's wine was also requisitioned, and the proximity of a war zone there enabled négociants to sell informally to soldiers behind the front lines. But in Burgundy as elsewhere, vineyards had been badly neglected for four years because of a shortage of labor and fertilizer. Those of the Jura suffered even more, as phylloxera ran rampant there during the war: twelve thousand hectares (thirty thousand acres) of vines in 1914 were reduced to seven thousand (seventeen thousand acres) by 1918.[45]

France's viticultural labor force was much diminished by 1918, and the names of vignerons and vineyard workers killed during the war can be read on memorials in the squares of wine villages throughout the country. Eighteen names of "fallen children" are inscribed on the memorial in the small town of Tavel, in Provence, now the heart of an appellation famous for its rosé wines. In the Bordeaux region, some 12,400 vineyard workers had died,[46] and many others were temporarily or permanently disabled. It was not only their physical work that was lost but also their knowledge and skills. Because of casualties and other population changes, Bordeaux's vineyard area lost a fifth of its workers between 1914 and 1918 and saw the sex ratio shift from a slight majority of men to a substantial majority of women. Throughout France, foreign workers were employed to replace the thousands of French men who had been killed. They flowed from Spain into Bordeaux—reversing the current of the phylloxera years—and between 1921 and 1936 the number of foreign workers and landowners (mainly Spanish but also Italian, Belgian, and Polish) in Bordeaux alone rose from nine thousand to thirty-six thousand.[47]

International export markets also needed urgent attention. Wine exports had plummeted, in the case of Bordeaux from sixty million liters (sixteen million gallons) in 1913 to fourteen million (four million gallons) in 1917. During the war, Bordeaux exported no wine to its two major prewar markets: Germany, for obvious reasons, and Belgium, which was occupied by

German forces. Shipping across the Atlantic, to the United States, Canada, and South America, was hazardous because of submarine activity. Britain became Bordeaux's main wartime export market, taking at least four million liters (one million gallons) of its wine each year.[48]

Rebuilding wine exports was difficult, as many markets had either contacted dramatically or disappeared entirely. Exports to Russia ended with the 1917 Revolution, when wealthy clients—including the imperial court and the nobles, who had been major purchasers of champagne—lost their buying power (and in many cases their lives). The new Bolshevik government continued into the mid-1920s the prohibition policies that the tsar had introduced at the outbreak of war, but even when they were relaxed, it treated alcohol as a threat to social order and economic productivity. Despite official bans, Russians drank illicit alcohol, but vodka was their preferred beverage and wine a minor item. Crimea had a small wine industry, and "Soviet champagne" was later popular, but there was no official tolerance at all of imported "bourgeois" wine until much later in the century.

French wine exports to the United States had declined before and during the war as one state after another adopted prohibition policies. Exports were cut off entirely when national prohibition took effect in 1920, although small volumes of French wine were smuggled in for consumption by better-off Americans in their homes or in clandestine clubs. Some (along with cognac and other spirits) was carried on freighters as far as American territorial waters, then ferried ashore at night by flotillas of small boats that evaded the Coast Guard. More wine arrived on transatlantic liners; the best wines served in Belle Livingstone's elegant night club on New York's Park Avenue were obtained from the captain of a French liner.[49] Clearly, well-off Americans accustomed to drinking French wine could obtain it during Prohibition—which was designed, according to Sarah Delano Roosevelt, the mother of the president under whom Prohibition was repealed, "to close saloons and not to deny those who wanted French wine with dinner."[50] But the volume of French wine that found its way into the United States between 1920 and 1933 was a mere trickle compared with American wine imports before Prohibition.

Prohibition policies that were introduced by Canada's provinces during World War I and lasted through to the late 1920s and 1930s (depending on province) reduced French wine exports to that market, while in other parts of the world the absence of French wine during the war helped stimulate local wine production. This was the case in Argentina, Chile, Australia, and South Africa. Exports of French wine to these countries in the 1920s were much lower than they had been before the war.

The European markets that had been so important for French wine exports before World War I were also problematic after the war. The Nordic countries experimented with prohibition for varying periods following the war through to the 1930s, but many other markets survived, although in diminished forms. Belgium and the Netherlands continued to import French wine in substantial volumes (despite a short period of postwar prohibition in Belgium) and were among its top three importers in the late 1920s. The other was Britain, even though many of the better-off British consumers of French wine—especially claret and champagne—had died during the war. In addition, the British raised excise taxes on luxury goods to help pay for the war; the duty on a dozen bottles of champagne rose fourfold, from seven shillings six pence to thirty-one shillings.

Elsewhere, many Austrians and Hungarians (such as the Habsburg nobility) who had purchased French wines before the war declined financially as a result of the dissolution of the Austro-Hungarian Empire. Finally, demand for French wine fell in Germany as it experienced a series of economic problems in the 1920s, notably the 1923 inflation that ruined many middle-class families. A "Drink German Wine" campaign, launched by the German wine industry in the mid-1920s, undercut sales of wine from France.[51]

Despite these postwar challenges, some French wine regions did well in the short term. Bordeaux's exports in 1919 were triple those of 1918, with big sales to Belgium, the Netherlands, and Scandinavia. But these were temporary gains, as merchants in these countries were replenishing stocks that had dwindled during the war. After putting up good figures in the early 1920s, Bordeaux's sales abroad languished until after World War II.

The challenges that the French wine industry was expected to face after the war go some way toward explaining why the Treaty of Versailles, which set out the peace terms between Germany and its wartime enemies, includes provisions dealing with French wine. Germany was required to allow the importation of French wine for three years at the most favorable tariff that had been applied to goods as of 31 July 1914. It was also required to respect "any regional appellation in respect of wine or spirits produced in the State to which the region belongs" and to take action to see that no German company breached appellation laws by counterfeiting products defined by appellation.[52] These conditions (which are also included in the treaties that France concluded with Germany's wartime allies) responded to French claims that before the war, German producers frequently labeled their wines and spirits with the names of French appellations, especially Champagne and Cognac.

As for the wine market in France itself, the war had cut a deep and wide swath through an important wine-drinking demographic: young men. Between 1914 and 1918, almost 1.4 million French men were killed in action, and a similar number were permanently disabled, while another 4.6 million were wounded but recovered. The nearly three million dead and permanently disabled represented six of every ten French males in the eighteen-to-twenty-eight-year-old age group. These losses were not only responsible for France's postwar labor shortage but also, because they were concentrated in a key drinking demographic, reduced domestic demand for wine. The belief that a pinard-drinking army would become a large wine-drinking population was predicated on the soldiers' surviving the war.

Low demand was a new problem facing French wine at the end of the war, but other challenges were of longer standing. One was fraudulent and counterfeit wine, which persisted decades after the phylloxera period that gave rise to so many dubious winelike beverages. It is likely that there was little raisin wine about in 1919, but additives were still an issue, French and foreign wines were still blended, and there was widespread confusion about the provenance of many wines. Although appellations were a guide to quality in the case of champagne and of wines from the better-known districts of Bordeaux and Burgundy, they were rarely used outside these most prestigious of France's wine regions—a far cry from the present, when French wines are more likely to be known by appellation than by grape variety. Before World War I, most French wine was sold to consumers in bulk (*en vrac*) or to négociants, who bought wine from a number of producers, blended it, and sold it under their own name, with or without an appellation. And most exported wine was shipped in barrels rather than in labeled bottles. In 1913, for example, bottled wine (including champagne) represented less than 4 percent of all wine (by volume) exported from France and only 7.5 percent of wine exported from Bordeaux.[53]

But even when an appellation appeared on a négociant's wine, it did not necessarily indicate where the grapes were grown, because a practice known as *équivalence* allowed a négociant to label a wine that had the character of wine from an appellation with its name. Thus, wines from any commune in Burgundy could be labeled "Pommard" as long as the négociant believed they had the character of Pommard wine. Appellation was to be read, then, not literally but as an indicator of style and quality. To that extent, it would not matter to consumers whether an appellation-labeled wine was made from grapes grown in that appellation or not. Of the twenty-nine villages in Burgundy's famed Côte de Nuits district, only twelve gave their name to wines before the 1920s. The wines from the other seventeen were sold under the names of one or more of the dozen better-known villages.

This situation began to change when, on 6 May 1919, the French government passed a law that was a step toward the recognition of appellation as the overriding indicator of wine identity and quality in France. It built on a 1913 draft bill, suspended when war broke out, that was a response to widespread fraud and misrepresentation in the labeling of French wines before the war and to concern about the appropriation of French appellation names by German producers. There was some urgency to pass the law in 1919: the Treaty of Versailles required German producers to respect appellations, and it was important to ensure compliance by French producers themselves—many of whom were no more fastidious than Germans were alleged to be when it came to using appellation names. As the concept of équivalence shows, stated appellations were not necessarily actual appellations, but at least this was a known and tolerated practice; some producers simply misrepresented the source of their wine without regard to its character or quality.

The 1919 law provided for the creation of appellations by giving the civil court in each district the power to define the territory within which its distinctive wines were made. The geographical features commonly associated with terroir today (such as soil and subsoil, exposure, and mesoclimate) did not come explicitly into play, and in most cases the boundaries of appellations followed existing administrative boundaries. Thus the limits of the Margaux (in Bordeaux) and Volnay (in Burgundy) appellations were essentially the same as the communes of Margaux and Volnay, modified to exclude zones unsuitable for viticulture.

There were precedents for this practice, notably the 1911 delimitation of the Bordeaux appellation, which simply followed the boundaries of the département of Gironde (as it does today). In 1909, it had been proposed to include Bergerac, Duras, and much of the Côtes du Marmandais (all to the east and southeast of the modern Bordeaux appellation) within the appellation. This seemed reasonable, as these areas had a long history of supplying wine, made from the same grape varieties as those grown on the left and right banks of Bordeaux, to négociants who would blend them with other wines and sell them as wines from Bordeaux. But opposition from Bordeaux producers led to the exclusion of any areas not in Gironde. This pleased the producers of Gironde but not the négociants, who needed the outside wine.

In 1913 and 1914, compromise agreements were reached that "small quantities" of non-Gironde wine could be added to a wine labeled "Bordeaux": "In Gironde, it is local, authentic and long-standing practice to maintain the appellation of origin of the finished wine, when the light addition of another wine simply has the result of making it conform better to the taste of the consumer, while respecting the distinct qualities that are common to all the wines of the origin indicated."[54] It was, effectively, a restatement of the idea of équivalence: a blend of wine from Bordeaux and other regions could be labeled "Bordeaux" because it had "the distinct qualities" expected of wine solely from Bordeaux.

The principle that underpinned this compromise—that such blending and labeling was in accord with "local, authentic and long-standing practice" ("usage local, loyal et constant")—became the key to defining appellations under the 1919 law: appellations were essentially to be made up of groups of producers whose vineyards were within a defined area and who followed common practices in geographical, ethical, and historical dimensions. These terms provided rich material for lawyers and extended litigation, as they raised more questions than they settled. How local was "local"? What defined an "authentic" practice? And how long was "long-standing": a decade, a century, longer?[55]

The 1919 law allowed associations (*syndicats*) of wine producers to apply to the civil courts for recognition of an appellation and permitted anyone who believed they were adversely affected by an appellation (such as by being excluded from it) to take legal action. The way was open for an unlimited number of appellations, not to mention numerous interminable lawsuits, as appellations were sought, granted, and contested and judgments rendered, appealed, and reappealed. The situation was aggravated by the fact that the judges who heard these cases were not necessarily familiar with the world of wine. They often found it difficult to determine whether a particular viticultural practice was or was not of long standing in a region, and many of these legal actions revolved on technical details that were argued on the basis of memory or insubstantial or ambiguous archival evidence.

The result was chaotic. In the commune of Arsac in Bordeaux, about nine kilometers (six miles) from Margaux, fifteen producers adopted the appellation "Margaux" for all their red wines and twenty-one for some of their red wines, while white wines were variously labeled "Margaux," "Arsac-Margaux," or "Arsac-Médoc." At Toulenne, in the Sauternes region, producers adopted appellations that included "Graves Supérieures," "Toulenne-Sauternes," "Preignac-Sauternes," and "Haut-Toulenne Sauternes," while wines from Saint-Martin-de-Sescas, in Entre-deux-Mers, carried appellations as diverse as "Entre-deux-Mers," "Côteaux Entre-deux-Mers," "Graves de Saint-Martin-de-Sescas," and "Graves de Perrey-

Saint-Martin-de-Sescas." Some producers simply invented appellations, like "Barjac" and "Desgraves."[56]

Giving civil courts the power to decide how producers could label their wines resulted in thousands of lawsuits regarding appellations, as either individual vignerons claimed the right to label their wines with particular appellations or associations of producers in those appellations tried to prevent outsiders from using their names. In Bordeaux, for example, the association of vignerons in Saint-Julien successfully obtained a court order forbidding the use of their appellation by producers in Saint-Laurent and Cussac. The latter appealed on the ground that some Saint-Julien producers sourced grapes from vineyards in Saint-Laurent and Cussac. They lost two appeals, but the whole process took years.

One of many lawsuits in Burgundy saw the vignerons of Monthelie complain in 1919 about their exclusion from the Côte de Beaune appellation and call the attention of the court to their fine wines. This was only the first shot in their campaign to have their wine recognized as having contributed to the reputation of their better-known neighbors like Meursault, Volnay, and Pommard. Monthelie's partisans insisted in 1923 that their produce was "the equal of these other wines, and that since time immemorial they have been sold under their own name as well as under more famous names like Pommard and Volnay."[57]

The owners of vines in the prestigious Richebourg appellation of Burgundy petitioned in 1922 to stop the owners of the Les Verouilles vineyard from selling their wine as Richebourg. But the appeals court ruled that as they had been doing it for many years, they could continue, because it had become "local, authentic and long-standing practice."[58] As we might expect, the legal battles that took place throughout the 1920s and early 1930s focused mainly on prestigious appellations, such as Pommard and Richebourg in Burgundy and Margaux and Saint-Julien in Bordeaux. If the reputation and quality—not to mention the price—of a wine were to be judged by its appellation, producers in the appellation had everything to gain, while producers excluded from it had everything to lose.

No region exemplified this better than Champagne, where the question of which regions should be included had not been fully resolved, despite a tentative agreement in 1911. That year, the département of Aube had been declared a "second zone" of Champagne, and its vignerons had wasted no time in taking action before the courts to have themselves fully integrated into the Champagne appellation on an equal basis with the département of Marne.[59] The debate, which took place not only in the courts but also in the press and in public spaces, drew in all manner of issues. The vignerons of

Marne represented themselves as the heirs of Dom Pérignon, the putative father of champagne, and declared wine from Aube inferior and made from inferior grape varieties such as gamay and gouais. They also declared that Aube was really part of Burgundy, to which the Aubois replied that if that were true, Alsace and Lorraine were really part of Germany. Underlying the arguments of the vignerons of Marne was anxiety that including Aube in the Champagne appellation at a time when markets were depressed would increase the supply of champagne and drive down prices even more.

The court decided in favor of Aube, and there were days and nights of festivities there, but in 1923 the vignerons of Marne launched an appeal on the grounds that the historical area of Champagne excluded Aube, which had no great and ancient négociant houses and whose practices were inconsistent with those of Marne. A lawyer for Marne expressed anxiety about an oversupply of champagne: "We do not need your wine, because we already have too much. You can make champagne a common drink, but we won't!"[60] Unable to get satisfaction from the court, both sides agreed in 1925 to arbitration by Édouard Barthe, a prominent socialist politician. Two years later, after an exhaustive evaluation of the various claims and numerous visits to the region, he presented a balanced judgment that included key parts of Aube in Champagne, but with qualifications. Much of Aube had been replanted with gamay after the phylloxera crisis, and noting objections to the use of this variety, Barthe proposed allowing it for eighteen years, after which any Aube vineyards still planted to it would be excluded from the Champagne appellation. The vignerons of both départements accepted his recommendations, but because the end of this long dispute was achieved outside the courts, it highlights the shortcomings of the 1919 law.

The 1919 law transformed the way the business of wine was carried out. It ended the practice of équivalence and required négociants to keep registers of appellations as they received wine and as they released it on to the market, so as to ensure that, for any appellation, no more wine was released than was received. It was a direct attack on powerful négociants: by restricting the use of an appellation's name to wines made from grapes grown there, it started the process of classifying wines not by the blending and marketing skills of négociants but directly by their geographic provenance.

In Burgundy, the négociants countered by dispensing with appellation names altogether and adopting new terms such as *Monopole, Excelsior, Réserve Ducale,* and *Carte d'Or.* The president of their association declared, "We shall simply let the names of Burgundy disappear."[61] Throughout the 1920s, associations of vignerons in Burgundy filed scores of lawsuits against négociants, restaurateurs, and fellow vignerons for breaching the appellation rules, and won most of them. It was a phase in the process that led to the eventual victory of the *appellation d'origine contrôlée* (AOC) system of classifying French wine in 1935.

Even in the 1920s, some associations of vignerons anticipated the AOC system, which includes regulations that encompass grape varieties and practices in the vineyard and winery rather than simply defining an appellation's territory, as the 1919 law largely did. In October 1923, the vignerons of Châteauneuf-du-Pape, led by Baron Le Roy of Château Fortia, adopted a code of practice for any wine that was to be labeled with that appellation's name. It included a list of thirteen approved grape varieties believed to make the region's best red wines and rules relating to cultivating vines, obligatory selective picking (*tris*) during harvest, a minimum alcohol level of 12.5 percent, and low levels of volatile acidity.[62]

In Bordeaux, a number of the most prestigious producers adopted an alternative way of differentiating themselves and promoting quality: bottling their wines themselves at their châteaux. Before the 1920s, only a few producers had tried this, to prevent adulteration at the hands of wine merchants, and most continued to sell their young wine to négociants, who would age and blend it before bottling it under the grower's label. Although wine makers are fond of saying that the vineyard accounts for 90 percent of a wine's quality, fermentation, aging, barrel selection, and blending play very important parts in the final wine, and leaving these stages to the négociants effectively gave them control over the end product. The old method had the advantage of providing producers with quick revenues, but it opened the door to shady practices, and in a period when counterfeiting and fraud were still rife, some of Bordeaux's top châteaux took action to protect their reputations. In 1924, Châteaux Mouton Rothschild, Margaux, and Haut-Brion declared that that year's vintage would be bottled on their own properties. Châteaux Lafite and Latour joined in the following year.[63] This was the origin of the phrase, now printed on many Bordeaux labels, "Mis en bouteille au château" (Bottled at the château); it might seem unremarkable today, when most wineries bottle their own wine, but it bore a great deal of significance in the 1920s and 1930s, when négociants handled most wine production and bottling. This was another step on the path toward guaranteeing the provenance of wine in France.

Throughout France, only a small percentage of the wine produced in the decade after the 1919 law came into force was labeled by appellation, as most was still sold to consumers in bulk or to négociants. Producers whose wines were already well known and appreciated for their quality probably saw no point or any commercial advantage in adding an appellation. The law did not materially affect producers who did not want to label their wines by appellation, except to forbid them to use terms like *château, domaine, tour, moulin, mont, côte,* and *cru,* which might lead consumers to believe that the wine was from an appellation. Even with restrictions such as these, it has been argued that the 1919 law favored producers of poor wines, many made from hybrid grape varieties, over those of quality wines: poor wines could benefit from the prestige of higher-quality wines in the same appellation.[64]

Following a number of scandals involving cheese and wine appellations, the 1919 law was amended in 1927. Appellation names could not be used for wines made from hybrid grape varieties,[65] and appellation wines could be made only from grapes grown on "land suitable to produce appellation wine."[66] This was a nod toward the concept of terroir. But the new law triggered another round of legal actions, as vignerons' associations in some appellations sought to prevent some producers from using their appellation's name. In Barsac, for example, producers whose vineyards were on the palus (drained marshlands) near Bordeaux were forbidden to label their wines "Barsac" because growing vines there was not a long-standing practice. In contrast, the courts upheld the right of producers on the palus to use "Saint-Émilion" on their labels, despite the objections of Saint-Émilion's association of vignerons.[67]

The uncertainty over appellations continued to generate lawsuits and countersuits until matters were clarified by a comprehensive AOC law passed in 1935. But it is unlikely that many French consumers at the time were concerned about appellations, as most bought their wine in bulk or from négociants. Disputes over appellations probably did no harm to exports of wine, either, as they were sluggish throughout the 1920s and 1930s. In the interwar period, the great bulk of French wine was sold without reference to appellation; on the eve of World War II, only about 10 percent of French wine was identified by simple appellation under the 1919 law.

Because the 1919 law did not regulate yields, French wine producers were free to make as much wine as they wanted, even though domestic demand was modest and export opportunities poor. There were two broad approaches within the French wine industry. One was to make "as much wine as possible," as vignerons in Muscadet were urged in February 1922. They had been thrilled when the 1921 harvest came in, as it was the largest of the 1920s, "the largest any vigneron could remember."[68] In contrast, other producers aimed for quality rather than volume, hoping to profit from higher prices for fewer bottles. In 1930, Muscadet producers shifted to this perspective and declared, "It is urgent to put a stop to poorly planned plantings and the drive for yields that are too high and harm the quality and reputation of French wines."[69]

But rather than improve quality and cut back on production to reduce oversupply, most producers encouraged French people in the late 1920s to drink more wine, specifically to drink the equivalent of a barrel a year each. The barrel in question was not specified, but it was more likely a 225-liter (59-gallon) barrique than a 600-liter (159-gallon) demi-muid. However, even 225 liters a year would have meant a big increase in annual per capita consumption, which ranged between 100 and 112 liters (26 and 30 gallons) at the time. One supporter of this barrel-a-year idea was Jules Alquier, the secretary-general of the Scientific Society of Food Hygiene. He noted in 1930 that although the doubling of French wine consumption in the previous hundred years sounded like good news, the consumption of other beverages had risen much more quickly in the same period: beer consumption had increased fivefold, tea sixfold, and coffee tenfold. He also noted that stocks of unsold wine amounted to about three hundred liters (seventy-nine gallons) for every man, woman, and child in France and added that an inexpensive "good family wine" was half the cost of meat in terms of calories.[70] In a similar vein, the agronomist Raymond Brunet noted that between 1910 and 1924, the consumption of wine in France had risen only 24 percent, while that of coffee had risen 46 percent and that of tea 147 percent. "Therein," he wrote, "lies a veritable national danger."[71]

With the exception of 1922, wine production in metropolitan France in the 1920s was robust (it averaged six billion liters, or 1.6 billion gallons, a year), and steadily increasing wine production in Algeria aggravated the imbalance between production and consumption; shipments of Algerian wine to metropolitan France doubled from four to eight hundred million liters (one to two hundred million gallons) between 1925 and 1929.[72] Faced with a serious oversupply, the French government began to promote wine consumption and to emphasize its health benefits. In 1928, when the League of Nations set out to study alcoholism on a transnational basis, the French government refused to participate if the research was to go beyond distilled spirits and include wine and beer. Because France was such an important alcohol-consuming country, its failure to participate would have rendered the league's study virtually meaningless, and the survey was dropped.

The government's position echoed the insistence by many nineteenth-century French politicians and physicians that only drinkers of spirits could be alcoholics, and the point that wine was nutritious was made over and over again. In 1929, when France issued a postage stamp depicting Joan of Arc, a detachable sticker below it read, "Wine is a food."[73] Post offices and other public buildings displayed posters bearing a similar message, and in the early 1930s the French post office used a cancellation mark that declared, "Wine is a food. Drink wine."

On the eve of the worldwide depression that began in the United States in 1929 and spread to France two or three years later, the French wine industry faced difficulties on several fronts. Exports were low, and production was significantly higher than consumption. At the organizational level, the appellation system was chaotic, and courts fielded hundreds of lawsuits from producers who wanted to be included in appellations and from producers who wanted to exclude others. The time was right for a wholesale reform of French wine law, and when that was achieved in 1935, it was one of the few positive developments interrupting the long line of troubles that afflicted French wine from the 1860s to the 1940s.

8. From Depression to Liberation

1930–1945

Between the Great Depression and the end of World War II, the French wine industry faced more in the series of challenges that had confronted it since the 1860s. The worldwide economic depression that began in 1929 intensified the slump in France's wine exports that had started during World War I. To make things worse, the Depression coincided with record grape harvests in France, which found itself producing more and more wine for fewer and fewer customers. To reduce fraud and to promote wine quality, it passed an *appellation d'origine contrôlée* (AOC) law in 1935. French wine exports slowly began to rebound as the Depression ebbed and the United States abandoned Prohibition, but in 1940 Germany invaded France, whose wine exports to anywhere but Germany effectively ceased. The German occupation, together with the policies of the collaborationist Vichy government, created additional problems for France's wine industry, and it was not until the 1950s that France's vignerons could look to the future with any optimism.

The Depression struck France later than many other countries, because its economy was still predominantly agricultural. And while unemployment soared in Britain, Germany, and elsewhere, the French government was able to mitigate this effect of the Depression by expelling thousands of the foreign workers who had been recruited to make up for the labor shortage caused by wartime losses. But the Depression still had profound effects on the French wine industry, coming as it did after a period of stagnant exports. As unemployment rose and real incomes fell throughout Europe and North America, consumer demand for discretionary goods like wine declined, and the already reduced markets for French wine contracted even further. In 1932, French wine exports amounted to about 675 million liters (178 million gallons), barely a third of the more than two billion liters

(528 million gallons) exported in 1924. Germany and Argentina virtually stopped importing wine in the first half of the 1930s, and even though the United States repealed national Prohibition in 1933, the depressed American economy prevented French imports from rebounding there as they might otherwise have been expected to. The United States imported more than two million liters (528,000 gallons) of Bordeaux wine in 1934, much of it expensive wine from prestigious estates, as importers expected high demand following thirteen years of virtually no French wine. But continuing economic problems limited the American market, and in 1938 only 1.1 million liters (291,000 gallons) of bordeaux made its way there.[1]

This was only one aspect of the broad-based setback that the wines of Bordeaux suffered during the Depression. In 1930, some forty million liters (eleven million gallons) of Bordeaux wines were exported, but that year's vintage and the following two were of poor quality. The owners of some Bordeaux estates were forced to sell; an American banker bought Château Haut-Brion in 1935. But others weathered the harsh economic climate. In 1934, Baron Philippe de Rothschild took the best of the wines remaining from the 1930, 1931, and 1932 vintages and bottled them under a new label, Mouton Cadet, which became one of Bordeaux's most successful brands.[2]

In 1933 and 1934, Bordeaux's exports were half of 1930's, and they did not exceed thirty million liters (eight million gallons) a year during the rest of the 1930s. Exports to Bordeaux's three main markets—Belgium, Britain, and the Netherlands—fell by half between 1929 and 1934. If the decline in exports was not bad enough, 1933 and 1934 saw two of the three biggest harvests ever recorded in the Bordeaux region. The result was that only about 3 percent of the wine produced in Bordeaux in those years was exported, and its figure for the 1930s as a whole—7 percent—was not much better.[3] Because many of Bordeaux's wines were relatively expensive, it fared worse than other French wine regions and represented a declining share of the value of French wine exports, from 40 percent in the late 1920s to 32 percent on the eve of World War II.

Similar problems beset Champagne, one of whose main markets, Britain, almost dried up. In 1931, Britain abandoned the gold standard, leading to a devaluation of the pound. This made imported goods that much more expensive, and even the well-off began to curb their spending. Sales of champagne fell, and in 1934, exports of champagne were less than a third of their immediate postwar numbers. Stocks of wine resting on its lees in Champagne's cellars rose, and by 1934 they totaled 147 million bottles, double the 72 million in 1919. Many of these bottles never went through disgorgement and second fermentation but were sold as still wines, simply so that the producers would get some return from them.[4]

As for the French domestic market, it seemed to be saturated. In 1930 the French consumed 121 liters (32 gallons) of wine (much of it Algerian) per capita, the highest level of any large state. Imported wines and blends of foreign and French wines created additional competition for French wine on the home market. Although the government could have halted foreign wine imports, as French vignerons wanted it to, it had to bear in mind the bigger commercial picture. In July 1931, for example, there was an attempt in the Chamber of Deputies to reverse a "scandalous" decision to allow the importation of three million liters (eight hundred thousand gallons) of white wine from Greece for blending with French wine. Opponents pointed to the vast volumes of wine languishing in cellars throughout the Midi and Algeria and argued that if Greece were allowed to export that much wine to France, Italy would expect to export as much and Spain even more. The minister of commerce argued that France had a favorable trade imbalance with Greece and that refusing the Greek wine could jeopardize hundreds of millions of francs in other French exports. The chamber agreed to confirm the imports of Greek wine. It was high in alcohol and would be blended with weak French whites and reds (with less than 8 percent alcohol) to make white or rosé wines with an alcohol level of at least 13 percent.[5]

The upshot of these various conditions—bumper harvests, flat domestic consumption, and poor exports—was that during the 1930s, French producers had more and more wine to export to fewer and fewer foreign consumers, leaving an impossibly large volume of wine for the domestic market to absorb. Year by year, as the surplus grew, prices fell. When the 1929 vintage of Château Léoville-Lascazes was put on the market in 1931, it sold for only two-thirds of its nine-thousand-franc *en primeur* price—the price consumers and merchants pay for a wine before it has finished aging and is released for general sale. Other en primeur prices fell by half or more: Saint-Emilion Second Growths fell from 4,500–5,500 francs in 1929 to 2,200–2,400 francs in 1935, and the prices of the First Growths of Graves fell similarly in the same period. Some Bordeaux négociants held fire sales to reduce their inventories; Denorus et Compagnie did so in May 1935, selling off 164 barriques and more than sixty-five thousand bottles of Bordeaux and Burgundy wines at heavily reduced prices.[6]

Again, Algeria complicated the French wine picture. Because Algeria was an integral part of France, it was able to sell its wine on the metropolitan French market in the same way as regions like Bordeaux and Languedoc. Even though some French vignerons regarded Algeria as a foreign, competitor country, it did not "export" wine to the markets of Paris and other French cities any more than Burgundy or the Midi did. Tariffs that had been levied on Algerian wine entering France had been removed in 1867, and metropolitan France proved such a profitable market for inexpensive Algerian wine that the area of Algeria's vineyards more than doubled during the 1920s, from 170,000 to 400,000 hectares (420,000 to 988,000 acres), and production tripled. Having higher yields than metropolitan France meant that Algeria was able to flood the metropolitan French market with cheap wine at a time of oversupply.[7]

Not that Algeria was the only French region to massively increase its contribution to the glut of wine. Between the end of World War I and 1935, land under vines in Languedoc more than doubled, with almost all producers turning out wine of mediocre quality for the mass market. The flood of inexpensive wine was a sore point for producers in other regions, but the government was unwilling to take direct action; it wanted to protect the interests of the French colonists in Algeria, many of whom owned vineyards and wineries, and was reluctant to confront the vignerons of Languedoc again. Instead, it tried to curb production by indirect means.

Beginning in the late 1920s and intensifying during the 1930s, measures were put in place to improve quality at the expense of quantity and thus indirectly to reduce the production of the mediocre wine that formed the bulk of what was on the market. Wines within appellations already sanctioned by the courts under the 1919 law were exempted from these regulations because they were assumed to be quality wines, but by the early 1930s they accounted for only a very small percentage of French wine production. One of the new measures, which came into force in 1929, lowered the amount of added sugar permitted in wine making and prohibited chaptalization outright in Bordeaux, southern France, and Algeria. Another, enacted the following year, set minimum alcohol levels for unblended French wines, so as to weed out the weak wines thought to be proliferating. France was divided into seven regions, and minimum alcohol levels for each were to be set annually, depending on the vintage; wines that did not meet the minimum could be sold and consumed only in the region where they were produced, but minimum levels were later established in those cases too. Other regulations required unblended wines to show their region of origin and banned the blending of French and foreign wines[8]—although this was sometimes permitted on a case-by-case basis, as we have seen with the Greek wines imported for blending.

As for enforcement of the rules, a 1930 law gave agents of the Service for the Repression of Fraud the right to inspect wineries and cellars without notice and without having to obtain a warrant. They had their work cut out for them, because wine fraud seems to have been widespread, as a 1930 cabaret song about muscadet suggests:

> Muscadet, well, what is it?
> You, monsieur, can you tell me?
> Pure juice from the Nantes countryside?
> You poor idiot, you make me laugh.
> Come with me to the wine merchant,
> and you'll see how it's made:
> Half noah, half gros plant,
> and to fill up the barrel,
> they top it up with muscadet.
> Then off it goes in an automobile,
> that mixture that's so lively.
> It's perfectly good for townspeople.[9]

Measures to improve quality and reduce production extended to vine-yards. In 1931, restrictions were placed on irrigation between 15 July and the end of harvest, largely to stop the practice of watering vines heavily just before harvest so as to increase the volume of juice. There were exceptions: irrigating vines was permitted on a département-by-département and com-mune-by-commune basis according to specific climatic conditions or where the practice was "local, authentic and of long standing." Irrigation was con-sidered to have such an impact on quality that wine from vineyards culti-vated that way had to be labeled "wine from irrigated vines."[10]

But all these measures made little impact on the wine surplus, and as prices fell because of continuing oversupply, so did the earnings of millions of small-scale vignerons and vineyard workers, thousands of coopers, and anyone involved in transporting and selling wine. The crisis was so broad based that the government could not ignore it. Grapes and wheat were known as "electoral crops," because so many French men were engaged in farming them that government policies toward them had serious effects on voting patterns. ("French men" because women did not get the vote in France until 1944.) Some 1.5 million vignerons worked France's vineyards, and they represented one in every six French families. When prices and incomes began to spiral down in the early 1930s, all levels of government came under pressure to act. Unable to do anything, municipal councils in wine-producing regions resigned en masse, and there were warnings that direct action by vignerons and wine industry workers would be even more violent and widespread than in 1907, when it was largely confined to Languedoc-Roussillon.

For all that the wine industry faced severe problems, wine—if we can both generalize and take words at face value—continued to have a semi-mystical place in common notions of French identity. The president of the General Confederation of Vignerons declared in 1930 that "the prolonged consumption of wine has certainly contributed to the formation and the development of the fundamental qualities of the French race: cordiality, frankness, gaiety, wit, good taste—which set it so profoundly apart from people who drink a lot of beer." Two years later, the prime minister, André Tardieu, asserted that bread and wine were "the culminating expressions of material and spiritual civilization."[11]

To protect this cultural heritage, but even more to balance supply and demand so as to stabilize prices and incomes, the government intervened directly and broadly in the wine market between 1931 and 1935. It replaced the free interplay of supply and demand with official direction and imposed regulations that were more wide ranging and rigorous than ever seen before in France. The government defended its interventionist policies as a sensible middle road between the nationalization of vineyards, which some socialists had proposed in 1907, and the market chaos that had resulted from unregulated market forces.

These measures included the time-honored response to wine gluts: limiting production. In June 1930 the government proposed a graduated scale of taxes on wineries with high yields. In its final form, enacted on 4 July 1931, producers with yields under 100 hectoliters of wine per hectare (1,069 gallons per acre), together with those making wine solely for family consumption, were exempt from the tax. Those with yields of 101 to 125 hectoliters per hectare (1,080 to 1,336 gallons per acre) were taxed at five francs a hectoliter, while production between 126 and 150 (1,347 and 1,604 gallons per acre) was taxed at ten francs a hectoliter. At the higher end, yields of 201 to 250 hectoliters (2,149 to 2,673 gallons per acre) were taxed at fifty francs a hectoliter, and production over 250 hectoliters per hectare attracted a punitive levy of one hundred francs a hectoliter.[12] (For comparison, the maximum yield for wine with *indication géographique protégée*, or IGP, status—granted to wine thought to express a broad regional character—in France today is ninety hectoliters per hectare, or 962 gallons per acre, for most varieties, and for AOC red burgundy fifty-five hectoliters per hectare, or 588 gallons per acre.) It is worth noting that average yields rose during the twentieth century despite the pulling out of high-cropping varieties, largely because many northern areas with low yields were no longer producing wine (see diagram 8.1).

The 1931 law also prohibited new vineyard plantings for the following ten years, although they were allowed in some circumstances, such as when

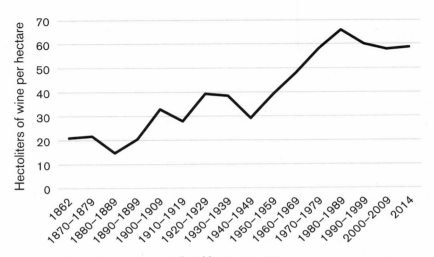

DIAGRAM 8.1.   Average vineyard yields, France, 1862–2014

the production of a vineyard was solely for family consumption or where it was a matter of replacing a vineyard damaged or destroyed during the war.[13] The draft law envisaged subjecting any new plantings to an annual tax of five thousand francs per hectare, but parliament defeated that part of the law, which would have effectively ruled out the extension of vineyards in marginal regions.[14] Not only were most new plantings prohibited, but a 1934 law provided a subsidy to pull up vineyards, and producers whose vineyards had increased by more than 5 percent since 1924 had to pull up 10 percent of their vines.

Another law of 1934 forbade using hybrid varieties for commercial wine. Hybrid varieties had been forbidden in appellation wines in 1927, and the extension of the ban to any wine destined for the market rendered useless much of the work on hybrids by French scientists during the late nineteenth century. Hybrids could be used only to make wine for family consumption, even though one of the justifications offered for the law was that wine made from those varieties could lead to insanity. The same 1934 law ordered the ripping out of American grape varieties. They had been a significant part of French wine production since being introduced during the phylloxera crisis: in the mid-1930s they accounted for six thousand hectares (fifteen thousand acres) of vines and produced three hundred million liters (seventy-nine million gallons) of wine,[15] a yield of fifty hectoliters a hectare (535 gallons per acre).

In addition to placing some controls on the extent and varietal character of France's vineyards, the government empowered itself to block the release of wine for sale when there was evidence of "dangerous overproduction for the domestic market." This was measured in relation to average wine consumption during the previous three years. The blocked wine could later be gradually released, but only at times determined by the government.[16] This rule applied to producers of more than forty thousand liters (eleven thousand gallons) a year with an average yield of more than eighty hectoliters per hectare (855 gallons per acre), meaning that it affected a minority of producers, since the majority owned no more than five hectares (twelve acres) of vineyards. The overall purpose of these policies was to reduce production while protecting small producers. If too much wine was produced despite these measures, the surplus would be released slowly on to the market so as to keep prices stable. Any surplus wine that was to be kept permanently from the market would be distilled into fuel.

Appellation wines were exempted from these measures, but there were still protests that it would be a "profanity" to allow "the pearls of a Château d'Yquem or the rubies of a Chambertin . . . [to] end up in the fuel-tank of a motor-car."[17] In fact, the exemption of appellation wines prompted many producers to seek that status, and by 1934 more than a fifth of France's wine was classified by simple appellation, double the percentage of less than ten years earlier.[18] In Muscadet, the association of vignerons noted that it was in the interest of producers to seek appellation status, and evidently many vignerons agreed: in 1925, only a handful had obtained the appellation Muscadet Grand Cru de Sèvre et Maine, but their number rose to 30 in 1927 and 130 in 1930. Following the new laws that exempted appellation wine from levies and other measures, the number of vignerons belonging to the appellation shot up to more than 1,600 in 1932.[19]

These various policies, especially the levies on production and bans on planting, were hotly contested and led to the formation of a new organization, the Confederation for the Defense of Viticulture and the Promotion of Wine, whose aim was to fight the government's program and to restrict or place high tariffs on Algerian and foreign wines. We should note, though, that the taxes on yields affected only a small number of producers; when the original draft was presented in 1928, it proposed starting the levy on yields at eighty hectoliters a hectare (855 gallons per acre), and the government calculated that fewer than 1 percent of metropolitan French producers and only 7 percent of those in Algeria would be affected.[20] As few as they were, even some of these escaped taxation when the final legislation set the threshold at one hundred hectoliters a hectare (1,069 gallons per acre).

Clearly, the government had big producers, not the 1.5 million small-production vignerons, in its sights. In the Chamber of Deputies and its committees, members attacked "big vineyard owners . . . capitalist companies who have industrialized the vine" and argued against limitations on planting vineyards because they would affect not "the proprietors of the great estates nor the corporations whom you reproach for their dividends" but "small vignerons and small landholders who wish to become vignerons."[21] The government also targeted Algerian producers, who on average had larger vineyards and obtained higher yields; the regulations affected 26 percent of the wine produced in metropolitan France but fully 87 percent of Algerian wine. These measures effectively halted the expansion of Algeria's vineyard area, which never went beyond the four hundred thousand hectares (988,000 acres) it reached in the mid-1930s. Having their wine blocked from immediate sale was a greater hardship for producers in Algeria than for those in metropolitan France, because of the higher temperatures they had to deal with.[22]

In practice, the complex of regulations did little to stabilize the French wine market. The first harvest following their adoption in July 1931 was a little higher than the year before, and in December the commission tasked with implementing the measures decided to hold back some wine from sale. But by then some producers had sold all their wine, so officials tried to block the sale of some wine by négociants, while other producers found all their wine blocked. Because the harvest had exceeded the seventy-five million hectoliters (two billion gallons) that triggered distilling, millions of liters of wine were sent to distillers, but they were soon unable to cope with the volume. The short-term result was uncertainty among producers and négociants, and the sale of wine virtually halted. Even though only a minority of producers had their wine blocked from sale or distilled, all producers were affected by the price of wine, which, instead of rising in the face of a smaller supply, fell instead. A hundred liters (twenty-six gallons) of red wine, which had fetched 180 francs in Montpellier and Perpignan in July 1931, could be bought for less than half that—between 72 and 90 francs—in December. By May of the following year, it was selling for about 67 francs.[23]

The size of harvests fluctuated in the early 1930s: they were low in metropolitan France and high in Algeria in 1932, and a little higher in both in 1933, but soared in 1934, when Algeria produced a record 2.2 billion liters (580 billion gallons) and metropolitan France had its second-highest harvest on record, at 7.8 billion liters (2.1 billion gallons). These were massive harvests, but there was little to be said for their quality. In 1935, the Nicolas chain of wine stores sent out a message to its customers:

For ordinary wines the year 1934 is not, as some people claim, a year of great quality. The fruit that these anemic wines start with disappears day by day; this is what excessive production gives us. And the market is positively flooded with it, at prices that challenge those of mineral water. Against this state of affairs, there is last autumn, and a négociant wanting to protect his reputation must take measures. Thus it is that the Nicolas Company, foreseeing this crisis of quality, has judged it necessary to ensure, at the right time, it has large stocks of old wines selected from among the best. . . . An anemic wine, no matter what its price, is always more expensive than a wine with good body.[24]

With each harvest, the government modified the regulations, changing the trigger points for market blockage and distilling and tinkering with replanting rules and other measures, all with the aim of getting the balance of supply and demand right. But equilibrium was elusive, and although wine prices fluctuated, they continued to drift downward. Retail prices did not always mirror trends in wholesale prices for wine, and there were suspicions that négociants and retailers were profiting as vignerons suffered. Even so, the government attempted to recruit consumers in the fight to stabilize the wine industry by encouraging them to drink more of the wine made available by bumper harvests and the decline of exports. But persuading the French to drink more wine, even at advantageous prices, was an optimistic goal. At 121 liters (32 gallons) per capita in 1930, the national consumption rate of wine in France was the highest in the world. It seemed unlikely that it could be increased significantly enough to have much impact on the wine accumulating in vats and barrels all over the country but, beginning in 1930, the French government determined to try.

Attempting to increase the consumption of any alcoholic beverage ran counter to almost all contemporary trends. It is true that the United States was on the verge of abandoning Prohibition, but no one there or elsewhere was calling for increased drinking—except for the chairman of England's Brewers' Society, Sir Edgar Sanders, who launched a campaign to increase beer consumption on the ground that it was beneficial to the health of drinkers.[25] In France, wine, not beer, was the healthy beverage, and there was a long-standing tradition of distinguishing between wine (portrayed as a natural and healthy beverage) and distilled spirits (which were believed to cause health and social problems).

Running against the contemporary trend elsewhere, the French medical profession continued to insist that wine had nothing but therapeutic and medicinal properties, and these positive qualities were deployed in the government's campaign to increase wine consumption. Eminent doctors formed an association called Médecins Amis du Vin to support the campaign by writing letters and articles for newspapers. Advertisements too stressed the health benefits of wine; one claimed that the average life expectancy of a wine drinker was sixty-five years, compared to fifty-nine years for a water drinker, and that 87 percent of hundred-year-olds were wine drinkers.[26]

Allied to this theme was the message that wine, which had been declared France's national beverage, was rooted in the French soil (occasionally irrigated with the blood of the country's martyrs), so consuming it was not only a healthy pleasure but a patriotic duty. And if drinking wine was patriotic, drinking more wine could only be more patriotic. Indeed, one doctor linked wine to the sheer existence of France in a brilliant non sequitur: "For over a thousand years, wine has been the national drink of the French and although they have been surrounded by enemies against whom they have fought more wars than any other people, the French have not only survived but they are among the two or three most important nations in the world."[27]

The drink-more-wine campaign used various means—posters, billboards at railway stations, newspaper advertisements, postage stamps, local festivals, and conferences—to convey its message, and it eagerly embraced the newest mass media (see figure 8.1). Four hundred flashing neon signs were erected in Paris with pithy messages such as "Make wine your preference" and "A meal without wine is like a day without sunshine." References to wine were encouraged in French movies, an early example of product placement. Between 1934 and 1937, the new state radio system broadcast a series of talks on the history of France through wine. Listeners learned that Louis XVI failed as a king not because his mismanagement of the state's finances led to the French Revolution but because he diluted his wine with water, which prevented him from thinking deeply enough. As for the great ideas of the Enlightenment, they came forth under the influence of wine, as one would expect.

No segment of the population that was perceived as able to drink more wine was spared the attention of the campaign. Young men would learn to drink wine while they did military service. Over the objections of some teachers' groups—and, of course, France's weak and ineffective temperance associations—the campaign even reached into schools. When children took dictation, they copied out Louis Pasteur's writings on the health benefits of wine, and when they took geography lessons, they learned the location of France's wine regions. Mathematics classes included equations such as "One liter [0.26 gallons] of wine at ten degrees [alcohol level] corresponds as a food-stuff to 900 grams [1.98 pounds] of milk, 370 grams [0.816 pounds] of

FIGURE 8.1. French postage stamps and cinderella stamps (used for advertising, not postage) issued in France between 1929 and 1939 to promote the consumption of wine. (In the author's possession.)

bread, 585 grams [1,29 pounds] of meat, and five eggs." It was even suggested that wine be provided to children during lunch and at breaks. The French Olympic Committee got on board the wine campaign and asked that French athletes at the 1932 Olympic Games in Los Angeles "be given the same consideration as French sailors in American ports. That is to say, that they be accorded a free daily allowance of a liter of wine." The team had French chefs, the committee noted, but "without wine, the food will not be the same."[28]

France's colonies were identified as underperforming in wine consumption. The pro-wine campaigners had not only the colonists in mind but also the indigenous populations, particularly in Algeria and France's sprawling possessions elsewhere in North Africa. Many, of course, were nondrinking Muslims, but it was thought that they could help the national cause by eating more French grapes and drinking grape juice. A conference to pursue this goal was held in Tunis in 1936, where speakers addressed topics such as making and conserving grape juice. Algeria was a particular problem because it was an integral part of France: most of the indigenous population were Muslims and nondrinkers and so could not help with wine consumption, and the small European population of vignerons contributed massively to the oversupply.

But the main force of the campaign was in metropolitan France and directed at those already drinking wine. Restaurants were encouraged to include some wine in the price of food and to price wine fairly. More retail outlets were permitted, and by 1931 the number of bars serving wine was back to the prewar level of 480,000. Four years later, there were 508,000.[29] Even without its sometimes outrageous proposals—like giving wine to schoolchildren and paying cyclists in the Tour de France to be seen drinking wine while they were racing—the campaign to increase wine consumption in France is astonishing because it ran directly counter to so many trends in the interwar period. As President Franklin Roosevelt was warning about a return to the bad old days after the repeal of Prohibition, the French government was urging its citizen to drink, drink, and drink more wine. Yet for all the effort and cost, the campaign foundered on the economic realities of the Depression, which depressed consumers' real income. During the 1920s, adult per capita wine consumption averaged 117 liters (30.9 gallons) a year in France; in the 1930s, despite the wide-ranging wine campaign, it averaged 118 liters (31.1 gallons). The French were unable or unwilling to drink more wine on demand.

Government efforts on both the production and the consumption fronts seem to have failed consistently, although it is possible that things would have been worse had the government not intervened. In the end, much of the failure of the policies can be attributed to the particular structure of the French wine industry. Vignerons who farmed only a few hectares of vines produced the bulk of French wine, and the ethos surrounding them and their land—not to mention a recent history of violent resistance—made legislators wary of imposing hardships on these small producers. Yet it was production by the great mass of vignerons that had to be contained; limiting the production and sale of wines made by large producers had a marginal impact on France's overall wine supply, although it had more effect in Algeria, where estates were larger on average. Even there, however, constraints on planting had little effect; although there was a slight decline from 1935 to 1936 (from 400,000 to 390,000 hectares, or 988,000 to 964,000 acres), vineyard area began to expand again the following year.

Then too, government policies were neither consistent nor, as far as we can tell, effectively implemented or enforced. Controlling the supply of wine on the market by blocking or distilling it made sense only once the size of the harvest was known and the probable excess over demand could be calculated. But this made government policy almost wholly reactive, and tailoring specific measures to the harvest introduced permanent insecurity to the market. Vignerons, continually anxious about the growing season and the size of the harvest, might now dread a good crop as much as they had once welcomed it, knowing that high numbers might provoke government intervention. This and the continual tinkering with policy, so that no one knew where they stood for more than a few months at a time, did little to improve market stability or relations between vignerons and the government.

While government efforts were directed at dealing with immediate problems of overproduction and securing a better long-term balance between production and demand, some regions focused on the challenges of marketing their wine. In Burgundy, new formulations of terroir were advanced to create a narrative linking the region's wine not only to the physical environment of the vineyards but also to the histories and cultures of wine making.[30] These efforts contributed to making Burgundy the French wine region that is most immediately and closely associated with the idea of terroir, such that the American wine commentator Matt Kramer writes, "One cannot make sense of Burgundy without investigating the notion of *terroir.*"[31] Terroir is often thought of only in terms of the physical environment of vineyards, but it was reformulated in interwar Burgundy to overcome the region's reputation, which was weighed down by wine scandals in the 1920s, and to sell more of its high-end wines.

At the heart of Burgundy's marketing initiative was the construction of an image that stressed its timelessness. Cultural historians have frequently described the process of fabricating or inventing traditions as a way of describing the world that was lost when modernity, in the forms of industrialization and government intervention, began to make itself felt in the rural world. Wine traditions were constructed in Burgundy that centered on the image of the small-scale vigneron tending his small vineyard with his family and making a humble living from the land, with which he and his ancestors had a special relationship. Here the connection of vigneron families to their land was portrayed as no less strong than that of aristocratic families to theirs, and vignerons were characterized as possessing the simple nobility of honest, hardworking peasants.

Bringing the vigneron and land to the foreground was a real shift in emphasis in the marketing of Burgundy's wine. Until the 1920s, wine was identified more with négociants, merchants who bought it from vignerons and sold it under their own name, than with the growers and wine makers themselves. But during the 1920s a number of scandals struck the region as négociants were discovered selling wine labeled as Burgundy that they had brought in from other regions. In some cases, vignerons were also complicit; some overstated the volume of wine they sold to négociants, giving them the opportunity to make up the difference with non-Burgundy wines. For much of the 1920s, more wine labeled as Burgundy was sold than was produced in the region. The appellation law of 1919 regulated the labeling of wines, and as we saw in the previous chapter, many négociants also created new names for their wines so that they could compete commercially with appellation-labeled wines. Even so, contraventions of the law were common, and hundreds of prosecutions resulted in convictions during the 1920s. This was one of the problems addressed by highlighting the vigneron rather than the merchant.

Burgundy seemed perfectly situated for the elaboration of such a tradition, because in the first half of the twentieth century thousands of proprietors owned its vineyards. Through the vagaries of inheritance, purchase, and marriage, vignerons might own a row of vines in one vineyard, two in another, and more in yet others. One of the justifications of the *ban de vendange*, which set the date of the harvest in each commune and forbade owners to go into vineyards in the preceding week, was to prevent the owner of one row of vines from taking grapes from adjacent rows while their owners were absent.

This pattern of ownership was anything but timeless. Before the French Revolution, much of the Burgundy vineyards were owned by the church, particularly the Cistercian order, which alone owned more than two thousand hectares (five thousand acres) of vines. When church lands were nationalized in 1790 and auctioned off, they were deliberately broken up into small units, in the expectation that sales of many small plots by auction would raise more money than the sale of fewer large vineyards. Small-scale vignerons owning and working their vines thus became a dominant feature of Burgundy in the nineteenth century, and the division of small holdings at each generation intensified this pattern of ownership.

But facts are unimportant when traditions are being invented, and the Burgundy tradition needed small-scale vignerons going back into the mists of time. As Gilles Laferté notes, "Images of winegrowing and Burgundy landscapes were stage-managed . . . [and] the winegrowing tradition was fabricated to win over national and international customers."[32] The nineteenth-century efforts of champagne producers to create traditions, especially that of Dom Pérignon, and of Bordeaux producers to establish an image of the aristocratic château are much better known than the more diffuse traditions created for regions such as Burgundy in the twentieth century. But it is clear that Burgundy's wine industry worked to establish a specific historical image as a vehicle for selling its wine and rehabilitating its reputation.

Terroir, its definition, and its implications for wine are much debated, and there is no ready consensus on what should be included within its scope. Some commentators stick rigorously to the physical characteristics of the vineyard, while others see cultural conditions as part of terroir. James Wilson, an American scientist who has written extensively on terroir, argues that "beyond the measurable ecosystem, there is an additional dimension—the spiritual aspect that recognizes the joys, the heartbreaks, the pride, the sweat, and the frustrations of [the vineyard's] history."[33] This said, discussions of terroir have often privileged the soil that vines grow in, and Burgundians gave pride of place to soil, explicitly or implicitly, when they talked of terroir in the interwar years.

The novelist Colette, a native of Burgundy, wrote that of all plants, only the grapevine expresses the true essence of the soil: "The secrets of the soil are expressed through the grape."[34] But although soil is referred to here in a material sense, as the very dirt in which vines grow, the force of the argument rests on soil as a metaphor: it embodies history and communicates tradition and meaning to the vines that grow in it and to the people who work it. That was the significance of soil and terroir that was constructed in interwar Burgundy, and it is far from the meaning of *soil* in modern terroir discourse, where it refers to limestone, granite, clay, and other types of geological substrata, as well as mineral content, drainage qualities, and exposure.

The cultural meaning of terroir was reinforced as links were made between Burgundy's folkways and the physical environment. The image that was promoted stressed the essentially rustic and traditional character of Burgundian society, the opposite of the modern France that was emerging in the 1930s—a France that was urban (the balance of population distribution tipped from rural to urban at this time) and industrial and was extending the modern ethic to farming, where paid laborers doing increasingly mechanized work for absentee proprietors were replacing owner-farmers. This was a restatement of the cultural nostalgia that had played out throughout the late 1800s in other parts of Europe, and as then, folklore was employed to sustain the narrative.[35]

At its heart was the Burgundian vigneron, a man (it was invariably a man) who was portrayed as rooted as deeply in the land as his vines and who was as much a part of the landscape as the vineyards. There was no polarity between "man" and "nature" here; man was part of nature, and in this sense, true Burgundians could be seen as intrinsic parts of the physical environment. Their work on the vines was different from the work of the sun and the rain, but it was essentially no less natural. These vignerons were at the core of a timeless peasant culture that was imagined and given life in celebrations and rituals, at fairs, feasts, and dances. Research into these folkways in the 1920s and 1930s suggested that contemporary cultural forms were largely built on the culture of the vigneron, placing wine at the heart of Burgundian culture.

As Philip Whalen has pointed out, a key figure in the broadening of terroir by linking work, workers, and their culture to the physical environment was Gaston Roupnel, a historian who spent most of his life in Burgundy. Roupnel wrote particularly about the countryside and insisted that there was a "holistic and ecological relationship between the Burgundian people and their natural milieu."[36] He also argued that wine and its culture represented this relationship and that wine itself "is a world larger than us. Because it contains the spirit of the past and is sustained by that which preceded it, its destiny is determined in proportion to its distant origins. . . . It transcends time and the brief passage of human life."[37]

This invented history was also linked to the growth of tourism, which, until the interwar period, stressed historical monuments and "natural" landscapes unspoiled by evidence of agriculture or other signs of human occupation. Until the 1920s, Burgundy's main centers, Dijon and Beaune, were mere stopovers for tourists traveling to Provence, the Riviera, or the Italian lakes, and there was no interest in visiting the region's vineyards, not even the twelfth-century Château du Clos de Vougeot. But in the 1920s, folklore, which included "traditional" costumes, songs, and gastronomy, was added to the list of tourist attractions. Folklore put people back into the landscape, while gastronomy opened the door to wine. One of the leaders of this movement was Gaston Gérard, the mayor of Dijon from 1919 to 1935, who gave more than six hundred public lectures on wine and Burgundy in thirty-two countries in the 1920s. In 1921 he cofounded the annual Foire Gastronomique de Dijon, which aimed to "revive the old culinary and gastronomic traditions of the Province of Burgundy, illustrated by its famous wines and the no less famous cuisine of its dukes."[38] The two-week-long fair attracted six hundred thousand visitors in 1925.

In a 1923 speech, Gérard linked tradition, wine, and land. France could not be a great business power and should not "Americanize" its business and commerce, he said, but "it must remain a country that does things very well. . . . It has its wines that will never be imitated, because to imitate them would be to take our land itself, and we have proved that is no easy matter."[39] The uniqueness of Burgundy's wine, then, was the land in which the vines grew. In the same speech, Gérard condemned "the laziness, the weakness, the filth, and the insurmountable horror of international cooking," and he probably thought much the same of foreign wines.

This emphasis on tradition and region replaced an emphasis on tradition and class. Until the 1920s, producers and négociants stressed family and lineage (with terms such as "Père et Fils" and "Frères") and aristocracy (with various legitimate and fabricated coats of arms). In the 1930s, this image was replaced by one that put the vigneron front and center. One of the initial mechanisms was the staging of the Paulée de Meursault, a gourmet meal that was made with Burgundian ingredients and served to journalists as folklore groups danced and sang to entertain them. (A *paulée* was originally a meal offered to vineyard workers at the end of a harvest.) Other initiatives included the creation of the Confrérie des Chevaliers du Tastevin ("Brotherhood of the knights of the *tastevin*," a reference to a small metal tasting cup), more elitist than popular, whose members wore elaborate faux-aristocratic costumes and observed rituals based on medieval models.

As Burgundy and other regions developed traditions to sell their wine, the French government was embarking on a major revision of national wine legislation, which resulted in the 1935 law that put regulated appellations of origin (*appellations d'origine contrôlée*, or AOCs) in a permanent form. This was the culmination of various measures dealing with appellations, most responding to widespread wine fraud. The 1919 law gave the civil courts the power to approve appellations, but the result was still chaotic in the early 1930s, when oversupply and falling prices led to another wave of wine fraud. Some merchants improved their income by labeling wine originating from regions that commanded low prices as coming from more prestigious regions that produced higher-priced wines; one sold wine from Spain's La Mancha region labeled as if it came from Chablis, a much more prestigious (and expensive) Burgundy appellation.

To combat fraud and misrepresentation and to introduce stability in the appellation system, a new AOC law was passed on 30 July 1935.[40] The driving force behind the law was Joseph Capus, a Bordeaux viticulturist who had entered politics and was successively a deputy, a minister of agriculture, and a senator. A bill that he introduced in March 1935 became the basis of the AOC law passed four months later. It aimed not only to identify wines by their geographic origin but also to guarantee their quality by regulating practices in the vineyard and winery. Only certain grape varieties were to be permitted for a wine labeled with a specific appellation name, and hybrids were totally forbidden. Where blends of varieties were allowed, minimum and maximum percentages of each variety were specified. Maximum yields, expressed as hectoliters of wine per hectare of vineyard, were established, and minimum alcohol levels were set. Rules governed other practices in the vineyard (such as planting vines at specific densities and irrigating) and in the winery (such as adding sugar to the must to raise the alcohol level of the finished wine).

Producers were required to keep thorough records, which could be audited, and inspectors were assigned to wine-producing départements to ensure that the rules were observed. Finally, wines were to be tasted by a panel before being released for sale so as to ensure that they had an acceptable level of quality. In short, the 1935 AOC law surrounded every aspect of wine, from planting vines to selling the finished product, with a set of regulations whose extent was unprecedented in France and unparalleled in any other wine-producing country.

In procedural terms, this law made the important change of removing decisions on appellations from civil courts. It created a new body, the Comité National des Appellations d'Origine, composed of representatives of vignerons, négociants, and the key government ministries (Agriculture, Justice, and Economy) concerned with the wine industry. The comité (which was renamed the Institut National des Appellations d'Origine, or INAO, in 1947) made decisions on appellations, which the Ministry of Agriculture then issued as decrees. It was also active in promoting wine and in combating wine fraud, but its regulatory role was most important. In May 1936, only a month after its composition was finalized, the comité approved the first appellations, most in the Jura, southern France (including Châteauneuf-du-Pape, Cassis, and Tavel), the southwest, and Cognac. By the end of the year, many of Bordeaux's and Burgundy's appellations had been approved, but completing the work with these complex regions of many small appellations took much longer. In Bordeaux, the sweet-wine appellations (such as Sauternes and Barsac) were approved in September 1936, followed by appellations in Médoc, in Entre-deux-Mers, and on the Right Bank, but the comité was still working on Bordeaux when France declared war on Germany three years later.[41]

The comité started by sending questionnaires to all vignerons' associations, asking for as much information as possible on such matters as their boundaries, grape varieties, yields, and alcohol levels, as well as suggestions on how the quality of their wines might best be assured. Some responses were straightforward, enabling appellations to be approved quickly, but others revealed disagreements within regions. In Burgundy, the vignerons of Pommard wanted the maximum yield for superior (cru) wines set at thirty hectoliters a hectare (321 gallons per acre), while those of Chambertin and Clos de Vougeot argued for forty hectoliters (428 gallons per acre). In some cases, the comité sent experts to appellations to look at the vineyards and listen to the vignerons' views before it made any decisions.

Inevitably, there were petitions from vignerons who would be excluded from this or that appellation. When the association in Pommard proposed basing the boundaries of its appellation on an 1860 map that was commonly used as a reference, one of the association's members complained that his vineyards would be excluded.[42] In the nearby commune of Meursault, well known for its white wines, there were three associations of vignerons, each with different ideas about how the appellation's rules should be defined. The mayor stepped in and sent the comité a compromise plan, but progress toward an appellation was derailed when individual vignerons appealed to the comité to halt its work until their cases were heard. One claimed that on the basis of tradition, his Les Combettes vineyard should be included in Meursault rather than Puligny-Montrachet, to which it had been assigned. His evidence included a mention in André Jullien's 1816 book on vineyards and a 1908 document from Louis Latour, the négociant, listing a "Combettes Meursault" wine. The claim was complicated by a counterpetition from the appellation of Puligny-Montrachet, which wanted to keep Les Combettes. In the end, the vineyard stayed in Puligny-Montrachet, but the complexities of Meursault's case were such that its appellation status was not approved until 1970.

The comité received hundreds of requests for appellations from all over France, and it worked remarkably efficiently. (It had an interest in doing so, as a two-franc-per-hectoliter levy on AOC wines financed its work, meaning that the more appellations it approved, the greater its budget became.) Although one of the comité's concerns was to prevent the proliferation of AOCs, it had the power to create new appellations when "their quality and reputation" would justify them.[43] But the great majority of requests for AOC status related to appellations with already defined borders, as the 1935 law encompassed existing "regional, subregional and communal" appellations that the courts had recognized before the new law was passed. Many of the AOC boundaries that the comité approved effectively rubber-stamped those that the courts had established earlier. Many others followed the administrative boundaries of communes, minus any zones unsuitable for viticulture. Others were drawn up by officials sent to survey the territory in question.

The overriding criteria for the definition of AOC boundaries were judicial and administrative. Very rarely was there any claim that characteristics now commonly associated with terroir—soil composition or topological features—should be taken into account. Geology was invoked in the case of Pouilly-sur-Loire, but that was a rare exception.[44] Similarly, when producers petitioned to be included in this or that AOC, they based their claims on tradition and history, not on having limestone or other soil type in common. Even when the vignerons of Barsac tried to exclude vineyards growing on the palus (reclaimed marshland) near Bordeaux from their appellation in the 1920s, it was not because that soil was thought to have a negative effect on the wine but because the palus was not part of Barsac's historic viticulture zone.

Not all the appellations that the courts had recognized up to 1935 applied for AOC status, meaning that from 1935 there coexisted two types of appellation for wine: a simple appellation, defined by the 1919 law almost solely by the territory of the vineyards, and another (AOC), adhering to a much wider set of criteria. In 1936, the first year of the AOC system, about eight hundred million liters (211 million gallons) of wine were from simple appellations and only one hundred million (26 million gallons) from AOCs. By 1939, when many more AOCs had been approved, the numbers had begun to close: there were 1.2 billion liters (317 million gallons) of simple appellation wine, against 350 million (92 million gallons) of AOC wines. AOC wines had gained on those from simple appellations, but they still accounted for only 5 percent of French wine production that year.

In the year and a half between May 1936 and November 1937, the comité issued 110 decrees announcing AOCs, but the number of appellations thus created was larger, as some were omnibus decrees; one of 11 September 1936 created five small Burgundy AOCs, including Romanée-Conti and Richebourg. But most concerned single AOCs. Champagne, which was a single AOC in its own right, had been given special status and was recognized by a decree of 28 September 1935, which predated the installation of the comité.

In addition to establishing geographic boundaries, the comité had to identify the grape varieties that would be permitted in each AOC, set maximum yields, and determine other criteria, and all these decisions entailed research and negotiations among various interested parties. In Bordeaux, for example, five grape varieties (cabernet sauvignon, merlot, cabernet franc, malbec, and petit verdot) were identified as the appellation's most important for red wine, and the appellation rules specified that they had to account for at least 80 percent of a wine labeled "Bordeaux." The maximum yield was initially set at fifty hectoliters per hectare (535 gallons per acre) for Bordeaux as a whole but thirty-six hectoliters (385 gallons) in Haut-Médoc, thirty-four hectoliters (363 gallons) in some Médoc appellations such as Saint-Julien and Pauillac, and thirty-eight hectoliters (406 gallons) in others. Soon after, in 1938, the maximum yield was standardized at thirty-six hectoliters throughout Médoc.[45]

In Burgundy, the commune of Monthelie, which had been frustrated in its attempt to be included in the Côte de Beaune appellation, applied in 1935 for its own AOC status and provided the adjudicating committee with information on the district's position, soil, and topography. Monthelie's producers undertook to limit their red grapes to pinot noir and some of its variants, and their whites to chardonnay and pinot blanc. They also agreed to standardize row spacing, practice "traditional" wine making, and ensure that their wine had a minimum 10.8 percent alcohol. But they drew the line at having their vines trained in one single fashion and at setting maximum yields. Vines should be trained according to where they grew, the vignerons argued, and they declared that they would not overproduce, because to do so would lower the quality of their wine.[46] Despite these efforts, Monthelie had not achieved AOC status when war broke out in 1939 and was successful only in 1970.

The producers of top-tier French wines welcomed the 1935 AOC law and its oversight by inspectors (even though there were very few, no more than twenty for the whole country in 1938). It provided a standardized set of criteria rather than the seemingly random rules that emerged from the courts applying the earlier appellation laws, and it was seen as protecting their brands and combating fraud more effectively than any mechanism devised up to that point. In contrast, producers whom the comprehensive 1935 rules excluded from AOCs chafed against the law. Many were disqualified because they were growing hybrids or other grape varieties not on the approved lists. Others were making styles of wine that did not qualify. When Sancerre gained appellation status in 1936, only its white wines were included; producers of red and rosé wines had to wait until 1961 before they could label their wines with the appellation's name. This highlights an important characteristic of the AOC system: it was developmental rather than static. Over time, the boundaries of appellations, lists of permitted grape varieties, and minimum alcohol levels have changed. In the few years between the application of the AOC law in 1936 and the invasion of France in 1940, however, the work of the comité focused on giving initial approval to appellations and defining authorized vineyard and wine-making practices.

Coming into force just as the Depression began to ebb and consumer markets began to recover, the AOC system must have seemed like a critical turning point in the fortunes of the French wine industry. Exports to the United States began to pick up after Prohibition was repealed. Champagne resumed shipments to the United States: almost eight million bottles in

1935–36 and nearly twelve million in each of the two following years.[47] Muscadet was described as one of the first wines, if not the first, to find its way to American tables "after that great penance called Prohibition."[48] It was in this period too that muscadet began to appear in the restaurants of Paris and other parts of France, where it became France's wine for seafood par excellence.

The stabilization of the appellation system and the gradual recovery of wine markets after the Depression must have seemed like the end of a nightmarish seven decades and the beginning of a period of promise. But it lasted only a few years. In September 1939, France declared war on Germany, which invaded France on 13 May 1940. On 5 June, Paris was occupied, and on 22 June an armistice was signed, allowing Germany to occupy the strategically important west and north of France (including Paris) and Italy to occupy a small area in the southeast. The rest of France (together with Algeria and French territories in Africa) was declared a "free zone," which was not occupied by German forces but administered by a collaborationist government headed by Marshal Philippe Pétain. A military hero of World War I, Pétain set up his government in the town of Vichy and governed at the pleasure of Germany from 1940 to 1942. When the Allied invasions of Africa in 1942 made southern France strategically more sensitive, German occupation was extended to most of the Vichy government's territory, and the Italian occupation in the southeast was expanded. From 1942 to 1944, Pétain continued to govern his original territory, but as a puppet of Germany, until he was relocated to Germany in 1944 after the liberation of France began. While it was in place, the Vichy government collaborated with Germany on a wide range of policies, including the transportation of French Jews to death camps, and in most respects the Vichy government was a conservative and repressive regime.

Wine was far from the most important issue at this time, but German and Vichy policies did have significant effects on French wine. One of the first measures taken by German forces when they occupied France was the expropriation of property owned by Jews. Château Mouton Rothschild was seized (a German garrison was established on the estate for the duration of the war), as were vineyards owned by Jews in other parts of France. Vineyards owned by nationals of countries at war with Germany—like Château Langoa, owned by the British Ronald Barton—were also expropriated. On the other hand, Adolph Segnitz, a Bremen wine merchant, was able to reclaim Château Chasse-Spleen, which had been confiscated as German property at the beginning of World War I, and the German former owners of the Mumm champagne house recovered that property.[49]

French vineyards experienced varying histories between 1940 and 1944. Most of the country's best-known wine regions, including Alsace, Champagne, the Loire valley, Burgundy, and parts of Bordeaux, lay in areas occupied by Germany in 1940. (Champagne was occupied by the German army for the third time in seventy years.) Others, notably the more eastern areas Bordeaux, Languedoc-Roussillon, the Rhône valley, and much of Provence, fell under the control of the Vichy government until 1942, when Germany and Italy occupied them (Italy taking Provence and the northern Rhône valley).

Although the Vichy government did not have day-to-day control over those parts of France that Germany and Italy occupied, its legislation in some matters, including wine, extended to occupied regions. Some of the Vichy regime's measures, such as the extension of appellations, were quite conventional. In Burgundy, the premier cru tier was created in 1943. In Bordeaux, a category of sparkling wine (Bordeaux Mousseux) was created in 1941, as was AOC Bordeaux Supérieur, a tier that had a lower yield per hectare and a slightly higher alcohol level than AOC Bordeaux. Other measures applied to Bordeaux were designed to improve wine quality. Destemming grapes before pressing became mandatory, and in 1943 the minimum alcohol level of Bordeaux wines was raised slightly across the board. New rules required maximum yields per hectare to be observed for each individual vintage, not as an average of three or five vintages, as the 1935 AOC law had specified.[50]

While reinforcing quality in some regions, Vichy wine law lowered it in others, thus widening the gap between the quality wine that France had become famous for and the bulk of French wine. Various laws lowered the minimum alcohol level of non-AOC wine, permitted more blending, and allowed the wider use of hybrid varieties. Measures like these had the potential of increasing the production of ordinary wine, but Pétain himself was ambivalent about wine, even though he had praised pinard for its contribution to victory in 1918: "For the soldiers, wine was the stimulant of moral strength as well as physical strength. In its own way, it helped us to our victory."[51] By the 1940s, he valued wine as an emanation of the soil of France and saw viticulture as representing all that was good in the French character: hard work and devotion to land and tradition.

Pétain also understood that wine was a staple of the French diet, and in his address of 12 August 1941, when acknowledging that workers were suffering shortages, he highlighted wine, meat, and tobacco. But he also believed that overindulgence in wine had sapped the French of their nobility and that widespread alcoholism was a symptom of his country's decadence. (By this time, many of France's oenophile physicians had abandoned the belief that alcoholism resulted only from drinking distilled spirits and that wine was a cure for alcoholism.) Perhaps it was indicative of his views on alcoholic beverages that Pétain set up his government in Vichy, a town famous not only for its spas but also for the mineral water whose growing popularity in the interwar years France's wine industry had so often deplored.

In the four years of its existence, the Vichy regime issued more than fifty laws, decrees, and edicts on wine, many of which growers, producers, and consumers quietly opposed. New rules included a reduction of the volume of tax-free wine that vignerons could keep for their family's consumption and restrictions on cafés and other drinking places. The number of public drinking places in France shrank by 40 percent during the war, from more than half a million to barely three hundred thousand.[52] Wine was included on the list of rationed goods; in 1940 the ration was two liters (0.53 gallons) of wine per adult each week, but later it was restricted to males. In 1941 there was talk of reducing the ration to a single liter of wine per adult male each week, but the German authorities opposed this for fear that it would turn public opinion even more against them. Rationing was implemented because even though stocks of wine were abundant, the Vichy government wanted to divert much of it for distilling into fuel. Similarly, grape juice was converted to grape sugar, and grape seeds were pressed for their oil.[53]

Needless to say, the war put an end to exports of French wines to then-enemy markets including Britain, Canada, and (from December 1941) the United States, and trade effectively stopped with German-occupied European countries such as Denmark, Norway, and Belgium, which had been significant importers of French wine. All that were left were neutral and nonbelligerent countries (such as Sweden and Spain), which had been only minor importers of French wine, and, of course, Germany. Germany had been one of the most important markets for French wine before the war, but once it had defeated France, the usual rules of commerce ceased to apply. The German government saw France, like the rest of occupied Europe, as a source of resources of all kinds, and designated France as its main supplier of agricultural products, including wine.

Much has been written of the looting of wine by German troops during the occupation, though less has been written of looting by Allied forces during the liberation. In anticipation of theft in 1940, some producers hid stocks of wine in the implicit hope that German occupation would end before the wine spoiled. In Vouvray, Philippe Poniatowski buried some of his best wines in his yard.[54] At Château Haut-Brion, which was used as a Luftwaffe rest home during the occupation, the entrances to some cellars filled with wine were hidden behind piles of rubbish, but the occupying troops did not even touch production during the war.[55] In Beaune, Maurice Drouhin built a wall in his cellar to hide his valuable stock of Romanée-Conti from the 1929 through 1938 vintages.[56] Other producers did not do as well. At the beginning of 1941, the vignerons of the small Burgundy commune of Monthelie recorded the catalog of misfortunes of 1940: freezing weather in January, heavy rain in April, then occupation by the German army in June, followed by the prompt seizure of their wine reserves. Such, they wrote, "is the balance sheet of a particularly catastrophic year." The Germans paid for the confiscated wine in occupation currency, which the vignerons rightly suspected was not worth very much.[57]

But looting and forced requisitions seem to have been sporadic and opportunistic, and most wine was bought, even if the prices paid were favorable to the Germans. Their acquisitions took two main forms: purchases directly by the German military authorities and by agencies such as the Gestapo and the Schutzstaffel (SS), and purchases by civilian merchants who obtained wine for the German domestic market. The German authorities shipped the equivalent of 320 million bottles of French wine a year to Germany during the war, the great bulk of it willingly sold by French négociants and vignerons. An economic services bureau in Paris oversaw these purchases, but German négociants or wine merchants who were installed in France's main wine regions selected the wines. The official charged with purchasing wine in Champagne was Otto Kläbisch, the manager of a German sparkling wine company and the brother-in-law of the Nazi foreign minister Joachim von Ribbentrop, who himself had been a representative in Germany of the Mumm and Pommery champagne houses. A wine merchant from Bremen looked after purchases from Burgundy, the Rhône, and Languedoc. In addition to these buyers, responsible for purchasing the bulk of French wine for German consumption, others from the SS, the Gestapo, and other agencies of the Nazi regime spread throughout France's regions to acquire wine for their own purposes.

We have only impressionistic accounts of the drinking habits of German soldiers in France during the war, and they need to be read in light of an enduring French portrayal of Germans as boorish drinkers. Wartime accounts refer to the occupation forces drinking deeply and to officers wining and dining regularly in the restaurants of Paris and occupied cities and towns in the provinces. French wine was served to German officers in their messes and at special occasions (see figure 8.2). Observers noted that officers were often seen drunk, late in the evenings. A historian living in Dijon during the war noted in his diary that German soldiers stationed in Côte de

Figure 8.2.   Undated photograph of German soldiers at a Christmas celebration, prominently featuring bottles of Bordeaux wine. (In the author's possession.)

Nuits drank the local wine all day long and that on one occasion in Volnay, four drunk soldiers beat up an officer and left him for dead, saying they had had enough.[58]

In many (perhaps most) cases, French vignerons and négociants seem to have been more than willing to do business with German authorities, whether civilian or military. In Champagne, the Germans at first demanded the shipment of 480,000 bottles a week, but the association of champagne houses managed to reduce the number to 250,000. Given additional sales from individual houses, some twenty million bottles of champagne were shipped to Germany each year of the war. They represented more than half of each year's production and depleted almost all of Champagne's reserves.[59] In Burgundy, one student of the period writes, soldiers, officers, and buyers for the SS "bought thousands of hectoliters—for millions of francs—that were then shipped to German négociants for the German domestic market and the German army."[60] Friedrich Dörrer, the official German wine buyer in Burgundy from 1940 to 1941, invited producers to let him know what they wanted to sell. Deluged with wine, he noted, "I do not have time to reply personally to all the houses that have kindly sent me samples, which I have tasted very carefully. I thank them sincerely for their efforts, which, by a careful selection, have made my job easy, all the while showing me their fraternal feelings." Even so, he complained that some had sent poor wines, especially those from the abundant 1934 and 1935 vintages, "which did not even have acceptable color."[61]

It is hardly surprising that producers were willing to sell to German buyers, as they represented virtually the sole opportunity for staying solvent in wartime conditions. Even if the Germans paid prices that were not generous, they paid promptly. A postwar French analysis estimated that between 1940 and 1944 the Germans bought eighty-six million bottles of still wine and 8.2 billion liters (2.2 billion gallons) of wine in bulk, as well as tens of millions of bottles of sparkling wine.[62] But any commercial relationship with German occupation authorities was risky, as it could be considered collaboration with the enemy. A 1941 Vichy law cleared the way for French citizens to do business with Germans, but many French people considered Pétain's administration illegitimate, and it was unlikely that this law would protect collaborators if Germany was defeated.

Despite widespread resistance to German occupation, it is clear that there was enthusiastic support for Marshal Pétain's government in many parts of France, as conservatives rallied to an ideology of authority, religion, and hierarchy that replaced the republican egalitarianism that had dominated France during the Third Republic (1870–1940). By 1942, more than two hundred streets, squares, and stadiums throughout France had been named after Pétain, and there was support for his regime within many circles of the French wine industry. Perhaps some wine producers thought it was not merely a coincidence that the Third Republic, which had governed in the tradition of the French Revolution, had come into being just as phylloxera began to ravage France's vineyards and that its seven-decade existence had seen one disaster after another for the French wine industry. Perhaps they hoped the demise of the Third Republic in 1940 and the establishment of Pétain's right-wing state would regenerate not only France but also French wine.

One of the more bizarre episodes of the Vichy period was the 1942 gift to Pétain of the Les Teurons vineyard, which had been part of the prestigious Hospices de Beaune estate since the seventeenth century. It was given by the département of Côte-d'Or, which purchased the vineyard specifically for that purpose from the Hospices de Beaune. Workers were hired to build a wall around the half hectare (1.2 acres) of pinot noir vines, making it into a clos, and it was renamed Le Clos du Maréchal Pétain. The gift of the vineyard, which was in German-occupied territory, was formalized at a ceremony in Vichy on 29 May 1942, when the leaders of the département, the mayors of Dijon and Beaune, and other members of Burgundy's political elite handed over the deed and a map of the vineyard.[63] The Hospices de Beaune undertook to look after the vines, harvest the grapes, and make the wine, and the purchase of another, larger vineyard compensated it for the sale of Les Teurons.

In itself the gift was unexceptional, as many regions, municipalities, and individuals showered Pétain with offerings of all kinds. In June 1942, the association of Burgundy négociants sent sixty-six six-bottle cases of their best wine to "the savior of France . . . as a sign of respect for you yourself, as evidence of obedience to your directives, to show its adherence to national unity."[64] Pétain also received thirty cases of beaujolais from the town of Villefranche-sur-Saône. But in his message of thanks for the Beaune vineyard, he wrote that of all the gifts, that of the vineyard was "the most charming and pleasing." He firmly situated it within the ideology that glorified the land, the peasantry, and hard work. Referring to his "love of the land," Pétain wrote, "If I do not have the soul of a Burgundian, my viticulturist's instinct brings me very close to it." (He was not actually a viticulturist, although his father was a farmer.)

The attachment of many of Burgundy's vignerons to this sort of rhetoric should not be surprising, as the creation of a folklore tradition centered on the vigneron and his land was one of the region's projects during the 1920s and 1930s. As we have seen, Gaston Roupnel was a leader in the articulation of an idealized image of the peasant tending his land, and this was essentially the ideology of Pétain's National Revolution, just as it was of the many doctrines of cultural nostalgia that fed into late nineteenth- and twentieth-century fascism. Whatever Roupnel's own attitudes toward Pétain and Vichy, his works were harnessed in support of Pétain's agrarian ideology and program.[65]

After the vineyard gift was made, the city of Beaune paid for a road to be constructed so that it could be accessed more easily as a destination of political pilgrimage. In May 1943, even as Vichy was more and more associated with growing repression and atrocities by German occupation forces, stone markers were installed at the Clos du Maréchal Pétain. The installation was the centerpiece of a week of festivities that included performances by a choir of fifty young people from Chablis, "united by their love of terroir," who sang Burgundian folk songs.[66] The marker was emblazoned with the fasces symbol common to fascist organizations in Europe and the initials "Ph.P.," for "Philippe Pétain." As for the wine from the Clos du Maréchal Pétain, the 1942 vintage in Burgundy was poor, and a négociant purchased the wine. Some bottles were sent to Pétain, but their arrival was overshadowed by the fact that the box was addressed to "Maréchal Pétain, Chef de la République, Vichy, Frankreich,"—that is, the address employed the term *République*, which was abhorrent to the Vichy regime, instead of *État* (state), and the German word for "France."

The 1943 harvest was more significant, as the stone marker made the clos official. Some of Burgundy's pro-Vichy political personalities visited it during the harvest, a much better one, and Pétain's wine filled four and a half barrels and an additional five liters (1.3 gallons)—a total of 1,031 liters (272 gallons), or 1,375 bottles. It is not known whether Pétain tasted any of the wine; it probably stayed in barrel until late 1944, by which time France had been liberated and Pétain had relocated to Germany to head a short-lived government-in-exile. The wine was sold at the Hospices de Beaune auction in 1946.

After the liberation of France, the gift of the clos to Pétain became a point of reference in charges of collaboration leveled against wartime leaders in Beaune and in Burgundy more generally. The mayor of Beaune, who had supported the gift, defended his role by saying that he had argued against it and had finally agreed only because it was a way of protecting the wines of the Hospices de Beaune from being stolen by the Germans. In 1946 the sale of the vineyard was annulled and it was renamed Beaune-Teurons.

The war and occupation had significant effects on wine production and consumption in France. Production dropped in this period, partly as a result of poor weather during the growing seasons; the 1939 vintage was widely regarded as one of the worst of the century to that point, and 1940's was not much better. Shortages of labor and materials also made an impact on wartime production. Vines suffered from mildew and mold when vignerons were unable to spray copper sulfate because the German authorities had requisitioned copper for military purposes. Fuel for tractors and other vehicles was tightly rationed, and because glass was in short supply, wine was bottled in whatever bottles producers could obtain. Under these constraints and suffering from food shortages and rationing, some vignerons went so far as to pull out vines so as to plant crops that would feed their families.

The period of occupation also disrupted the prewar wine market and distribution networks, which led to shortages outside wine-producing regions. In 1940, wine was rationed and price controls placed on non-AOC wine. Then, as the availability of AOC wines declined and their prices rose, they too were subjected to price controls. (Price controls were not removed until 1947.) As one would expect, the shortage of higher-quality wines led to a black market, but black market prices were well beyond the means of the mass of French people, who struggled to make do during the war. Given the poor wartime harvests and the extent of German wine requisitions, per capita wine consumption in France must have declined markedly. Two broad measures (admittedly indirect and imprecise) were a decrease in hospital admissions for alcoholism (3,495 in 1939, 626 in 1943) and a decline in the incidence of cirrhosis of the liver during the war.[67]

The end of World War II brought to a close almost a century of challenges to the French wine industry. The final decade and a half saw it beset by uncertainty in domestic markets and by very limited opportunities for exports, first because of the Depression and then because of World War II. But these conditions forced the French state to step in to regulate the wine industry on a scale and with a breadth not seen before. Although there were, and continued to be, complaints about government intervention in wine production and commerce and the restrictions that the AOC system imposed, measures such as the 1935 law provided a secure foundation for the reconstruction of the French wine industry after the war.

9. French Wine Reinvented

1945 to the Present

Anyone wanting to identify a period in the history of French wine as a golden age might well settle on the most recent half century, even though the imperative of nostalgia generally places a golden age of anything in a more distant past. As far as the years since World War II are concerned, it might be argued that any period would look good after eight decades of the challenges that the French wine industry experienced up to 1945: a catastrophic vine disease, chronically chaotic wine markets, violence in the vineyards, dismal export figures, and three wars in which German armies (and Italian armies in one) invaded and occupied French wine regions.

Yet considered in its own right, the period between the early 1960s and the early twenty-first century saw a French wine industry that generally enjoyed robust sales and exports, together with a global reputation for quality at the higher end and good value at the lower. The total area under vines contracted, but there was an increase in the proportion of AOC wines, which may be considered a general if not wholly reliable indication of better quality. In contrast, the mass of poor *vins de table* (the lowest category of wine) that had been the mainstay of French wine drinkers for centuries disappeared as many underperforming grape varieties were pulled out and areas only marginally suitable for viticulture were taken out of production. There were, of course, fluctuations that accompanied economic cycles and broad changes in the wider world of wine that harmed the sales of French wine. But overall the French wine industry echoed the prosperity that many European and non-European wine consumers experienced following World War II.

The immediate postwar period started with the reconstruction of French vineyards. World War II had been fought over a much wider area of France than World War I, but it had seen little fighting in most of France's wine regions. The total area under vines had declined only slightly from 1939 to 1945 (from 1,494,000 to 1,434,000 hectares, or 3,692,000 to 3,543,000 acres),[1] but even though war-related damage was limited in 1945, many vineyards were in a state of neglect as a result of shortages of labor, fertilizers, and pesticides during the war. Ironically, vineyards planted with hybrid varieties, which accounted for as much as a quarter of France's vines at the beginning of the 1950s, had survived better than others, because hybrids were bred to be climate hardier and more resistant to the various diseases and other problems that routinely affect vineyards.

The first three postwar vintages, of 1945, 1946, and 1947, were of good quality, with 1947's widely considered one of the best of the twentieth century in Bordeaux. But all, especially the first two, were small in quantity. In Bordeaux, efforts were made to take advantage of the quality to regenerate wine exports, but producers had to wait for the normalization of economic and social conditions in the 1950s as Western European countries—including important markets for French wine such as Britain, Belgium, and the Netherlands—rebuilt their economies. Over the short term, poverty was extensive in much of Europe and food rationing continued for several years. In 1948 and 1949, France experienced a currency crisis and a period of high inflation that raised the cost of export goods and made it that much more difficult to sell French wine on foreign wine markets.

While the wine industry faced these economic challenges, the Institut National des Appellations d'Origine (INAO), the body formed to create and regulate appellations, resumed the work that it had all but suspended during the war. Only six AOCs were established between 1941 and 1944, among them Petit Chablis, Bordeaux Supérieur, and Bandol. This was a pale shadow of the scores of AOCs created each year before France was invaded. Some modifications enacted by the Vichy regime that altered prewar AOC regulations were repealed, and the INAO resumed its primary functions of approving new appellations and modifying the rules applied to those already approved. In a number of cases the changes involved expanding appellations to encompass more communes, as when Saint-Germain-la-Rivière was included in Côtes de Fronsac in 1954 and Haillan in Graves in 1956. Completely new appellations in Bordeaux included Margaux, established in 1954, and Côtes de Castillon, in the following year. Satellite appellations, such as Montagne-Saint-Émilion and Puisseguin-Saint-Émilion, were created around Saint-Émilion.[2]

The INAO began work with a flourish immediately after the war and created nineteen appellations between 1945 and 1949. Most defined new appellations (such as Alsace, Givry, and Madiran), while some referred to specific wine styles, such as Pacherenc du Vic-Bilh sec AOC, a dry white wine, contrasted with the sweeter wines permitted in the Pacherenc du Vic-Bilh AOC, which was created at the same time. The pace at which the INAO created AOCs slackened during the 1950s and 1960s—only sixteen new ones appeared in the two decades between 1950 and 1969, a period of change in many vineyards—but it picked up thereafter: there were fifty new AOCs in the 1970s (nineteen in 1970 alone), twenty-one in the 1980s, and twenty-nine in the 1990s.

Other institutional changes affected classification schemes. The approach of the centenary of the 1855 Bordeaux Classification seems to have concentrated attention on the fact that it includes wines from only the Médoc, Graves (represented only by Château Haut-Brion), and Sauternes districts. This was a long-standing grievance of vignerons and château owners in other Bordeaux appellations, and in the early 1950s some set up their own classification systems. In 1953 a classification of Graves was announced, followed by Saint-Émilion (with a fine sense of timing) in 1955. As the centenary of 1855 drew closer, Bordeaux's *Sud Ouest* newspaper polled people prominent in the Médoc wine industry on whether the century-old classification should be revisited. Not surprisingly, most owners of classified châteaux were happy with the status quo, but some less embedded in Bordeaux's elite, such as Alexis Lichine, who owned Château Prieuré-Lichine, were in favor of a revision.[3] In the event, the 1855 classification was not revised then and has not been since.[4] Its only change since it was drawn up was the elevation in 1973 of Château Mouton Rothschild from Second to First Growth.

The owner of that winery, Baron Philippe de Rothschild, is an example of the entrepreneurship that a few owners showed after the war. He had scarcely recovered his estate, confiscated as Jewish property when the German army occupied Bordeaux, when he developed a plan to promote his wine. Starting with the 1945, he commissioned an artist to create a label for each vintage of Château Mouton Rothschild. The first of them, Philippe Jullien, then an obscure artist and later better known as a dramatist, produced a label with stylized grape vines and leaves around a letter *V* (for *Victoire*), in whose angle "1945 ANNÉE DE LA VICTOIRE" was printed. It was more design than art, but soon the Mouton Rothschild labels featured work by some of the world's best-known artists, including Jean Cocteau (on the 1947 vintage), Georges Braque (1955), Salvador Dalí (1958), Jacques Villon (1960), Henry Moore (1964), Joan Miró (1969), Marc Chagall (1970), Pablo Picasso (1973, the year of Picasso's death, when his 1959 *Bacchanale* was featured), and Andy Warhol (1975).[5]

Independent organizations (that is, organizations not sponsored by the state) had been forbidden during the war, but as soon as the Vichy regime and German occupation ended, associations and syndicates of vignerons were revived or created. The immediate postwar period also saw initiatives to promote the culture of wine in Bordeaux. A group of scholars, professionals, and artists established the Académie du Vin de Bordeaux in 1948 to do this through historical research, publications, colloquia, and exhibitions. The next year saw the founding of a confrerie, the Commanderie du Bontemps de Médoc, modeled on a similar organization that had been set up in Burgundy in the 1930s. Members of the commanderie, prominent members of the wine industry, dress in medieval-style robes for elaborate ceremonies and banquets, and it regularly admits honorary members from other wine industries, the worlds of politics and business, and the media. The members consider themselves the heirs of centuries of tradition, and their prime purpose is to promote the interests of the wine industries of Médoc, Graves, Sauternes, and Barsac.[6] The commanderie was soon followed by similar organizations in other Bordeaux appellations, such as the Hospitaliers de Pomerol and the Gentilshommes de Fronsac.

The wine producers of Beaujolais decided to accelerate the prosperity of their region in a more populist way. One of its profitable products was a young wine that went on sale in November, only weeks after its fermentation was complete. This was classified as a *primeur* wine, one released for sale before the spring following the harvest; others were produced in regions as diverse as Burgundy and Gaillac. (The wines shipped to England from Bordeaux in the Middle Ages were primeur wines.) When Beaujolais gained AOC status in 1937, it had continued to sell primeur wines, as well as wines that aged longer before release, but in 1951 the INAO ruled that AOC wines could be not released for sale until 15 December of the year of harvest. (There is an echo here of the 15 December embargo that Bordeaux merchants placed on High Country wines in the Middle Ages.) Associations of vignerons in several appellations petitioned against the new rule, which was amended only months after it was issued, to allow the release of certain wines before 15 December, with no earliest date specified. The exemption applied not only to Beaujolais but also to wines such as the whites of Gaillac and aligoté in Burgundy. In Beaujolais, the new ruling was the go-ahead for what became known as "beaujolais nouveau," a fruity red wine (also a rosé since 2007) made from the gamay grape variety and intended to be consumed while it was very young.

From 1951, beaujolais nouveau was released on various dates, usually in early November, but in 1967, 15 November was agreed on as the date when it could go on sale. In the 1960s it was decided to promote this wine by staging a race from Beaujolais to Paris, and in 1966 the Nicolas chain of wineshops in the capital held events to celebrate the arrival of the wine. The association of Beaujolais producers adopted the slogan "Le Beaujolais nouveau est arrivé!" (The beaujolais nouveau has arrived!) By the 1980s, beaujolais nouveau was being shipped to other European countries in time to be released on 15 November, and before long it was being sent to North America and around the world, including to Australia and Japan. In 1985 the release date was changed to the third Thursday in November, and beaujolais nouveau can now be sold from 12:01 AM on that day.

Wine professionals often summarily dismiss beaujolais nouveau as an inferior wine that is good only for quaffing (an attitude that calls to mind the centuries-old prejudice against gamay) and that is mass-produced with little attention to quality. But however it is judged, it has proved a mainstay of Beaujolais. In the 1950s, about two million bottles of beaujolais nouveau were produced each year, but by 2013, production of both beaujolais nouveau and beaujolais-villages nouveau had risen to more than thirty million bottles. This accounts for half of Beaujolais AOC and a third of Beaujolais-Villages AOC production and means these primeur wines are an important source of income for wine producers in Beaujolais, although some regret that their success has led many consumers to associate the region with only these young, fruity wines rather than its wines of other quality levels, especially those from designated communes such as Morgon and Fleurie.

While these cultural and commercial initiatives were beginning in some regions in the 1950s, vignerons throughout France were working to bring their vineyards back to full production, despite continued shortages of equipment and material. Some had to pull out varieties that were no longer permitted under AOC rules. One was baco noir, which had been bred in 1902 and banned for use in AOC wines in 1935 but was still widely planted throughout France, especially in Burgundy, the Loire valley, and Landes, south of Bordeaux. Vignerons often used baco noir to make wine for their families, but it also found its way into some commercial wines. Other varieties, high-yielding but mediocre, were replaced by those that would make better wine. Aramon had been one of the staple grapes of Languedoc-Roussillon (especially Hérault), where it produced yields as high as four hundred hectoliters to the hectare (4,276 gallons per acre). It made a wine that was pale, thin, and low in alcohol—the sort that needed to be blended with the altogether more robust wines of Algeria to be marketable. The area planted with aramon, about 150,000 hectares (370,000 acres) in the late 1950s, began a steady decline to 35,000 hectares (86,000 acres) in 1998, but even then it was France's sixth-most-planted variety. By 2013, fewer than three thousand hectares (seven thousand acres) remained. It was largely replaced by carignan, also a high-yielding variety, but one that produces wines with more color, body, alcohol, and structure.

The removal of hybrids such as baco noir and poor performers such as aramon provided an opportunity for replanting with varieties that would produce better wines. In Languedoc and the southeast, syrah, grenache, and cinsault were more widely planted. In Bordeaux, the AOC-approved grape varieties were distributed throughout the region, but the distinction between the merlot-dominant Right Bank (especially Saint-Émilion, Pomerol, and Fronsac) and the cabernet sauvignon–dominant Left Bank (mainly Médoc and Graves) became sharper. The ratios of varieties planted shifted all over France in response to regional and local conditions and vignerons' plans or aspirations. The picture was complicated, but if there was an overarching tendency, it was toward an increase in lower-yielding varieties with the potential to produce higher-quality wine. Quality is relative, of course. It was not that every region in France aspired to become a source of top-tier wines with the reputation of some appellations in Bordeaux, Burgundy, and the northern Rhône valley. But there appears to have been a collective sense among France's hundreds of thousands of vignerons that the days of barely drinkable wines were numbered.

Compulsory tastings were required for some appellations in order to control quality, and wines that failed were unable to use the appellation name that they had applied for. Prospective Saint-Émilion grand cru first underwent this process in 1955, which had the effect of reducing the volume of wine so labeled by 3.8 million liters (1 million gallons). Hundreds of producers withdrew their wines from consideration before the first year's tasting, and 9 percent of the remaining wines did not pass. In the 1955 and 1956 vintages, only 2 percent and 6 percent, respectively, of the volume was rejected, suggesting that either quality had quickly improved or producers of inferior wines had learned not to put them forward for tasting.

In some key regions, the proportion of AOC wines, which ought to have been of higher quality than others, declined. In the late 1940s, for example, vineyards making AOC wines accounted for 72 percent of viticultural land in Bordeaux, but that share fell to 60 percent in 1950 and 53 percent in 1953 before settling at 57 percent for the rest of the decade. This is not to say that the non-AOC wines were of poor quality. The early 1950s saw big and good harvests, and the yields of AOC and non-AOC vineyards in Bordeaux were almost the same: AOC vineyard yields were lower by only two hectoliters a hectare (twenty-one gallons per acre).[7]

In the early 1950s—as vineyards were reconstituted, harvests began to grow, and Europe recovered from the war—foreign wine markets took more and more French wine. Bordeaux recovered some foreign markets, but its sales to the rest of France proved more important: in 1954, shipments outside France accounted for only a quarter of the region's total production, and Parisians alone drank almost as much wine from Bordeaux as all its exports combined. Important French markets for Bordeaux's wine included the industrial northeast, Normandy, Lyon, and the regions around Gironde, but in the south only Marseille bought significant volumes. Most of the Bordeaux wine sold in France was not classified as AOC, but it nonetheless fetched higher prices than the wines from Languedoc that also poured into the cities of northern France. As for export markets, Belgium quickly resumed its place as one of Bordeaux's best customers, while the Netherlands, whose economy recovered more slowly from the war, began to place significant orders only in the later 1950s. British wine merchants also placed significant orders, particularly for the more expensive appellations, and exports to Scandinavia expanded.

The United States was to all intents and purposes a new market for French wines after World War II. Wine exports to the United States had ended with the start of Prohibition in 1920 and were sluggish between 1933, when Prohibition was repealed, and 1940, when France was invaded. A new market and a small market—wine drinkers were a very small minority of the American population—the United States was nonetheless a good market in the 1950s, as it was generally prosperous and the war had affected its economy less than Europe's. Better-off American wine drinkers wanted French wine from Bordeaux above all, and imports from there accounted for two-thirds of all American wine imports from France. One characteristic of the American market was a marked preference for wine to be shipped already bottled, even though most wine shipped in the 1950s, whether to domestic or to foreign destinations, was transported in barrels and bottled on arrival. Even in Great Britain, where there was a preference for the more expensive Bordeaux wines, which were more likely to be bottled at the châteaux, only 7 percent of the Bordeaux wine imported during the 1950s had been shipped in bottles.

As the French wine industry was starting to find its feet, ten years after the end of the war, there was a major setback: a devastatingly harsh winter in 1956. Three weeks of freezing weather in early February affected many wine regions. In Burgundy the temperature dropped to −25 degrees Celsius (−13 degrees Fahrenheit), while in Bordeaux the daily minimum temperature rose above zero (32 degrees Fahrenheit) only twice during February, with most daily minimums falling between −6 and −15 degrees Celsius (21.2 and 5 degrees Fahrenheit). Some districts suffered more than others. In Bordeaux, the temperature dropped to −15 in Sauternes and −23 (−9.4 degrees Fahrenheit) at Libourne on 15 February. Although these temperatures were not as cold as those in 1709, they persisted for weeks and had particularly devastating effects in low-lying areas of vineyards, where the cold air settled. Throughout the Bordeaux region, some 45 percent of the vines were killed, and another 45 percent were lightly or seriously damaged. Other wine regions throughout France also lost high proportions of their vines, and only the Rhône valley, Provence, and Languedoc were unaffected.

The replanting needed after 1956 gave further impetus to the replacement of hybrids with *Vitis vinifera* varieties and the distribution of grape varieties according to appellation. The Right Bank of Bordeaux was seriously affected by the winter—most of the vines in Pomerol were killed—and the INAO agreed that merlot should be the dominant grape of the area. Cabernet franc was permitted to occupy a third of the vineyards, with cabernet sauvignon relegated to a small percentage.

Yet although there was a steady shift in the 1950s toward planting *Vitis vinifera* vines and making better wine, much of what was available in metropolitan France at the time was Languedoc wine blended with Algerian. The French wine (most still made from aramon) was thin, pale, and low in alcohol and contributed volume but not much more, while the Algerian wine's contributions of body, color, and alcohol made the blend marketable. As we have seen, wine production was encouraged in Algeria to compensate for the wine shortages in metropolitan France during the phylloxera crisis, but Algeria continued to produce vast volumes of wine long after phylloxera had ceased to be anything but a sporadic problem in some French localities. In the 1930s it produced an average of 1.7 billion liters (450 million gallons) of wine a year and metropolitan France 5.8 billion (1.5 billion gallons), meaning that Algeria was responsible for more than a fifth of the total French production. Algeria's vineyards contracted during World War II as overproductive vines were grubbed up, but they expanded after the war, and during the 1950s Algeria returned to contributing about the same percentage of France's wine: on average 1.6 billion liters (420 million gallons) annually, which were added to the 5.3 billion liters (1.4 billion gallons) that the vineyards of metropolitan France produced each year.[8]

If Algeria is considered as a wine-producing region in its own right, it was the world's fourth biggest in 1960, following Italy, metropolitan France, and Spain. Similarly, if its shipments to metropolitan France are regarded as exports rather than as shipments within France (like wines of Languedoc sent to Paris), Algeria was by far the largest wine exporter in the world. In the early 1960s it shipped wine representing 41 percent of the world's total wine exports; France's wine exports, which were the next biggest, represented only 14 percent.[9]

But the early 1960s were the high point for Algeria's external wine sales. After a vicious war between Algerian nationalists and French forces, Algeria won independence in 1962, and its wine lost the automatic access to the metropolitan French market that it had had since the mid-1800s. Much of the Algerian wine industry was owned and operated by French citizens whose families had lived in Algeria since the late nineteenth century, and many of them left for France following independence. As they and almost all the other Europeans (including hundreds of thousands of French troops) left Algeria, they abandoned their vineyards and wineries. The production of 1.3 billion liters (340 million gallons) of wine a year of the early 1960s fell to half that in the following decade and declined precipitously from then: by the early 1980s, annual production was 150 million liters (40 million gallons), which might sound like a lot but was only 10 percent of the yearly production of two decades earlier.[10] The exodus of 90 percent of the European population suddenly contracted the Algerian domestic wine market, because most Algerians were nondrinking Muslims.

Even though Algeria had been politically an integral part of France, the experience of its wine industry is a classic example of colonial dependency. Wine made up half of its nonoil offshore earnings, and its viticulture had flourished at the expense of other sectors of agriculture. The loss of the metropolitan French market made Algeria's economy and much of its labor force vulnerable. In principle, this should not have happened, because the independence agreement signed in 1962 gave Algerian wine access to France on a commercial basis. This was advantageous to Algeria, where the sudden disappearance of the wine industry would have caused an economic crisis. It was also advantageous to France, much of whose wine would have been unmarketable if it could not have been blended with the more robust Algerian wine. But in 1963, the first full year of independence, shipments of Algerian wine to France were only half of what they had been the year before. The reason was not a shortage of wine, because Algeria's production did not decline appreciably until 1967, but rather pressure from the French wine lobby, which now included aggrieved former Algerian winery owners and wine makers, to restrict imports of Algerian wine.

To deal with the problem, an agreement was signed in 1964 to allow larger imports of Algerian wine, which would decline steadily over five years. The figure for 1964 was set at 875 million liters (231 million gallons), which would decline by 50 million liters (13 million gallons) a year to 675 million liters (178 million gallons) in 1968. In 1964 the French government also encouraged the planting in French vineyards of new varieties that would make wines of a style that would compensate for the loss of Algerian wine. Not only was there style to think about, but the absence of Algerian wine meant that far less wine would be available on the French market. But French vignerons did not respond, and rather than expanding, land under vines declined slowly but steadily right through the 1960s and 1970s. As we shall see, this mirrored a long-term decline in French wine consumption.

Relations between Algeria and France were complicated in 1967 when the French government briefly introduced regulations that limited the volume of blended French-Algerian wines. They were repealed after only a few months, but in that year and 1968 the French breached the 1964 agreement by taking only half the agreed-upon volume of Algerian wine. Algeria responded with sanctions on French goods, and soon wine was the object of a trade war. Algeria was able to export small volumes of wine to Germany and other European countries, and the Soviet Union helped it out in 1968 by agreeing to purchase five hundred million liters (132 million gallons) of wine a year for the following seven years. But the price that the Soviet Union agreed to was much lower than what France and other European countries had paid. Although France did take more Algerian wine in the early 1970s, pressure from its wine lobby and conflict over oil prices and the nationalization of French oil companies led to the virtual disappearance of Algerian wine from France. Known primarily as a producer of ordinary, inexpensive wine, Algeria was unable to develop export wine markets once the French market effectively closed to it. From more than a billion liters (290 million gallons) a year in the early 1960s, Algerian wine production fell to a mere 3 million liters (800,000 gallons) in the early 2000s, and its exports virtually ceased.

During the 1960s and 1970s, then, the French wine supply was reduced by the 20 percent that Algeria had contributed. But it lost more than simply that percentage, because fifty-fifty blends of Languedoc-Algerian wine accounted for 40 percent of the wine available to French wine drinkers in the preceding decades. Divorcing weak Languedoc wine from its robust Algerian partner deprived the French market of up to two-thirds of its wine, depending on the blending ratio, leaving 20 percent unacceptably thin and low in alcohol. Actual French wine production, as distinct from the volume that was marketable, remained stable, with the usual annual variations that reflected the vagaries of weather. There were small harvests

262 / Chapter Nine

in 1961, 1969, and 1977 and big harvests in 1962, 1970, and 1976, with a massive harvest in 1979 (8.4 billion liters, or 2.2 billion gallons), which easily exceeded the bumper harvests of 1934 and 1935.

The loss of Algerian content—metropolitan French–Algerian blends were sold almost exclusively to consumers in metropolitan France—was partly offset by a decline in French wine consumption that began in the 1960s and has continued steadily since. In the late 1930s, the per capita consumption of wine in France was 170 liters (45 gallons) a year (half a liter, or 0.13 gallons, a day), which fell during the war because of shortages. Consumption began to rebound in the late 1940s and reached 150 liters (40 gallons), almost its prewar level, in the early 1950s, but instead of rising or even stabilizing at that point, it went into a long-term decline. By the 1970s it had fallen to 110 liters (29 gallons) per capita, by the early 2000s it was 57 liters (15 gallons), and by 2014 it was only 43 liters (11 gallons), the equivalent of one four-ounce glass of wine a day.

In sixty years, then, the per capita consumption of wine in France has fallen by more than 60 percent, but it is still the highest of any large nation-state. It is, however, exceeded by states with much smaller populations, such as Vatican City (fifty-four liters, or fourteen gallons, per capita in 2012) and Andorra (forty-six liters, or twelve gallons).

To put the French experience in context, other European (and non-European) countries with high per capita wine consumption rates have also seen significant declines over the same period. Italian wine consumption fell 70 percent, from 110 to 33 liters (26 to 9 gallons) a head, between the 1950s and 2014. In the same period, per capita consumption fell by a third in Spain and Portugal and a quarter in Greece. These declines contributed to a decrease in Europe's share of global wine consumption: from 74 percent at the end of the 1980s to just over 60 percent in 2014. (The other contributor to that shift was a general increase in per capita consumption of wine in the non-European world.)

Per capita rates of wine consumption, as we have noted, have limited usefulness, because not all demographic groups consume at the same rate. Women drink less than men, and some men and women drink more than others. A shift in the age structure also necessarily changes per capita rates of wine consumption. Even if French men had continued to consume wine at the same rate during the 1950s and 1960s, per capita consumption would have fallen somewhat because of the larger proportion of children in the population, the result of the postwar baby boom. And since the 1960s, France has witnessed a large immigration of North African Muslims, most of whom abstain from all forms of alcohol or drink rarely and little. But even controlling for these variables, wine consumption by French adults has declined steadily.

An increasing proportion of the wine produced in France in the 1950s and 1960s came from cooperatives, organizations of vignerons who shared production facilities and usually sold their wine under a single label. Much of the cooperative-produced wine was sold in bulk (en vrac) and was (and is) priced according to the alcohol level. Hundreds of wine cooperatives had been formed earlier in the twentieth century, notably in the 1930s, but a new generation sprang up in the 1950s. Vignerons' need to mechanize partly drove the surge, as tractors began to replace horses in vineyards and (on larger properties) mechanical harvesters replaced the thousands of men, women, and children who had historically picked grapes by hand. There was also a general drive for better quality, which meant renovating wine-making facilities: buying gentler presses, replacing or renovating concrete fermentation vats and sometimes installing stainless steel tanks, and buying new, better, and often smaller barrels. All of this was expensive, too expensive for hundreds of thousands of small-scale vignerons, but the cost was manageable when shared among dozens, scores, or hundreds of them organized into cooperatives.

Although wine from cooperatives is often thought to be, by definition, of poor quality, it is important to note that vignerons were motivated to join cooperatives not only for the efficiency and financial benefits they offered (some provided loans to members) but also so they could make higher-quality (and more expensive) wines. Cooperatives were also important as a means for small-scale vignerons to participate in the widening scope of AOC wines. An individual vigneron might have difficulty achieving the necessary quality on his or her own, but cooperatives provided consultants to improve vineyard practices and professional wine makers in the winery. Just as important, they provided marketing expertise; many smaller cooperatives relied on local sales, but the wines of larger cooperatives could get on to domestic and international markets that individual vignerons could never have reached with their own resources. Some cooperatives also distilled excess wine into brandy, so that producers would receive some return even from unsold wine.

From 1945, hundreds of new cooperatives were formed, bringing the total in France to nearly a thousand, with more than two hundred thousand members. Most were in Languedoc-Roussillon, but there were concentrations in Bordeaux, the southern Rhône valley, Burgundy, Alsace, and Champagne. They were sparse in the Loire valley and the southwest. The largest cooperative was Marsillargues, in Hérault, which had some seven hundred members and a storage capacity of 150 million liters (40 million gallons) of wine, but many others also had hundreds of members.

In some regions, cooperatives were vital engines of reconstruction. In Cahors, which had produced full-bodied red wines from the côt (malbec) variety for centuries, the vineyards were replanted after phylloxera mainly with hybrid varieties because of their disease resistance. This enabled small-scale vignerons to make a living, but the wines of Cahors virtually disappeared from all but its regional market. In 1947 the Les Côtes d'Olt cooperative was formed, and after it identified an appropriate rootstock, its members began to graft côt vines and reestablish Cahors's prephylloxera vineyards. They also experimented with other varieties and identified merlot, tannat, syrah, and jurançon rouge as suitable for blending with côt. In 1951 the INAO granted Cahors producers *vin délimité de qualité supérieure* (VDQS) status, a probationary stage on the way to becoming an AOC, and in 1971 it was elevated to full AOC status.[11] At that time Cahors had 507 hectares (1,253 acres) of vines in production, but the AOC certification quickly encouraged further planting. Vineyard area tripled within ten years, and by the end of the 1990s the vines of Cahors covered more than four thousand hectares (9,884 acres).[12]

Cahors was not a unique example. The work of cooperatives was vital in establishing the preconditions for AOCs in many other regions of France. They included Buzet in the southwest, Poitou in the Loire valley, and Hautes-Côtes de Beaune and Marsannay in Burgundy. By the mid-1980s there were more than 1,100 cooperatives in France. The biggest concentration was still in Languedoc-Roussillon, but there was no significant wine-producing département that did not have at least one cooperative. Their success is indicated by the fact that while the total viticultural area of France declined significantly between 1950 and 2000 (from 1.3 million to just 1 million hectares, or 3.2 million to 2.5 million acres), the area cultivated by cooperatives remained stable. As this suggests, the proportion of French wine made by cooperatives increased steadily, and by the end of the 1990s two-fifths of French vignerons were members of cooperatives, which made half the wine in France. The 140 cooperatives in Champagne make just over half the champagne produced, and a number of them have developed very successful brands, such as Jacquart and Nicolas Feuillatte.

It is noteworthy too that cooperatives have made an increasing proportion of AOC wine. In the early 1950s, 72 percent of the total AOC wine was made by independent growers and larger privately owned wineries and 28 percent by cooperatives. By the 1990s those percentages had converged, and cooperatives were responsible for 40 percent of all AOC wines, with 60 percent made by noncooperative growers. This was more or less in line with the rising profile of cooperatives in the French wine industry. Over the same period, the percentage of vignerons belonging to cooperatives rose from 16 to 37 percent, and the cooperatives' share of total production increased from 31 to 46 percent.

The rise of cooperatives is one of the often neglected stories of French wine, partly because of a long-standing belief that wines produced by cooperative are not—indeed, cannot be—as good as wines produced by individual vignerons. To a large extent this belief rests on the residual power of the romantic image of the solitary vigneron working his land (the vigneron is always portrayed as a man) like his ancestors—the sort of belief that was fostered in Burgundy in the 1920s and 1930s. It ignores the realities of farming and the general corporatization of France's wine industry, but it still has a strong hold on the imaginations of many wine professionals and consumers. The issue of terroir also comes into it, as the vineyards of cooperative members may cover wide tracts of land. For terroir purists, blending wines from many sites overrides the effects of terroir and tends to make the resulting wines homogenized and commercial. There was sometimes also a political agenda underlying the prejudice against cooperatives: they look like socialist or collective organizations, in contrast with the entrepreneurial and independent spirit often attributed to the individual vigneron.

French wine is produced by cooperatives, by wineries owned by individuals, and by wineries owned by corporate entities, a three-way division that overlays a long-term two-way division: "quality wines" (*vins de qualité*) and "commercial wines" (*vins courants*). This distinction was made as far back as the early modern period, but for most of the past five hundred years it has been made in only the most general terms. Perhaps the most important criterion was grape variety: some had the potential to make quality wine, but others did not. This was clear in the fourteenth and fifteenth centuries, when gamay was banished from the Côtes of Burgundy to its refuge in Beaujolais. Quality wines could be made from pinot noir but not from gamay under any circumstances, and the reason that was cited over and over was that gamay yielded crops that were too large. Quality was associated with low quantity—almost a truism in the world of wine, although there is no strict correlation between the two. Over time, quality wines were identified by other criteria: the grapes were good, low-yielding varieties grown in the right soil and climatic conditions, and the wine making was careful.

These criteria—grape variety, crop yields, and location—underlie AOC laws, and because of them AOCs became indicators not simply that a wine was from a certain place but that it was a quality wine. The distinction between AOC and non-AOC wines opened a major division in the French wine industry in the 1950s. This is a fractious industry that has been riven by conflicts, which have taken the form of some regions attempting to block the sale or transportation of wine from other regions in the early modern period, allegations of fraudulent practices in the late nineteenth and early twentieth centuries, and litigation both to exclude some districts from and to include some districts in appellations in the 1920s and 1930s.

In the 1950s the major fault line was between the supporters of AOC wines and the supporters of non-AOC wines. Producers and partisans of AOC wines began to describe non-AOC wines as "industrial"—a word that harked back to the nineteenth century, when the wine lobby referred to distilled spirits as "industrial" to distinguish them from "natural" fermented beverages, notably wine. In the postwar period this industrial-natural dichotomy was deployed to distinguish two broad categories of wine. It implied that non-AOC wines were a sort of fifth column within French wine and that the state and other entities ought to throw their support behind the AOC category. A coalition of technocrats, appellation wine supporters, and health experts began to argue in the early 1950s that "industrial" wine was responsible for more than half of the alcoholism in France. Joseph Bohling suggests that state technocrats and AOC-supporting groups employed this threat to justify both state intervention in the largely non-AOC wine industry of Languedoc-Roussillon and the exclusion of inexpensive foreign wines from the French market.[13]

The debate on AOC and non-AOC wines was generally framed in terms of quality, but it drew in many other concepts that are used in the wine world to distinguish wines with high cultural value from the rest. A complex superstructure of values associated quality wines with notions such as authenticity and artisanship and made strong connections between wine, land, and vigneron. The concept of terroir is critical here, of course, and Marion Demossier has convincingly argued that since the 1970s in particular, terroir has been "the pillar of French wine production and national drinking culture."[14]

But terroir is a dynamic and evolving concept, and in the past fifty years a number of "terroir"s have competed with one another. One refers not only to the physical environment in which the vines grow but also to the human contribution, as the vigneron mediates between the soil and the wine. In this formulation, the "soil" might be soil in a material sense, but it is also metaphorical, representing the timelessness of the land that produces the wine. A second formulation of *terroir* treats the soil in a wholly scientific manner and focuses on soils and subsoil to explain wine character. It has often been observed that vineyards of the same grape variety planted only meters apart produce wines that differ in flavor or style. Geology is thus seen as the determining element, and differences in such factors as vine age, vineyard exposure, wine making, and barrel variation are considered less important or not taken into account at all. A third approach, largely imported from the New World, attempts to identify the effects of soil on wine character with more precision than ever before. "Earthy" qualities in wine are attributed to soil types, "minerality" to the presence of limestone, and "fiery" character to the volcanoes on whose slopes the vines grow.[15]

Even when links between soil and wine were not made with such precision, French producers highlighted their terroir as what made their wines distinctive. This was not new, as the idea had been part of French wine discourse for centuries.[16] But terroir took on a new force at a time of globalization, when wines from Australia, California, and other New World countries were challenging the preeminence of French wine. In the last decades the twentieth century, most of these wines were inexpensive, mediocre, and sometimes produced in large volumes. France's AOC producers regarded them in the same way that they regarded the mass-produced wines of Languedoc: as commercial, industrial, and generally deplorable. For their part, many New World producers scorned the idea of terroir, even though they often described their pinot noirs and chardonnays as "Burgundian" and called their blends "Bordeaux blends" and their sparkling wines "champagne." Over time, however, New World regions adopted the language of terroir, and even when they did not use the term, they spoke of their wines as having "a sense of place" or expressing "regionality."

Discourses of terroir often stress the unchanging nature and timelessness of great wine regions, and many advertisements, promotional materials, and wine bottle back labels refer to wine being made in a "traditional" way. Yet after World War II, many French wine makers embraced technologies that were anything but traditional. They included customized yeasts, more efficiently calibrated filtering, reverse osmosis, and micro-oxidation. Others reacted against the trend by reducing the scale of intervention in the vineyard and winery, and a number of formal and informal approaches to making wine emerged to challenge mainstream, conventional (and often, but not always, large-scale-production) methods, which, they argued, produced "industrial" or "fabricated" wines.

One was the organic wine movement, which not only reflected concern about the widespread use of synthetic materials in vine growing and wine making but also intersected with growing anxiety about the environment that started in the 1960s. A number of producers argued that the excessive and long-term use of chemical fertilizers and pesticides in French vineyards had ruined the soil—an allegation leveled at agriculture generally. Demand increased for organic products of all kinds, with the result that there was a steady growth in organic wines—although organic products are still quite a small part of most markets. To be labeled "organic," a wine must be certified by a recognized organization as having been made from grapes grown in vineyards that are not treated with (or exposed to) chemical fertilizers, pesticides, or fungicides and having been produced in a winery where chemicals are not used for purposes such as cleaning the equipment. There is an important difference between organic wine and wine made from organically grown grapes: organic wine is the result of organic practices in both vineyard and winery, but wine made from organic grapes may be produced in a winery where organic practices are not followed. Organic wine makers also tend to use wild yeasts in fermentation and often avoid filtering their wine.

Although organic viticulture is now widespread, some producers who follow organic practices are reluctant to be certified as such, in case they need to resort to a chemical solution to a vineyard disease or pest. Instead, many wine producers practice and acknowledge "sustainable" viticulture, which is less rigorous than organic and includes minimizing the application of chemicals, conserving and recycling water, using renewable sources of energy, and promoting biodiversity in the vineyard.

Far less common is biodynamic viticulture and wine making. To be recognized as a biodynamic producer, a winery must be certified by the Demeter Association, an internationally recognized body. The movements of the moon and stars and other natural phenomena guide biodynamic vine growers in their planting, growing, and harvesting schedules. Following the principles set down by Rudolf Steiner in the 1920s, they make preparations from cow dung and other material, some of which are buried in cow horns in the vineyard before being stirred into water and applied to the vines. Biodynamic producers typically make their own compost and foster living organisms in the soil and among the vines. Although only a small proportion of wine makers have adopted biodynamic practices (there are about five hundred worldwide), they include some well-known French producers, such as Nicolas Joly in the Loire valley and Michel Chapoutier in the Rhône valley.

The natural wine movement takes a third approach, reducing human intervention to a minimum. It looks back to wine making in antiquity, when grapes grew without much human attention and ambient, wild yeasts fermented the must. Over time, according to its supporters, this "natural" wine (bearing in mind that wine is a product of human activity) became increasingly artificial: conventional modern wine production involves substantial human intervention in the vineyard and the winery. In contrast, makers of "natural wine" intervene as little as possible. They farm their vines organically (and some biodynamically) and in the winery add no sulfur or additives such as acids or tannins, and wild yeasts ferment their wines.

Natural wine supporters look to Jules Chauvet, who was a wine maker and négociant in Beaujolais, as the founder of the French natural wine movement. Trained in chemistry, he worked on many aspects of wine making and the theory of tasting, and in the 1950s he designed the ISO (International Organization for Standardization) wine tasting glass that has become the standard, widely used by professionals and in wine competitions. Most of Chauvet's technical work was published after his death in 1989, but in interviews he made it clear that he opposed the direction of most French wine making in the postwar period. He advocated cultivating vineyard soils to make them healthier, eliminating the use of sulfur during fermentation, and thinking of wine as "a reflection of its soil."[17] A small number of natural wine producers in France and elsewhere have followed Chauvet's principles.

Whether or not organic, biodynamic, or "natural" wines are better than those made with more common methods is a matter of debate, but there is no doubt that during the 1970s and 1980s the French government and wine industry tried to promote quality in French wine. This aspiration was in line with a tendency among other European wine-producing countries, and over time the European Union gained some jurisdiction over their wines, harmonizing policies that individual member countries had enacted. Faced with an oversupply of wine in the 1980s, the EU in 1988 adopted a policy to reduce the size of Europe's vineyards. It compensated vignerons who pulled out vines that were producing unmarketable wines, and it contributed to the reduction of the French viticultural area from just over 1,000,000 hectares (2,500,000 acres) in 1986 to 792,000 hectares (1,960,000 acres) in 2015.

The oversupply had resulted in part from declining per capita wine consumption in Europe's three main wine-consuming countries, France, Italy, and Spain. There was also a decline in demand for inexpensive European wine on foreign markets. California was supplying inexpensive wine for the whole of the United States, while key European markets, such as the United Kingdom, the Low Countries, and Scandinavia, had growing imports of wines from Australia, South Africa, and California and substantial volumes from Chile and Argentina by the 1990s. The rise in exports from these New World producers had little effect on the export of higher-quality wines from France's more prestigious regions, but they did cut into France's ability to export less-expensive wines. By the early 2000s, French wine exports had begun to slump under the impact of New World competition.

Oversupply and the drive to achieve more overall quality by eliminating poorer wines are related to the general decline in wine consumption in France. One way of describing the decline is as a result of the preference for quality wine: the decline in consumption of vins de table, the lowest-ranking French wine, was far more rapid than that of AOC wines. In the early 1950s only 11 percent of French wines were labeled as AOCs, but by the end of the century that was true of more than a quarter. By 2015 more than half the wine produced in France fell within the AOC category. While AOC classification is not a guarantee of quality, AOC wines are subject to tightly administered rules that regulate grape varieties, yields, and wine making, and they are more expensive than their non-AOC counterparts. The decision to spend more per bottle goes some way toward explaining the decline in the volume of wine consumed. As is often said, the French are drinking less wine, but they are drinking better wine. France is, however, a nation of remarkable regional variation, and there remain strong markets for table wine in the southeast, the southwest, and Paris. These were also the robust wine-drinking regions of the nineteenth century, when consumption among rural and urban workers was particularly high.

Between 1950 and the early 2000s, immense social changes took place in France and other major European wine-producing countries such as Italy, Spain, and Portugal. Even though large numbers of their populations remained poor, an increasing proportion shared in the benefits of postwar prosperity and participated in the consumer economy that accompanied it. As lifestyles changed, so did the place of wine, although the precise mechanism here has not been satisfactorily explained. Wine ceased to be the integral part of the diet that it had been for centuries and became instead only one of several beverage options for French consumers.

Perhaps most surprising is the decline of wine as the beverage that French people choose to accompany their meals. To an extent that would have appalled those in the earlier 1900s who defined wine as quintessentially French and who registered their horror at the advances made by tea, coffee, and spirits, their late twentieth-century compatriots became water drinkers. In part this reflected the improved supply of good tap water in France since the 1950s, but commercially bottled water production has also soared, to both meet and generate demand. In the 1950s a third of French people had a glass of water, not wine, at hand as they sat at the meal table, but that was true of three-quarters of them in the 1990s.[18]

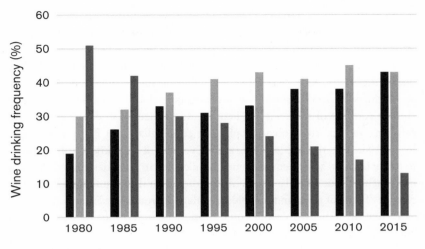

■ Never drink wine

■ Drink wine occasionally (once or twice a week or less often)

■ Drink wine every day or nearly every day

DIAGRAM 9.1.   Frequency of drinking wine, France, 1980–2015

Although many French people might have been drinking tap water, the decline of wine consumption coincided with the advent of bottled water as a product of mass consumption. In 1957 the government passed rigorous regulations regarding standards of hygiene in the bottling of water and set out clearer definitions of "natural," "spring," and "mineral" waters. Other regulations governed the advertising, labeling, and pricing of bottled water. Like those of some other foods and drinks, the price of mineral water was strictly controlled: between 1958 and 1978 its pretax price increased by only 30 percent, compared to a 230 percent rise in the cost of living.[19] From the 1950s to the 2000s there was a steady increase in the per capita annual consumption of bottled water in France, from less than 20 liters (5.3 gallons) in the 1950s to 50 liters (13 gallons) in 1972, 100 liters (26 gallons) in 1995, and more than 150 liters (40 gallons) in 2006.[20] This was the inverse of the trajectory of wine consumption over the same period. Wine was only one beverage among several that were available, and its share of family budgets fell as purchases of water rose.

It was not only in French homes that patterns of wine drinking changed: wine also lost some of its appeal as a public drink. The most dramatic manifestation of this is the rapid decline in the number of French cafés licensed to sell alcohol. Still one of the most common associations that foreigners make with France, the sidewalk café offering a glass of wine is increasingly rare. In the 1960s about two hundred thousand French cafés were licensed to sell wine, but by the 1990s there were only sixty thousand such cafés and by 2014 only about thirty-three thousand. The disappearance of cafés speaks to a dramatic shift in patterns of sociability in France, and to changes in demography. The café was an important meeting place in rural villages in France, but since World War II there has been a marked movement of population from country to town: in 1945, 30 percent of French people lived in areas designated as rural, but that was true of only 6 percent by 1990. Rural depopulation led to the closure of tens of thousands of cafés in villages throughout France.

Other influences on wine consumption included more rigorous laws against drinking and driving and against the advertising of alcohol of all kinds. These laws became more stringent as automobile ownership increased. More severe penalties for driving while intoxicated were introduced in 1978, and in 1983 the maximum blood alcohol concentration (BAC) was set at 0.08 (eighty milligrams of alcohol per hundred milliliters of blood) for drivers. In 1990, random breath testing was introduced, and in 1995 the maximum BAC was reduced to 0.05. Some French alcohol lobby groups unsuccessfully opposed these restrictions as potentially ruinous to cafés, bars, and restaurants.

Their fears seem to have been borne out, however. The public drinking common to French urban workers, overwhelmingly men, who settled down to a few glasses of red wine with their workmates and neighbors has given way to new patterns. To some extent, domesticity has replaced neighborhood sociability, manifested by French people's increasingly entertaining in their homes rather than meeting their friends in public places like cafés and restaurants. It is easy to romanticize the past and to overlook the personal, family, and social consequences of heavy drinking by males in cafés and bars, but it is nonetheless undeniable that a sea change has taken place, not only in the amount of wine consumed in France but also in the contexts in which it is consumed.[21]

Wine was also included in restrictions on alcohol advertising. The rigorous Évin Law (named after the then–minister of health), adopted in 1991, banned the advertising of all alcohol on television and in cinemas and forbade alcohol companies to sponsor sports events. Wine could still be advertised on billboards and at events such as wine fairs and exhibitions, and in 2009 the law was modified to permit wine advertisements on France-based websites, as long as they were not directed at children. Most French winery websites, in fact, ask visitors to confirm that they are of the minimum legal drinking age, although there is, of course, no way of verifying that online.

As the consumption of wine declined, there was a significant shift in French wine culture. It would be wrong to say that very few French people thought about the wine they were drinking before World War II, but it is fair to say that their exposure to anything like the full range of wines was very limited. The French wine market was highly regionalized, so that consumers in Burgundy, for instance, were virtually unable to buy wines other than those made in their region. It was largely the same in other wine regions, while in the parts of France where wine was not made, most wines came from one or two regions. As its consumption declined, there seems to have been a growth in interest in wine. French television broadcast programs on various wine-related topics with increasing frequency between 1950 and 2000. Before the mid-1980s the focus tended to be on aspects of production, such as the state of individual harvests and mechanical innovations in viticulture, but then the emphasis shifted to consumption. Between 1987 and 1994 a number of documentaries, such as *Vins de femmes*, considered women as consumers and producers, while other programs explored wine tasting, the language of wine, and oenology.[22]

There have been some countervailing influences on consumption. Throughout the late 1980s and the 1990s, for example, the case was again made for the potential health benefits of drinking wine. Wine came to medical attention for its role in explaining "the French paradox," the fact that the French have low rates of heart disease despite eating a diet that should predispose them to high rates. The critical variable, many researchers argued, was resveratrol, a compound found in wine, especially French wine. There has been continuing debate on this issue, much of it centering on whether other forms of alcohol are as beneficial as wine and whether red and white wines are equally effective. Although it is recognized that excessive drinking can be harmful to health, the consensus among medical authorities is that the regular consumption of wine in moderate quantities and as part of a healthy lifestyle helps to reduce the likelihood of coronary disease and heart attack.[23]

French wine found a new position not only in French culture as wine consumption declined but also within the changing global wine culture. Until the 1960s, Europe was the undisputed heart of global wine production, and within Europe the reputation of France as making the best wine was virtually unchallenged. The wine regions that had stood out in the seventeenth century—Bordeaux, Burgundy, and Champagne—were still regarded as the best, although from the 1990s some appellations in the Loire valley and the northern Rhône valley began to be ranked as highly as any. Such was the continuing hold of the three best-known French wine regions on the global imagination that wine producers in places as diverse as California, New Zealand, and South Africa appropriated their names. "Champagne" became a generic term for any sparkling wine, whether or not it was made by the method used in Champagne, and wines were labeled "Burgundy" and "Bordeaux" no matter where or with which grape varieties they were made.

These wines, many bearing faux-French names, were for the most part sold in their countries of origin before the mid-twentieth century. There was a modest wine trade from former British colonies, especially Australia and South Africa, to the United Kingdom, and much of this wine was fortified into styles reminiscent of sherry and port. The bulk of the international wine trade emanated from France. In the early 1960s, total world wine exports (excluding Algerian shipments to metropolitan France) were about 1.6 billion hectoliters (42 billion gallons). France was the single biggest exporter, shipping 370 million liters (97 million gallons, or 24 percent of the world total), while Italy and Spain together exported a similar volume, 360 million liters (95 million gallons, or 23 percent).[24]

Although New World wine-producing countries were minor players in this trade, they produced increasing volumes of wine in this period. Wines from Chile and Argentina tended to be low in quality and made largely for domestic consumption. California wine, which throughout the 1950s often meant that of the massive Gallo company (which made 25 percent of American wine as late as the 1990s), was consumed in California and elsewhere in the United States. Much of Australia's wine production (like New Zealand's and South Africa's) was fortified and consumed on the domestic market, although some was exported to the United Kingdom.

There was a veritable wine revolution in these countries in the 1980s and 1990s as *Vitis vinifera* grape varieties replaced hybrids and better wine-making practices were adopted. The New World was following the path that the French wine industry had embarked upon forty years earlier. The revolution was gradual and often unnoticed, and when it was noticed, certain individuals and specific wineries were thought to have set the pace of change even though they might have been simply the most visible signs of it. They included Penfolds in Australia, Robert Mondavi in California, Cloudy Bay in New Zealand, and Eduardo Chadwick in Chile. One way or another, though, the quality level of non-European wines rose steadily during the 1980s and 1990s, and some began to make inroads into markets where imported wines were mostly French.

For California, which accounted for more than 90 percent of the wine production of the United States, a critical moment in its rise to global recognition was the comparative tasting of Californian and French wines organized by Steven Spurrier and held in Paris in 1976. Often called "the Judgment of Paris," this blind tasting pitted some of the most prestigious and expensive wines of each country against one another.[25] The white wines were six chardonnays from California and four from Burgundy, while in the red wine category the judges compared six cabernet sauvignons (or cabernet sauvignon–dominant blends) from California and four from the Left Bank of Bordeaux. Two of the Bordeaux wines were First Growths (including those of Château Mouton Rothschild, which had been promoted to First Growth status three years earlier), and the others were Second Growths.

When the scores of the nine French judges were averaged, a California wine came out on top in both the white and the red wine categories, even though most of the judges had placed one of the French wines at the top of their individual rankings. The results horrified the judges, who (like most of the wine-drinking world at the time) believed that French wine was incomparable and that it was impossible to make wine outside France to the best French standards. The French media largely ignored the results, but they were widely reported in the United States and gave California credibility as a region that could produce world-class wines. This not only boosted the California wine industry but also benefited other New World wine-producing countries by demonstrating that France did not have a monopoly on the production of fine wines.

A combination of conditions contributed to the growing presence of New World wines on international markets. For the most part, they were not imported into the three major European wine-producing countries, but Scandinavia, the Netherlands, the United Kingdom, and Germany were soon receptive to them. In the United Kingdom, where wine consumption doubled each decade starting in the 1970s, only a quarter of the additional wines consumed were European; most came from former colonies (Australia, New Zealand, and South Africa) and from California, Chile, and Argentina.

The French wine industry generally regarded New World wines with hostility, not least because wine laws there were far less rigorous than AOC regulations. Producers in Chile, California, Australia, and elsewhere were virtually free to grow whichever grape varieties they liked, could irrigate, chaptalize, and acidify at will, and were not limited by maximum yields or minimum alcohol levels. French producers at once resented the restrictions of AOC rules and defended them as necessary to ensure high-quality wine. In general, French wine makers embraced attitudes that echoed the position many of their predecessors had adopted with regard to additives and blending in the nineteenth and early twentieth centuries: the relatively lax wine laws of the New World were tantamount to unfair business practices, and New World wines were essentially fraudulent.

There were exceptions, including the number of French wine producers who entered into collaborative ventures with New World counterparts. One such was the partnership, begun in 1979, of Robert Mondavi and Baron Philippe de Rothschild to create the Opus One vineyard and winery in California's Napa Valley. Other examples were simple investments, such as those by Moët and Chandon in sparkling wine production in Argentina and Australia. In 1998 several French wine makers, headed by the consultant wine maker Michel Rolland, purchased 850 hectares (2,100 acres) in Argentina's Mendoza wine region to make wine under the Clos de los Siete brand. In 2000, Henri Bourgeois, a prominent producer of sauvignon blanc wines in Sancerre, bought ninety-eight hectares (242 acres) of sheep pasture in Marlborough, New Zealand, where he established his Clos Henri winery and began to produce wines made from sauvignon blanc and pinot noir.

On the other hand, some French wine makers were hostile to the intrusion of non-French producers into France. In 2000, local opposition prevented Mondavi from clearing forest and garrigue in the département of Hérault to plant vineyards not far from Languedoc's highly rated Mas de Daumas Gassac winery in Aniane. There was also anxiety that distinctively French styles of wine were being eroded as producers shifted to "New World styles" (more concentrated and made for earlier consumption) that would sell better on the increasingly important United States market. The American wine critic Robert Parker was alleged to have too much influence on wine-buying decisions there, and some French producers were accused of "Parkerizing" their wine—making it in a style to which Parker would give high marks.

Competition came not only from the New World but also from the other wine-producing countries in Europe. An example was Spain, where cava, a sparkling wine, has been made in the northeast since the 1920s, using the same method as champagne but usually indigenous grape varieties. Cava saw a steady increase in production, rising from fifty million to more than two hundred million bottles a year between 1960 and 2000. But exports rose more rapidly than domestic sales: negligible exports in the early 1970s became fifty million bottles a year by the late 1980s and one hundred million bottles in 1999, meaning that they had risen from a third to a half of total production.[26]

Cava was not necessarily competition to champagne, which has an exclusive brand and generally costs substantially more, but some cava producers began to sell their sparkling wine in the United Kingdom under the name "Spanish champagne." This reflected the widespread tendency to refer to any sparkling wine as "champagne," no matter what grape varieties it is made from and whether or not the second fermentation has taken place in the bottle, as the Champagne method requires. Champagne producers sued Spanish producers in the United Kingdom in 1958, 1959, and 1960 on the ground that only sparkling wine from Champagne can be labeled "champagne," while the Spanish argued that "champagne" is a generic name that can be applied to any sparkling wine. Two of three judgments went against the Spanish cava producers.

Producers of champagne have been more active than their counterparts in other French wine regions in protecting the name of their wine, because theirs has such high cultural value and is therefore more likely than others to be appropriated. In 1993 they successfully sued Yves Saint Laurent for branding a perfume "Champagne" and, adding insult to appropriation, packaging it in a bottle reminiscent of a champagne cork and its wire cage. (The company renamed the perfume "Yvresse," which combines its corporate name with *ivresse*, the French word for "drunkenness.") Champagne producers have also prevented producers of nonchampagne sparkling wine from using the term "Champagne method," even if they do make it by the method used in Champagne (a second fermentation in the bottle). Non-Champagne producers of sparkling wine now use terms such as "traditional method" or "classic method" instead.

Champagne producers have reached a number of agreements with other sparkling wine–producing jurisdictions to prevent their use of the "champagne" name. One was with the United States in 2006, and another was with Russia in 2011, the latter putting an end to the use of "champagne" in the labeling of the Russian sparkling wine known as "Soviet champagne." First made in 1928, it was a staple wine produced by state-owned wineries right through the Soviet period, and its name survived the collapse of the Soviet Union in 1991, as privately owned wineries in Russia, Belarus, Moldova, and Ukraine continued to use it.

Champagne's actions against cava producers in the late 1950s and early 1960s were the beginning of a sustained effort by the French wine industry to protect the names of its appellations from use by outside producers. As we have noted, this had already been achieved within France itself.

Champagne producers had prevented other French makers of sparkling wine from appropriating the name "champagne," while the end of équivalence in Burgundy and elsewhere had stopped the labeling of wine with the names of appellations where the grapes had not grown. The creation and growth of the European Union (and its predecessors) helped the process of protecting appellations, as all its members had an interest in protecting their own. The Spanish wanted to protect appellations such as Cava and Jerez (Sherry) as much as the French wanted to protect Champagne and Burgundy. Protecting French appellations from appropriation by producers outside the EU was a more difficult and longer struggle.

At the end of the twentieth century, champagne became the focus of anxiety that was, for some people, even greater than that caused by the Y2K computer problem, which, it was feared, would crash hard drives and make airliners fall from the sky as one millennium turned into the next. The worry was that there would not be enough champagne for everyone who wanted to celebrate the advent of the new millennium with the French wine that was a byword for celebration. There were many media reports that champagne sales had started to increase early in 1999 and that by the end of the year it would be impossible to buy many brands, especially the small-production, high-end labels such as Moët et Chandon's Dom Pérignon and Louis Roederer's Cristal.

But the champagne houses had been preparing for years, setting aside stocks that would be ready for disgorgement in time to be shipped around the world for the millennium. In 1999, a record 327 million bottles of champagne were sold, an increase of 35 million over the year before. This was possible because the champagne houses had managed their reserves throughout the 1990s. Healthy harvests in 1992, 1993, and 1994 enabled them to put aside tens of millions of bottles, and even though they had to release some to compensate for a low crop in 1997, they were still able to put on the market seventy-four million bottles from their reserves at the beginning of 1999. The result was that despite significantly increased demand in champagne's export markets, there was more than enough to go around. Exports to the United Kingdom and the United States, which were champagne's biggest importers, rose by about a third in 1999, and to Scandinavia by about a half. In contrast, sales of champagne in France rose by less than a tenth.

As French producers wrestled with the realities of a global wine market with many more players than ever before, the INAO introduced new categories of French wine. In the 1970s a *vin de pays* level was introduced between vin de table—the basic category of wine, which bears no reference to vintage or grape variety—and the highly regulated AOC level. The rules governing vins de pays mirrored those of AOCs but were much less rigorous. They could be made from only an approved number of grape varieties, but it was not as restrictive as the AOC's, yields were generally about twice those permitted for AOC wines, and minimum levels of alcohol were lower.

In all, there were more than 140 named vins de pays, each associated with a region, like AOC wines. Many were named for départements, such as vin de pays de l'Hérault and vin de pays de l'Ardèche. There were also four named for broader zones: vin de pays d'Oc (from Languedoc), vin de pays du Jardin de la France (Loire valley), vin de pays du Comté Tolosan (southwest France), and vin de pays des Comtés Rhodaniens (southeast France, including Beaujolais, Jura, and the northern Rhône valley). The vin de pays category quickly represented a significant segment of French wine production, between a quarter and a third by the early 2000s.

In 2010, however, further changes to French (and European) wine law saw a renaming of all the quality categories of French wine. Vin de table, the lowest, was replaced by *vin de France*, and these wines could be labeled by grape variety, although they could show only France, not a region, as their provenance. This was a response to the declining production of vins de table and the difficulty of exporting them, as their labels showed neither grape variety nor vintage. The middle tier in the French classification, vin de pays, was replaced by *indication géographique protégée* (IGP, or "protected place of origin"), while the top, AOC category was renamed AOP (*appellation d'origine protégée*). The changes in terms did not alter the regulations governing viticulture and wine making for the two upper levels. A fourth category, VDQS, which had been granted to wine regions on their way to AOC status, was abolished in 2007. France's emphasis on quality wine was signaled in 2009 when the INAO was renamed the Institut National d'Origine et de Qualité.

There was also a general relaxation in France of what information French wine labels can display. Historically, AOC wines were labeled only by appellation, although information on grape varieties could be shown on the back label. The exception was Alsace, whose AOC wines could show grape variety on the front label. The rules were changed to allow all AOC wines to show grape variety on the front label, and it was hoped that this would improve sales in most export markets, where consumers are more accustomed to buying wine by grape variety than by appellation. In general, however, only large-volume producers of AOC wines have added grape varieties to their labels.

As we have seen, French wine underwent important changes in the period following World War II. At the level of infrastructure, the total area of France's vineyards shrank from 1,434,000 hectares (3,543,000 acres) in 1945 to 792,000 (1,957,000 acres) in 2014, a loss of 642,000 hectares (1,586,000 acres), or close to half of the country's land under vines. Almost all the lost vineyards had been responsible for producing poor vins de table, and their disappearance left France's wine industry smaller, more efficient, and producing a higher proportion of AOC or quality wine than ever before. Perhaps that is enough to qualify the most recent phase of the history of French wine as a golden age.

Conclusion

Viticulture and wine making in France go back two and a half millennia, but there is nothing like a smooth, seamless history between the small vineyards planted by Greek and Roman proprietors and today's massive French wine industry, between the Roman perception of the beer-drinking Celts as barbarians and the general sense today that French wine is integral to France's culture and style. A simple measure of the progress of French wine might be the extent of French land under vines, but as we have seen, there has been no linear trend of expansion. Instead, vineyard area has expanded in some periods and contracted in others—the latter notably as a result of the Black Death, the Hundred Years' War, and especially the phylloxera crisis. At a little under eight hundred thousand hectares (two million acres) today, France's national vineyard has been slowly shrinking since the 1990s, and it is now less than a third of the almost 2.5 million hectares (6.2 million acres) planted with vines in the mid-1870s.

Consistent linear trends cannot be discerned in any of the other measurable themes this book covers, such as the extent of wine production or patterns of wine consumption in France. And not only is it difficult to find consistent trends, but it is also difficult to generalize about French wine in any given period, because it is so multifaceted. One need only look at the current state of French viticulture to see how complicated it is. As far as wine appellations are concerned, some of the five hundred or so are very well known, and others are well known, while many others are little known. Bordeaux, Burgundy, and Champagne are the best known, and smaller appellations within these regions, such as Saint-Émilion and Saint-Julien in Bordeaux and Pommard and Nuits-Saint-Georges in Burgundy, are well recognized among wine aficionados. Wines from appellations such as these are highly coveted and fetch high prices on world markets. But there are scores of appellations, such as Pacherenc du Vic-Bilh, Saint-Péray, L'Étoile, Clairette de Bellegarde, and Palette, that are known only locally or by those who immerse themselves in French wine.

There is a similar patchwork of grape varieties, as each appellation has its own list, approved by the authorities that regulate appellations. Some have only one or two approved varieties (Condrieu, in the northern Rhône valley, makes only white wine and only from viognier), others have a few (six varieties are approved for red wine in Bordeaux), and yet others can draw from a bigger range, such as the thirteen varieties that the red wines of Châteauneuf-du-Pape may include. Chaptalization (the addition of sugar to grape must to boost the resulting wine's potential alcohol) is permitted in some regions, acidification is allowed in others, and rules specify vineyard yields, trellising, and other practices for each appellation.

Each of these wine regions and appellations has its own history, and their collective histories make up the history of French wine. But although a national history such as this book strives to generalize and to identify the main trends, we must always be aware of qualifications and exceptions, whether they are stark or nuanced. Some French wine regions established themselves as regionally and locally important and have mainly remained that way, while others became significant exporters of wine to other parts of France (notably Paris), Europe, and the wider world. Participation in the international wine trade was largely confined to a handful of wine regions until the second half of the twentieth century, when the inexpensive wines of Languedoc-Roussillon were launched on to world markets. Now all of France's wine regions vie for a share of the international market.

Despite the regionalism and localism that lie at the heart of French wine, several events affected the whole of the French wine industry, even if their effects varied in scale and intensity from region to region. The dramatic population loss caused by the Black Death in the fourteenth century reduced both vineyard labor and demand for wine throughout France. The two world wars of the twentieth century each also saw a general retrenchment in viticulture and wine production, even though the contexts were entirely different. World War I deprived vineyards throughout France of labor and resources while the government requisitioned billions of liters of wine to provide rations for its troops. World War II also saw shortages of labor and resources, but while the occupation authorities requisitioned wine for their troops and for consumption in Germany, the collaborationist Vichy regime actively discouraged the production and consumption of wine, such that the number of public drinking places in France shrank by almost half during that war.

But it was the phylloxera crisis and its aftershocks that really transformed French wine, and it is no exaggeration to say that this was the key turning point in the long-term history of French wine. The size of France's national vineyard began its decline at that time, and vineyards in many parts of northern France, where viticulture had been marginal, contracted or (in some regions) disappeared entirely. In contrast, viticulture in parts of Mediterranean France experienced a boom. The arrival of the railroad and its ability to transport wine quickly from the massive vineyards of Languedoc-Roussillon to the industrial cities of northern France had boosted the fortunes of southern France a couple of decades before phylloxera arrived, and phylloxera accelerated and intensified the process.

The replanting made necessary by the ravages of phylloxera transformed many vineyards and became the basis of the general pattern of viticulture in France during the twentieth century. As we have seen, replanting after phylloxera was nothing like the regular replanting undertaken in ordinary circumstances to replace old and dying vines and vineyards. It was necessary to find rootstocks that were resistant to phylloxera and that performed well in the specific soil and climatic conditions of each region. Vignerons and viticulturists paid more attention to grape varieties at this time than they ever had before, despite sporadic attempts in the eighteenth century to classify grape varieties and to identify those that produced the best wine in specific regions.

One of the results of replanting was the tendency to focus on a narrower range of varieties than had been cultivated before the arrival of phylloxera. Just as some regions abandoned viticulture because it was marginal and unprofitable in the face of a growing national market for wine, so some varieties were abandoned as not worth replanting. Some were only marginally suited to their growing conditions and failed to ripen fully, others made poor wine, and others produced yields that were too high or too low, depending on the vigneron's needs. A notable example was carmenère, which disappeared from Bordeaux's vineyards even though it remained on the list of approved grapes when the AOC rules for Bordeaux were drawn up in the 1930s. Carmenère is a late-ripening variety that too often did not reach full maturity in Bordeaux's often cool growing conditions. With their experiences as a guide, France's vignerons took the opportunity that the necessity of wholesale vineyard renewal offered to replant the grape varieties that performed best in ripening and yield and in making wine of the style and quality they were looking for. That meant high-quality wine from low-yielding vines in some cases and mediocre wine from high-yielding vines in others. But everywhere there was a greater consciousness and deliberation in the selection of grape varieties.

There was also a new pattern of planting vines: planting vineyards (or parcels within vineyards) with just one variety so that the grapes would all ripen at once and could be harvested at that time. Until the postphylloxera replanting, most French vineyards seem to have been multivarietal and cultivated randomly, with all the grapes—ripe, underripe, and overripe, because the varieties ripened at different times—harvested at the same time and then fermented together. Separating varieties in replanted vine-yards enabled vignerons to harvest grapes as they ripened, to ferment each variety separately, and to make varietal wines either as finished wines or for blending. It is not possible to estimate how far that shift in viticulture and wine making had gone before phylloxera struck. But viticultural works throughout the 1800s urged vignerons to adopt these practices, suggesting that multivarietal vineyards and field-blend wines were widespread (and perhaps the norm) until the last decades of the nineteenth century.

To the extent that this is true, the modern French wine industry owes a great deal to the phylloxera crisis; there were more changes in the organi-zation of vineyards, in methods of wine making, and in wine styles in the decades following the 1880s than in all the centuries before. Moreover, the number of fraudulent and counterfeit wines posing as French wines from the 1800s provoked many producers to persuade the state to take action. One of the direct effects of the phylloxera crisis was the elaboration of regulations to guarantee quality and provenance, which culminated in the AOC legislation enacted in the mid-1930s. The period from 1870 to 1935, then, was transformative in the history of French wine. In 1801, Jean-Antoine Chaptal wrote that it was "scarcely a century since perceptible progress has been made in the famous estates" of France. There might well have been improvements at the level of luxury wines, but there is no evi-dence of change in the mass of French vineyards and wineries during the eighteenth century. And these changes at the top end of French wine pale against the radical restructuring of French vineyards, regions, wine styles, and regulations that unfolded as a result of the phylloxera crisis.

This perspective should make us realize that although the history of French wine dates back more than two thousand years, the roots of the modern French wine landscape and industry are much shallower. This is not at all to deny the importance of the longer-term history, which saw the definition of wine regions, the initial selection of grape varieties, the crea-tion of a wine culture in France, and the creation of domestic, European, and intercontinental wine trades. But it is to draw attention to the importance of the phylloxera crisis as a turning point, a hinge in the long-term narrative of French wine. The restructuring that took place in the three or four decades after the crisis peaked led to vineyards being reorganized physically and in terms of grape varieties, increased yields as ill-chosen varieties were pulled out and regions unsuited to viticulture abandoned it, the virtual disappearance of adulterated and counterfeit wines, the cooperative movement, and the AOC regulatory system. Whether or not all of these changes are thought to be positive, they are the face of modern French wine, and they were responses to the conditions that the phylloxera crisis provoked.

This turning point had critical consequences for the representation of French wine because there was a recognition among those involved in marketing it that the postphylloxera period entailed not just a reorganization or even a renewal but a new departure. Following the phylloxera crisis and the many scandals of wine fraud that accompanied it, French wine needed to be reinvented as both a beverage and a cultural symbol. History is often a complex fabric woven of continuities and discontinuities, and there are of course threads that link the pre- and postphylloxera periods. As far as wine is concerned, not much might have changed between 1900 and 1950 on the great estates of Bordeaux, in the vineyards of Champagne, or in the *climats* (the defined vineyards) of Burgundy. But most of France's vineyards— those that were left—were transformed, and so were the wines they produced, in style and in quality.

New vineyards, new vines, and new wines ran counter to the image of French wine as rooted in centuries of history, making it necessary for wine industry organizations to construct new traditions and histories to override the innovations that phylloxera brought about. The producers of Bordeaux embraced the château as a symbol of lineage, nobility, and permanence. Their counterparts in Burgundy turned to folklore and created traditions and events that associated their wines with the soil of the region and the noble character of the vigneron. Champagne houses focused on the royal and aristocratic associations of their wine while appealing to the growing market of middle-class consumers.

These examples suggest one of the overriding, if perhaps obvious, points about the history of French wine: it is inseparable from the history of France. One of the few linear trends that one might perceive in the long-term history of French wine is its increasing integration into the economy, culture, and material life of France. Wine has been an increasingly important part of France's economy and an increasingly significant element of French identity, and French wine has been a more and more widely recognized emblem of French culture and civilization in the wider world.

France's vineyard area is shrinking, and France is no longer consistently the biggest producer of wine in the world. The French are drinking less wine, and more French people are not drinking wine at all. But the standard-bearing regions and estates are as prestigious as ever, even if they are the leading formation of a diminishing army, and French wine generally has a more solid reputation than the wines of any other country. Yet we should remember that the history of French wine is punctuated by discontinuities and periodic departures from apparently well-established trends, and we should not expect its future to be any different.

Notes

1. FROM THE BEGINNINGS TO 1000 CE

1. This section draws on Patrick E. McGovern et al., "Beginning of Viticulture in France," *Proceedings of the National Academy of Science* 110 (2013): 1047–52.
2. Stefano Bruni, "Seafaring: Shipbuilding, Harbors, the Issue of Piracy," in *The Etruscan World*, ed. Jean MacIntosh Turfa (London: Routledge, 2013), 767.
3. Max Nelson, *The Barbarian's Beverage: A History of Beer in Ancient Europe* (London: Routledge, 2005), 50.
4. A. Trevor Hodge, *Ancient Greek France* (Philadelphia: University of Pennsylvania Press, 1999), 121.
5. Information provided by Michel Gassier, Château de Nages, AOC Costières de Nîmes.
6. Jeremy Patterson, "Wine (Greek and Roman)," in *Oxford Classical Dictionary*, ed. Simon Hornblower and Anthony Spawforth (Oxford: Oxford University Press, 1996), 1622.
7. Rod Phillips, *A Short History of Wine* (London: Penguin, 2000), 43–45.
8. Nelson, *Barbarian's Beverage*, 27–28.
9. Hodge, *Ancient Greek France*, 214–15.
10. Marcel Lachiver, *Vins, vignes et vignerons: Histoire du vignoble français* (Paris: Fayard, 1988), 28–29.
11. André Tchernia, *Le vin de l'Italie romaine: Essai d'histoire économique d'après les amphores* (Rome: École Française de Rome, 1986), 63.
12. Robert Étienne, "Les importations de vin campanien en Aquitaine," in *Vignobles et vins d'Aquitaine: Histoire, économie, art* (Bordeaux: Fédération Historique du Sud-Ouest, 1970), 24.
13. Roger Dion, *Histoire de la vigne et du vin en France: Des origins au XIXe siècle* (Paris: Flammarion, 1977), 98.
14. Ibid., 105–16.
15. Guy Lavignac, *Cépages du Sud-Ouest: 2000 ans d'histoire* (Arles: Éditions du Rouergue / INRA Éditions, 2001), 20.

16. Tchernia, *Le vin de l'Italie romaine*, 88.

17. Nicolas Purcell, "The Way We Used to Eat: Diet, Community, and History at Rome," *American Journal of Philology* 124 (2003): 336–37.

18. Keith Nurse, "The Last of the (Roman) Summer Wine," *History Today* 44 (1994): 4–5.

19. Dion, *Histoire de la vigne et du vin*, 129–31.

20. Tim Unwin, *Wine and the Vine: An Historical Geography of Viticulture and the Wine Trade* (London: Routledge, 1991), 117.

21. Sandrine Lavaud, *Bordeaux et le vin au Moyen Âge: Essor d'une civilisation* (Bordeaux: Éditions Sud Ouest, 2003), 13.

22. Lachiver, *Vins, vignes et vignerons*, 43.

23. Tim Unwin, *Wine and the Vine*, 118.

24. Raphaël Schirmer, *Muscadet: Histoire et géographie du vignoble nantais* (Bordeaux: Presses Universitaires de Bordeaux, 2010), 26.

25. Dion, *Histoire de la vigne et du vin*, 148.

26. Lavignac, *Cépages du Sud-Ouest*, 24.

27. Dion, *Histoire de la vigne et du vin*, 120–21.

28. Lachiver, *Vins, vignes et vignerons*, 34–35; Jancis Robinson, Julia Harding, and José Vouillamoz, *Wine Grapes* (New York: Harper Collins, 2012), 1023–27.

29. Lavignac, *Cépages du Sud-Ouest*, 176–77.

30. Dion, *Histoire de la vigne et du vin*, 137–38.

31. For a discussion of wine in Rome, see Phillips, *Short History of Wine*, 29–65.

32. 1 Timothy 5:23.

33. Jean-Charles Sournia, *A History of Alcoholism* (Oxford: Basil Blackwell, 1990), 10.

34. Nelson, *Barbarian's Beverage*, 71–74.

35. Edward Gibbon, *The History of the Decline and Fall of the Roman Empire*, ed. David Womersley (London: Penguin, 1994), 238.

36. Tim Unwin, "Continuity in Early Medieval Viticulture: Secular or Ecclesiastical Influences?," in *Viticulture in Geographical Perspective*, ed. Harm Jan de Blij (Miami: Miami Geographical Society, 1992), 9.

37. Lavignac, *Cépages du Sud-Ouest*, 25.

38. J.M. Wallace-Hadrill, *The Barbarian West, 400–1000* (London: Hutchinson, 1952), 153.

39. Georges Duby, *Rural Economy and Country Life in the Medieval West* (London: Edward Arnold, 1968), 42.

40. Lavignac, *Cépages du Sud-Ouest*, 25.

41. On monastic diets, see Dianne M. Bazell, "Strife among the Table-Fellows: Conflicting Attitudes of Early and Medieval Christians toward the Eating of Meat," *Journal of the American Academy of Religion* 65 (1997): 73–99.

42. Kathy L. Pearson, "Nutrition and the Early-Medieval Diet," *Speculum* 72 (1997): 15.

43. Lachiver, *Vins, vignes et vignerons*, 45–46.

44. Nelson, *Barbarian's Beverage,* 74–76.

45. Ibid., 80.

46. Desmond Seward, *Monks and Wine* (New York: Crown, 1979), 25–35.

47. Lachiver, *Vins, vignes et vignerons,* 49–53.

48. Ibid., 52–53.

49. Unwin, *Wine and the Vine,* 124.

50. Dion, *Histoire de la vigne et du vin,* 171.

51. Lachiver, *Vins, vignes et vignerons,* 46.

52. Seward, *Monks and Wine,* 29.

53. Yitzhak Hen, *Culture and Religion in Merovingian Gaul,* AD *481–751* (Leiden: Brill, 1995), 236–37.

54. Pierre Riche, *Daily Life in the World of Charlemagne* (Philadelphia: University of Pennsylvania Press, 1978), 177.

55. Ibid., 176.

56. Hen, *Merovingian Gaul,* 240.

57. John T. McNeill and Helena M. Gamer, *Medieval Handbooks of Penance* (New York: Octagon Books, 1965), 230.

58. Ibid., 275, 308.

2. THE MIDDLE AGES

1. Emmanuel Le Roy Ladurie, *Histoire du climat depuis l'an mil,* vol. 1 (Paris: Flammarion, 1983), 40–43.

2. D.B. Grigg, *Population Growth and Agrarian Change: An Historical Perspective* (Cambridge: Cambridge University Press, 1981), 53.

3. William Chester Jordan, *The Great Famine: Northern Europe in the Early Fourteenth Century* (Princeton: Princeton University Press, 1998), 34.

4. Jean Guilly, *Vignerons en pays d'Auxerre autrefois: Histoire et témoignages* (Lyon: Horvath, 1985), 43.

5. Raphaël Schirmer, *Muscadet: Histoire et géographie du vignoble nantais* (Bordeaux: Presses Universitaires de Bordeaux, 2010), 43–62.

6. Jancis Robinson, Julia Harding, and José Vouillamoz, *Wine Grapes* (New York: Harper Collins, 2012), 236, 623.

7. Jean-François Bazin, *Histoire du vin de Bourgogne* (Paris: Éditions Jean-Paul Gisserot, 2013), 21.

8. Rosalind Kent Berlow, "The 'Disloyal' Grape: The Agrarian Crisis of Late Fourteenth-Century Burgundy," *Agricultural History* 56 (1982): 426–38.

9. Bazin, *Histoire du vin de Bourgogne,* 21–22.

10. Ibid., 22.

11. Mack P. Holt, "Wine, Community, and Reformation in Sixteenth-Century Burgundy," *Past and Present* 138 (1993): 73.

12. Roger Dion, *Histoire de la vigne et du vin en France: Des origines au XIXe siècle* (Paris: Flammarion, 1977), 328–29.

13. Marcel Lachiver, *Vins, vignes et vignerons: Histoire du vignoble français* (Paris: Fayard, 1988), 158.

14. *The Exchequer Rolls of Scotland*, vol. 6, ed. George Burnett (Edinburgh: H.M. General Register House, 1883), 644.

15. Thorough discussions of medieval *clairet*/claret are Marcel Lachiver, "Autour du vin clairet," in *Le vin des historiens: Actes du 1ᵉʳ symposium "Vin et histoire,"* ed. Gilbert Garrier (Suze-la-Rousse: Université du Vin, 1990), 135–42; and Jean-Bernard Marquette, "Le 'vin de Gascogne' au XIVᵉ siècle," in *Le vin à travers les ages: Produit de qualité, agent économique* (Bordeaux: Fréret, 2001), 81–92.

16. Marquette, "Le 'vin de Gascogne,'" 91.

17. Jean-Bernard Marquette, "La vinification dans les domaines de l'archevêque de Bordeaux à la fin du Moyen Âge," in *Géographie historique des vignobles: Actes du colloque de Bordeaux, octobre 1977,* ed. A. Huetz de Lemps, vol. 1 (Paris: Éditions du Centre National de la Recherche Scientifique, 1978), 131.

18. Lachiver, "Autour du vin clairet," 136.

19. Ibid., 135.

20. Much of the following description of wine making is from Olivier de Serres, *Théâtre d'agriculture et ménage des champs* (Paris, 1600), 214–20.

21. Ibid., 216.

22. Marquette, "Le 'vin de Gascogne,'" 91.

23. Susan Rose, *The Wine Trade in Medieval Europe, 1000–1500* (London: Continuum, 2011), 85.

24. Sandrine Lavaud, *Bordeaux et le vin au Moyen Âge: Essor d'une civilisation* (Bordeaux: Éditions Sud Ouest, 2003), 93–96.

25. Rose, *Wine Trade in Medieval Europe,* 69.

26. F.W. Carter, "Cracow's Wine Trade (Fourteenth to Eighteenth Centuries)," *Slavonic and East European Review* 65 (1987): 537–78.

27. Rod Phillips, *A Short History of Wine* (London: Penguin, 2000), 84–115.

28. Lachiver, *Vins, vignes et vignerons,* 62–63.

29. Guilly, *Vignerons en pays d'Auxerre autrefois,* 66.

30. Rose, *Wine Trade in Medieval Europe,* 90–92.

31. Antoni Riera-Melis, "Society, Food and Feudalism," in *Food: A Culinary History from Antiquity to the Present,* ed. Jean-Louis Flandrin and Massimo Montanari (London: Penguin, 2000), 260–61.

32. Constance Hoffman, *Medieval Agriculture, the Southern French Countryside, and the Early Cistercians: A Study of Forty-Three Monasteries* (Philadelphia: American Philosophical Society, 1986), 93.

33. Béatrice Bourély, *Vignes et vins de l'Abbaye de Cîteaux en Bourgogne* (Nuits-Saint-Georges: Éditions du Tastevin, 1998), 101.

34. Philip Ziegler, *The Black Death* (New York: John Day, 1969), 96–109.

35. Emmanuel Le Roy Ladurie, *Montaillou: Cathars and Catholics in a French Village, 1294–1324,* trans. Barbara Bray (London: Penguin, 1980), 9, 15.

36. Lavaud, *Bordeaux et le vin au Moyen Âge,* 128–29.

37. Ibid., 133.

38. Martine Maguin, *La vigne et le vin en Lorraine, XIVᵉ–XVᵉ siècle* (Nancy: Presses Universitaires de Nancy, 1982), 199–215.

39. Georges Duby, *Rural Economy and Country Life in the Medieval West* (London: Hutchinson, 1952), 65.

40. Richard Unger, *Beer in the Middle Ages and the Renaissance* (Philadelphia: University of Pennsylvania Press, 2007), 129.

41. Lavaud, *Bordeaux et le vin au Moyen Âge*, 134–36.

42. P.W. Hammond, *Food and Feast in Medieval England* (Stroud, Gloucestershire: Alan Sutton, 1993), 127.

43. Billy Kay and Caileen MacLean, *Knee-Deep in Claret: A Celebration of Wine and Scotland* (Edinburgh: Mainstream Publishing, 1983), 9.

44. Patricia Labahn, "Feasting in the Fourteenth and Fifteenth Centuries: A Comparison of Manuscript Illumination to Contemporary Written Sources" (PhD diss., Saint Louis University, 1975), 60.

45. Yuval Noah Harari, "Strategy and Supply in Fourteenth-Century Western European Invasion Campaigns," *Journal of Military History* 64 (2000): 302.

46. A. Lynn Martin, *Alcohol, Violence, and Disorder in Traditional Europe* (Kirksville, MO: Truman State University Press, 2009), 57, table 3.8.

47. Christine Jéhanno, "Boire à Paris au XVe siècle: Le vin à l'Hôtel-Dieu," *Revue Historique* 276 (1986): 4–28.

48. Lachiver, *Vins, vignes et vignerons*, 140.

49. Rose, *Wine Trade in Medieval Europe*, 113–32, has a good summary of wine consumption statistics.

50. Lachiver, *Vins, vignes et vignerons*, 102–5, describes the "Battle of the Wines."

51. Ibid., 104.

52. Rose, *Wine Trade in Medieval Europe*, 113–22.

53. Hammond, *Food and Feast*, 74.

54. This section draws on Allen J. Grieco, "Le goût du vin entre doux et amer: Essai sur la classification des vins au Moyen Âge," in Garrier, *Le vin des historiens*, 89–97. Much of Grieco's work is based on Italian sources, but general medical views were held across Europe, and his conclusions align with the views of contemporary French physicians.

55. Ibid., 91–92.

56. Marie-Thérèse Lorcin, "Les usages du vin à la fin du Moyen Âge (XIIIe– XVe siècles)," in Garrier, *Le vin des historiens*, 102.

57. Jean Dupebe, "La diététique et l'alimentation des pauvres selon Sylvius," in *Pratiques et discours alimentaires à la Renaissance*, ed. J.-C. Margolin and R. Sauzet (Paris: G.-P. Maisonneuve et Larose, 1982), 41–56.

58. Lorcin, "Les usages du vin," 100–101.

59. Terence Scully, "Medieval France: The North," in *Regional Cuisines of Medieval Europe*, ed. Melitta Weiss Adamson (New York: Routledge, 2002), 58–59.

60. Constance B. Hieatt and Robin F. Jones, "Two Anglo-Norman Culinary Collections Edited from British Library Manuscripts Additional 32085 and Royal 12.C.xii," *Speculum* 61 (1986): 877.

61. Terence Scully, ed., *The Viandier of Taillevent: An Edition of All Extant Manuscripts* (Ottawa: University of Ottawa Press, 1988), 90–91, 295–96, 94–95.

62. Lorcin, "Les usages du vin," 99–100.

63. Ibid., 104.

64. Jeremy duQuesnay Adams, *Patterns of Medieval Society* (Englewood Cliffs, NJ: Prentice Hall, 1969), 111.

3. NEW WINES, NEW REGIONS

1. Philip Benedict, *The Huguenot Population of France, 1600–1685: The Demographic Fate and Customs of a Religious Minority* (Philadelphia: American Philosophical Society, 1994), 98.

2. Thomas Pinney, *A History of Wine in America: From the Beginnings to Prohibition* (Berkeley: University of California Press, 1989), 11.

3. Ibid., 101.

4. "Huguenots of Abbeville, South Carolina," Geni, accessed 4 February 2015, www.geni.com/projects/Huguenots-of-Abbeville-South-Carolina/12850.

5. Jean Bonoeil, *His Majesties Gracious Letter to the Earl of South-Hampton . . . Commanding the Present Setting Up of Silke Works, and Planting of Vines in Virginia* (London: Felix Kyngston, 1622), 2.

6. Ibid., 37–50.

7. Louis de Saint Pierre, *The Art of Planting and Cultivating the Vine; as Also, of Making, Fining, and Preserving Wines According to the Most Approved Methods in the Most Celebrated Wine-Countries in France* (London: J. Wilkie, 1772), title page.

8. Henri Enjalbert, "La naissance des grands vins et la formation du vigno-ble moderne de Bordeaux, 1647–1767," in *Géographie historique des vignobles: Actes du colloque de Bordeaux, octobre 1977*, ed. A. Huetz de Lemps, vol. 1 (Paris: Éditions du Centre National de la Recherche Scientifique, 1978), 63–64.

9. The law is 23 Hen. 8, c. 7.

10. A. D. Francis, *Wine Trade* (London: A. and C. Black, 1972), 29–30.

11. Marcel Lachiver, *Vins, vignes et vignerons: Histoire du vignoble français* (Paris: Fayard, 1988), 133–34.

12. Ibid., 151.

13. *Œuvres de Michel de Montaigne*, ed. J.-A.-C. Buchon (Paris: Auguste Desrez, 1838), 641.

14. Lachiver, *Vins, vignes et vignerons*, 149–50.

15. Nicolas de Nicolay, *Description générale de la ville de Lyon et des anciennes provinces du Lyonnais et Beaujolais* (Lyon: Mougin et Rusand, 1881), 185.

16. Lachiver, *Vins, vignes et vignerons*, 156.

17. Ibid., 158–59.

18. *Félix et Thomas Platter à Montpellier, 1552–1559, 1595–1599: Notes de voyage de deux étudiants balois*, ed. Léon Gaudin (Montpellier: C. Coulet, 1892), 58.

19. Ibid., 39.

20. Ibid., 48.

21. Enjalbert, "La naissance des grands vins," 62.

22. Henriette De Bruyn Kops, *A Spirited Exchange: The Brandy Trade between France and the Dutch Republic in Its Atlantic Framework* (Leiden: Brill, 2007), 180.

23. Enjalbert, "La naissance des grands vins," 63–64.

24. English cartoons of the seventeenth and eighteenth centuries portray the Dutch as frogs, and John Arbuthnot calls his stereotyped Dutchman "Nic Frog" in *The History of John Bull* (London: Printed for John Morphew, 1712).

25. Enjalbert, "La naissance des grands vins," 66.

26. Ibid., 65.

27. William T. Harper, *Origins and Rise of the British Distillery* (Lewiston, NY: Edwin Mellen, 1999), 13–17.

28. Francis, *Wine Trade*, 74.

29. See Rod Phillips, *Alcohol: A History* (Chapel Hill: University of North Carolina Press, 2014), 123–31.

30. De Bruyn Kops, *Spirited Exchange*, 179.

31. François Brumont, "Aux origins de la production des eaux-de-vie d'Armagnac," in *L'univers du vin: Actes du colloque de Bordeaux (4–5 octobre 2012)*, ed. Bernard Bodinier, Stéphanie Lachaud, and Corinne Marache (Rennes: Presses Universitaires de Rennes, 2014), 331.

32. Ibid., 333.

33. Francis, *Wine Trade*, 74.

34. Enjalbert, "La naissance des grands vins," 73–74.

35. Christian Wolff, *Riquewihr: Son vignoble et ses vins à travers les âges* (Ingersheim: Société d'Archéologie de Riquewihr, 1967), 71.

36. Marie-Noëlle Denis, "Vignoble et société en Alsace depuis la Guerre de Trente Ans," in *Les boissons: Production et consommation aux XIXe et XXe siècles* (Paris: Comité des Travaux Historiques et Scientifiques, 1984), 11–12.

37. Jean Richard, "Aspects historiques de l'évolution du vignoble bourguignon," in Huetz de Lemps, *Géographie historique des vignobles*, 190–91.

38. Jean-François Bazin, *Histoire du vin de Bourgogne* (Paris: Jean-Paul Gisserot, 2013), 26.

39. Lachiver, *Vins, vignes et vignerons*, 284.

40. "Comptes d'Antoine Rougier" (CC1692) and "Pièces justificatives des comptes d'Antoine Rougier" (CC1695), Comptabilité communal (1619–1620), Archives Municipales de Lyon, accessed 13 January 2015, www.archives-lyon. fr/static/archives/contenu/old/fonds/cc/127.htm.

41. Jean Clavel, *Le 21e siècle des vins du Languedoc: Du monde gréco-romain à Internet* (Saint-Georges-d'Orques: Causse, 1999), 57–58.

42. *Vignobles et vins d'Aquitaine: Histoire, économie, art* (Bordeaux: Fédération Historique du Sud-Ouest, 1970), 107.

43. Lachiver, *Vins, vignes et vignerons*, 287.

44. Thomas Brennan, "The Anatomy of Inter-regional Markets in the Early Modern French Wine Trade," *Journal of European Economic History* 23 (1994): 584–87.

45. Ibid., 591.

46. Jean-Jacques François, *Au temps des vignes et des vignerons du pays chartrain, 840–1920*, vol. 3 (Luisant: Durand, 2003), 15.

47. Martin Wolfe, *The Fiscal System of Renaissance France* (New Haven: Yale University Press, 1972), 325–26.

48. Kolleen Guy, *When Champagne Became French: Wine and the Making of a National Identity* (Baltimore: Johns Hopkins University Press, 2003), 28–29.

49. Fynes Moryson, *An Itinerary Containing His Ten Yeeres Travell through the Twelve Dominions . . .* , vol. 1 (Glasgow: James MacLehose, 1908), 43.

50. Emmanuel Le Roy Ladurie, *Histoire du climat depuis l'an mil*, vol. 1 (Paris: Flammarion, 1983), 82–83.

51. Ibid., 84–85.

52. Enjalbert, "La naissance des grands vins," 74.

53. See Norbert Elias, *On the Process of Civilization* (Dublin: University College Dublin, 2012).

54. Enjalbert, "La naissance des grands vins," 59.

55. Charles Ludington, *The Politics of Wine in Britain: A New Cultural History* (New York: Palgrave Macmillan, 2013).

56. Samuel Pepys, diary, 10 April 1663.

57. Ludington, *Politics of Wine in Britain*, 85. Locke has conflated Haut-Brion and Pontac here, as Pontac wine came from Pez, in Saint-Estèphe, which is in the Médoc. He must have intended "Médoc and Haut-Brion," unless he was using "Pontac" to refer to the owner.

58. Ibid., 84–85.

59. Lachiver, *Vins, vignes et vignerons*, 155–56.

60. Roger Dion, *Histoire de la vigne et du vin en France: Des origines au XIXe siècle* (Paris: Flammarion, 1977), 473.

61. Pierre Pegeot, "Le vin des chanoines montbéliardais (1498–1530)," in *L'église, la vigne et le vin dans le massif jurassien: Actes de la table ronde de Lons-le-Saunier, avril 1990* (Besançon: Néo Typo, 1991), 104.

62. Jean Calvin, *Institutes of the Christian Religion*, ed. J.T. McNeill, trans. Ford Lewis Battles, vol. 2 (London: SCM Press, 1961), 1425.

63. John Calvin, *Theological Treatises*, ed. and trans. J.K.S. Reid (London: SCM Press, 1954), 81.

64. Mack P. Holt, "Wine, Community, and Reformation in Sixteenth-Century Burgundy," *Past and Present* 138 (1993): 78.

65. John, 15:1, 15:5.

66. Holt, "Wine, Community, and Reformation," 78.

67. Ibid., 80.

68. Calvin, *Institutes of the Christian Religion*, 1264.

69. Daniel Rivière, "Le thème alimentaire dans le discours proverbial de la Renaissance française," in *Pratiques et discours alimentaires à la Renaissance,* ed. J.C. Margolin and R. Sauzet (Paris: G.-P. Maisonneuve et Larose, 1982), 201–18, passim.

70. Jean-Robert Pitte, *La bouteille de vin: Histoire d'une revolution* (Paris: Taillandier, 2013), 122–23.

71. *The Diary of John Evelyn,* ed. William Bray, vol. 1 (New York: M. Walter Dunne, 1901), 67, 71–72.

72. Jean-Louis Flandrin, "Médicine et habitudes alimentaires anciennes," in Margolin and Sauzet, *Pratiques et discours alimentaires,* 86.

73. Ibid., 87.

74. Ibid., 85.

75. Ibid.

76. Rivière, "Le thème alimentaire," 203.

77. *Œuvres de Michel de Montaigne,* 639.

78. Jean Dupebe, "La diététique et l'alimentation des pauvres selon Sylvius," in Margolin and Sauzet, *Pratiques et discours alimentaires,* 41–56, passim.

79. Henri de Buttet, "Le vin des Invalides au temps de Louis XIV," in *Les boissons,* 39–51.

80. Michel Reulos, "Le premier traité sur le cidre: *De vino et pomaceo,* de Julien le Paulmier, traduit par Jacques de Cahaignes (1589)," in Margolin and Sauzet, *Pratiques et discours alimentaires,* 97–103.

4. ENLIGHTENMENT AND REVOLUTION

1. A.D. Francis, *The Wine Trade* (London: A. and C. Black, 1972), 124–25.

2. *The Diary of John Hervey, First Earl of Bristol: With Extracts from His Book of Expenses, 1688 to 1742* (Wells: Ernest Jackson, 1894), 170–71.

3. "L'hiver de 1709," Porte du Médoc, accessed 6 March 2015, http://portedumedoc.free.fr/index.php?option=com_content&view=article&id=785&Itemid=910.

4. Emmanuel Le Roy Ladurie, *Histoire du climat depuis l'an mil,* vol. 1 (Paris: Flammarion, 1983), 112–13.

5. Marcel Lachiver, *Vins, vignes et vignerons: Histoire du vignoble français* (Paris: Fayard, 1988), 326–27.

6. Armand Bourgeois, *Le vin de Champagne sous Louis XIV et sous Louis XV, d'après des lettres et documents inédits* (Paris: Bibliothèque d'Art de "La Critique," 1897), 43.

7. Lachiver, *Vins, vignes et vignerons,* 330.

8. Pierre Dejean, "L'exportation des vins béarnais dans les pays du Nord au XVIIIe siècle: La 'Compagnie patriotique pour le commerce des vins de Béarn,'" *Revue d'histoire moderne* 11 (1936): 217.

9. Lachiver, *Vins, vignes et vignerons,* 333.

10. Ibid., 338–39.

11. Dewey Markham Jr., *1855: A History of the Bordeaux Classification* (New York: John Wiley and Sons, 1998), 213–15.

12. Quoted in Claudine Wolikow, "Du vin pour tous! La palette des vins en Champagne méridionale à la fin de l'Ancien Régime," in *De la vigne en Champagne au vin de Champagne: De l'âge du Bronze à l'âge industriel*, ed. Patrick Demouy and Marie-Hélène Morell (Dijon: Éditions Universitaires de Dijon, 2013), 182.

13. Jean-Antoine-Claude Chaptal, *Traité théorique et pratique sur la culture de la vigne*, vol. 1 (Paris: Delalain, 1801), 161.

14. Lachiver, *Vins, vignes et vignerons*, 335.

15. Jancis Robinson, Julia Harding, and José Vouillamoz, *Wine Grapes* (New York: Harper Collins, 2012), 236, 153.

16. William Franck, *Traité sur les vins du Médoc et les autres vins rouges et blancs du département de la Gironde*, 3rd. ed. (Bordeaux: P. Chaumas, 1853), 56.

17. François-Alexandre Aubert de La Chesnaye-Desbois, *Dictionnaire universel d'agriculture et de jardinage*, vol. 2 (Paris: David le Jeune, 1751). The following paragraphs draw on 119–25.

18. Ibid., 119–20.

19. Ibid., 124.

20. Edme Beguillet, *Œnologie, ou Discours sur la meilleure méthode de faire le vin et de cultiver la vigne* (Dijon: Defay, 1770), 102–3.

21. Raphaël Schirmer, *Muscadet: Histoire et géographie du vignoble nantais* (Bordeaux: Presses Universitaires de Bordeaux, 2010), 80.

22. Loïc Abric, *Le vin de Bourgogne au XIXᵉ siècle: Aspects économiques, sociaux, culturels* (Précy-sous-Thil: Éditions de l'Armançon, 1993), 24.

23. Aubert de La Chesnaye-Desbois, *Dictionnaire universel d'agriculture*, 121.

24. Beguillet, *Œnologie*, 104–5.

25. Robert Forster, "The Noble Wine Producers of the Bordelais in the Eighteenth Century," *Economic History Review* 14 (1961): 22.

26. Ibid.

27. Wolikow, "Du vin pour tous!," 181.

28. Peter McPhee, *Revolution and Environment in Southern France: Peasants, Lords, and Murder in the Corbières, 1780–1830* (Oxford: Oxford University Press, 1999), 22–23, table 1.2.

29. *Journal d'un bourgeois de Bégoux: Michel Célarié, 1771–1836*, ed. Christiane Constant-Le Stum (Paris: Publisud, 1992), 106.

30. Arthur Young, *Travels during the Years 1787, 1788, and 1789* (Bury St. Edmund's: J. Rackham, 1792), 388.

31. Maurice Gresset, "Un document sur le rendement des vignes bisontines dans la seconde moitié du XVIIIᵉ siècle," in *Les boissons: Production et consommation aux XIXᵉ et XXᵉ siècles* (Paris: Comité des Travaux Historiques et Scientifiques, 1984), 30.

32. Lachiver, *Vins, vignes et vignerons*, 385.

33. Ibid., 386–87.

34. Young, *Travels*, 384.

35. Le Roy Ladurie, *Histoire du climat*, 87–89.

36. M. Maupin, *Essai sur l'art de faire le vin rouge, le vin blanc et le cidre* (Paris, 1767), 80–90.

37. See the cases in Thomas E. Brennan, ed., *Public Drinking in the Early Modern World: Voices from the Tavern, 1500–1800*, vol. 1, France (London: Pickering and Chatto, 2011).

38. Quoted in ibid., 39.

39. See ibid., 183–86.

40. Roderick Phillips, *Family Breakdown in Late Eighteenth-Century France: Divorces in Rouen, 1792–1803* (Oxford: Clarendon, 1980), 116–17.

41. Josef Smets, "À la table d'un seigneur languedocien en 1766: Les comptes du cuisinier," *Revue d'histoire moderne et contemporaine* 48 (2001): 37.

42. Young, *Travels*, 457.

43. A. Boyer, *The Compleat French Master for Ladies and Gentlemen* (London, 1744), 268–73.

44. Young, *Travels*, 19.

45. Bernard Ginestet, *Thomas Jefferson à Bordeaux: Et dans quelques autres vignes d'Europe* (Bordeaux: Mollat, 1996), 27–34, 123–26.

46. Philippe Roudié, *Vignobles et vignerons du Bordelais, 1850–1980* (Bordeaux: Presses Universitaires de Bordeaux, 1994), 16.

47. Fabienne Moreau, "Les enjeux du commerce international des vins de Champagne: Exemple de la Maison Veuve Clicquot Ponsardin," in Demouy and Morell, *De la vigne en Champagne*, 204–5.

48. Dejean, "L'exportation des vins béarnais," 219.

49. Ibid., 225.

50. Henri Enjalbert, "Comment naissent les grands crus: Bordeaux, Cognac, Porto (première partie)," *Annales: Économies, Sociétés, Civilisations* 3 (1953): 327.

51. Jean Richard, "L'Académie de Dijon et le commerce du vin au XVIIIe siècle à propos d'un mémoire présenté aux États de Bourgogne," *Annales de Bourgogne* 47 (1975): 222.

52. It was subsequently published as François Rozier, *De la fermentation des vins, et de la meilleure manière de faire l'eau-de-vie* (Lyon: Frères Perisse, 1770).

53. J.B. Gough, "Winecraft and Chemistry in Eighteenth-Century France: Chaptal and the Invention of Chaptalization," *Technology and Culture* 39 (1998): 96–97.

54. Enjalbert, "Grands crus," 329.

55. Robert Forster, *The Nobility of Toulouse in the Eighteenth Century: A Social and Economic Study* (Baltimore: Johns Hopkins University Press, 1960), 99.

56. Gough, "Winecraft and Chemistry," 83–84.

57. *Jugement de M. le lieutenant général de police, commissaire du conseil en cette partie, du 24 Mars 1751* (Paris: G. Lamesle, 1751), 1.

58. *L'Albert Moderne, ou nouveaux secrets éprouvés et licites* (Paris: Veuve Duchesne, 1772), 321–22.

59. Louis Leméry, *Traité des alimens,* vol. 1 (Paris: Durand, 1755), 31.

60. Benoît Musset, "Vins de Champagne et autres 'vins de distinction': Le renouvellement de la consommation vinicole des élites en France," in Demouy and Morell, *De la vigne en Champagne,* 168–69.

61. François Aignan, *Traité de la goutte dans son état naturel* (Paris: Claude Jombert, 1777), 113.

62. Ibid., 100.

63. Barbara Ketchum Wheaton, *Savoring the Past: The French Kitchen and Table from 1300 to 1789* (Philadelphia: University of Pennsylvania Press, 1983), 215.

64. Robert Forster, *The House of Saulx-Tavanes* (Baltimore: Johns Hopkins University Press, 1971), 212–20.

65. Forster, *Nobility of Toulouse,* 99.

66. Musset, "Vins de Champagne," 170–71, tables 3 and 4.

67. *Encyclopédie, ou Dictionnaire raisonné des sciences, des arts et des métiers* (Paris, 1751–65), s.v. "vin."

68. Gough, "Winecraft and Chemistry," 81.

69. Wheaton, *Savoring the Past,* 215.

70. Lachiver, *Vins, vignes et vignerons,* 352–53.

71. This theme is deftly explored in Noelle Plack, "Liberty, Equality and Taxation: Wine in the French Revolution," *Social History of Alcohol and Drugs* 26 (2012): 5–22.

72. *Cahiers de doléances, région Centre,* ed. Denis Jeanson, vol. 5, *Loire-et-Cher,* pt. 2 (Tours: Denis Jeanson, 1989), 480.

73. Schirmer, *Muscadet,* 88.

74. Quoted in Plack, "Liberty, Equality and Taxation," 116.

75. Noelle Plack, *Common Land, Wine and the French Revolution: Rural Society and Economy in Southern France, c. 1789–1820* (Farnham: Ashgate, 2009), 141.

76. Margaret Darrow, "Economic Terror in the City: The General Maximum in Montauban," *French Historical Studies* 17 (1991): 515.

77. Peter McPhee, *Revolution and Environment,* 175–77.

78. Ibid., 177–78.

79. Plack, *Common Land,* 20–21.

80. Peter McPhee, "Les Corbières en révolution, 1780–1830: Révolution paysanne, viticulture et environnement," *Bulletin de la Société d'études scientifiques de l'Aude* 95 (1995): 167.

81. Archives départementales de la Côte d'Or, M13 IX a/1, Viticulture.

82. Plack, *Common Land,* 141–46.

83. McPhee, *Revolution and Environment,* 198.

84. Archives départementales de la Côte d'Or, Q74, Biens nationaux.

85. Archives départementales de la Côte d'Or, Q213, Biens nationaux.

86. Jean Bart, *La Révolution française en Bourgogne* (Clermont-Ferrand: La Française, 1996), 312.

87. Richard Olney, *Romanée-Conti: The World's Most Fabled Wine* (New York: Rizzoli, 1995), 31.

88. Young, *Travels*, 390.

89. Claire Desbois-Thibault, "La modernité vitivinicole en Champagne au début du XIXe siècle: L'exemple de Jean-Remy Moët (1792–1832)," in Demouy and Morell, *De la vigne en Champagne*, 213.

90. For a discussion of this point, see Kolleen Guy, *When Champagne Became French: Wine and the Making of a National Identity* (Baltimore: Johns Hopkins University Press, 2003), 10–11.

91. W. Scott Haine, "The Priest of the Proletarians: Paris Café Owners and the Working Class, 1820–1914," *International Labor and Working-Class History* 45 (1994): 17.

92. Circular from the Commission des Subsistances et Approvisionnements de la République, 19 germinal II / 8 April 1794, Archives départementales de la Côte d'Or, L544, Subsistances.

93. Markham, *1855*, 226.

94. Archives départementales de la Côte d'Or, L465, Fête d'agriculture.

95. Circular "Prix nationaux d'agriculture" (Rouen, Year III / 1794–95), Archives départementales de la Côte d'Or, L574, Agriculture.

96. Archives départementales de la Côte d'Or, L1401, Maximum.

97. Louis Laurent, "Les maisons religieuses et le vin à Orgelet du XVIIe au XIXe siècle," in *L'église, la vigne et le vin dans le massif jurassien: Actes de la table ronde de Lons-le-Saunier, avril 1990* (Besançon: Néo Typo, 1991), 121–22.

98. Marcel Couturier, *Le vignoble en Eure-et-Loir, 1789–1815* (Société Archéologique d'Eure-et-Loir 1962), n.p.

5. STABILITY AND GROWTH

1. Hugh Johnson, *The Story of Wine* (London: Mitchell Beazley, 1989), 371.

2. Cyrus Redding, *A History and Description of Modern Wines* (London: Henry G. Bohn, 1851), 82.

3. Marcel Lachiver, *Vins, vignes et vignerons: Histoire du vignoble français* (Paris: Fayard, 1988), 594–99.

4. Ibid., 604–9.

5. Antoine-Alexis Cadet-de-Vaux, *L'art de faire le vin, d'après la doctrine de Chaptal* (Paris: Bureau de la Décade Philosophique, Littéraire et Politique, an IX [1801]), 1.

6. Ibid., 2.

7. Ibid.

8. Ibid., 24.

9. Ibid., 9.

10. Ibid., 11.

11. Ibid., 14.
12. Ibid.
13. Ibid., 16.
14. Ibid., 15.
15. Ibid., 16.
16. Ibid., 27.
17. Jean-Antoine-Claude Chaptal, *Traité théorique et pratique sur la culture de la vigne* (Paris: Delalain, 1801), vi–viii.
18. Ibid., 22–23.
19. Ibid., 10.
20. Ibid., 265–66.
21. Ibid., 161.
22. Ibid., 74.
23. Ibid., 340–44.
24. Lachiver, *Vins, vignes et vignerons,* 358.
25. Ibid., 395, table.
26. Redding, *Modern Wines,* 158.
27. M.P. Maigne, *Nouveau manuel complet du sommelier et du marchand de vins* (Paris: Roret, 1884), 123.
28. Ibid., 122.
29. Robert Druitt, *Report on the Cheap Wines from France, Italy, Austria, Greece, Hungary, and Australia* (London: Henry Renshaw, 1873), 56–57.
30. William Franck, *Traité sur les vins du Médoc et les autres vins rouges et blancs du département de la Gironde,* 3rd ed. (Bordeaux: P. Chaumas, 1853), 37–41.
31. Ibid., 198.
32. Dewey Markham Jr., *1855: A History of the Bordeaux Classification* (New York: John Wiley and Sons, 1998), 207–346.
33. Franck, *Traité sur les vins,* 199–202.
34. Markham, *1855,* 81–82.
35. Compare the rankings in ibid., 207–346.
36. Ibid., 52.
37. The best single work on the 1855 Bordeaux Classification is Markham, *1855.* The following discussion draws heavily on this work.
38. Quoted in ibid., 30.
39. Quoted in ibid., 33.
40. Ibid., 115.
41. Didier Nourrisson, *Le buveur du XIXe siècle* (Paris: Albin Michel, 1990), 30.
42. Lachiver, *Vins, vignes et vignerons,* 410.
43. Nourrisson, *Le buveur du XIXe siècle,* 25.
44. Quoted in Louis Chevalier, *Labouring Classes and Dangerous Classes in Paris during the First Half of the Nineteenth Century,* translated by Frank Jellinek (London: Routledge and Kegan Paul, 1973), 360.

45. Phillips, *Alcohol: A History* (Chapel Hill: University of North Carolina Press, 2014), 176–77.
46. Quoted in Chevalier, *Labouring Classes*, 264.
47. Nourrisson, *Le buveur du XIXe siècle*, 27.
48. Honoré de Balzac, *Illusions perdues* (Paris: Garnier, 1961), 126.

6. PHYLLOXERA AND RENEWAL

1. The best work on phylloxera is George Gale, *Dying on the Vine: How Phylloxera Transformed Wine* (Berkeley: University of California Press, 2011). See also Gilbert Garrier, *Le phylloxéra: Une guerre de trente ans, 1870–1900* (Paris: Albin Michel, 1989); George Ordish, *The Great Wine Blight* (London: Dent, 1972); and Roger Pouget, *Histoire de la lutte contre le phylloxéra de la vigne in France (1868–1895)* (Paris: Institut National de la Recherche Agronomique, 1990).
2. Quoted in Gale, *Dying on the Vine*, 17.
3. Quoted in ibid.
4. Ibid., 26–50, has a fascinating account and analysis of this debate.
5. The following paragraphs draw heavily on ibid., 58–78.
6. Swanzie Agnew, "The Vine in Bas-Languedoc," *Geographical Review* 36 (1946): 73.
7. Leo A. Loubère, Paul Adams, and Roy Sandstrom, "Saint-Laurent-de-la-Salanque: From Fishing Village to Wine Town," *Agricultural History* 62 (1988): 54.
8. Elizabeth Heath, *Wine, Sugar, and the Making of Modern France: Global Economic Crisis and the Racialization of French Citizenship, 1870–1910* (Cambridge: Cambridge University Press, 2014), 68.
9. Quoted in Gale, *Dying on the Vine*, 111.
10. "Vine Cultivation in the Gironde," *Bulletin of Miscellaneous Information (Royal Gardens, Kew)* 33 (1889): 228.
11. Quoted in Gale, *Dying on the Vine*, 135.
12. *Le progrès agricole et viticole: Journal d'agriculture méridionale*, 12 April 1891, 312.
13. The best discussion of "foxiness" is Thomas Pinney, *A History of Wine in America: From the Beginnings to Prohibition* (Berkeley: University of California Press, 1989), 443–47.
14. Philippe Roudié, *Vignobles et vignerons du Bordelais, 1850–1980* (Bordeaux: Presses Universitaires de Bordeaux, 1994), 154–55.
15. Raphaël Schirmer, *Muscadet: Histoire et géographie du vignoble nantais* (Bordeaux: Presses Universitaires de Bordeaux, 2010), 108–10.
16. Harry W. Paul, *The Science of Vine and Wine in France, 1750–1990* (New York: Cambridge University Press, 1996), 10.
17. Marcel Lachiver, *Vins, vignes et vignerons: Histoire du vignoble français* (Paris: Fayard, 1988), 416.

18. Ibid., 496–97.

19. Quoted in Gale, *Dying on the Vine*, 53

20. Ibid., 76.

21. Lachiver, *Vins, vignes et vignerons*, 448, table.

22. Quoted in Paul Birebent, *Hommes, vignes et vins de l'Algérie française (1830–1962)* (Nice: Éditions Jacques Gandini, 2007), 83.

23. Ibid., 84.

24. Ibid., 86.

25. Ibid., 222, "Evolution du vignoble algérien, 1830–1962" table.

26. Lachiver, *Vins, vignes et vignerons*, 582–83, "Le vignoble français" table.

27. Ibid., 449–54.

28. Roudié, *Vignobles et vignerons du Bordelais*, 243.

29. Abhijit Banerjee et al., "Long-Run Health Impacts of Income Shocks: Wine and Phylloxera in Nineteenth-Century France," *Review of Economics and Statistics* 92 (2010): 714–28.

30. Didier Nourrisson, *Le buveur du XIXᵉ siècle* (Paris: Albin Michel, 1990), 25.

31. Christophe Lucand, *Le pinard des poilus: Une histoire du vin en France durant la Grande Guerre (1914–1918)* (Dijon: Éditions Universitaires de Dijon, 2015), 20.

32. W. Scott Haine, *The World of the Paris Café: Sociability among the French Working Class, 1789–1914* (Baltimore: Johns Hopkins University Press, 1999), 91.

33. Ibid., 93.

34. Frédéric Le Play, *Les ouvriers européens*, vols. 5–6 (Tours: Alfred Mame et Fils, 1878), passim.

35. Patricia E. Prestwich, "Female Alcoholism in Paris, 1870–1920: The Response of Psychiatrists and of Families," *History of Psychiatry* 14 (2003): 328–29.

36. See especially Patricia E. Prestwich, *Drink and the Politics of Social Reform: Antialcoholism in France since 1870* (Palo Alto: Society for the Promotion of Science and Scholarship, 1988); also Rod Phillips, *Alcohol: A History* (Chapel Hill: University of North Carolina Press, 2014), 192–215.

37. Prestwich, *Drink and the Politics of Social Reform*, 20.

38. Prestwich, "Female Alcoholism in Paris," 324.

39. General works are Doris Lander, *Absinthe: The Cocaine of the Nineteenth Century* (Jefferson, NC: McFarland, 1995); and Jad Adams, *Hideous Absinthe: A History of the Devil in a Bottle* (London: Tauris Parke, 2008).

40. Prestwich, *Drink and the Politics of Social Reform*, 62.

41. Kevin D. Goldberg, "Acidity and Power: The Politics of Natural Wine in Nineteenth-Century Germany," *Food and Foodways* 19 (2011): 294–313.

42. A. Andréadès, "The Currant Crisis in Greece," *Economic Journal* 16 (1906): 41.

43. Lachiver, *Vins, vignes et vignerons*, 439–42.

44. Quoted in James Simpson, "Selling to Reluctant Drinkers: The British Wine Market, 1860–1914," *Economic History Review* 57 (2004): 97.

45. The following paragraphs draw heavily on Alessandro Stanziani, "Information, Quality, and Legal Rules: Wine Adulteration in Nineteenth-Century France," *Business History* 51 (2009): 280–84.

46. Quoted in ibid., 282.

47. Ibid., 277.

48. A. E. Bateman, "A Note on the Statistics of Wine Production in France," *Journal of the Statistical Society of London* 46 (1883): 119.

49. Simpson, "Selling to Reluctant Drinkers," 83, table 1.

50. Ibid., 88.

51. Ibid., 94.

52. Ibid., 97.

53. Ibid., 96, table 2.

54. Bateman, "Wine Production in France," 119.

55. Dewey Markham Jr., *1855: A History of the Bordeaux Classification* (New York: John Wiley and Sons, 1998), 30; William Franck, *Traité sur les vins du Médoc et les autres vins rouges et blancs du département de la Gironde*, 3rd ed. (Bordeaux: P. Chaumas, 1853), 200–204.

56. Cyrus Redding, *A History and Description of Modern Wines* (London: Henry G. Bohn, 1851), 377; Markham, *1855*, 102–3; *Wine and Spirit Merchant: A Familiar Treatise on the Art of Making Wine* (London: W. R. Loftus, [1864]), 139.

57. Markham, *1855*, 213, classification 3.

58. Eveline Schumpeter, quoted in Pierre Bourdieu, *Distinction: A Social Critique of the Judgment of Taste*, translated by Richard Nice (Cambridge, MA: Harvard University Press, 1984), 53.

59. Quoted in Nicholas Faith, *The Story of Champagne* (London: Hamish Hamilton, 1988), 78.

60. Serena Sutcliffe, *Champagne: The History and Character of the World's Most Celebrated Wine* (New York: Simon and Schuster, 1988), 121, illustration.

61. Kolleen Guy, "'Oiling the Wheels of Social Life': Myths and Marketing in Champagne during the Belle Epoque," *French Historical Studies* 22 (1999): 211–39.

62. Kolleen Guy, *When Champagne Became French: Wine and the Making of a National Identity* (Baltimore: Johns Hopkins University Press, 2003), 129.

63. Ibid., 119.

64. Jean Sagnes, "Le mouvement de 1907 en Languedoc-Roussillon: De la révolte viticole à la révolte régionale," *Le Mouvement Social* 104 (1978): 7–10.

65. Lachiver, *Vins, vignes et vignerons*, 466–67.

66. Ibid., 453.

67. Ibid., 467.

68. Sagnes, "Le mouvement de 1907," 3.

69. Pierre Bosc, *Le vin de la colère* (Paris: Éditions Galilée, 1976) is an account of the episode.

70. Lachiver, *Vins, vignes et vignerons,* 476–77.
71. Guy, *When Champagne Became French,* 158–59.
72. Ibid., 161.

7. PINARD AND POSTWAR FRANCE

1. Information provided by Professor Geoffrey Giles, University of Florida.
2. Michael Marrus, "Social Drinking in the *Belle Époque,*" *Journal of Social History* 7 (1974): 120.
3. Nicolas Marty, *L'invention de l'eau embouteillée: Qualités, normes et marchés de l'eau en bouteille en Europe, XIXᵉ–XXᵉ siècles* (Brussels: Peter Lang, 2013), 361, table 1.
4. Pierre Viala, *L'avenir viticole de la France après la guerre: Le vin et l'hygiène—le vin au front,* 2nd ed. (Paris: Bureaux de la "Revue de viticulture," 1916), 47–48.
5. Ibid., 52–53.
6. Patricia E. Prestwich, *Drink and the Politics of Social Reform: Antialcoholism in France since 1870* (Palo Alto: Society for the Promotion of Science and Scholarship, 1988), 172.
7. Christophe Lucand, *Le pinard des poilus: Une histore du vin en France durant la Grande Guerre (1914–1918)* (Dijon: Éditions Universitaires de Dijon, 2015), 43.
8. *Journal officiel de la République française: Débats parlementaires, Chambre des députés,* 30 September 1916, 1952.
9. Average for 1910–19. Marcel Lachiver, *Vins, vignes et vignerons: Histoire du vignoble français* (Paris: Fayard, 1988), 608–9, table; 618, table.
10. *Ordinaires: Livre de cuisine militaire aux manœuvres et en campagne* (Paris: Henri Charles-Lavauzelle, 1915), 22.
11. Henri Chatinière, *Pour sa santé: Ce qu'un poilu doit savoir* (Paris: Charles Lavauzelle, 1916), 47–48.
12. I thank Adam Zietnek for this information.
13. Personal communication from Zietnek.
14. *Bulletin officiel du ministère de la guerre—Mouvements et transports: Organisation générale aux armées,* vol. 2, *Transports stratégiques* (Paris: Imprimerie Librairie Militaire, 1914), 37.
15. *Aide-mémoire de l'officier du génie en campagne* (Paris: Imprimerie Nationale, 1915), vol. 1, 38, section 60.
16. Ibid., vol. 2, 36, section 47 (uppercase in the original).
17. *Journal officiel de la République française: Débats parlementaires, Chambre des députés,* 30 September 1916, 1951–52.
18. Ibid., 1953.
19. Ibid., 1952.
20. "Vive le Pinard," quoted in Lucand, *Le pinard des poilus,* 140.
21. Viala, *L'avenir viticole de la France,* 41.

22. *Australian Words and Their Origins,* ed. Joan Hughes (Melbourne: Oxford University Press, 1989), 416.

23. Gilbert Garrier, *Histoire sociale et culturelle du vin* (Paris: Larousse, 1998), 366.

24. Adam Zietnek kindly supplied this information.

25. Patricia E. Prestwich, "Female Alcoholism in Paris, 1870–1920: The Response of Psychiatrists and of Families," *History of Psychiatry* 14 (2003): 328–29.

26. Lachiver, *Vins, vignes et vignerons,* 484.

27. Vicente Pinilla, "Wine Historical Statistics: A Quantitative Approach to Its Consumption, Production and Trade, 1840–1938," American Association of Wine Economists, Working Paper No. 167 (August 2014), tables T4 and T6.

28. Asa Briggs, *Wine for Sale: Victoria Wine and the Liquor Trade, 1860–1984* (Chicago: University of Chicago Press, 1985), 93.

29. Circulaire ministérielle, 11 August 1916, in *Guerre de 1914: Documents officiels, textes législatifs et réglementaires,* vol. 12 (Paris: Dalloz, 1915–18), 132.

30. D. Zolla, "Revue des questions agricoles," *Revue politique et parlementaire* 83 (1915): 156–66.

31. Jean-Jacques Becker, *The Great War and the French People* (New York: Berg, 1985), 128.

32. W. Scott Haine, "Drink, Sociability, and Social Class in France, 1789–1945: The Emergence of a Proletarian Public Sphere," in *Alcohol: A Social and Cultural History,* ed. Mack Holt (Oxford: Berg, 2006), 137.

33. Anne Combaud and Alain Marre, "Impacts des deux guerres mondiales sur les territoires viticoles champenois: Cas du versant nord de la Montagne de Reims," in *La construction des territoires du Champagne (1811–1911–2011),* ed. Serge Wolikow (Dijon: Éditions Universitaires de Dijon, 2013), 133–38.

34. Viala, *L'avenir viticole de la France,* 16.

35. Ibid.

36. Ibid., 17–18.

37. André Simon, *The History of Champagne* (London: Octopus Book, 1962), 115.

38. Rod Phillips, *A Short History of Wine* (London: Penguin, 2000), 64–65.

39. Alphonse Nicot, *La Grande Guerre de 1914–1918,* vol. 2 (Tours: Alfred Mame et Fils, n.d.), 67.

40. Viala, *L'avenir viticole de la France,* 20.

41. There is a tasting note in Per-Henrik Mansson, "Swiss Company Sells Costly Sunken Champagne to Public," *Wine Spectator,* 17 May 1999, www.winespectator.com/webfeature/show/id/Swiss-Company-Sells-Costly-Sunken-Champagne-to-Public_20283.

42. Simon, *History of Champagne,* 113–14.

43. Kolleen Guy, *When Champagne Became French: Wine and the Making of a National Identity* (Baltimore: Johns Hopkins University Press, 2003), 187.

44. Quoted in Lucand, *Le pinard des poilus,* 114.

45. Ibid., 115.

46. Philippe Roudié, *Vignobles et vignerons du Bordelais, 1850–1980* (Bordeaux: Presses Universitaires de Bordeaux, 1994), 244–45.

47. Ibid., 247–49.

48. Ibid., 248–51.

49. Ellen NicKenzie Lawson, *Smugglers, Bootleggers, and Scofflaws: Prohibition and New York City* (Albany: State University of New York Press, 2013), 41.

50. Ibid., 105.

51. Daniel Deckers, *Im Zeichen des Traubenadlers: Eine Geschichte des deutschen Weins* (Mainz: Philipp von Zabern, 2010), 85–86.

52. Treaty of Versailles, Articles 269, 274, and 275.

53. Pinilla, "Wine Historical Statistics," table T6.

54. Jean-Claude Hinnewinkel, "Les usages locaux, loyaux et constants dans les appellations viticoles du nord de l'Aquitaine: Les bases des aires d'appellations d'origine," in *Le vin à travers les ages: Produit de qualité, agent économique* (Bordeaux: Fréret, 2001), 134–36.

55. Ibid., 133–34.

56. Roudié, *Vignobles et vignerons du Bordelais*, 251–52.

57. AD Côte-d'Or M 13 IX d/1, Syndicat Agricole de la Commune de Monthelie.

58. Charles Curtis, *The Original Grands Crus of Burgundy* (New York: WineAlpha, 2014), 129.

59. A compelling account is Claudine Wolikow, "Pour l'Aube en Champagne! Les mobilisations judiciaires dans l'Aube, 1919–1927," in *La construction des territoires du Champagne (1811–1911–2011)*, ed. Serge Wolikow (Dijon: Éditions Universitaires de Dijon, 2013), 147–66. The next paragraphs draw on this article.

60. Quoted in ibid., 160.

61. Gilles Laferté, "The Folklorization of French Farming: Marketing Luxury Wine in the Interwar Years," *French Historical Studies* 34 (2011): 701.

62. Aude Lutun, *Châteauneuf-du-Pape* (Paris: Flammarion, 2001), 14–15.

63. Nicholas Faith, *Château Margaux* (London: Mitchell Beazley, 1991), 52.

64. Roudié, *Vignobles et vignerons du Bordelais*, 256.

65. *Journal officiel de la République Française: Débats parlementaires, Chambre des députés*, 12 July 1927, 1013–14.

66. Hinnewinkel, "Les usages locaux, loyaux et constants," 141.

67. Roudié, *Vignobles et vignerons du Bordelais*, 257.

68. Raphaël Schirmer, *Muscadet: Histoire et géographie du vignoble nantais* (Bordeaux: Presses Universitaires de Bordeaux, 2010), 124.

69. Ibid., 126.

70. "French Wine Consumption," *The Queenslander* (Brisbane, Australia), 30 October 1930, 6.

71. Raymond Brunet, *Nos vins de France: Comment les classer, les vinifier, les conserver, les présenter*, 3rd ed. (Paris: Librairie Agricole de la Maison Rustique, 1934), 110–11.

72. Giulia Meloni and Johan Swinnen, "The Rise and Fall of the World's Largest Wine Exporter—and its Institutional Legacy," *Journal of Wine Economics* 9 (2014): 12, figure 5. This article refers to "exports" of wine from Algeria to France, which obscures the fact that Algeria was constitutionally an integral part of France.

73. Prestwich, *Drink and the Politics of Social Reform*, 212.

8. FROM DEPRESSION TO LIBERATION

1. Philippe Roudié, *Vignobles et vignerons du Bordelais, 1850–1980* (Bordeaux: Presses Universitaires de Bordeaux, 1994), 267.

2. Michael Broadbent, "Bordeaux," in *A Century of Wine: The Story of a Wine Revolution*, ed. Stephen Brook (London: Mitchell Beazley, 2000), 80.

3. Roudié, *Vignobles et vignerons du Bordelais*, 265.

4. André Simon, *The History of Champagne* (London: Octopus Books, 1962), 122–23.

5. *Journal officiel de la République française: Débats parlementaires, Chambre des députés*, 3 July 1931, 3650–53; also available at http://gallica.bnf.fr/ark:/12148/bpt6k62369311/f20.

6. Roudié, *Vignobles et vignerons du Bordelais*, 267.

7. Giulia Meloni and Johan Swinnen, "The Rise and Fall of the World's Largest Wine Exporter—and Its Institutional Legacy," *Journal of Wine Economics* 9 (2014): 22, table 4.

8. Charles K. Warner, *The Winegrowers of France and the Government since 1875* (New York: Columbia University Press, 1960), 95.

9. Raphaël Schirmer, *Muscadet: Histoire et géographie du vignoble nantais* (Bordeaux: Presses Universitaires de Bordeaux, 2010), 153. Noah is an indigenous American variety first planted in Muscadet in the 1880s and still grown there today.

10. Loi du 4 juillet 1931 ("Loi sur la viticulture et le commerce des vins"), Article 1.7, in *Journal officiel de la République française: Lois et décrets*, 5 July 1931, 7282–84, also available at http://gallica.bnf.fr/ark:/12148/bpt6k6541733 m/f2.

11. Robert O. Paxton, *French Peasant Fascism: Henry Dorgères's Greenshirts and the Crises of French Agriculture, 1929–1939* (Oxford: Oxford University Press, 1997), 47–48.

12. Loi du 4 juillet 1931, Article 1.1.

13. Ibid., Article 9.

14. Warner, *Winegrowers of France*, 249n5.

15. George Gale, *Dying on the Vine: How Phylloxera Transformed Wine* (Berkeley: University of California Press, 2011), 203.

16. Ibid., 94–95.

17. Sarah Howard, "Selling Wine to the French: Official Attempts to Increase Wine Consumption, 1931–1936," *Food and Foodways* 12 (2004): 203.

18. Florian Humbert, "La naissance du système des AOC: Étude de la mise en place du Comité Nationale des Appellations d'Origine (1935–1938)," in *Territoires et terroirs du vin du XVIIIe au XXIe siècles: Approche international d'une construction historique,* ed. Serge Wolikow and Olivier Jacquet (Dijon: Éditions Universitaires de Dijon, 2011), 316.

19. Schirmer, *Muscadet,* 127.

20. Warner, *Winegrowers of France,* 101.

21. Ibid., 103.

22. Meloni and Swinnen, "World's Largest Wine Exporter," 22–23.

23. Warner, *Winegrowers of France,* 111.

24. Undated circular from Établissements Nicolas, in the author's possession.

25. John Burnett, *Liquid Pleasures: A Social History of Drinks in Modern Britain* (London: Routledge, 1999), 136.

26. Howard, "Selling Wine to the French," 209, figure 1.

27. Ibid., 211.

28. *Eugene (OR) Register-Guardian,* 15 June 1932, 6.

29. Patricia E. Prestwich, *Drink and the Politics of Social Reform: Antialcoholism in France since 1870* (Palo Alto: Society for the Promotion of Science and Scholarship, 1988), 211.

30. Philip Whalen, "'Insofar as the Ruby Wine Seduces Them': Cultural Strategies for Selling Wine in Inter-war Burgundy," *Contemporary European History* 18, no. 1 (2009): 67–98.

31. Matt Kramer, *Making Sense of Burgundy* (New York: W. Morrow, 1990), 39–40.

32. Gilles Laferté, "The Folklorization of French Farming: Marketing Luxury Wine in the Interwar Years," *French Historical Studies* 34 (2011): 681.

33. James E. Wilson, *Terroir* (Berkeley: University of California Press, 1998), 55.

34. Colette, *Les vrilles de la vigne* (Paris: Éditions de "La vie parisienne," 1908), 47.

35. See, e.g., Fritz Stern, *The Politics of Cultural Despair: A Study in the Rise of the Germanic Ideology* (Berkeley: University of California Press, 1974).

36. Philip Whalen, "'A Merciless Source of Happy Memories': Gaston Roupnel and the Folklore of Burgundian *Terroir,*" *Journal of Folklore Research* 44, no. 1 (2007): 26.

37. Quoted in ibid., 26–27.

38. Laferté, "Folklorization of French Farming," 695.

39. Ibid.

40. See Marcel Lachiver, *Vins, vignes et vignerons: Histoire du vignoble français* (Paris: Fayard, 1988), 490–96.

41. Roudié, *Vignobles et vignerons du Bordelais,* 284.

42. Olivier Jacquet, *Un siècle de construction du vignoble bourguignon: Les organisations vitivinicoles de 1884 aux AOC* (Dijon: Éditions Universitaires de Dijon, 2009), 235–36.

43. Law of 30 July 1935, Article 21, in *Journal officiel de la République française: Lois et décrets*, 31 July 1935, 8314–19, also available at http://gallica.bnf .fr/ark:/12148/bpt6k65489715/f2.

44. Humbert, "La naissance du système des AOC," 332.

45. Roudié, *Vignobles et vignerons du Bordelais*, 286.

46. Archives Départementales de la Côte-d'Or, 13 IX d/1, Syndicat Agricole de la Commune de Monthelie.

47. Simon, *History of Champagne*, 125.

48. Schirmer, *Muscadet*, 129.

49. Giles MacDonogh, "Wine, Politics, and Economics," in Brook, *Century of Wine*, 29.

50. Roudié, *Vignobles et vignerons du Bordelais*, 288–89.

51. Quoted in Howard, "Selling Wine to the French," 206.

52. Information kindly provided by W. Scott Haine.

53. Warner, *Winegrowers of France*, 158–62.

54. Don Kladstrup and Petie Kladstrup, *Wine and War: The French, the Nazis and the Battle for France's Greatest Treasure* (New York: Broadway Books, 2001), 8.

55. Asa Briggs, *Haut-Brion: An Illustrious Lineage* (London: Faber and Faber, 1994), 179–80.

56. Kladstrup and Kladstrup, *Wine and War*, 26.

57. Archives Départementales de la Côte-d'Or, 13 IX d/1, Syndicat Agricole de la Commune de Monthelie, 12 January 1941.

58. Henri Drouot, *Notes d'un Dijonnais pendant l'occupation allemande (1940–1944)* (Dijon: Éditions Universitaires de Dijon, 1998), 41.

59. Gilbert Garrier, *Histoire sociale et culturelle du vin* (Paris: Larousse, 1998), 367.

60. Quoted in Jean Vigreux, *La vigne du maréchal Pétain* (Dijon: Éditions Universitaires de Dijon, 2005), 61.

61. Quoted in Christophe Lucand, "La Champagne et la Bourgogne à l'épreuve de la Seconde Guerre Mondiale: Deux itinéraires comparés de territoire vitivinicoles durant l'occupation (1940–1944)," in *La construction des territoires de Champagne (1811–1911–2011)*, ed. Serge Wolikow (Dijon: Éditions Universitaires de Dijon, 2013), 188–89.

62. Quoted in ibid., 194.

63. Vigreux, *La vigne du maréchal Pétain*, 31–34. This is the best single source on this episode.

64. Ibid., 30.

65. Ibid., 41.

66. Ibid., 47.

67. Patrice Liquière, *Restaurer, réformer, agir: La France en 1945* (Paris: La Documentation Française, 1995), 116.

9. FRENCH WINE REINVENTED

1. The 1939 figure does not include the vineyards of Alsace and Lorraine, while the 1945 figure does. The decline was therefore slightly greater than it appears here.

2. Philippe Roudié, *Vignobles et vignerons du Bordelais, 1850–1980* (Bordeaux: Presses Universitaires de Bordeaux, 1994), 297–98.

3. Ibid., 299.

4. Gary M. Thompson and Stephen A. Mutkoski suggest a reclassification based on wine ratings in "Reconsidering the 1855 Bordeaux Classification of the Médoc and Graves Using Wine Ratings from 1970–2005," *Journal of Wine Economics* 6 (2011): 15–36.

5. All the labels can be viewed at www.chateau-mouton-rothschild.com/label-art/discover-the-artwork.

6. See Emmanuel Cruse, "Introduction by Our Grand Master," Commanderie du Bontemps de Médoc, des Graves, de Sauternes et de Barsac, www.commanderiedubontemps.com/en/commanderie-du-bontemps_accueil.html.

7. Roudié, *Vignobles et vignerons du Bordelais*, 302.

8. Giulia Meloni and Johan Swinnen, "The Rise and Fall of the World's Largest Wine Exporter—and Its Institutional Legacy." *Journal of Wine Economics* 9 (2014): 22, table 3, table 4.

9. Ibid., 6, table 1.

10. Keith Sutton, "Algeria's Vineyards: A Problem of Decolonization," *Méditerranée* 65 (1988): 56, table 1.

11. Marcel Lachiver, *Vins, vignes et vignerons: Histoire du vignoble français* (Paris: Fayard, 1988), 542.

12. Pierre Capdeville, *Le vin de Cahors: Des origines à nos jours* (Cahors: Dire Éditions, 1999), 125.

13. Joseph Bohling, "'Drink Better, But Less': The Rise of France's Appellation System in the European Community, 1946–1976," *French Historical Studies* 37 (2014): 504–5.

14. Marion Demossier, "Beyond *Terroir:* Territorial Construction, Hegemonic Discourses, and French Wine Culture," *Journal of the Royal Anthropological Institute* 17 (2011): 691.

15. Alex Maltman, "The Role of Vineyard Geology in Wine Typicity," *Journal of Wine Research* 19 (2008): 1–17.

16. In *Tasting French Terroir: The History of an Idea* (Oakland: University of California Press, 2015), Thomas Parker examines the idea of terroir up to the end of the eighteenth century.

17. Jamie Goode and Sam Harrop, *Authentic Wine: Toward Natural and Sustainable Winemaking* (Berkeley: University of California Press, 2011), 145.

18. This is a general theme of Michael Steinberger, *Au Revoir to All That: Food, Wine, and the End of France* (New York: Bloomsbury, 2010).

19. Nicolas Marty, *L'invention de l'eau embouteillée: Qualités, normes et marchés de l'eau en bouteille en Europe, XIXe–XXe siècles* (Brussels: Peter Lang, 2013), 273.

20. Ibid., 365, graphique 6.

21. Steinberger, *Au Revoir to All That*, 87.

22. Marion Demossier, *Wine Drinking Culture in France: A National Myth or a Modern Passion?* (Cardiff: University of Wales Press, 2010), 118–22.

23. See Gene Ford, *The French Paradox and Drinking for Health* (New York: Wine Appreciation Guild, 1993); also the discussion in Harry W. Paul, *Bacchic Medicine: Wine and Alcohol Therapies from Napoleon to the French Paradox* (Amsterdam: Rodopi, 2001), 269–304.

24. Meloni and Swinnen, "World's Largest Wine Exporter," 6, table 1.

25. See George M. Taber, *The Judgment of Paris* (New York: Scribner, 2006).

26. Gemma Mollevi, "Cava versus Champagne," in *La construction des territoires du Champagne (1811–1911–2011)*, ed. Serge Wolikow (Dijon: Éditions Universitaires de Dijon, 2013), 209.

Selected Bibliography

This is a list of the main sources consulted that are substantially devoted to the subject of French wine. The notes acknowledge other works.

ARTICLES AND CHAPTERS

Agnew, Swanzie. "The Vine in Bas-Languedoc." *Geographical Review* 36 (1946): 67–79.

Banerjee, Abhijit, Esther Dillo, Gilles Postek-Vinay, and Tim Watts. "Long-Run Health Impacts of Income Shocks: Wine and Phylloxera in Nineteenth-Century France." *Review of Economics and Statistics* 92 (2010): 714–28.

Berlow, Rosalind Kent. "The 'Disloyal' Grape: The Agrarian Crisis of Late Fourteenth-Century Burgundy." *Agricultural History* 56 (1982): 426–38.

Bohling, Joseph. "'Drink Better, But Less': The Rise of France's Appellation System in the European Community, 1946–1976." *French Historical Studies* 37 (2014): 501–30.

Bordenave, Louis, Thierry Lacombe, Valérie Laucou, and Jean-Michel Boursiquot. "Étude historique, génétique et ampélographique des cépages Pyrénéo Atlantiques." *Bulletin de l'OIV* 920–22 (2007): 553–86.

Brennan, Thomas. "The Anatomy of Inter-regional Markets in the Early Modern French Wine Trade." *Journal of European Economic History* 23 (1994): 581–617.

Brumont, François. "Aux origines de la production des eaux-de-vie d'Armagnac." In *L'univers du vin: Actes du colloque de Bordeaux (4–5 octobre 2012)*, edited by Bernard Bodinier, Stéphanie Lachaud, and Corinne Marache, 325–37. Rennes: Presses Universitaires de Rennes, 2014.

Brun, Jean-Pierre. "L'oléiculture et la viticulture antiques en Gaule: Instruments et installations de production." In *La production du vin et de l'huile en Méditerranée: Actes du symposium international Aix-en-Provence et*

Toulon, 20–22 novembre 1991, edited by M.-C. Amouretti and Brun, 307–41. Paris: de Boccard, 1993.

Crowley, William K. "Changes in the French Winescape." *Geographical Review* 83 (1993): 252–68.

Dejean, Pierre. "L'exportation des vins béarnais dans les pays du Nord au XVIIIᵉ siècle: La 'Compagnie patriotique pour le commerce des vins de Béarn.'" *Revue d'histoire moderne* 11 (1936): 212–36.

Delafosse, Marcel. "Le commerce du vin d'Auxerre (XIVᵉ–XVIᵉ siècles." *Annales de Bourgogne* 13 (1941): 203–30.

Demossier, Marion. "Beyond *Terroir*: Territorial Construction, Hegemonic Discourses, and French Wine Culture." *Journal of the Royal Anthropological Institute* 17 (2011): 685–705.

Dietler, Michael. "Driven by Drink: The Role of Drinking in the Political Economy and the Case of Early Iron Age France." *Journal of Anthropological Archaeology* 9 (1990): 352–406.

Dion, Roger. "Métropoles et vignobles en Gaule romaine: L'exemple bourguignon." *Annales: Économies, Sociétés, Civilisations* 7 (1952): 1–12.

Forster, Robert. "The Noble Wine Producers of the Bordelais in the Eighteenth Century." *Economic History Review* 14 (1961): 18–33.

Fourcade, Marion. "The Vile and the Noble: On the Relation between Natural and Social Classifications in the French Wine World." *Sociological Quarterly* 53 (2012): 524–45.

Gergaud, Olivier, and Victor Ginsburgh. "Natural Endowments, Production Technologies and the Quality of Wines in Bordeaux: Does Terroir Matter?" *Journal of Wine Economics* 5 (2010): 3–21.

Gough, J. B. "Winecraft and Chemistry in Eighteenth-Century France: Chaptal and the Invention of Chaptalization." *Technology and Culture* 39 (1998): 74–104.

Gresset, Maurice. "Un document sur le rendement des vignes bisontines dans la seconde moitié du XVIIIᵉ siècle." In *Les boissons: Production et consommation aux XIXᵉ et XXᵉ siècles*, 23–38. Paris: Comité des Travaux Historiques et Scientifiques, 1984.

Guy, Kolleen. "'Oiling the Wheels of Social Life': Myths and Marketing in Champagne during the Belle Epoque." *French Historical Studies* 22 (1999): 211–39.

Haine, W. Scott. "Drink, Sociability, and Social Class in France, 1789–1945: The Emergence of a Proletarian Public Sphere." In *Alcohol: A Social and Cultural History*, edited by Mack Holt, 121–44. Oxford: Berg, 2006.

Hinnewinkel, Jean-Claude. "Terroirs et qualité des vins: Quels liens dans les vignobles du nord de l'Aquitaine?" *Sud-Ouest Européen* 6 (1999): 9–19.

———. "Les usages locaux, loyaux et constants dans les appellations viticoles du nord de l'Aquitaine: Les bases des aires d'appellations d'origine." In *Le vin à travers les ages: Produit de qualité, agent économique*, 133–46. Bordeaux: Féret, 2001.

———. "Vignes et vins de la Porte de l'Entre-deux-Mers: La fin d'une longue histoire?" Paper presented at "La rive droite de Bordeaux," thirteenth "L'Entre-deux-Mers et son identité" conference, 2011. Posted 23 January 2013. https://halshs.archives-ouvertes.fr/halshs-00780053.

Holt, Mack P. "Wine, Community, and Reformation in Sixteenth-Century Burgundy." *Past and Present* 138 (1993): 58–93.

Howard, Sarah. "Selling Wine to the French: Official Attempts to Increase Wine Consumption, 1931–1936." *Food and Foodways* 12 (2004): 197–224.

Jacquet, Olivier, and Gilles Laferté. "Le contrôle républicain du marché: Vignerons et négociants sous la Troisième République." *Annales: Histoire, Sciences Sociales* 61, no. 5 (2006): 1147–70.

Jéhanno, Christine. "Boire à Paris au XVᵉ siècle: Le vin à l'Hôtel-Dieu." *Revue Historique* 276 (1986): 4–28.

Laferté, Gilles. "The Folklorization of French Farming: Marketing Luxury Wine in the Interwar Years." *French Historical Studies* 34 (2011): 679–712.

———. "La mise en folklore des vins de Bourgogne: La 'Paulée' de Meursault." *Ethnologie française* 33 (2003): 435–42.

Loubère, Leo A., Paul Adams, and Roy Sandstrom. "Saint-Laurent-de-la-Salanque: From Fishing Village to Wine Town." *Agricultural History* 62 (1988): 37–56.

Lucand, Christophe. "La Champagne et la Bourgogne à l'épreuve de la Seconde Guerre Mondiale: Deux itinéraires comparés de territoire vitivinicoles durant l'occupation (1940–1944)." In *La construction des territoires de Champagne (1811–1911–2011)*, edited by Serge Wolikow, 185–95. Dijon: Éditions Universitaires de Dijon, 2013.

Maltman, Alex. "The Role of Vineyard Geology in Wine Typicity." *Journal of Wine Research* 19 (2008): 1–17.

Marrus, Michael. "Social Drinking in the *Belle Époque*." *Journal of Social History* 7 (1974): 115–41.

McGovern, Patrick E., Benjamin P. Luley, Nuria Rovira, Armen Mirzoian, Michael P. Callahan, Karen E. Smith, Gretchen R. Hall, Theodore Davidson, and Joshua M. Henkin. "Beginning of Viticulture in France." *Proceedings of the National Academy of Science* 110 (2013): 1047–52.

Meloni, Giulia, and Johan Swinnen. "The Rise and Fall of the World's Largest Wine Exporter—and Its Institutional Legacy." *Journal of Wine Economics* 9 (2014): 3–33.

Pinilla, Vicente. "'Old' and 'New' Producing Countries in the International Wine Market, 1850–1938." Paper presented at the International Economic History Conference, Helsinki, 2006.

———. "Wine Historical Statistics: A Quantitative Approach to Its Consumption, Production and Trade, 1840–1938." American Association of Wine Economists, Working Paper No. 167, August 2014.

Plack, Noelle. "Liberty, Equality and Taxation: Wine in the French Revolution." *Social History of Alcohol and Drugs* 26 (2012): 5–22.

Racine, Pierre. "Vigne e vini nelle Francia medievale." In *La civiltà del vino: Fonti, temi e produzioni vitivinicole dal Medioevo al Novecento*, edited by G. Archetti, 15–66. Brescia: Centro Culturale Artistico di Franciacorta e del Sebino, 2001.

Renouard, Y. "Les relations de Bordeaux et de Bristol au Moyen-Âge." *Revue Historique de Bordeaux* 6 (1957): 97–112.

Richard, Jean. "L'Académie de Dijon et le commerce du vin au XVIIIᵉ siècle à propos d'un mémoire présenté aux États de Bourgogne." *Annales de Bourgogne* 47 (1975): 221–41.

Sagnes, Jean. "Le mouvement de 1907 en Languedoc-Roussillon: De la révolte viticole à la révolte régionale." *Le Mouvement Social* 104 (1978): 3–30.

Simpson, James. "Selling to Reluctant Drinkers: The British Wine Market, 1860–1914." *Economic History Review* 57 (2004): 80–108.

Smith, J. Harvey. "Agricultural Workers and the French Wine-Growers' Revolt of 1907." *Past and Present* 79 (1978): 101–25.

Stanziani, Alessandro. "Information, Quality, and Legal Rules: Wine Adulteration in Nineteenth-Century France." *Business History* 51 (2009): 268–91.

Sutton, Keith. "Algeria's Vineyards: A Problem of Decolonization." *Méditerranée* 65 (1988): 55–66.

Thompson, Gary M., and Stephen A. Mutkoski. "Reconsidering the 1855 Bordeaux Classification of the Médoc and Graves Using Wine Ratings from 1970–2005." *Journal of Wine Economics* 6 (2011): 15–36.

Whalen, Philip. "'Insofar as the Ruby Wine Seduces Them': Cultural Strategies for Selling Wine in Inter-war Burgundy." *Contemporary European History* 18, no. 1 (2009): 67–98.

———. "'A Merciless Source of Happy Memories': Gaston Roupnel and the Folklore of Burgundian *Terroir*." *Journal of Folklore Research* 44, no. 1 (2007): 21–40.

BOOKS

Abric, Loïc. *Le vin de Bourgogne au XIXᵉ siècle: Aspects économiques, sociaux, culturels.* Précy-sous-Thil: Éditions de l'Armançon, 1993.

Aubert de La Chesnaye-Desbois, François-Alexandre. *Dictionnaire universel d'agriculture et de jardinage.* Vol. 2. Paris: David le Jeune, 1751.

Bazin, Jean-François. *Histoire du vin de Bourgogne.* Paris: Éditions Jean-Paul Gisserot, 2013.

Beguillet, Edme. *Œnologie, ou Discours sur la meilleure méthode de faire le vin et de cultiver la vigne.* Dijon: Defay, 1770.

Bertall [d'Arnoux, Charles Albert]. *La vigne: Voyage autour les vins de France.* Paris: E. Plon, 1878.

Berthier, Marie Thérèse, and John-Thomas Sweeney. *Histoire des hospices de Beaune: Vins, domains et donateurs.* Paris: Guy Trédaniel, 2012.

Birebent, Paul. *Hommes, vignes et vins de l'Algérie française (1830–1962).* Nice: Éditions Jacques Gandini, 2007.

Bodinier, Bernard, Stéphanie Lachaud, and Corinne Marache, eds. *L'univers du vin: Actes du colloque de Bordeaux (4–5 octobre 2012)*. Rennes: Presses Universitaires de Rennes, 2014.

Bourgeois, Armand. *Le vin de Champagne sous Louis XIV et sous Louis XV, d'après des lettres et documents inédits*. Paris: Bibliothèque d'Art de "La Critique," 1897.

Brennan, Thomas. *Burgundy to Champagne: The Wine Trade in Early Modern France*. Baltimore, Johns Hopkins University Press, 1997.

———. *Public Drinking and Popular Culture in Eighteenth-Century Paris*. Princeton: Princeton University Press, 1988.

———, ed. *Public Drinking in the Early Modern World: Voices from the Tavern, 1500–1800*. Vol. 1, *France*. London: Pickering and Chatto, 2011.

Briggs, Asa. *Haut-Brion: An Illustrious Lineage*. London: Faber and Faber, 1994.

Cadet-de-Vaux, Antoine-Alexis. *L'art de faire le vin d'après la doctrine de Chaptal*. Paris: Bureau de la Décade Philosophique, Littéraire et Politique, an IX [1801].

Capdeville, Pierre. *Le vin de Cahors: Des origines à nos jours*. Cahors: Dire Éditions, 1999.

Chaptal, Jean-Antoine-Claude. *L'art de faire le vin*. Paris: Delalain, 1801.

———. *Traité théorique et pratique sur la culture de la vigne*. Vol. 1. Paris: Delalain, 1801.

Colette. *Les vrilles de la vigne*. Paris: Éditions de "La vie parisienne," 1908.

Craeybeckx, Jan. *Un grand commerce d'importation: Les vins de France aux anciens Pays-Bas (XIIIᵉ–XVIᵉ siècle)*. Paris: SEVPEN, 1958.

Cullen, Carmen, Gary Pickering, and Roderick Phillips, eds. *Bacchus to the Future: The Inaugural Brock University Wine Conference—Proceedings of the Conference, May 23–25, 2002*. St. Catharines, Ontario: Brock University, 2002.

Cullen, L.M. *The Brandy Trade under the Ancien Régime: Regional Specialization in the Charente*. Cambridge: Cambridge University Press, 2002.

Curtis, Charles. *The Original Grands Crus of Burgundy*. New York: WineAlpha, 2014.

De Bruyn Kops, Henriette. *A Spirited Exchange: The Brandy Trade between France and the Dutch Republic in Its Atlantic Framework*. Leiden: Brill, 2007.

Deckers, Daniel. *Im Zeichen des Traubenadlers: Eine Geschichte des deutschen Weins*. Mainz: Philipp von Zabern, 2010.

Demossier, Marion. *Wine Drinking Culture in France: A National Myth or a Modern Passion?* Cardiff: University of Wales Press, 2010.

Deroudille, Jean-Pierre. *Le vin face à la mondalisation*. Paris: Hachette, 2003.

Dion, Roger. *Histoire de la vigne et du vin en France: Des origines au XIXᵉ siècle*. Paris: Flammarion, 1977.

———. *Le paysage et la vigne: Essais de géographie historique*. Paris: Payot, 2004.

Faith, Nicholas. *Château Margaux*. London: Mitchell Beazley, 1991.
————. *The Story of Champagne*. London: Hamish Hamilton, 1988.
Francis, A. D. *The Wine Trade*. London: A. and C. Black, 1972.
Franck, William. *Traité sur les vins du Médoc et les autres vins rouges et blancs du département de la Gironde*. 3rd ed. Bordeaux: P. Chaumas, 1853.
François, Jean-Jacques. *Au temps des vignes et des vignerons du pays chartrain, 840–1920*. Vol. 3. Luisant: Durand, 2003.
Gale, George. *Dying on the Vine: How Phylloxera Transformed Wine*. Berkeley: University of California Press, 2011.
Garrier, Gilbert. *Histoire sociale et culturelle du vin*. Paris: Larousse, 1998.
————. *Le phylloxéra: Une guerre de trente ans, 1870–1900*. Paris: Albin Michel, 1989.
————, ed. *Le vin des historiens: Actes du 1er symposium "Vin et histoire."* Suze-la-Rousse: Université du Vin, 1990.
Gaubert, P. *Étude sur les vins et les conserves: Suivie du compte rendu de la séance de dégustation tenue par les membres de la onzième classe de l'Exposition universelle*. Paris: Croissant, 1857. Also available at http://babel.hathitrust.org/cgi/pt?id=uc1.31175014769122.
Ginestet, Bernard. *Thomas Jefferson à Bordeaux: Et dans quelques autres vignes d'Europe*. Bordeaux: Mollat, 1996.
Guilly, Jean. *Vignerons en pays d'Auxerre autrefois: Histoire et témoignages*. Lyon: Horvath, 1985.
Guy, Kolleen. *When Champagne Became French: Wine and the Making of a National Identity*. Baltimore: Johns Hopkins University Press, 2003.
Haine, W. Scott. *The World of the Paris Café: Sociability among the French Working Class, 1789–1914*. Baltimore: Johns Hopkins University Press, 1999.
Heath, Elizabeth. *Wine, Sugar, and the Making of Modern France: Global Economic Crisis and the Racialization of French Citizenship, 1870–1910*. Cambridge: Cambridge University Press, 2014.
Huetz de Lemps, A., ed. *Géographie historique des vignobles: Actes du colloque de Bordeaux, octobre 1977*. Vol. 1. Paris: Éditions du Centre National de la Recherche Scientifique, 1978.
Jacquet, Olivier. *Un siècle de construction du vignoble bourguignon: Les organisations vitivinicoles de 1884 aux AOC*. Dijon: Éditions Universitaires de Dijon, 2009.
James, Margery Kirkbride, and Elspeth M. Veale. *Studies in the Medieval Wine Trade*. Oxford: Clarendon, 1971.
Jefferson, Thomas. *Thomas Jefferson's European Travel Diaries*, edited by James McGrath Morris and Persephone Weene. Ithaca, NY: Isadore Stephanus, 1987.
Kladstrup, Don, and Petie Kladstrup. *Wine and War: The French, the Nazis and the Battle for France's Greatest Treasure*. New York: Broadway Books, 2001.
Kramer, Matt. *Making Sense of Burgundy*. New York: W. Morrow, 1990.
Lachiver, Marcel. *Vin, vigne et vignerons en région parisienne du XVIIe au XIXe*

siècle. Pontoise: Société historique et archéologique de Pontoise, du Val d'Oise et du Vexin, 1982.

———. *Vins, vignes et vignerons: Histoire du vignoble français*. Paris: Fayard, 1988.

Laferté, Gilles. *La Bourgogne et ses vins: Image d'origine contrôlée*. Paris: Belin, 2006.

Lavaud, Sandrine. *Bordeaux et le vin au Moyen Âge: Essor d'une civilisation*. Bordeaux: Éditions Sud Ouest, 2003.

Lavignac, Guy. *Cépages du Sud-Ouest: 2000 ans d'histoire*. Arles: Éditions du Rouergue / INRA Éditions, 2001.

Lecoutre, Matthieu. *Ivresse et ivrognerie dans la France moderne*. Rennes: Presses Universitaires de Rennes / Presses Universitaires François-Rabelais de Tours, 2011.

Legeron, Isabelle. *Natural Wine: An Introduction to Organic and Biodynamic Wines Made Naturally*. London: Cico, 2014.

L'église, la vigne et le vin dans le massif jurassien: Actes de la table ronde de Lons-le-Saunier, avril 1990. Besançon: Néo Typo, 1991.

Le Roy Ladurie, Emmanuel. *Histoire du climat depuis l'an mil*. Vol. 1. Paris: Flammarion, 1983.

Les boissons: Production et consommation aux XIXe et XXe siècles. Paris: Comité des Travaux Historiques et Scientifiques, 1984.

Le vin à travers les âges: Produit de qualité, agent économique. Bordeaux: Fréret, 2001.

Loubère, Leo A. *The Red and the White: The History of Wine in France and Italy in the Nineteenth Century*. Albany: State University of New York Press, 1978.

Lucand, Christophe. *Le pinard des poilus: Une histoire du vin en France durant la Grande Guerre (1914–1918)*. Dijon: Éditions Universitaires de Dijon, 2015.

Ludington, Charles. *The Politics of Wine in Britain: A New Cultural History*. New York: Palgrave Macmillan, 2013.

Lutun, Aude. *Châteauneuf-du-Pape*. Paris: Flammarion, 2001.

Markham, Dewey, Jr. *1855: A History of the Bordeaux Classification*. New York: John Wiley and Sons, 1998.

Marty, Nicolas, *L'invention de l'eau embouteillée: Qualités, normes et marchés de l'eau en bouteille en Europe, XIXe–XXe siècles*. Brussels: Peter Lang, 2013.

Maupin, M. *Essai sur l'art de faire le vin rouge, le vin blanc et le cidre*. Paris, 1767.

Nelson, Max. *The Barbarian's Beverage: A History of Beer in Ancient Europe*. London: Routledge, 2005.

Nourrisson, Didier. *Le buveur du XIXe siècle*. Paris: Albin Michel, 1990.

Olney, Richard. *Romanée-Conti: The World's Most Fabled Wine*. New York: Rizzoli, 1995.

Ordish, George. *The Great Wine Blight*. London: Dent, 1972.

Parker, Thomas. *Tasting French Terroir: The History of an Idea*. Oakland: University of California Press, 2015.

Paul, Harry W. *Bacchic Medicine: Wine and Alcohol Therapies from Napoleon to the French Paradox*. Amsterdam: Rodopi, 2001.

Paxton, Robert O. *French Peasant Fascism: Henry Dorgères's Greenshirts and the Crises of French Agriculture, 1929–1939*. Oxford: Oxford University Press, 1997.

Phillips, Rod. *Alcohol: A History*. Chapel Hill: University of North Carolina Press, 2014.

———. *A Short History of Wine*. London: Penguin, 2000.

Pitte, Jean-Robert. *Bordeaux/Burgundy: A Vintage Rivalry*. Berkeley: University of California Press, 2008.

———. *La bouteille de vin: Histoire d'une revolution*. Paris: Taillandier, 2013.

Plack, Noelle. *Common Land, Wine and the French Revolution: Rural Society and Economy in Southern France, c. 1789–1820*. Farnham: Ashgate, 2009.

Pouget, Roger. *Histoire de la lutte contre le phylloxéra de la vigne in France (1868–1895)*. Paris: Institut National de la Recherche Agronomique, 1990.

Poux, Matthieu, Jean-Pierre Brun, and Marie-Laure Hervé-Monteil, eds. "La vigne et le vin dans les Trois Gaules." Special issue, *Gallia* 68 no. 1 (2011).

Prestwich, Patricia E. *Drink and the Politics of Social Reform: Antialcoholism in France since 1870*. Palo Alto: Society for the Promotion of Science and Scholarship, 1988.

Redding, Cyrus. *A History and Description of Modern Wines*. London: Henry G. Bohn, 1851.

Renouard, Yves. *Histoire médiévale d'Aquitaine*. Vol. 2, *Vin et commerce du vin de Bordeaux*. Monein: Éditions des Régionalismes, 2010.

Robinson, Jancis, Julia Harding, and José Vouillamoz. *Wine Grapes*. New York: Harper Collins, 2012.

Rose, Susan. *The Wine Trade in Medieval Europe, 1000–1500*. London: Continuum, 2011.

Roudié, Philippe. *Vignobles et vignerons du Bordelais, 1850–1980*. Bordeaux: Presses Universitaires de Bordeaux, 1994.

Rozier, François. *De la fermentation des vins, et de la meilleure manière de faire l'eau-de-vie*. Lyon: Frères Perisse, 1770.

Sagnes, Jean, ed. *La viticulture française aux XIXᵉ et XXᵉ siècles: Colloque national d'histoire, Béziers, le 30 mai 1992*. Béziers: Presses du Languedoc, 1993.

Saint Pierre, Louis de. *The Art of Planting and Cultivating the Vine; as Also, of Making, Fining, and Preserving Wines According to the Most Approved Methods in the Most Celebrated Wine-Countries in France*. London: J. Wilkie, 1772.

Schirmer, Raphaël. *Muscadet: Histoire et géographie du vignoble nantais*. Bordeaux: Presses Universitaires de Bordeaux, 2010.

Serres, Olivier de. *Théâtre d'agriculture et ménage des champs*. Paris, 1600.

Simon, André. *The History of Champagne*. London: Octopus Books, 1962.

Stanziani, Alessandro, ed. *La qualité des produits en France (XVIIIᵉ–XXᵉ siècles).* Paris: Belin, 2003.

Sutcliffe, Serena. *Champagne: The History and Character of the World's Most Celebrated Wine.* New York: Simon and Schuster, 1988.

Unwin, Tim. *Wine and the Vine: An Historical Geography of Viticulture and the Wine Trade.* London: Routledge, 1991.

Viala, Pierre. *L'avenir viticole de la France après la guerre: Le vin et l'hygiène— le vin au front.* 2nd ed. Paris: Bureaux de la "Revue de viticulture," 1916.

Viallon-Schoneveld, Marie, ed. *Le boire et le manger au XVIᵉ siècle: Actes du XIᵉ colloque du Puy-en-Velay.* Saint-Étienne: Presses Universitaires de Saint-Étienne, 2004.

Vignobles et vins d'Aquitaine: Histoire, économie, art. Bordeaux: Fédération Historique du Sud-Ouest, 1970.

Vigreux, Jean. *La vigne du maréchal Pétain.* Dijon: Éditions Universitaires de Dijon, 2005.

Warner, Charles K. *The Winegrowers of France and the Government since 1875.* New York: Columbia University Press, 1960.

Wilson, James E. *Terroir.* Berkeley: University of California Press, 1998.

Wolff, Christian. *Riquewihr: Son vignoble et ses vins à travers les âges.* Ingersheim: Société d'Archéologie de Riquewihr, 1967.

Wolikow, Serge, ed. *La construction des territoires du Champagne (1811–1911– 2011).* Dijon: Éditions Universitaires de Dijon, 2013.

Wolikow, Serge, and Olivier Jacquet, eds. *Territoires et terroirs du vin du XVIIIᵉ au XXIᵉ siècles: Approche international d'une construction historique.* Dijon: Éditions Universitaires de Dijon, 2011.

Index

Note: Some Bordeaux producers are identified as "Château" (their current name) even though they adopted the designation only in the late nineteenth century.